Human Rights and
Transnational Solidarity
in Cold War Latin America

Critical Human Rights

Series Editors

Steve J. Stern ❧ Scott Straus

Books in the series **Critical Human Rights** emphasize research that opens new ways to think about and understand human rights. The series values in particular empirically grounded and intellectually open research that eschews simplified accounts of human rights events and processes.

How does the rise of human rights as a normative force in world culture relate to ideas of political community? In *Human Rights and Transnational Solidarity*, Jessica Stites Mor and her collaborators engage this question for the important case of Cold War Latin America. They show that human rights emerged within a broader story—the making of transnational "solidarity" values and relationships by social actors rooted in particular urgent contexts, even as they built an emerging idea of the global "South." This fresh approach yields striking results. It flips the common idea of human rights as values and empathy emanating from the global North, while assessing how activists in Latin America, by forging an alternative transnational solidarity from below, shaped human rights and political community.

Human Rights and Transnational Solidarity in Cold War Latin America

Edited by

Jessica Stites Mor

The University of Wisconsin Press

Publication of this volume has been made possible, in part, through support from the Anonymous Fund of the College of Letters and Science at the University of Wisconsin–Madison.

The University of Wisconsin Press
1930 Monroe Street, 3rd Floor
Madison, Wisconsin 53711-2059
uwpress.wisc.edu

3 Henrietta Street
London WC2E 8LU, England
eurospanbookstore.com

Library of Congress Cataloging-in-Publication Data
Human rights and transnational solidarity in Cold War Latin America / edited by Jessica Stites Mor.
    p.   cm. — (Critical human rights)
    Includes bibliographical references and index.
    ISBN 978-0-299-29114-3 (pbk. : alk. paper) — ISBN 978-0-299-29113-6 (e-book)
    1. Human rights advocacy—Latin America—International cooperation—Case studies. 2. Solidarity—Latin America—Case studies. 3. Latin America—Politics and government—20th century. 4. Cold War—Social aspects—Latin America. I. Stites Mor, Jessica. II. Series: Critical human rights.
    JC599.L3H815   2013
    323.098'09045—dc23
                                                                                        2012013284

To Patricia Pessar

Contents

Acknowledgments   ix

*Introduction: Situating Transnational Solidarity within
Critical Human Rights Studies of Cold War Latin America*   3
Jessica Stites Mor

PART I. CRITICAL PRECURSORS TO
TRANSNATIONAL SOLIDARITY

1. The Puerto Rican Nationalist Party, Transnational
   Latin American Solidarity, and the United States
   during the Cold War   21
   Margaret Power

2. Latin America Encounters Nelson Rockefeller:
   Imagining the *Gringo Patrón* in 1969   48
   Ernesto Capello

3. The Mexican Student Movement of 1968:
   National Protest Movements in International
   and Transnational Contexts   74
   Sara Katherine Sanders

PART II. SOLIDARITY IN ACTION

4. Cosmopolitans and Revolutionaries:
   Competing Visions of Transnationalism
   during the Boom in Latin America   101
   Russell Cobb

5. Transnational Concepts, Local Contexts:
   Solidarity at the Grassroots in Pinochet's Chile   120
   Alison J. Bruey

6. Cuba's Concept of "Internationalist Solidarity":
   Political Discourse, South-South Cooperation with
   Angola, and the Molding of Transnational Identities   143
   Christine Hatzky

PART III. THE INFLUENCE OF TRANSNATIONAL
SOLIDARITY ON POSTNATIONAL
RESPONSIBILITIES

7. "As the World Is My Witness": Transnational Chilean
   Solidarity and Popular Culture   177
   Brenda Elsey

8. The Politics of Refuge: Salvadoran Refugees and
   International Aid in Honduras   209
   Molly Todd

EPILOGUE

9. Desire and Revolution: Socialists and the Brazilian
   Gay Liberation Movement in the 1970s   239
   James N. Green

Selected Bibliography   269
Contributors   285
Index   287

Acknowledgments

In the process of editing a volume with such a wide scope, I've incurred numerous debts, only a small fraction of which I am able to recognize here. My intellectual debts began in 2007, when Tufts University hosted a symposium on indigenous movements and intellectuals in the Americas at which José Antonio Lucero presented a paper titled "The 'African' Origins of Indianismo?" The paper made a strong concluding statement that begged further consideration: that national liberation and decolonization across the Americas depended on producing transnational solidarity and consciousness, and that this challenge was in fact more important than creating actual political communities that transcended national boundaries. Having come across this piece, I was struck by the inherent issue raised by such a statement: how solidarity participated in the work of resisting forms of colonialism in various local contexts. I am grateful to José Antonio for his intellectual generosity in sharing his thoughts and writings with me and for sparking the interest that eventually led to this present work.

This project, compelled by Lucero's statement, began to take shape in earnest in a panel that I organized for the Vancouver meeting of the Canadian Latin American and Caribbean Studies Association in 2008. Participants included political scientist Thomas Olesen, historian Christine Hatzky, geographer Catherine Nolin, and sociologist Patricia Tomic. The conversation that followed the panel opened the issue even farther than I had initially intended, which convinced me even further that a more detailed historical study was in order. I am indebted to Eric Zolov, Greg Grandin, Victoria Langland, Heidi Tinsman, and Gilbert Joseph for making valuable suggestions of inclusions and thought matter in the volume's early conceptual stages. I am equally grateful to Steve Stern, Jeffrey Gould, Pablo Yankelevich, Luis Roniger, Raanan Rein, Florencia Mallon, Paul Gootenberg, Arun Agrawal, Horacio Tarcus, Eric

Hershberg, Nichole Stahlmann, and Jorge Nállim for communicating their valuable thoughts, commentary, and suggestions as the volume developed. Comments from audience members at the American Historical Association and Latin American Studies Association meetings that hosted papers by various contributing authors are also gratefully acknowledged.

The University of British Columbia's commendable generosity toward junior faculty allowed me to take advantage of a reduced teaching load during the completion of this project and facilitated the hiring of two outstanding research assistants, Sasha Johnston and Stephanie Tissot, who each contributed to the delivery of the final work. I am especially grateful to Cynthia Mathieson, Peter Wylie, and Peter Urmetzer for their unflagging support of this project, and to my colleagues in the history and Latin American studies departments, of which James Hull, Francisco Peña, James Rochlin, and Margo Tamez each provided valuable advice and timely suggestions. I am also grateful to my students, in particular Ashley Black and Bethany Wade, for raising challenging questions in my seminar courses, which forced me to think about the work in different ways.

In the final stages of editing and polishing up the final draft of the manuscript, I would like to acknowledge the wonderful care and shepherding of the project by Gwen Walker, Sheila McMahon, and the series editors at the University of Wisconsin Press. I am also thankful for the assistance of Carla Miranda and Barbara Camps at the Museo de Solidaridad Salvador Allende, who graciously facilitated permission to reproduce the image on the cover of the book.

From the early moments of this project, Christine Hatzky provided an intellectual companionship and enthusiasm that made the project feel more like an adventure than work. And finally, Brenda Elsey was an incomparable sounding board and provided sustaining intellectual support and camaraderie throughout the entire process. I am especially appreciative of her many interventions and her remarkable sense of humor. During the course of this project, however, an important *compañera* in the field passed away. Patricia Pessar was a model of the kind of intellectual solidarity that inspires young scholars to embark on the study of Latin American resistance. This book is dedicated to her memory.

Human Rights and
Transnational Solidarity
in Cold War Latin America

Introduction

Situating Transnational Solidarity within Critical Human Rights Studies of Cold War Latin America

JESSICA STITES MOR

One of the central problems of political life in the twentieth and now the twenty-first centuries has been that of
what determines the unity of a political community. When direct actions
of political collaboration and solidarity occur between distant, unequal, or
often quite different parties to create new notions of political community,
these relationships have the potential to challenge existing power structures.
Transnational ties often evolve as the result of finding a common cause, such
as class struggle or a mutual enemy, and sometimes as the result of a newly
formed bond of affection or empathy in the aftermath of crisis or devastation.
An earthquake or a famine might have the power to bring together communities around the globe to provide immediate relief for victims of disaster,
while high-profile cases of human rights abuse or politically motivated violence might spark support from networks of activists around the globe that
hope to utilize the weight of extra-national political resources to influence
local outcomes. This kind of solidarity is sometimes described as "project-
related solidarity," a matter of special problem, or "target-oriented," and it has

been demonstrated to lead to diminishing ties of solidarity, rather than long-term ties.[1]

In contrast, strategic reciprocities and solidarities that tend to have greater staying power tend to be the result of long-standing constructions of political community, most often those that have been codified into law or legitimized by cultural practice, that agents of change are able to turn or to broaden to include a new circumstance or a previously excluded group. For instance, abolitionists on both sides of the Atlantic extended to men of color inclusion in concepts of citizenship and rights of man that had long been considered to apply only to propertied white men. Likewise, solidarity campaigns to provide relief or asylum for refugees of political violence are often premised on notions of protection of civil liberties that are well established within the community providing refuge. Political theorist Enrique Dussel argues in his landmark essay "From Fraternity to Solidarity: Towards a *Politics of Liberation*" that the essence of the problem of crafting unity and mutual support, parallel to the paradox of the Talmudic account of the good Samaritan, is the question of "who establishes the subject-subject relation as proximity." In other words, what kind of collective political unity allows for the identification of an otherwise distant or excluded "other" as like subject, and how does the other enter into social consciousness as one to whom responsibilities are owed?[2] Often, this relation of proximity is described as a set of universal rights and duties, and defending such rights of the other becomes a central feature of political organizing.

The authors whose contributions are included in this work all engage the problem and the promise of the transnational as a means of constructing more useful or alternative political unities to the nation-state. The work as a whole underscores and explores the notion that transnational solidarities and sympathies are derived from common or shared understandings at the local level, that is, within grounded national, regional, or community contexts. The book presents such individual moments of collaboration and encounter as they are intimately tied to meta-narrative contextual frames, such as the Cold War, colonialism, or civil and human rights movements, as the volume asks the central question: How do solidarity movements contribute to the emergence of more democratic, rather than hierarchical, forms of political community? It examines the implications of global frameworks of human rights and rights-based transnational advocacy in promoting equitable and empowering political participation in the Global South. As editor, I hope that the work assembled here helps to establish a theoretical frame for the study of transnational solidarity in Cold War Latin America and to inform the intellectual currents of human rights and citizenship struggles from this perspective.

The Cold War is a distinctive and key period of political change in Latin America, given the polarizing influence of the competition between two aggressive and powerful states for spheres of influence in the region. This book reveals the way that multiple sectors in Latin America resisted and responded to Cold War pressures, both ideological and material, and uncovers the relationship of this transnational history to the shaping of a renewed agenda for the left in Latin America. It challenges much of the existing literature on this period, which suggests that the left that survived and rebuilt after the Cold War was the product of looking outward to universal notions of rights and models of democratic institutions in the North. This book argues that the re-emerging left and new social movements that characterized the post–Cold War period were not primarily the result of the heavy involvement in local affairs of transnational nongovernmental organizations but, rather, emerged from strategic engagement of the left with transnational solidarity activism. The individual case studies in this work pose new research questions and present new sources that challenge former perspectives on the left, instead concentrating on the multiple ways that the left used the transnational to raise its own organic challenges to Cold War realities. This volume demonstrates that social actors rooted in specific networks and communities on the ground shaped Cold War struggles into languages of anticolonialism, socioeconomic rights, and identity that transformed political subjecthood and built a kind of alternative transnational solidarity from below—by and for the socially excluded and activist leaders within the Global South.

This volume asks of the historiography of the period that it not overlook the key contributions of social actors, such as Latin American community organizers, party members, intellectuals, novelists, priests, students, artists, urban *pobladores*, refugees, migrants, and common people, to the growth of new visions of political community and human rights in participatory democracy. Transnational networks frequently provided the external validation that local campaigns needed to refine and renegotiate political community and responsibility within local contexts. This work makes the case that solidarity values and related notions of citizenship were developed and adapted within the vernacular and existing practices of specific political communities and organizations to provoke change and mobilize social movements. Specifically, the momentum of transnational solidarity campaigns facilitated the broadening of the social agenda, focusing the attention of a revitalizing left on the otherwise uncelebrated victims of poverty and social exclusion that the neoliberal economic policies of the global Cold War produced.

Transnational Political Community and Universal Rights

Jean Quataert, pointing to the work of Mary Midgley, argues that, in the arena of global politics, "human rights consciousness defied the odds" in becoming one of the most visible and effective mediums by which the quotidian struggles of social movements have been able to articulate resistance. Quataert asserts that the development of a legal framework of international rights has come to "represent an alternative non-territorial source of sovereignty that limits state actions."[3] The very claim that human rights have the ethical wherewithal to transcend legal systems of nation-states and even international governing bodies, she argues, signals a monumental change in the way that civil society has been able to organize and maintain viable networks for advocacy, challenging states, administrations, local governments, and legal systems closed to popular and oppositional participation. Most scholars of human rights, however, have tended to envision the progress of this transnational agency as a byproduct of international relations and of the triumph of Western democratic ideals. When human rights scholars have tended to think about historical context, they frequently look toward major legal documents, constitutions, declarations, and treaties, such as the U.S. Declaration of Independence or United Nations resolutions, as signaling major shifts in rights protections across the globe, casually omitting local contributions and on-the-ground experiences.

Rather than presume that transnational civil society evolves principally via the institutions, processes, and technologies of global governance or the proliferation of a specifically European-derived global humanitarian ethic, this volume focuses its attention on the importance of local contexts and situations to the formation of transnational identities, concentrating on variables that have received relatively little critical examination, such as the contributions of local activist communities, popular culture, and social movements to shaping meanings of shared responsibility. This project de-centers understandings of the spread of humanitarian ideals by focusing on the dialectical processes by which formulations of citizenship and human rights frameworks have translated into local practices and everyday understandings of transnational codes of ethics, specifically in relation to responses to U.S. intervention and to the ideological struggles of the Cold War. Further, the volume examines, through a variety of case studies, the way in which the hegemonic status of human rights as a discourse has the power to occlude alternative epistemologies of responsibility and political agency. As Gayatri Chakravorty Spivak has argued, the problem of human rights is not so much their uneven enforcement but the way in which they privilege rights-based cultural formulations over those based in notions of responsibility.[4] Human rights as a discursive framework for political participation has been critiqued by feminists, indigenous scholars, and theorists of postcolonialism, among others, who point out that rights-based notions of political community derive from a decidedly Western model of political and economic development, one that values individualism over community and one that is ill suited to deal with diversity and difference.[5] These critics call for a rethinking of rights-based notions of citizenship to better situate agency within pluralist body politics and to move beyond the implication of such formulations that the individual be tied to the nation-state as the natural and exclusive guarantor of rights and welfare.

For the nation-state, the binding relationship that developed between parties aligned with the interests of the state was that of a national citizenship. The notion of the national citizen, a mode of constructing bonds between discrete and often distant communities within newly formed geographies of statehood, was a notion suited to address the postcolonial struggles of state formation. However, the consolidation of the national citizen in Latin America gave rise to fiercely competitive constructions of nationalism across the region and became increasingly tied up in the protection of state bureaucracies that operated on behalf of the privileged few. Increasingly in the twentieth century, the development and integration of global financial markets, trade, transportation, and telecommunications further pushed the limits of the nation-state, weakening its position of authority over individual subjects and privileging multinational entities that could evade local legislation. Critiques of the limitations of national citizenship to protect and define the rights and responsibilities of communities both within and beyond borders have even led to calls for postnational political identities to replace or reconfigure notions of citizenship tied to states.

The spaces, flows, and movements of the transnational have forcefully articulated a new set of roles and responsibilities for the individual premised on the expansion of practical opportunities for transnational interaction. Calls for transnational political identities, sometimes described as a cosmopolitan humanism, are most often modeled on the notion of a social contract of duties and responsibilities, rights and freedoms encoded in the language of citizenship. The immediate problem the *global* citizen faces has been to deal with the fate of those who lacked access to the protections of a more universal social contract, such as refugees of war, immigrants, excluded minorities, exiles, the stateless, the colonized, and citizens of nations "beyond the pale." The emergence of these sensibilities and the contradictions that they implied initiated new social and ideological perspectives about the role of global civil society and the purpose and nature of transborder affinities and alliances, specifically in terms of networks of political solidarity and the conception of a global collective responsibility. The transnational struggle for the protection of human rights has intersected with a variety of challenges to citizenship practices and exclusions at the level of the state, emerging as one of the most prominent—but also controversial—spaces within the political imaginary of the Latin American left up to today. During the Cold War, as struggles for legitimate democracy and citizenship against dictatorship were often international in scale, human rights advocacy and transnational solidarity emerged as two of the most prominent modes of opposition to repressive regimes and to external intervention. These also proved to be spaces that shifted the battlefield for oppositional politics, creating a new space for leftism that had not previously been possible under the heavy intervention of the United States and the dominance of military regimes "combating communism" and political "subversion" across the region.

South-South Solidarity in Cold War Latin America

Latin America saw first the expansion of transnational defense of rights and human liberty as early as the push for Pan American resistance to Spanish rule, but, during the Cold War, the international push for recognition of human rights became entangled with visions for economic justice and redistribution of wealth. Economic development strategies encouraged by international lending agencies favored urban industrial growth tied closely to foreign capital, forcing an unprecedented level of internal and external migration. During this period, human rights protections became increasingly important, as dissenters and economic migrants seeking justice, fair treatment, and political relief pushed the boundaries of the application of human rights guarantees and protections beyond the nation-state, frequently in territories where they were not citizens.[6] The fall of Salvador Allende's government, in 1973, and the military rule that followed was something of a watershed in terms of the articulation of an international human rights platform. Transnational actors, such as the estimated 200,000 Chilean exiles who formed a diasporic community in more than 140 countries, were certainly essential in forming the social network of alliances for political action.[7] The coup itself sparked protests across the globe, 250,000 people marched in Buenos Aires and 100,000 in Mexico City,[8] and the fall of Allende's experiment in socialist government solidified a set of operating principles that connected traditions of human rights and solidarity activism rooted in the Latin American left. The coup in Chile was a critical moment during which a variety of distinct approaches to rights advocacy found a powerful voice in transnational advocacy networks. This moment has been described by many historians of Latin America as the beginning of the rise of nongovernmental organizations as key actors in the politics of the late Cold War.[9]

Jürgen Habermas argues that cosmopolitan solidarity arises primarily out of a shared moral indignation, such as the response to dramatic human rights abuses or mass violence, and that it is because these ties of solidarity are mobilized in a very contingent and temporary way that they are less meaningful in terms of organizing and negotiating political life.[10] Sporadic activity, rather than long-term engagement in socially inclusive projects and reforms, relies on a sympathy generated around a focal point that is often far removed from its social context and historical particularities. In this way, human rights law has provided a crucial frame for legitimizing collective responses to the violation of shared values, such as freedom from torture, genocide and mass violence, but fails to make clear how existing structures and institutions are implicated in the perpetuation of such events. Other critics have focused on the way in which the dominance of a discourse of human rights has overshadowed basic subsistence rights and global socioeconomic justice.[11] This concern is echoed by James Green, who writes that the "term *human rights*, tied as it was to torture and state violence in the 1970s, seemed to exclude a broader definition," such as everyday forms of exclusion from participation and denials of equality under the law.[12] Likewise, Greg Grandin asserts, "state terror . . . played an unexpected role in bringing forth the kind of subjectivity on which appeals to human rights can be based. Government repression disaggregated powerful collective movements into individual survival strategies, extracted leaders from their communities and redefined the relationship of self to society."[13] The legitimacy of claims to human rights improvements must be measured by enforcement and by whether or not individuals and communities are able to utilize new policy to change their daily circumstances. In many cases these movements limited rather than expanded roads to inclusivity and socioeconomic justice.

In some contexts, the political discourse of solidarity and human rights came into common usage as a substitute for direct calls for socialism. Partially as a consequence of and reaction to repression, human rights struggles temporarily eclipsed traditional social movements as a mode of organizing on the left during this period. This challenge to what theorists like Carol Gould have lauded in the human rights moment and the transnational as spaces for more democratic interactions between nation-states is echoed in the work of scholars and other observers of Latin America.[14] Political scientists such as Saskia Sassen, Thomas Olesen, Margaret Keck, and Katherine Sikkink have also identified modes of communication and new spaces for exchange as a means of escaping the power of states to control or restrict mobilization but have cautioned against the implications of the transcendence of the transnational, arguing that these networks should reinforce good government of states, rather than replace state government or accountability.[15] John Guidry further examines the way that political opportunity structures that arise from globalization have given rise to what Sassen describes as "economic citizenship" for multinational corporations alongside privation of citizenship rights for individuals living and working in transnational contexts. He argues that disruptions of democratic processes, while paradoxically also creating a new transnational public sphere that potentiates the activity of a more global civil society, can be ultimately harmful to democratic civil life. Echoing Habermas's and, later, Richard Rorty's concern with the nature of solidarity and contingency, Guidry posits that the lack of specific ties to community has the potential to result in *uncivil* society. For example, theorists of labor politics have argued that, despite the increasing capacity of workers to organize across borders, signaling a crucial new moment of actualizing an alternative form of citizenship, this same capacity allows multinational corporations to sidestep local labor laws and safety protections. The field of critical human rights, speaking to the way that transnational social movements, such as ethnic, diasporic, or gender-based struggles, fit into a broader debate about the usefulness of human rights as a mobilizing device, thus is crucial to understanding this phenomenon in Latin America.[16]

Much of this literature suggests that an organic sense of human rights and a constitutionally based definition of citizen rights and responsibilities were the product of looking outward to international convention and to mediated discussions of these legal frameworks. However, using the comparative or global lens to construct historical paradigms overvalues the meta-narrative frame and fails to account for the critical nuances of local practice. Scholars of Cold War Latin American history and, more broadly, of U.S. imperialism in the region have argued that the postcolonial turn in scholarship, by identifying the "range, inner complexity, and fluidity of the subjects and locations involved in imperial encounters," has given voice to the "fragmentation, ambiguity, and disjunctures" that are characteristic of complex and sometimes competing political systems.[17] This volume addresses the way transnational activism has intersected on the ground with understandings of human rights, global and national citizenship, and citizenship demands and exclusions. It responds to the call of immigration, diaspora, and borderlands scholars to consider critically the ethical implications of what is sometimes referred to as planetary humanism,[18] as a common ethics transcending the confines of nationality, race, ethnicity, class, and states, and to question the negotiated and precarious relationships these universal demands and calls to human rights responsibilities construct on the ground with local actors and institutions.

To this end, the book argues that historical paradigms used to examine solidarity organizing must better reflect the variety of solidarity organizing and of meanings of solidarity, which differ greatly from region to region and from locality to locality. Much of the existing theoretical literature on solidarity is based exclusively on North-South solidarity, and South-South interactions and encounters have long been an understudied and undertheorized dimension of transnational history. This work confronts this gap by examining notions and practices of solidarity situated in the local, the national, and specifically, South-South solidarity actions. It builds on theory advanced by James Sidaway of the imagined regional community of the Global South as a new way to conceptualize "Third World" solidarities, sometimes known as Third Worldism, during the course of the Cold War.[19] The history and construction of shared meanings of political solidarity across the region reframe transnational solidarity theoretically. Beyond challenging the proximity question of distant-issue movements with roots in unresolved historical conflicts, Latin American solidarity projects tended to deviate substantially from the model of nonreciprocal humanitarianism understood as North-to-South solidarity. As this volume argues, political solidarity was energized, often, by the activism of extremely marginalized social groups and responded to local dimensions of transregional struggle in ways that were transformative of political unities on the ground.

Solidarities across the Americas and between the Americas and other parts of the Third World also challenge what Sally Scholz calls "parasitical solidarity," or the use of social justice motifs to stand in for any real positive duties of political solidarity,[20] largely because these distant alliances were often critically tied to factions within political parties, diasporic communities of exiles, and ongoing social movements committed to direct political action. As such, examining the question of how these particular solidarities have manifested within and become part of political organization and ideological shifts within the Latin American left may reveal the distinctiveness of South-South solidarity and its continued relevance to contemporary politics. It reveals South-South solidarity as a transnational force quite distinct from North-to-South solidarity in its ability to challenge, rather than reinforce, hierarchal and hegemonic structures of power such as the state or U.S. foreign policy. This volume challenges solidarity theorists to consider constructions of political unity from within, from without, and in the in-between spaces of human interaction, and, by doing so, it suggests the potential of South-South campaigns to resist the pitfalls of project-related, temporary solidarities that tend to diminish more rapidly over time. Because these campaigns more frequently emerge from locally based notions of political unity extended outward, rather than adapting to a universalizing or normative frame of rights, they tend toward more lasting and often more politically useful ties of alliance.

Organization of the Volume

The work is organized around a set of key new research directions on the study of transnational solidarity and human rights during the Cold War period. It examines key precursors and shaping events prior to the human rights movements of the 1980s. It considers in rich detail the fashion in which different individuals, organizations, and governments throughout Latin America contributed to the reshaping left's vision of solidarity in relation to the politics of resistance, anticolonialism, and social justice movements. The first chapter, by Margaret Power, explores the efforts of the Puerto Rican Nationalist Party to build and employ Latin American solidarity in its struggle against U.S. colonialism on the island during the 1950s. This piece generates a conversation with the following chapters by Ernesto Capello, Sara Katherine Sanders, and Russell Cobb about the multiple meanings of anticolonialist movements within the frame of local and national struggles against U.S. intervention.

While Power examines the anticolonialist movement in Puerto Rico, a case much closer to home than the war in Vietnam or the anticolonialist struggles in Africa, Capello reverses the theoretical gaze by looking at the ill-fated journeys of Governor Nelson Rockefeller of New York to twenty Latin American countries on a "fact-finding tour" for the new Nixon administration. Sanders's treatment of the Mexican student movement of 1968 similarly problematizes the construction of an historical memory of 1968 as a framing narrative of the left in the period that followed by rethinking the national and locally specific meanings of anticolonialism operating within this frame. Where Power asks specifically what meaning anticolonialism conveyed to Latin Americans in solidarity with Puerto Rico's Nationalist Party (PN), drawing on strategic relationships that the PN had built since the 1920s, principally with other political parties and groups that the United States, by the 1950s, identified as "communist," Capello examines a series of unexplored solicitation letters sent to Rockefeller in the wake of his travels that illuminate the degree to which philanthropic, humanitarian, and cultural diplomatic activities shaped the development of cross-cultural empathy from the bottom up. Sanders's piece, a history of radical university politics in 1960s Mexico, further illustrates the conscious borrowing of resistance models to reveal a highly diverse moment of social mobilization based on discrete national concerns, as well as a shared and hybrid mobilizing framework of "global" revolution.

A second major concern of the volume is to explore the way in which cultural politics between the everyday and the transnational informed the development of sensibilities of solidarity and shaped everyday meanings of the Cold War struggle in Latin America. Just as Capello's piece unearths the voice of common people, from taxi drivers to single mothers, demonstrating a people's tangible desire to transcend the polarized Cold War framework that enveloped the clashes on the street, Russell Cobb's contribution addresses the construction of a public sphere for Latin American intellectuals responding to the call of the Cuban Revolution to artists to solidarity. His chapter explores the so-called Boom generation of writers in the 1960s and 1970s for whom the Cuban Revolution gave to writing a sense of urgency and engagement that caught the world's attention and reshaped popular engagement with the work of writers cum transnational activists such as Gabriel García Márquez and Pablo Neruda. Alison Bruey's contribution similarly engages this question of postnational political identity, exploring the way that solidarity offered an alternative type of citizenship in poor and working-class urban communities torn asunder by repression, fear, and economic misery under Augusto Pinochet's regime. She examines the use of popular conceptions of solidarity in the underground organizing networks affiliated with religious institutions in Santiago's poor and working-class neighborhoods and their success in crafting viable notions of postnational rights and responsibilities. Christine Hatzky's chapter looks closely at Cuban involvement in Angola between 1975 and 1991, observing, via one of the largest "proxy wars" of the Cold War in Africa, a hitherto unique example of a transatlantic, Latin American–African cooperation between two formerly colonized countries. Using testimony from individual participants from a variety of backgrounds, she uncovers the practical challenges of political identity formation via solidarity networks and reveals the means by which Cuban "internationalist solidarity" offered an alternative view of political unity in South-South solidarity movements.

The third part of the book explores transnational activism as a political resource. Brenda Elsey's essay moves the question of popular culture into the period of intense transnational human rights organizing of the 1970s and 1980s, examining the movement as a powerful yet problematic transnational political identity and tool. Elsey's work examines the Soviet Union's first boy-cott of the World Cup in protest of Chile's human rights violations in 1973 and the controversy that ensued, highlighting the role of popular culture in the construction of an international "human rights community." She asserts that, in the 1970s, the Chilean solidarity movement constituted a formative experience for many human rights activists and a benchmark in the expansion of universal jurisdiction to enforce human rights. Elsey argues that popular culture served as a vehicle for building empathy, which was crucial to the ac-ceptance of human rights standards. Molly Todd examines the complicated postnational responsibilities and attendant identities surrounding Cold War refugees and displaced persons. Her essay on Salvadoran refugees and interna-tional aid in Honduras underscores the cultural construction of the refugee in the late 1970s and 1980s. Using documentation from the refugee camps, oral history interviews, and internal records of the UN High Commissioner for Refugees, Todd, like Hatzky and Elsey, reveals a stark contrast between high-profile actors' perceptions of and approaches to refugees on the one hand and the perceptions and actions of the victims of Cold War conflicts on the other. Rather than view war flight solely as an act of desperation, this contribution examines flight and exile as conscious strategies of resistance to state-sponsored citizenship exclusion and violent political repression. By elaborating commu-nal governance structures in the refugee camps, distributing newsletters, and coordinating protest actions, among other activities, they insisted on their own agency and asserted themselves as participants not only in all realms of their life in exile but also on the Salvadoran national scene.

The volume concludes with an epilogue by James N. Green, crafted from a self-interview on the subject of his time as an activist in the struggle against authoritarianism in Latin America and for gay rights across the Americas. As a member of a radical Quaker group, Green joined solidarity groups in opposi-tion to torture and repression in Brazil beginning in 1971, while he was still in Philadelphia. His quest to merge sexual and political identities was central to his activism in the United States and Brazil. Decades later, the interview high-lights the need for further scholarship related to sexual liberation movements in Latin America and their relationship to transnational solidarity organizing and human rights struggle. Green's piece builds on the momentum of the Power, Capello, Hatzky, and Todd pieces by exploring the tense relationship between gay rights movements and leftists; he considers the competing politi-cal identities and everyday concerns that were very much a part of the struggle to define and organize a New Left in Brazil. His reflections on the emergence of two important vehicles, SOMOS and *Lampião da Esquina*, are invaluable to constructing the history of the transnational gay rights movement but also shed light on denials of equality and participation for minorities in solidarity organizing during the Cold War. Green's piece adds a crucial dimension to our understandings of the social history of rights-based struggle, responding to the question posed by Dussel of how responsibilities to distant others are constructed and framed and, at least in a very specific case, by whom.

Conclusion

What this volume pleads for is a sustained conversation about the nature and challenge of the transnational in Latin American Cold War history. By exploring campaigns waged on behalf of distant others by discrete translocal networks, political communities, and social actors in Latin America, the book attempts to illuminate the way that longstanding leftist notions of anti-imperialism, pan-regionalism, solidarity, and social and economic justice found a way to compete with the powerful discursive frame of human rights and democracy whose tone was often set by the imperialist ambitions of the United States, complicit nation-states, and military regimes. Popular groups and literary figures reshaped notions of cosmopolitan ethics to include their own leftist critiques of capitalism, embracing the global as an arena of social responsibility while resisting the global as a preeminent source of authority over local markets and national interests. Politically active Catholic communities in Latin America extended solidarity to non-Catholics by broadening the existing ideological commitments that were codified in religious doctrine and existing social responsibilities practiced by activists within the church, resulting in relatively successful transnational campaigns on behalf of human rights victims and refugees across the region during the Cold War. Similarly, refugees and political exiles were active participants in constructing understandings of transnational responsibility to the displaced and to socially excluded minority and ethnic groups. Participating in solidarity during this period was often transformative for individuals and communities, just as the transnational connections and alliances organizations and communities made were transformative of their local struggles.

The heterogeneity of calls for justice and transnational solidarity during the Cold War in Latin America speaks volumes about the way that the shifting landscape of political economy on the ground created spaces for new political imaginaries and new political subjecthoods. As the left reemerged after decades of repression and dirty war, it had to respond to these new subject positionings and visions of community that already were giving rise to social movements, international truth tellings, and collective memory debates. The Cold

War pushed the left to confront its own concerns about the consequences of conceiving of political communities in terms of citizenship and rights. This volume argues that transnational solidarity activism was a key site of political encounter, negotiation, exchange, and, sometimes, empowerment in the struggles that came to characterize the re-emergent left and new social movements of the post-Cold War period.

This volume is being written at a time when solidarity between peoples across long distances figures prominently in the media, when technologically mediated interactions are worming for grip on our understanding of how human relations are forged across space and time. As greater trust is placed on transnational modes of interaction, it becomes ever more crucial for us to understand the consequences of moving beyond state and local authority. Kwame Anthony Appiah argues that "there are many reasons to think that living in political communities narrower than the species is better for us than would be our engulfment in a single world-state: a cosmopolis of which we cosmopolitans would not be figurative but literal citizens."[21] In the case of South-South solidarity, it is clear that the goal of activism is not participation in a global democracy or the eventual dissolution of state and local authority, but rather the use of transnational alliances to better democratic institutions and to promote socioeconomic justice on the ground. This form of transnational solidarity from below is far more prevalent than has been recognized in earlier literature on the subject, and it is hoped that this volume will encourage more scholarly interest in the subject.

Notes

The author would like to thank the University of British Columbia for a generous internal grant, which facilitated the coordination and publication of this book, and Steve Stern, Gwen Walker, Margaret Power, and Brenda Elsey for their insightful comments on the introduction. I would also like to thank David Jefferess and Thomas Olesen for their early support and engagement with the project in its conceptual stages.

1. Klaus Peter Rippe, "Diminishing Solidarity," *Ethical Theory and Moral Practice* 1.3 (1998): 355–73.

2. Enrique Dussel, "From Fraternity to Solidarity: Toward a *Politics of Liberation*," *Journal of Social Philosophy* 38, no. 1 (Spring 2007): 80.

3. Jean Quataert, *Advocating Dignity: Human Rights Mobilizations in Global Politics* (Philadelphia: University of Pennsylvania Press, 2009), 3–5.

4. Giyatri Chakravorty Spivak, *A Critique of Postcolonial Reason* (New York: Routledge, 1999).

5. Spike V. Peterson, "Whose Rights? A Critique of the 'Givens' in Human Rights Discourse," *Alternatives* 15, no. 3 (Summer 1990): 304–5.

6. David Jacobson, *Rights across Borders: Immigration and the Decline of Citizenship* (Baltimore, MD: Johns Hopkins University Press, 1996).

7. Patrick William Kelly, "'When the People Awake': The Transnational Solidarity Movement, the Pinochet Junta, and the Human Rights Movement of the 1970s" (lecture, University of Chicago Latin American History Seminar, March 19, 2009), http://humanrights.uchicago.edu/Baro/Patrick-Kelly-Martin-Baro-Essay.pdf.

8. Margaret Power, "The U.S. Movement in Solidarity with Chile in the 1970s," *Latin American Perspectives* 36, no. 6 (2009): 46–66.

9. Steve Stern, *Battling for Hearts and Minds: Memory Struggles in Pinochet's Chile, 1973–1988* (Durham, NC: Duke University Press, 2006), 102.

10. Jürgen Habermas, "The Postnational Constellation and the Future of Democracy," in *The Postnational Constellation: Political Essays*, ed. Jürgen Habermas (Cambridge, MA: MIT Press, 2001), 108.

11. Jeffrey Flynn, "Human Rights, Transnational Solidarity, and Duties to the Global Poor," *Constellations* 16, no. 1 (2009): 68.

12. James Green, "(Homo)sexuality, Human Rights, and Revolution in Latin America," in *Human Rights and Revolutions*, 2nd ed., ed. Jeffrey N. Wasserstrom, Lynn Hunt, Marilyn B. Young, and Gregory Grandin (New York: Rowman and Littlefield, 2007), 146.

13. Greg Grandin, "Human Rights and Empire's Embrace," in *Human Rights and Revolutions*, 2nd ed., ed. Jeffrey N. Wasserstrom, Lynn Hunt, Marilyn B. Young, and Gregory Grandin (New York: Rowman and Littlefield, 2007), 205.

14. Carol C. Gould, "Transnational Solidarities," *Journal of Social Philosophy* 38, no. 1 (Spring 2007): 148–64.

15. See the discussion in Saskia Sassen, *Territory, Authority, Rights* (Princeton, NJ: Princeton University Press, 2006); Thomas Olesen, *International Zapatismo* (London: Zed Books, 2005); Margaret Keck and Kathryn Skikink, *Activists without Borders: Advocacy Networks in International Politics* (Ithaca, NY: Cornell University Press, 1998). See also the argument made by Arjun Appadurai in "Sovereignty without Territoriality: Notes for a Post-national Geography," in *The Geography of Identity*, ed. Patricia Yaeger (Ann Arbor: University of Michigan Press, 1997), 337–50.

16. See for instance Cecilia Lesgart, *Usos de la transición a la democracia: Ensayo, ciencia y política en la década del '80* (Rosario, Arg.: Homo Sapiens Ediciones, 2003); Alison Brysk, *The Politics of Human Rights in Argentina: Protest, Change, and Democratization* (Stanford: Stanford University Press, 1994); Katherine Hite, *When the Romance Ended: Leaders of the Chilean Left, 1968–1998* (New York: Columbia University Press, 2008); Oscar Landi et al., *Los derechos humanos como política: Encuentro realizado el 20 y 21 de Junio de 1984 en Santiago de Chile* (Buenos Aires: Ediciones La Aurora, 1985); Luis Roniger, "Human Rights Violations and the Reshaping of Collective Identities in Argentina, Chile and Uruguay," *Social Identities* 3.2 (1997): 221–46; Sally J. Scholz, *Political Solidarity* (University Park: Pennsylvania State University Press, 2008); Stern, *Battling for Hearts and Minds*; Eric Zolov, "Expanding our Conceptual Horizons: The Shift from an Old to a New Left in Latin America," *Acontracorriente* 5.2 (2008): 47–73.

17. Fernando Coronil, "Foreword," in *Close Encounters of Empire: Writing the*

Cultural History of U.S.-Latin American Relations, ed. Gilbert M. Joseph, Catherine Legrand, and Ricardo Salvatore (Durham, NC: Duke University Press, 1998), xi.

18. Paul Gilroy, *Postcolonial Melancholia* (London: Routledge, 2004).

19. James Sidaway, *Imagined Regional Communities: Integration and Sovereignty in the Global South* (New York: Routledge, 2002).

20. Scholz, *Political Solidarity*, 5.

21. Kwame Anthony Appiah, "Loyalty to Humanity," reply to Martha Nussbaum's essay "Patriotism and Cosmopolitanism," *Boston Review* 19, no. 5 (October/November 1994): 10.

Part I

Critical Precursors to Transnational Solidarity

The Puerto Rican Nationalist Party, Transnational Latin American Solidarity, and the United States during the Cold War

MARGARET POWER

In June 1958, Carlos Padilla Pérez, a member of the Puerto Rican Nationalist Party, addressed a gathering of Argentines organized by the Amigos pro Libertad de Puerto Rico in Buenos Aires. He thanked them, his "fellow citizens of Our América," for their solidarity and evoked the image of a shared history and a common heritage. Just as the Argentines "crossed the Andes in pursuit of the enemies of freedom" during the wars of independence in the 1800s, so, too, did Puerto Ricans join the continental fight against Spanish colonialism. The Puerto Rican general Antonio Valero de Bernabe "fought for the independence of Mexico" and then hastened to continue the battle against Spanish colonialism alongside "the Liberator Bolivar in whose army he achieved positions of distinction." Recognizing that the historical moment has changed—"the patriotic armies are no longer intertwined along the paths of Our América as they once were"—Padilla nonetheless urged Argentines to support Puerto Rico's ongoing struggle against colonialism, now directed against the United States. Above all, he emphasized that Puerto Rico is part of Latin America and that the U.S. occupation of the island nation represents a threat to the entire region. "[Freedom of Puerto Rico] is of critical importance to each of you because the United States threatens to extend the colonial regime that it has imposed on Puerto Rico under the name of the 'free associated state' over all the peoples of Our America. We are conscious . . . that as long as Puerto Rico awaits its freedom and is prevented from exercising its powers as a sovereign people, then the goal of unity that we pursue is blocked because it prevents us from joining the Latin American family."[1]

Puerto Rico became a U.S. colony in 1898, following the Spanish-American War. In order to ensure its control of the island, the U.S. Congress passed the Foraker Act in 1900 and the Jones Act in 1917. The Foraker Act ended U.S. military rule in Puerto Rico and established a civilian government, with North American governors appointed by the United States, while the Jones Act made Puerto Ricans U.S. citizens.[2]

By and large, the Puerto Rican response to these acts was muted. During the first three decades of U.S. colonialism in Puerto Rico, various political figures and parties called for independence. However, their demands, weakened by internecine political fights and the absence of a unified political strategy, were ineffective. Pedro Albizu Campos's ascension to secretary general of the Nationalist Party in 1930 radically altered the situation.[3] Under his leadership, the Nationalist Party transformed what had been inchoate dreams for independence into a determined fight to actually achieve it.

The Nationalist Party did not advocate either capitalism or socialism, and, despite allegations to the contrary, the party was not fascist.[4] Many in the party, including Albizu Campos, were fervent Catholics.[5] However, the glue that held the party together was the desire to establish Puerto Rico as a sovereign nation, not agreement as to what economic system they would implement once independence was achieved.

Nationalists defined Puerto Rico as part of the "Latin American family" and sought a sovereignty anchored in the joint history and the future of what they perceived to be a shared transregional reality. They identified with the former colonies of Spain, now independent republics, because they shared a common language, culture, religion, and history. They also confronted the same enemy: the United States. The Nationalist Party understood that Puerto Rico was a small Antillean nation confronting a formidable imperial power in the region. In order to strengthen efforts to end U.S. colonialism, the Nationalists consciously sought—and received—solidarity from democratic, leftist, anticolonial, and anti-imperialist individuals, organizations, and governments across Latin America.

The Nationalist Party ceased to participate in elections in the 1930s, which has made it difficult to gauge concretely what percentage of the Puerto Rican population belonged to or supported it. It is also a challenge to determine the social makeup of the party. However, police records of Nationalist Party members and sympathizers arrested after the October 1950 revolt, which is discussed in greater detail later, offer some clues. Following the uprising, the Puerto Rican police arrested 1,106 people.[6] The police recorded brief descriptions of those they arrested, noting such information as their skin color, size, position within the party, place of origin, residence, and work. Information on these cards reveals that the party attracted Puerto Ricans from across the island, from the capital, San Juan, to the small towns and farms in the mountainous interior. It also shows that peasants, small landowners, intellectuals, shopkeepers, professionals, students, and laborers joined or sympathized with the party. Puerto Ricans of all races and both genders were members of the party.[7] Miñi Seijo Bruno analyzed the 140 combatants who took part in the insurrection. Her detailed study reveals that male fighters outnumbered female ones but that "non whites," which is how the census characterized Puerto Ricans of African descent, "had a greater degree of representation in the insurrection than the white race, when compared to their percentage in the 1950 census."[8]

This chapter examines trans–Latin American solidarity with Puerto Rican independence and the Nationalist Party in the 1950s, during the height of the Cold War. It reveals the deep bonds of solidarity that existed among and between Latin Americans, the importance that people throughout the hemisphere placed on securing a free and independent Puerto Rico, and the profound anger that many Latin Americans felt at the U.S. government's imprisonment of Puerto Rican Nationalists who fought to end colonialism in their country.

The existence and persistence of Latin American solidarity with the struggle for Puerto Rican independence during the Cold War exposes cracks in U.S. efforts to extend hegemonic control over the region and the world. At a time when the U.S. government was vociferously cloaking itself in the mantle of democracy, its colonial hold over Puerto Rico clearly contradicted its own discourse and sharply challenged its efforts to portray itself as a trustworthy supporter of those nations in Africa and Asia that were struggling against European colonialism or that had recently achieved national independence. The U.S. government both failed to understand and was unable to extinguish Latin American solidarity with Puerto Rico. Support for Puerto Rican independence and demands for the release of Nationalist Party political prisoners extended throughout the continent and involved individuals, organizations, parliamentarians, and governments of various political stripes. It drew on a historical legacy of regional support for anticolonial and anti-imperialist struggles and

reflected the determined efforts of members of the Nationalist Party to gener-
ate support for their struggle. Latin American solidarity with Puerto Rico persisted despite the attempts of the U.S. government to obviate or overcome it
through the political changes it engineered in Puerto Rico or through the
construction of tighter alliances with repressive, anticommunist governments.
The endurance of this solidarity with Puerto Rican independence simultaneously makes manifest the weaknesses of U.S. Cold War rhetoric and policies,
speaks to the perseverance of a transregional identity, highlights a shared opposition to foreign rule, and anticipates and prefigures the continental spirit of
anti-imperialist revolution that erupted following the 1959 Cuban revolution.

Much of the literature on Latin America unfortunately overlooks Puerto
Rico—the only remaining U.S. colony in the hemisphere—when discussing
the United States and Latin America.[9] As a result, it describes dynamics that do
not reflect the Puerto Rican reality and ignores the important connections that
existed between Puerto Rico and the rest of the region. For example, in their
discussion of Latin America from 1944 to 1948, Leslie Bethell and Ian Roxborough argue that much of Latin America experienced a period of "democratization, a shift to the Left, and labor militancy" in the years immediately following World War II. However, they point out, by 1948 (and for some countries
as early as 1945), government repression increased, and "the popular forces, the
Left, and democracy suffered a historic defeat."[10] While this description applies
to much of Latin America, it clearly does not fit Puerto Rico for the obvious
reason that Puerto Rico was a U.S. colony, before, during, and after the war.
Puerto Rico did not enjoy a democratic spring after the war; instead, Nationalist political prisoners languished in U.S. and Puerto Rican jails. Certainly, the
island shared the wave of repression that hit Latin America in the late 1940s
and 1950s, but this was not new, since Nationalists had been experiencing
similar attacks for decades.[11] When Greg Grandin makes an important critique
of "historians of U.S. policy toward the region [Latin America]" who focus on
"what preoccupied U.S. policymakers," it appears that he is not taking Puerto
Rico's colonial status into sufficient consideration. He calls on historians to pay
attention to "what was being fought over in Latin America itself."[12] Yet, what
the Nationalists were fighting for was independence from the United States, so
it would be difficult, if not impossible, to discuss politics in Puerto Rico and
ignore the U.S. government's role in it.

Puerto Rico represented a particular challenge to the United States and
its efforts to dominate the region politically and ideologically. Members of
the Nationalist Party refused to renounce the struggle for Puerto Rican independence.[13] Their repudiation of U.S. rule demonstrated to Latin America
and the rest of the world that some Puerto Ricans were willing to undertake

bold and dramatic actions, at great personal sacrifice, to liberate their nation. Their commitment to independence and Puerto Rico's status as a colony revealed the hypocrisy of the United States at a time when Washington was loudly proclaiming the virtues of democracy, defending human rights, and defining itself as the friend of the global movement against colonialism.[14] This contradiction, combined with the sympathy and political support that individuals, parties, and governments throughout Latin America expressed for the colonized Caribbean island and for the political prisoners jailed by the United States for resisting Puerto Rico's subordinate status, mattered to politicians and government officials in Washington. It explains, in part, why the U.S. Congress allowed Puerto Ricans to vote for their own governor and worked with the Popular Democratic Party to engineer Puerto Rico's transition from an outright colony to a more disguised one as a Free Associated State. It also contributed to saving the life of Oscar Collazo, the Puerto Rican Nationalist who received the death penalty following his attack on Blair House, the temporary residence of President Harry Truman, in November 1950.

Trans–Latin American Solidarity with the Puerto Rican Nationalist Party in the 1920s and 1930s

Latin American solidarity with the Nationalists in the 1950s reflected, in part, the work of pro-independence forces in the 1920s and 1930s. Pedro Albizu Campos and the Nationalist Party understood that Latin American solidarity was critical for Puerto Rico to obtain independence. To that end, they promoted opposition to U.S. imperialism and support for Puerto Rican independence across the Americas. From 1927 to 1929, Albizu Campos traveled throughout the region in a "patriotic pilgrimage" to meet with "the people of our race."[15] As the party newspaper reported, he would begin his trip in the "heroic Dominican homeland from where he will continue his travels through Ibero-América." (During his travels, Albizu Campos visited the Dominican Republic, Haiti, Cuba, Mexico, and Peru.)[16] Albizu Campos undertook this trip to inform Latin Americans about "the protests of a country that refuses to accept the shameful enslavement that the imperialists from the north have imposed on it." He and the Nationalist Party wanted the peoples of the continent to learn about "the island's tragedy"; they also hoped to expose the "false Yankee democracy so that [Latin Americans] could better prepare themselves against the imperialist economic policies from the North."[17] Albizu Campos's mission bore fruit. During his 1927 visit to Cuba, illustrious Cubans such as Dr. Enrique José Varona, Dr. Emilio Roig de Leuchsenring, Dr. Enrique Gay Galbó, and Juan Marinello Vidaurreta, among others, formed the Junta Nacional Cubana pro Independencia de Puerto Rico.[18] Strong bonds of mutual support existed between many Cubans and Puerto Ricans. Both Puerto Rico and Cuba had remained Spanish colonies throughout the nineteenth century, long after 1824, when Madrid's other American possessions had achieved independence. United in a common struggle, they had organized joint pro-independence committees, such as the Junta Revolucionaria in New York City, and fought together on the battlefield to end colonial control of their nations. This common heritage explains why anti-imperialist Cubans committed themselves to securing the independence of their sister Antillean nation. However, Cubans were not the only Latin Americans to form organizations and conduct campaigns in opposition to U.S. colonialism and repression in Puerto Rico, as events during the 1930s made clear.

During the 1930s, conflict between the Nationalist Party and the U.S. government increased. The Nationalist Party garnered greater popular support and stepped up its militant activities against U.S. colonial rule in response to increased U.S. government repression against the party. Across Latin America, anti-imperialist and antifascist forces took up the cause of Puerto Rico and the Nationalist political prisoners. In 1936, leaders of the Nationalist Party were accused and convicted of seditious conspiracy and sentenced to between six and ten years in the federal penitentiary in Atlanta, Georgia.[19] Pro-independence events were held in Mexico, Peru, and Uruguay in support of the Nationalists.[20] In Argentina, in 1936, the University Federation of Argentina sent a petition to U.S. Secretary of State Cordell Hull "demanding the release of the Nationalist leader Juan Antonio Corretjer." They also demanded "an end to the unjustified repression by the North American regime against the Nationalists."[21] And, in Costa Rica, the Communist Party dedicated one week to "the struggle for Puerto Rican independence." It called on its members to "raise money to send cables to the governor of Puerto Rico to protest the abuses that North American authorities have carried out against Puerto Rican Nationalists."[22] The Confederation of Anti-Imperialist Students of America, which was meeting in Mexico, wrote to President Franklin Delano Roosevelt in 1937 "to bring to your attention the immense clamor of protest that has risen in our hearts over the unjust incarceration of Pedro Albizu Campos, Juan Antonio Corretjer, and other leaders of Puerto Rican Nationalism, now banished to the Federal Penitentiary at Atlanta, Georgia, accused of the most honorable act which any man could accomplish—to struggle for the Independence of his country."[23] The relationships that the Nationalists built with Latin Americans in the 1920s and 1930s persisted through the 1940s and 1950s.

The 1950s: Defiance and Solidarity at the Height of the Cold War

The United States emerged from World War II as a major power in the world and the dominant force in the western hemisphere. The United States' position as one of two superpowers allowed it to expand its political reach, economic penetration, and military operations around the globe. Nevertheless, it continued to view Latin America as a foreign yet integral and essential extension/ possession of itself. The United States had profound economic ties with, even a dependency on, Latin America. Indeed, as Bethell and Roxborough point out, referring to the postwar period, "Latin America remained the United States' most important export market and source of imports and, after Canada, the area in which most U.S. capital was invested."[24]

Puerto Rico played an important military and geopolitical role in the U.S. government's plans for the hemisphere. The U.S. Navy viewed its bases at Roosevelt Roads and Vieques as critical to its outward defense against "communism," both on the mainland and throughout the western hemisphere. As Vice Admiral William Barby warned at a 1947 Lions Club luncheon in San Juan, the United States needed to prepare for a "possible attack from overseas." Alerting his audience to the very real "danger of invasion in the next seven to ten years," he added, "this danger required readiness in the Caribbean," specifically at the U.S. Navy bases in Puerto Rico.[25]

However, the United States colonial rule in Puerto Rico undermined Washington's efforts to portray itself as a supporter of democracy and freedom in opposition to communist totalitarianism and repression. The Nationalist Party knew that the United States' possession of Puerto Rico weakened the latter's image as the leader of the "free world." This understanding, combined with its history of working with anticolonial and anti-imperialist forces across Latin America, allowed the party to call upon sympathetic sectors throughout the region (and the world) to support its demand for sovereignty.

The Nationalist Party's work in the United Nations exemplified its recognition of the importance of hemispheric and global support for its struggle. In a 1948 interview, Pedro Albizu Campos remarked on the power exerted by the United States and other colonial powers, a group he referred to as the "United Front to render a restricted interpretation of Chapter 11" in the United Nations. (Chapter 11 and particularly Article 73 said that the imperialist powers "are bound to respect the political, economic, and cultural aspirations of the nations intervened in by their armed forces.") At the same time, he affirmed the importance of the international body since "it is of general knowledge that all the Latin American countries, and, in fact, all the nations of the world—

with the exception of the colonial powers—are willing, when the opportune moment arises, to implement the principle of the independence of all subjugated countries like Puerto Rico. That principle is incorporated in the Charter of the United Nations Organization, and its recognition is binding upon the despotism of the United States which shackles us."[26]

As part of its efforts to secure international support, the Nationalist Party designated Thelma Mielke, a New Yorker who supported Puerto Rican independence, to represent it in the international body.[27] The party believed that the United Nations offered it an important platform from which to inform the world of Puerto Rico's colonial status and to call on nations, particularly those in the region, for solidarity. Furthermore, Latin American nations had substantial influence in the international institution, since they "represented two fifths of the votes—20 out of 51—, . . . making [them] the most important single voting bloc."[28] The Nationalist Party's appeals for support posed a problem to the United States as it attempted to exert its influence over Latin America. As Ivonne Acosta-Lespier notes, "the plans the United States had for the hemisphere were hindered by the campaign in the United Nations of Puerto Rican Nationalists and independence activists who portrayed the United States as a colonial power."[29]

In order to clean up its public image and do away with the perception that its colonial hold over Puerto Rico contradicted its self-designation as the number one defender of freedom, the U.S. government implemented a two-prong strategy to effect changes in Puerto Rico's status so that it would appear that the island was no longer a U.S. colony and to silence the voice of those who most determinedly opposed ongoing U.S. colonialism, the Nationalist Party. To accomplish the first goal, Washington worked with like-minded Puerto Ricans to transform Puerto Rico's status so that it would appear that the United States no longer colonized it. In 1946, President Harry Truman appointed the first Puerto Rican governor, Jesús Piñero, a close collaborator of Luis Muñoz Marín, the leader of the Popular Democratic Party (PPD). Then, in 1948, after fifty years of U.S. colonial rule, Muñoz Marín became the first elected Puerto Rican governor.[30] Muñoz Marín had abandoned his support for independence during the 1940s and tied his political wagon to his relationship with the United States. Cognizant of the contradictions that U.S. colonialism in Puerto Rico posed to the emerging superpower, Muñoz Marín "sought to take advantage of the need of the United States to address the worldwide rise of anticolonial and anti-imperialist sentiment."[31] He presented himself as the man who would end colonialism by converting Puerto Rico into a Free Associated State.

The road to the Free Associated State involved a number of legislative changes. In 1950, President Truman signed Public Law 600, which allowed Puerto Ricans to vote for their own constitution. A referendum was held in Puerto Rico on the new constitution in 1952. Of 783,610 registered voters, 463,828 (59.0 percent) cast ballots; 373,594 (47.1 percent of total registered voters and 81.5 percent of those voting) supported the terms set forth in the constitution, and 82,877 (11.0 percent of total registered and 18.5 percent of those voting) opposed them.[32] As a result of the vote, the constitution went into effect on July 25, 1952, the anniversary of the day in 1898 when the United States had invaded Puerto Rico during the Spanish-American War.

Muñoz Marín and the U.S. government seized the opportunity to declare that Puerto Rico was no longer a U.S. colony, since Puerto Rico now had its own constitution and was a Free Associated State.[33] Although this change did result in the devolution of some governing functions to Puerto Ricans, it did not fundamentally change the island's colonial relationship to the United States. As a Free Associated State, which is an anomaly in U.S. history, Puerto Rico could now direct its own internal political affairs, such as local and gubernatorial elections. However, the U.S. government continued to exert control over all federal matters, foreign relations, and economic and military issues. For example, Puerto Ricans have had no voice in favor of or against any U.S. decision to go to war, since they cannot vote for any federal officials, yet they were subject to the draft when it was in effect.[34] The new arrangement worked to the benefit of the United States and Muñoz Marín. As Ayala and Bernabe note, "the U.S. State Department . . . looked favorably upon legislation that would allow the United States to argue Puerto Rico was no longer a colony while not reducing its ultimate rights over the island."[35]

The U.S. government (along with Muñoz Marín and the PPD) understood that the establishment of the Free Associated State alone would not convince the world that Puerto Rico was no longer a U.S. colony. This realization led to the second part of Washington's two-pronged strategy: the elimination of the Nationalist Party as the voice and symbol of resistance to U.S. colonialism. The measures that would facilitate the wave of repression that engulfed the Nationalist Party in the 1950s began in the late 1940s, in Washington, D.C. In 1948, the U.S. Congress passed and imposed on Puerto Rico Law 53, frequently referred to as the Gag Law. This law made it a felony to "encourage, defend, counsel, or preach, voluntarily or knowingly, the need, desirability, or convenience of overturning, destroying, or paralyzing the Insular Government, [the local Puerto Rican government] or any of its political subdivisions, by way of force or violence; and to publish, edit, circulate, sell, distribute, or publicly exhibit with the intention to overturn [the Insular Government]."[36] This law effectively made it illegal to struggle for or even speak in favor of the independence of Puerto Rico. The arrests of hundreds in Puerto Rico and the United States following the insurrection on the island on October 30, 1950, and the November 1950 attack on Blair House in the U.S. capital amply demonstrated the full scope of this law.

However, even before the uprising, the Nationalist Party was subject to increased repression and anticipated that more attacks were to come. In May 1950, the Nationalist Party issued a statement in which it denounced U.S. government plans to carry out "the immediate assassination of Dr. Pedro Albizu Campos . . . and of the other leaders of [the Nationalist] party, and the dissolution of the same."[37] As Oscar Collazo wrote in his memoirs, speaking of the period just before the insurrection, "the persecution and harassment against the Nationalists had arrived at such an extreme that they had to use force to defend themselves."[38]

The Nationalist Party understood the change from an outright colony to a Free Associated State to be merely cosmetic; at the same time it was alarmed that the transformation could and, according to the vote for the constitution, apparently did deceive people, both in Puerto Rico and around the world, leading them to believe that colonialism had indeed ended in Puerto Rico. This perception, combined with the growing number of party members arrested and fears that the U.S. government had plans to imprison or assassinate Pedro Albizu Campos, convinced the party leadership that only a dramatic and substantial rejection of the political changes being carried out in or planned for Puerto Rico would notify their compatriots and the world that the island remained a U.S. colony and that patriotic Puerto Ricans would resist both the repression and the new status. It is against this backdrop that the Nationalists launched the insurrection on October 30, 1950, in Puerto Rico and attacked Blair House in Washington, D.C., on November 1, 1950.

The Nationalist Party Attacks in the 1950s

Blanca Canales was a social worker who had supported Puerto Rican independence since she was nine years old. In her memoirs, she recalls that her favorite thing to do when she was young was to "stand on the balcony behind the house and harangue the neighborhood kids about patriotism." She received military training after she joined the Nationalist Party in 1931 and stored munitions for the party in her home. In 1950, she led the Nationalist uprising in Jayuya, her hometown of about 1,500 people, situated in the mountainous interior of the island. Years later, she recalled that she, like other Nationalists, launched the attack for two reasons. "We thought that they [the 'puppet government and the U.S. empire'] would try and imprison Albizu Campos, something for which they would pay a heavy price [this time] since when don Pedro was arrested in the 1930s he asked us all to remain calm." They also rose up to protest "the plan to approve the law that would establish the Free Associated State."[39]

According to some sources, the date for the uprising was moved forward several months as a result of growing U.S. attacks against the party.[40] Estanislao Lugo was a member of the Nationalist Party, a trusted compañero of Albizu Campos, and one of the party's seven military commanders. According to him, the Nationalists initiated the "Revolution" because they got word on October 29, 1950, that the police "were going to search the houses of the Nationalists and arrest those who had arms." To prevent this from happening, he and his men retreated to a farm to await orders. The police got wind of their presence and arrested them on October 30.[41]

When other military units of the Nationalist Party heard the news of their arrest, they followed instructions and attempted to attack colonial institutions, such as post offices and police stations, in seven other small towns in the interior of the island, as well as the governor's palace in San Juan.[42] The attacks were generally unsuccessful. Only in Jayuya were the Nationalists able to "attack the police headquarters, burn the Selective Service cards and the Federal Post Office, and proclaim the Republic of Puerto Rico."[43]

Luis Muñoz Marín, the governor, called the attacks a "conspiracy against democracy helped by the Communists" and "a criminal conspiracy by a group of fanatics."[44] The U.S. government sent planes to bomb Jayuya and Utuado, another town in the mountains of Puerto Rico, and the National Guard to attack the Nationalists. By November 1, 1950, most of the fighting was over; sixteen Nationalists, seven police, and one National Guard were killed; nine Nationalists, twenty-three police, six National Guard, and eleven civilians were wounded.[45] The government then applied the Gag Law and arrested 1,106 people, including Pedro Albizu Campos and the leadership of the Nationalist Party, and members of the Communist Party and of the Puerto Rican Independence Party, another pro-independence party. Although the majority of the detained were released soon thereafter, over one hundred people served lengthy prison terms. In 1962, thirty-one Puerto Ricans were still held in Puerto Rican or U.S. prisons.[46] Blanca Canales, for example, spent twenty years in jail.[47]

In New York City, two members of the Nationalist Party, Oscar Collazo and Griselio Torresola, learned of the unsuccessful uprising and decided to act to defend it. According to Collazo, who was head of the Nationalist Party in New York City, Torresola commented that newspaper reports "made it appear as if the fighting was nothing more than an issue exclusively among Puerto Ricans. Nothing mentioned the direct part the United States was playing in the genocide." He added that they needed to act quickly because "it is urgent that the world's attention be focused on Puerto Rico and that we expose [U.S.] imperialism as the principal protagonist in the tragedy."[48] Thus, without much planning or training, fueled by their indignation and by their desire to expose what they considered the "slaughter" then taking place in Puerto Rico, Collazo and Torresola went to Washington, D.C., to call attention to what the United States was doing in Puerto Rico. Security guards at Blair House, President Truman's temporary residence, confronted them as they approached the house, a gunfight ensued, and Torresola was killed and Collazo severely wounded.[49] Following his trial, Collazo was found guilty of "first degree murder, assaulting the residency of the president of the United States, and of carrying illegal arms" and sentenced to die.[50]

In 1954, four Nationalists, led by Lolita Lebrón, fired shots in the U.S. Congress to tell the world that Puerto Rico "is a colony."[51] "We went," said Rafael Cancel Miranda, one of the four, "because we wanted to call the attention of the world to our reality." Their timing and motivation underscore the importance the Nationalist Party placed on world opinion. The attack occurred shortly after the United States had "reported to the United Nations that Puerto Rico was a sovereign nation, and at the same time as the Organization of American States was meeting in Caracas, Venezuela."[52] They wanted the world to know not only that some Puerto Ricans considered this untrue but also that they were willing to sacrifice their lives to expose what they considered the colonial reality of their homeland.

Latin American Solidarity with the Nationalists

The late 1940s and the 1950s were a difficult period for left and anti-imperialist forces in Latin America. Determined to secure its control over the hemisphere, the United States government practiced the Truman Doctrine, which dictated that the goal of U.S. foreign policy was to "halt the spread of communism" through containment.[53] Working with pro-capitalist forces and the military across the region, the United States encouraged or sponsored the rise to power of conservative, anticommunist governments. By the end of 1954, dictatorial rule had replaced democratic governments in eleven countries.[54] Repression of the left became the order of the day. In Chile, which was technically democratic, the government of Gabriel González Videla moved against his coalition partners in the Communist Party, sending scores of them to camps.[55] Repression was not limited to the left. The U.S. government considered the reformist government of Jacobo Arbenz in Guatemala to be such a threat that it organized its overthrow and instigated the imposition of a military dictatorship in 1954.[56]

The United States influenced how Latin American nations voted in the United Nations. Both the U.S. government and leaders of the Popular Democratic Party, the party of Luis Muñoz Marín, were eager to remove Puerto Rico from the UN's list of non-self-governing territories.[57] In January 1953, the United States informed the secretary general that "it is no longer necessary or appropriate for the United States to continue to transmit information on Puerto Rico" to the United Nations.[58] In a clear indication of the power the United States exerted over the United Nations, the General Assembly voted to remove Puerto Rico from the list of non-self-governing territories. The majority of Latin American states voted in favor of the resolution, with only Mexico and Guatemala opposing it.[59]

However, it would be a mistake to think that this conservative atmosphere and repressive reality defined the totality of Latin America in this period. Various expressions of the left and anti-imperialism persisted throughout the region. Solidarity with Puerto Rican independence and support for the Nationalist prisoners were evident across the hemisphere. In fact, solidarity with the Nationalist prisoners was one significant way to expose and oppose U.S. imperialism in the region. Just as they had done in the 1930s, democratic and anti-imperialist Latin Americans responded to the appeal and actions of the Nationalist Party and signed petitions, wrote letters, staged demonstrations, and formed solidarity committees that demanded an end to U.S. colonialism, freedom for the Nationalist prisoners, and the commutation of the death penalty for Oscar Collazo.

Cubans responded rapidly and forcefully to news of the October 30, 1950, uprising. On October 31, the Cuban House of Representatives "named a commission composed of leaders of all the political parties to discuss the feasibility of sending a three-man congressional mission to San Juan to 'end the persecution of the Nationalists' and 'protect the life of Albizu Campos.'" The commission planned to ask President Carlos Prío Socarrás of Cuba for "a Cuban army airplane to fly the mission to San Juan" should the project be approved. On the same day, President Prío sent a cable to Governor Muñoz Marín "asking him to guarantee the safety and lives of nationalist leader Albizu Campos and his compañeros."[60] Muñoz Marín dismissively rejected the proposed visit of the Cuban congressmen, saying they "are profoundly misled regarding the political situation in Puerto Rico" and that they were operating on a "base of information that is maliciously false. Naturally, such an investigation would definitively lack any approval or sympathy on the part of this government."[61]

The Cuban historian Emilio Roig de Leuchsenring, who had worked in solidarity with Puerto Rican independence since Albizu Campos's 1927 visit to the island, angrily shot off a telegram to Muñoz Marín stating, "Secure that I am interpreting the feelings of the Cuban people, I send you and your gang of accomplices in the Yankee barbarism [the repression that followed the October 30 uprising] the strongest protest possible for the murder of Puerto Rican patriots and the persecution of Doctor Pedro Albizu Campos, brothers of the democratic and liberatory ideals of Martí and Hostos." He signed himself President of the Cuban National Junta for the Independence of Puerto Rico.[62]

In November 1950, eighty-seven lawyers practicing in Havana met to form the Committee of Lawyers in Support of Puerto Rican Independence. In an April 1951 message to the Fourth Meeting of the Ministers of Foreign Relations of the American Republics, they called on the delegates to "take all necessary measures to secure the immediate release of Dr. Pedro Albizu Campos and all the Puerto Rican political prisoners and to organize the Republic of Puerto Rico as soon as possible . . . [actions] which will strengthen the fraternal relations among the American nations and the sense of democracy in our hemisphere."[63]

Leaders of the Nationalist Party found refuge in Cuba in the early 1950s. Juan Juarbe Juarbe, the party's secretary of foreign relations, took up residence in Cuba and conducted his work and the party's international business from Havana. In March 1951, he wrote a message to the Fourth Meeting of the Ministers of Foreign Relations of the American Republics asking the delegates to present the case of Puerto Rico to the Organization of American States so that "this nation will have the opportunity to freely and openly determine its own future."[64]

Cuban and Latin American demands for the release of the Puerto Rican political prisoners continued. In 1953, writers from across Latin America met in Havana, Cuba, on the centenary of the birth of José Martí, "the Apostle of Antillean Independence." The writers from the Caribbean and from Central and South America sent a letter to President Dwight Eisenhower "respectfully soliciting a complete amnesty for all those imprisoned for the last two years, in prisons on the Island and in the United States, for the persecuted and exiled members of the Nationalist Movement of Puerto Rico who have fought for the independence of their homeland. Among them is their leader, Doctor Pedro Albizu Campos, whose state of health, under the prison regime to which he is submitted, ensures his death in the very near future."[65]

Cuban solidarity with the Nationalists continued; concern for Pedro Albizu Campos's health increased as his physical condition deteriorated. Following their arrests in the 1950s, Albizu Campos and other prisoners, such as Isabel

Rosado and Ruth Reynolds, all developed physical symptoms consistent with exposure to radiation. In order to diagnose Albizu Campos's condition, determine the cause of his illness, and prescribe treatment, Dr. Orlando Daumy, at the time president of the Cuban Association of Cancer, traveled to Puerto Rico to examine Albizu Campos. Upon his return to Havana, he wrote to Laura Meneses de Albizu, Albizu Campos's Peruvian wife, to inform her of his findings.[66] He concluded that Albizu's wounds were burns, the result of radiation, and that his general state "corresponded to someone who had received intense radiation."[67]

Members and supporters of the Nationalist Party worked very hard to educate people about U.S. colonialism in Puerto Rico and the situation of the prisoners. Lydia Collazo is the daughter of Oscar Collazo. Like her mother and sisters, she was detained after Oscar Collazo's arrest in Washington, D.C., in 1950.[68] She was released soon thereafter, but her mother, Rosa, served almost seven years in prison. Lydia Collazo was active in campaigns to save her father's life and to release all the Nationalist prisoners.[69] She used to write to supporters in South America: "When my father was in prison, I inherited all the people that he used to write to. I was forced to answer those letters [and] I had to write in my bad Spanish. It was terrible!"[70]

One of the groups she corresponded with was the Argentine Asociación de Amigos pro Libertad de Puerto Rico (Argentine Association of Friends for the Freedom of Puerto Rico), a solidarity organization led by two Argentines, Rito D. Luna (president) and Naldo Espeleta (secretary).[71] The group formed on August 4, 1956, and had an office, a telephone number, and statutes that described the group's goals, officers, membership requirements, and subcommittees.[72] In 1956, the group sent a letter to Lydia Collazo and Ruth Reynolds, a North American pacifist who had a long history of working in support of Puerto Rican independence. Both she and Lydia Collazo belonged to the American Committee for the Independence of Puerto Rico. (The government convicted Ruth Reynolds of "advocating the violent overthrow of the U.S. government" following the October 30 uprising in Puerto Rico, and she served eighteen months in jail in Puerto Rico.)[73] They wrote in the letter, "We are aware that your committee has the same goal as ours: the independence of Puerto Rico. Let's exchange publications. Here are some of ours."[74]

The Argentine Association of Friends campaigned for the release of the Nationalist prisoners and the independence of Puerto Rico. In 1956 and 1957, the association raised particular concerns regarding the health of Pedro Albizu Campos and expressed the widely held fear that he might die in prison. In December 1956, the association wrote to Governor Muñoz Marín, insisting that he release Albizu Campos, "due to [his] advanced illness . . . and his imminent death at any moment."[75] The organization published the bulletin *Puerto Rico Libre* and, in 1958, was planning its National Congress.[76]

In order to understand more specifically how the Nationalist Party promoted solidarity with its cause throughout Latin America, we turn to the activities of Carlos Padilla Pérez. Carlos Padilla Pérez, selections of whose speech open this chapter, was a student at the University of Puerto Rico when the October 30 uprising occurred. He joined the revolt, was arrested, and was jailed in the infamous La Princesa jail in San Juan from 1950 to May 1952, along with many of the Nationalist prisoners. Upon his release, the Nationalist Party assigned him to work in the party's Secretariat of Foreign Relations, a job he carried out during much of the 1950s. He was in Cuba in 1954 when the Nationalists attacked the U.S. Congress. The Fulgencio Batista government arrested and tried him, but he was found not guilty. Nevertheless, he was forced to leave Cuba, so he went to Central America. He left Guatemala after the 1954 overthrow of the Arbenz government and traveled to South America to conduct "an intense campaign in favor of the freedom of his homeland."[77]

During his "exile," he worked as a journalist, which allowed him to acquire "a deep knowledge of the problems of Latin America." He built ties with politicians in Ecuador; lived in Argentina for many years, where he worked closely with the Association of Friends of Puerto Rico; traveled to Chile to talk about the prisoners; wrote articles about Puerto Rico; spoke in universities and schools across the region; and published at least two books in Argentina to educate his fellow Latin Americans about the colonial situation of Puerto Rico.[78]

In Ecuador, he worked closely with anti-imperialist politicians who sponsored a "Solidarity Agreement with the Peoples of Algeria and Puerto Rico" in 1957. Displaying the sense of a shared trans–Latin American identity that characterized many of the regional statements in support of Puerto Rican independence, the document proclaimed, in its first point, that "the Nation of Puerto Rico has the total right to fight to constitute itself as an Independent Republic and to reintegrate itself into our family of sovereign Latin American peoples." Point 4 reflected the important role that Ecuador and, most likely, other Latin American countries believed was available to the United Nations in furthering this goal. It stated that Puerto Rico had the right "to ask those international bodies that they carry out in the strictest manner possible the Charter of the United Nations, which allows the people of Puerto Rico to determine, free from any pressure, their sovereign future."[79]

The proposed resolution elicited much support as well as serious reservations from members of the Ecuadorean Parliament. Congressman Otto Arosemena Gómez, as well as other congressmen, questioned whether the Ecuadorean Parliament could pass a bill that possibly contradicted the position of either the president or the chancellery, although he pointed out that he did not know what their position was. Congressman Jorge Luna Yépez, one of the agreement's main advocates, affirmed the ties that Ecuadoreans have with Puerto Ricans, who are "our brothers," since they share the same "blood, tradition, and culture." He then pointed out that the same parliamentary body had previously passed resolutions in support of international events such as the Bolivian Revolution. Luna Yépez reminded his fellow congressmen that they had unanimously approved an agreement backing don Pedro Albizu Campos, "the last of the Liberators of Hispanoamérica," who now "lies in prison." Concluding that the House must take stances "consistent with what it has done in previous years," he urged his co-parliamentarians "not to forget that [Puerto Rico] is the last of the nations that speaks our language, has the same legacy, shares our culture, [and] still lacks an independent government." Therefore, he concluded, "we who represent the Ecuadorean people" need to pass this agreement, which should "encourage the Executive" to carry out a similar action.[80] The debate continued, with passionate arguments for and against it. When the vote was taken, an "overwhelming majority" voted in favor of the resolution.[81]

The agreement received widespread coverage in Ecuador and Puerto Rico and throughout Latin America. *El Siglo*, the newspaper of the Communist Party of Chile, published an article titled "Ecuadorean Deputies Support Independence for Puerto Rico." It noted that this declaration "joins at this time with the continental clamor of the most democratic voices, demanding a complete amnesty for all the prisoners, persecuted and exiled, of the Movement for the Liberation of Puerto Rico, among whom is Doctor Pedro Albizu Campos." The article paid particular attention to the poor health of Albizu Campos, "who was recently the object of a continental-wide homage, under the auspices of the World Organization of Freedom, upon the celebration of his sixty-sixth birthday, in prison." The list of Chileans who signed the Manifesto in favor of Puerto Rican independence included Clotario Blest, the labor leader who subsequently contributed to the formation of the Movement of the Revolutionary Left (MIR); Salvador Allende, a leader of the Socialist Party and future president of Chile; and Rafael Tarud, a senator from the Independent Left party, among others.[82]

The ongoing imprisonment of the Puerto Rican Nationalist prisoners generated considerable concern and protests from politicians, activists, students, and intellectuals across Latin America. In 1959, the Third National Conference of Socialist Youth held its meeting in Buenos Aires. The group passed a Declaration that condemned the Free Associated State "as a disguise which obscures the colonial regime that exists in the Island." It also demanded "the liberty of all imprisoned Puerto Rican patriots, among whom is found Dr. Pedro Albizu Campos."[83]

A delegation of Ecuadoreans was so concerned about the fate of Puerto Rico and the prisoners that they visited the island. Jorge Luna Yépez, "an eminent jurist and head of the ARNE (Acción Revolucionario Nacionalista Ecuatoriano) Movement" and "the author of the resolution on Puerto Rican independence approved by the Ecuadorean Cámara de Diputados," said he would not leave Puerto Rico "without hugging Pedro Albizu Campos."[84] The Ecuadorean delegates were able to visit Pedro Albizu Campos in the Presbyterian Hospital in San Juan. Finding him in very poor health, "a human ruin," the four delegates began to sob, and one of the deputies was so upset he could not attend a meeting following the visit; another suffered a heart attack, from which he recovered sufficiently to return to Ecuador two days later.[85] The delegates returned to Ecuador convinced that "Puerto Rico does not enjoy sovereignty."[86]

Hemispheric attention did not focus exclusively on Pedro Albizu Campos; it also extended to Oscar Collazo, the Nationalist who had attacked Blair House, where President Truman was staying in Washington, D.C, and who, following his conviction in a U.S. court, received the death penalty. The U.S.-based "Committee to Save the Life of Oscar Collazo" understood the importance of generating international opposition to his death sentence. At one of the organization's meetings, the group agreed to "ask the United Nations to appeal to [President] Truman to commute the sentence." They group also decided to "send a letter to the Latin American diplomats in Washington, D.C., asking them to intercede with the North American Chief Executive." A speaker at the meeting read two telegrams, one from Mexico and the other from the University Alliance of Montevideo, Uruguay, sent to express the senders' backing of the goals of the event.[87]

Many people throughout Latin America mobilized to save the life of Oscar Collazo. The Committee to Save the Life of Oscar Collazo called on Puerto Ricans to attend an event on July 10, 1952, a few weeks before he was scheduled to die. To encourage Collazo's compatriots to attend, the leaflet for the event pointed out that "the call to save Oscar Collazo's life is international. Governmental entities, prominent personalities, workers' unions, and student congresses in Argentina, Uruguay, Peru, San Salvador, Spain, Cuba, and other American nations have demanded that the President of the United States commute his sentence."[88] Both the Guatemalan and Uruguayan Congresses passed resolutions supporting Collazo. The Mexican intellectual and writer José Vasconcelos, a long-time supporter of the Nationalist Party, wrote an article in favor of Collazo titled "Puerto Rico Is Spanish America."[89]

Believing that the death sentence was about to be carried out, the Uruguayan Group for the Freedom of Puerto Rico wrote to Collazo's wife, Rosa, offering her and her family their "deepest solidarity and spiritual presence . . . on the eve of this painful event that will add a new name to the list of those who have been sacrificed for the cause of a free and dignified Iberoamérica." The letter continued, "Oscar Collazo will not offer his life only [to impact] the destiny of Puerto Rico, rather [his death will have an effect] on all the Americans who carry out the same struggle in all the corners of the continent."[90] On July 24, 1952, the death sentence was changed to life in prison as a result of "the broad scope and the international support" that the campaign to save his life had generated.[91] When the organization heard that the death penalty against Oscar Collazo had been vacated, it sent Rosa Collazo a telegram welcoming the decision.[92] The Foreign Relations Secretariat of the Nationalist Party issued a statement thanking all those who had contributed to saving "the precious life of the patriot Oscar Collazo." It particularly thanked "the Spanish American nations [that] raised their voice regarding the life of this extraordinary man."[93]

During the 1950s and 1960s, the Nationalist prisoners were released gradually. Not wishing to have Albizu Campos die in jail and thus become a martyr, Muñoz Marín pardoned him in November 1964, and he died in April 1965. The four Nationalist prisoners who attacked the U.S. Congress and Oscar Collazo remained prisoners until the late 1970s. President Jimmy Carter approved Andres Figueroa Cordero's release in 1978, when he was dying of cancer. Responding to national and international demands, most especially those emanating from Latin America, Carter granted the remaining four Nationalists an unconditional pardon in 1979. Oscar Collazo was a political prisoner in U.S. jails for twenty-nine years, making him, at the time, the longest-held political prisoner in the western hemisphere.

Conclusion

The Nationalist Party drew on a common history of Spanish colonialism, a shared sense of being Latin American, and a joint antipathy to U.S. imperialism to build trans–Latin American solidarity with Puerto Rican independence and anticolonial political prisoners. Further, it referenced a shared identity based on a common language, culture, and religion. Latin American solidarity was important to the Nationalist Party for two reasons. First, the Nationalist Party considered Puerto Rico to be a part of Latin America and believed that U.S. colonial rule wrongly prevented it from fully participating with its sister republics of the hemisphere as a sovereign and equal member of the American

family of nations. Latin American solidarity with the Puerto Rican independence movement affirmed this position by rejecting the right of the United
States to colonize Puerto Rico. Second, the Nationalist Party knew that, in
fighting to end U.S. colonial rule, it was up against one of the most powerful nations on earth, if not the most powerful. To enhance the possibility of
achieving victory, it turned to supportive forces throughout the continent,
expecting that they could function as a counterweight to the United States.

For many Latin Americans, in turn, colonized Puerto Rico was a powerful
symbol of U.S. imperialism in the region. U.S. domination of Puerto Rico
clearly exposed the hollowness of the U.S. government's claims to uphold democracy, human rights, and anticolonialism. Puerto Rico was a potent symbol
for progressive forces in Latin America because it resonated with a reality they
shared, understood, and repudiated. It represented a particularly blatant example of the hegemonic control that the United States hoped to exert over the
entire continent. Because the chasm between the U.S. government's portrayal
of itself and the colonial reality of Puerto Rico was so stark, independence for
Puerto Rico and freedom for the Nationalist prisoners were key demands of
democratic, leftist, and anti-imperialist forces across the western hemisphere
during the 1950s.

The U.S. government understood that its colonization of Puerto Rico discredited its claims to promote democracy and human rights. In an effort to
conceal its relationship with Puerto Rico, the U.S. government worked with
Luis Muñoz Marín and the Popular Democratic Party to (supposedly) end
Puerto Rico's colonial status. To that end, it created the legislative anomaly
of a Free Associated State—and proceeded to imprison those members of the
Nationalist Party who resisted its attempts to mask colonialism behind the
façade of an elected Puerto Rican governor and a new name.

The 1950s are typically defined and viewed as a time of repression and U.S.
hegemony in the Americas; a period when anticommunist governments ruled
and leftist and anti-imperialist voices were silenced. This chapter shows that, as
with most totalizing appraisals of the past, the United States did not reign supreme; across the Americas, voices of solidarity spoke out against U.S. colonialism. From Cuba to Ecuador to Argentina to Chile, Latin Americans protested
U.S. control in Puerto Rico and the imprisonment of the Nationalists. They
sent cables, wrote letters, and published articles demanding independence
for Puerto Rico and freedom for the Nationalist political prisoners. Lauding Pedro Albizu Campos as "a symbol of the as yet unfree but indomitable
Latin America," as Ernesto "Che" Guevara characterized him when he spoke
at the United Nations in 1964, they clamored for an end to the deplorable and
inhumane conditions he suffered in jail, just as they worked to save the life

of Oscar Collazo.[94] And, in some cases, they succeeded. Oscar Collazo spent twenty-nine years in prison, but he did not die there. Latin American solidarity, combined with support from many other people from around the world and the work of anticolonial Puerto Ricans, helped to save his life, just as it contributed to securing the release of other Nationalist political prisoners. And, in doing so, Latin Americans joined with pro-independence Puerto Ricans to defy U.S. imperialist attempts to convince the world that Puerto Rico was not a U.S. colony and that those who were captured fighting for its independence were not political prisoners.

Notes

I would like to thank Jessica Stites Mor, César Rosado, and Antonio Sotomayor for their helpful suggestions on an earlier draft of this chapter. I also thank the American Philosophical Society for awarding me a Franklin Research Grant, which allowed me to conduct research in the CEP archives.

1. Presentation by Carlos Padilla Perez, Buenos Aires, June 27, 1958, box 4, file 2, Ruth Reynolds Papers, Centro de Estudios Puertorriqueños (hereafter cited as CEP), Hunter College, City University of New York. Although the document does not identify whom he is addressing, it is more than likely that it was Argentine members of the Asociación de Amigos pro Libertad de Puerto Rico and other supporters. In a June 24, 1958, letter, Rito D. Luna, the president of that organization, wrote about his conversations with Padilla and the fact that the group "is very busy working on a public event." See Letter from Rito D. Luna to Ruth Reynolds, Buenos Aires, June 24, 1958, box 4, folder 2, Ruth Reynolds Papers, CEP.

2. It was not until 1946 that a U.S. president, Harry Truman, appointed a Puerto Rican, Jesús Piñero, as governor. In 1947, the United States allowed Puerto Ricans to elect their own governor, Luis Muñoz Marín. See César J. Ayala and Rafael Bernabe, *Puerto Rico in the American Century: A History since 1898* (Chapel Hill: University of North Carolina Press, 2007), 158–59. To this day, Puerto Rican citizenship is, to put it bluntly, odd. Puerto Ricans living on the island cannot vote in any federal elections, although Puerto Ricans who migrate to the mainland can. Thus, Puerto Ricans living in Puerto Rico cannot vote in presidential, senatorial, or congressional elections. They can, however, serve in the U.S. military and pay taxes.

3. The Nationalist Party had formed in 1922.

4. Gordon Lewis and Luis Angel Ferrao both characterized the Nationalist Party as fascist. See Gordon Lewis, *Puerto Rico: Freedom and Power in the Caribbean* (New York: Monthly Review Press, 1963), 136; Luis Angel Ferrao, *Pedro Albizu Campos y el nacionalismo puertorriqueño* (San Juan: Editorial Cultural, 1990). In fact, as we shall see, many of the party's firmest supporters throughout Latin America were communists or socialists.

5. Ayala and Bernabe, *Puerto Rico in the American Century*, 105.

6. Marisa Rosado, *Las llamas de la aurora* (San Juan: Ediciones Puerto, 2006), 200.

7. Archivos Fotográficos, Departamento de Justicia, Documentos relacionados con los sucesos nacionalistas, Tarea 90-29, Tomo 2, Archivo General de Puerto Rico. Pedro Albizu Campos was the son of a former slave and a Basque landowner.

8. Miñi Seijo Bruno, *La insurrección nacionalista en Puerto Rico 1950* (Rio Pedras, PR: Editorial Edil, 1989), 243.

9. One exception is Laura Briggs, who argues for the centrality of Puerto Rico for students of U.S. foreign relations. "Puerto Rico is a good place to think about the meanings of colonialism and globalization because it has for a century been where the U.S. has worked out its attitudes toward its own expansionism." Laura Briggs, *Reproducing Empire: Race, Sex, Science, and U.S. Imperialism in Puerto Rico* (Berkeley: University of California Press, 2002), 2.

10. Leslie Bethell and Ian Roxborough, *Latin America between the Second World War and the Cold War, 1944–1948* (Cambridge: Cambridge University Press, 1992), 2.

11. As in many other Latin American countries, local and national forces carried out the repression, not the United States directly. Thus, Puerto Rican police attacked and arrested members of the Nationalist Party. However, the orders to do so came from Washington.

12. Greg Grandin, "Off the Beach: The United States, Latin America, and the Cold War," in *A Companion to Post 1945 America*, ed. Jean-Christophe Agnew and Roy Rosenzweig (Malden, MA: Blackwell, 2002), 426.

13. The Puerto Rican Independence Party (PIP), which formed in 1946, also advocated an end to U.S. colonialism in Puerto Rico. Many of its members left the Popular Democratic Party in the 1940s when it became clear that Muñoz Marín had abandoned his earlier support for independence. Ayala and Bernabe, *Puerto Rico in the American Century*, 157–58.

14. For a discussion of how U.S. race relations and the civil rights movement challenged U.S. government claims to support freedom and anticolonialism, see Thomas Borstelmann, *The Cold War and the Color Line: American Race Relations in the Global Arena* (Cambridge, MA: Harvard University Press, 2001).

15. "La cruzada nacionalista," *El Nacionalista de Ponce*, June 24, 1927. For Albizu Campos and the Nationalist Party, race had nothing to do with genetics or "biology." Race was defined by "our culture, our values, our nobility, and our Catholic civilization." "Concepto de la Raza," *La Palabra* (Puerto Rico), October 19, 1935, 27, as reproduced in Pedro Albizu Campos, *Escritos*, ed. Laura Albizu-Campos Meneses and Mario A. Rodríguez León (Hato Rey, PR: Publicaciones Puertorriqueñas, 2007), 26.

16. For a description of his trip, whom he met, and what he did in these various countries, see Ramón Medina Ramírez, *El movimiento libertador en la historia de Puerto Rico*, vol. 1 (San Juan: Imprenta Nacional, 1964), 73–81.

17. "La cruzada nacionalista," *El Nacionalista de Ponce*, June 24, 1927; Ayala and Bernabe, *Puerto Rico in the American Century*, 107.

18. "El caso de Puerto Rico es el atentado más grave que ha hecho Estados Unidos contra Ibero América," *El Mundo*, November 26, 1927. Enrique José Varona was one

of the founders of the Junta Revolucionaria pro Independencia de Cuba y Puerto Rico in New York, along with José Martí and Ramón Emeterio Betances. Roig de Leuchsenring was the famous historian of Havana, whose support for Puerto Rican independence continued into the 1950s and beyond. See also Medina Ramírez, *El movimiento libertador en la historia de Puerto Rico*, 78–79.

19. Luis Nieves Falcón, *Un siglo de represión política* (San Juan: Optimática, 2009), 96; Ché Paralitici, *Sentencia impuesta* (San Juan: Ediciones Puerto, 2004), 66–68.

20. "Gran mitin en Uruguay por la independencia de Puerto Rico," *La Palabra*, March 16, 1936.

21. "La Federación Universitaria Argentina Solicita," *El Mundo*, May 20, 1936.

22. "La fraternidad Iberoamericana en acción," *La Palabra*, June 8, 1936.

23. Letter from Natalio Vázquez, Secretary General of the Confederation of Anti-Imperialist Students of America, to President Roosevelt, June 24, 1937, Mexico City, Mexico, box 4, folder 2, Ruth Reynolds Papers, CEP.

24. Bethell and Roxborough, *Latin America between the Second World War and the Cold War*, 24.

25. César Ayala Casás and José Bolívar Fresneda, "The Cold War and the Second Expropriations of the Navy in Vieques," *Centro Journal* 18, no. 1 (Spring 2006): 19. See also Katherine T. McCaffrey, *Military Power and Popular Protest: The U.S. Navy in Vieques, Puerto Rico* (New Brunswick, NJ: Rutgers University Press, 2002).

26. Fernando González Alberty, "An Interview with Albizu Campos," *El Imparcial*, January 4, 1948.

27. Thelma Mielke, interview with author, New York City, July 6, 2007. Following the 1950 uprising in Puerto Rico, Mielke sent an urgent request to Trygve Lie, Secretary General of the United Nations, asking him to "bring the Puerto Rican revolt before the Security Council as a matter endangering international peace." A U.S. delegate dismissed her appeal, claiming that the "Puerto Rican developments were entirely a local affair" and that "the case could not be brought before the world organization." "Island Rebel Asks U.N. to Investigate," *New York Times*, November 3, 1950.

28. Bethell and Roxborough, *Latin America between the Second World War and the Cold War*, 24.

29. Ivonne Acosta-Lespier, "The Smith Act Goes to San Juan: *La Mordaza*, 1948–1957," in *Puerto Rico under Colonial Rule*, ed. Ramón Bosque-Pérez and José Javier Colón Morera (Albany: State University of New York Press, 2006), 60.

30. Ayala and Bernabe, *Puerto Rico in the American Century*, 158.

31. Ibid.

32. An analysis of these results is beyond the scope of this chapter; however, the number of Puerto Ricans voting for the constitution indicates a certain degree of disagreement with the Nationalist Party's rejection of the constitution and its advocacy of the ongoing struggle for independence. See Humberto García Muñiz, "Puerto Rico and the United States: The United Nations Role 1953–1975," *Revista Jurídica de la Universidad de Puerto Rico* 53 (1984): 9.

33. Ibid., 10.

34. For a discussion of the legal ramifications and contradictions of U.S. colonialism in Puerto Rico, see Christina Duffy Burnett and Burke Marshall, eds., *Foreign in a Domestic Sense* (Durham, NC: Duke University Press, 2001).

35. Ayala and Bernabe, *Puerto Rico in the American Century*, 162.

36. Acosta-Lespier, "The Smith Act Goes to San Juan: *La Mordaza*, 1948–1957," 59. The law was modeled on the Federal Smith Act, "which made it illegal to advocate the violent overthrow" of the U.S. government. See Ayala and Bernabe, *Puerto Rico in the American Century*, 160.

37. Partido Nacionalista de Puerto Rico, "The Nationalist Party of Puerto Rico Denounces the Plans of the United States," San Juan, May 20, 1950, box 29, folder 4, Ruth Reynolds Papers, CEP.

38. Oscar Collazo, *Memorias de un patriota encarcelado* (San Juan: Fundación Francisco Manrique Cabrera, 2000), 274.

39. Blanca Canales, *La constitución es la revolución* (San Juan: Comité de Estudios Congreso Nacional Hostosiano, 1997), 3, 20, 24.

40. For a detailed discussion of the uprising based on interviews with participants, see Seijo Bruno, *La insurrección nacionalista en Puerto Rico, 1950*. Her work conveys both the detailed planning that preceded the event and the inevitably spontaneous actions that accompanied it.

41. Estanislao Lugo, interview with author, San Juan, May 21, 2008.

42. Rosado, *Las llamas de la aurora*, 200. These attacks corresponded to plans and tactics that the military leadership of the party had previously developed.

43. Seijo Bruno, *La insurrección nacionalista en Puerto Rico*, 252.

44. "Revolt Flares in Puerto Rico; Soon Quelled with 23 Dead," *New York Times*, October 31, 1950, 1.

45. Ibid., 17; José Enrique Ayora Santaliz, "La insurrección nacionalista del año 1950," unpublished manuscript, October 2000, personal archive, Ponce, Puerto Rico.

46. Letter from Carlos Santiago, "Dear Friend," July 1962, box 28, folder 6, Ruth Reynolds Papers, CEP.

47. Canales, *La constitución es la revolución*.

48. Collazo, *Memorias de un patriota encarcelado*, 279.

49. In the shooting, one White House guard was killed and two were wounded. "President Resting," *New York Times*, November 2, 1950.

50. Collazo, *Memorias de un patriota encarcelado*, 287.

51. After her release from prison, in 1979, Lolita Lebrón returned to Puerto Rico, where she campaigned for an end to U.S. colonialism, the U.S. Navy bombing of Vieques, and the imprisonment of Puerto Rican political prisoners. She died in August 2010 and is buried near Pedro Albizu Campos, in San Juan, Puerto Rico.

52. Rafael Cancel Miranda, in conversation with author, San Juan, March 12, 2006.

53. Peter H. Smith, *Talons of the Eagle: Latin America, the United States, and the World*, 3rd ed. (New York: Oxford University Press, 2007), 116.

54. Dictatorships ruled Guatemala, El Salvador, Honduras, Nicaragua, Panama,

Cuba, the Dominican Republic, Venezuela, Colombia, Peru, and Paraguay. Bethell and Roxborough, *Latin America between the Second World War and the Cold War*, 18.

55. See Tomás Moulian, *La forja de ilusiones: El sistema de partidos, 1932–1973* (Santiago: ARCIS and FLACSO, 1993), 96; Lessie Jo Frazier, *Salt in the Sand: Memory, Violence, and the Nation-State in Chile: 1890 to the Present* (Durham, NC: Duke University Press, 2007), 165–67; Karin Rosemblatt, *Gendered Compromises: Political Cultures and the State in Chile, 1920–1950* (Chapel Hill: University of North Carolina Press, 2000).

56. Piero Gleijeses, *Shattered Hope: The Guatemalan Revolution and the United States, 1952–1954* (Princeton, NJ: Princeton University Press, 1991); Greg Grandin, *The Blood of Guatemala: A History of Race and Nation* (Durham, NC: Duke University Press, 2000); Stephen Schlesinger and Stephen Kinzer, *Bitter Fruit: The Story of the American Coup in Guatemala* (Cambridge, MA: Harvard University Press, 2005).

57. See García Muñiz, "Puerto Rico and the United States," 10–18. According to Chapter XI of the United Nations Charter, in the early 1950s, the U.S. government had to submit an annual report on the status of Puerto Rico, as well as on Alaska, American Samoa, Hawaii, the Panama Canal Zone, and the American Virgin Islands. Ibid., 20.

58. Ibid., 26.

59. Ibid., 58. It was not until 1973 that the General Assembly again considered the status of Puerto Rico. Ibid., 169.

60. "Desea enviar comisión aquí," *El Mundo*, November 1, 1950.

61. "Muñoz dice eso tocaría a camaras," *El Mundo*, November 2, 1950.

62. "Leuchsenring envía protesta al gobernador," *El Mundo*, November 2, 1950.

63. "Mensaje del 'Comité de abogados pro independencia de Puerto Rico' de Cuba a la IV Reunión de Consulta de los Ministros de Relaciones Exteriores de las Repúblicas Americanas," Havana, Cuba, April 4, 1951, box 46, Campos file, number 1, Vito Marcantonio Papers, New York Public Library (NYPL).

64. "Mensaje del Partido Nacionalista de Puerto Rico a la Cuarta Reunión de Consulta de los Ministros de Relaciones Exteriores de las Repúblicas Americanas," Havana, Cuba, March 14, 1951, p. 3, box 46, Campos file, number 1, Vito Marcantonio Papers, NYPL.

65. Letter from Writers of América to President Dwight Eisenhower, Havana, Cuba, February 25, 1953, Puerto Rico (2): Nationalists, Ralph T. Templin Collection, United Methodist Church Archives—GCAH, Madison, NJ.

66. Laura Meneses de Albizu was living in Mexico at the time because the U.S. government had cancelled her U.S. citizenship in 1948 and subsequently expelled her from the country. See Laura de Albizu Campos, *Albizu Campos y la independencia de Puerto Rico* (Hato Ray, PR: Publicaciones Puertorriqueñas, 2007), 137.

67. Letter from Laura de Albizu Campos to Ruth Reynolds, Mexico City, August 6, 1957, box 4, folder 3, Ruth Reynolds Papers, CEP.

68. "Widow of Assassin Seized as Plotter on Hunger Strike," *New York Times*, November 4, 1950.

69. Her mother's cellmate in New York City was Ethel Rosenberg, with whom she

became close friends. Lydia Collazo, in conversation with author, Levittown, Puerto Rico, May 25, 2008.

70. Ibid.

71. Progressive Argentine forces had a long history of anti-imperialism in general and support for Puerto Rican independence in particular. For more on this practice, see Florencia Ferreira de Cassone, *Claridad y el internacionalismo Americano* (Buenos Aires: Editorial Claridad, 1998), esp. 256–61; and Alfredo L. Palacios, *Nuestra América y el imperialismo* (Buenos Aires: Editorial Palestra, 1961), esp. 274–283, 321.

72. "Estatutos," Buenos Aires, August 4, 1956, box 19, folder 8, Ruth Reynolds Papers, CEP.

73. "Ruth M. Reynolds," *Centro de Estudios Puertorriqueños Bulletin* 2, no. 2 (Winter 1987): 41.

74. Letter from the Asociación de Amigos pro Libertad de Puerto Rico, Buenos Aires, August 16, 1956, box 19, folder 3, Ruth Reynolds Papers, CEP.

75. "Release of Albizu Asked from Argentina," *El Imparcial*, December 21, 1956, as cited in FBI Files, "Quarterly Summary Report," San Juan, January 31, 1957, 105-11898-NR. The FBI kept very close tabs on news in Latin America about the Nationalist Party.

76. Letter from Rito Luna to Ruth Reynolds, Buenos Aires, June 24, 1958, box 4, folder 2, Ruth Reynolds Papers, CEP. The Committee had previously put out a bulletin "at the time of Nixon's [May 1958] visit."

77. Carlos Padilla Pérez, *Puerto Rico: Al rescate de su soberanía* (Buenos Aires: Publicaciones del Partido Nacionalista de Puerto Rico, 1958), 7–8. I thank Andres Bisso for informing me about Padilla Pérez's publications.

78. Ibid.

79. Ibid., 103.

80. Ibid., 105–6.

81. Ibid., 131.

82. *El Siglo*, September 14, 1957, cited in Padilla Pérez, *Puerto Rico*, 139.

83. Declaration of the Third National Conference of Socialist Youth, Buenos Aires, May 28–30, 1959, box 4, folder 2, Ruth Reynolds Papers, CEP.

84. "Diputados Ecuatorianos prometen luchar por la independencia de Puerto Rico," *El Imparcial*, December 22, 1957, cited in Padilla Pérez, *Puerto Rico*, 159–60.

85. "Ecuatorianos lloran en visita a Albizu Campos," *El Imparcial*, December 22, 1957, cited in Padilla Pérez, *Puerto Rico*, 160–62.

86. "Una lección objetiva," *El Imparcial*, December 23, 1957, cited in Padilla Pérez, *Puerto Rico*, 162–63.

87. "Comités Collazo irán a Washington y a las N. Unidas," *La Prensa*, July 19, 1952.

88. "Hay que salvar a Oscar Collazo," n/d, box 20, folder 1, Ruth Reynolds Papers, CEP.

89. Nationalist Party of Puerto Rico, Foreign Relations Secretariat, "Our Gratitude," Havana, July 28, 1952, box 29, folder 4, Ruth Reynolds Papers, CEP.

90. Letter from Raúl F. Abadie-Aicardi to Rosa Collazo, Montevideo, July 9, 1952, box 20, folder 2, Ruth Reynolds Papers, CEP.

91. Paralitici, *Sentencia impuesta*, 158.

92. Telegram from Alianza Universitaria Federación Latinoamericana to Rosa Collazo, Montevideo, July 10, 1952, box 40, folder 2, Ruth Reynolds Papers, CEP.

93. Nationalist Party of Puerto Rico, Foreign Relations Secretariat, "Our Gratitude," Havana, July 28, 1952.

94. Ernesto Che Guevara, *Che Guevara Reader: Writings on Politics and Revolution*, ed. David Deutschmann (North Melbourne, Australia: Ocean Press, 2003), 285.

2

Latin America Encounters Nelson Rockefeller

Imagining the Gringo Patrón *in 1969*

ERNESTO CAPELLO

In August 1969, Gustavo Borja Moncayo, a middling bureaucrat at the Ministerio de Industrias y Comercio in Quito, Ecuador, learned that he had a severe stomach ulcer. His doctors recommended a delicate surgery that would cost the exorbitant sum of U.S. $1,500 and necessitate a journey abroad. This crisis propelled Borja to take a chance. Putting pen to paper, he wrote Governor Nelson A. Rockefeller of New York, who had recently concluded a frenzied listening tour of Latin America. Citing his cordial relationship with Rockefeller's well-known friend Galo Plaza, the Ecuadorian head of the Organization of American States, Borja requested help to secure a job in the United States, where he could not only receive treatment but also educate his children. Borja couched his solicitation as the natural result of his admiration for the United States and the deplorable conditions of his homeland, with its high cost of living and its lack of available jobs. In the United States, on the other hand, "everyone works, which is an ideal situation that reflects equal opportunity for all peoples."[1]

This tribute to an egalitarian United States with guaranteed employment and an unrivaled educational system may have startled Rockefeller's advisers after the trail of blood that had followed the governor during his 1969 presidential mission to Latin America. Suggested originally by Plaza, Rockefeller's listening tour to twenty countries sought to inform the Nixon administration's initiative to replace the roundly criticized Alliance for Progress, which had failed to propel regional development. However, his four visits were besieged by negative publicity as protesting students clashed with military forces from Honduras to Haiti. His refusal to curtail the visits despite the violence led to egomaniacal caricatures in the press and cost congressional support for the recommendations of increased hemispheric collaboration developed in the *Rockefeller Report on the Americas*, released that fall.

For an ailing bureaucrat like Borja, however, both Rockefeller and the United States maintained the luster of exceptional economic promise. Despite receiving a dry form letter refusing his request, signed by Rockefeller's chief of office staff, Louise Boyer, Borja enthusiastically wrote twenty more petitions over the next two years. These letters not only repeated the original appeal for medical assistance but also presented an increasingly detailed account of his daily life, his children, his multiple relocations to increasingly distant sectors of the city, and his physical deterioration. Most also reiterated his esteem for the United States, including a touching account of a frustrated attempt to meet the governor at his official reception at the Hotel Quito. Whereas this tale softened Mrs. Boyer's usual reserve and resulted in a personal refusal from Rockefeller's special assistant, Stewart Anderson, Borja received no other encouragement. Eventually, his ongoing letters were marked "NAN" or "No answer necessary" by the office staff, until they abruptly and ominously stopped in April 1971.

Borja is but one correspondent among several thousand who petitioned Rockefeller in the wake of his presidential mission. Hailing almost exclusively from the twenty countries visited by the governor in 1969, the authors range from students to cab drivers to nurses to priests to potential émigrés to civil servants. For these individuals, Rockefeller's repeated mantra that he had come to Latin America simply "to listen" invited a torrent of descriptions of everyday troubles, political manifestos, and aid requests. Like Borja, hundreds maintained their correspondence long after receiving the ubiquitous Boyer denial. Some seemed to cling to hope that they might arouse the great man's sympathy. Others wrote to detail and express their personal circumstances. Almost all couched this correspondence in political terms, seeing themselves as either allies or enemies of the wealthy American and his country. Still others positioned themselves as armchair political scientists, explaining to Rockefeller the precise roots of their nation's conflicts and offering advice on future policy.

A smaller group offered to serve as foot soldiers in the Cold War crusade or, alternately, decried American policy as nefarious imperialism.

The variety and scope of these responses suggests a tangled web of associations that transcends the obsession with the ritualistic violence that colored the contemporary press and that dominates the minimal historical scholarship on the subject. The lack of critical attention to the complexity of these encounters stems partly from an extended delay in processing the relevant files at the Rockefeller Archive Center, which hampered studies such as Peter Bales's dissertation on Nelson Rockefeller's lifelong interest in inter-American unity; Bales was forced to rely on newspaper accounts of the 1969 mission.[2] Other studies have been colored by the politics of the Cold War itself, particularly a dependency framework highlighting the insidious spread of U.S. hegemony through cultural as well as economic means. This approach, for example, underlies Gerald Colby and Charlotte Dennet's description of the tour as the "Rocky Horror Road Show," a reference to the chaotic sadomasochism of Jim Sharman's cult film.[3] For Colby and Dennett, the tour's failure serves to underscore its importance in cementing the expanding U.S. military aid that would prove disastrous during the next decade's political violence.[4]

Such analyses fail to take into account a methodological shift that has dominated inter-American histories for the past fifteen years. Inspired by postcolonial studies, scholars have begun to complicate the binaries that both positivist historians and the dependency school had deployed as analytical frameworks. The consideration of culture and the propagation and consumption of culture proved particularly fruitful to this endeavor, resulting in examinations of the multifarious processes through which U.S. hegemony began slowly to be articulated across the nineteenth and early twentieth centuries in art, literature, and political discourse. More recently, historians have begun to engage the Cold War more directly, elaborating a general interrogation of what might be seen as a scholarly frontier still dominated by the very Manichean language of the era.[5] Sandhya Shukla and Heidi Tinsman, for example, call for a transnational frame in the study of the Americas that seeks to decenter both the United States and dependency theory.[6] In an equally direct challenge, Hal Brands argues that Latin America's upheaval resulted less from the dichotomous conflicts between an imperial hegemon and its helpless victims than from "the multisided and mutually reinforcing nature of the conflicts that comprised Latin America's Cold War [including] foreign intervention, internal instability, and ideological extremism on both Left and Right."[7]

This chapter forms part of a broader study of the Rockefeller mission in which I argue the need to reevaluate Rockefeller's presidential mission to Latin America as a critical juncture in the Latin American Cold War, during which a transnational imaginary captivated a significant portion of the population. While the clashes in the street between right and left dominated media coverage, a pliable center engaged the journey by situating itself at a transcendent hemispheric nexus, in the process imagining an America of hemispheric solidarity and possibility. The high-profile regional involvement of both Nelson Rockefeller and the Rockefeller Foundation as patrons of postwar Latin America served as a central inspiration for this vision. However, the most striking quality of this correspondence concerns attempts to generalize a personal narrative within this transnational saga.[8] The letters thus not only demonstrate attempts to curry favor with a notoriously rich and powerful American but also an ambivalent vision of the United States marked by individuated representations of the Cold War itself.

The chapter begins by locating the mission among a relatively neglected history of U.S. goodwill tours to Latin America, which serve not only as propagandistic spectacles but also as significant barometers of U.S. interest in Latin America. Next, it considers the genesis and course of the presidential mission as a failed attempt to transcend this history, perhaps best exemplified by the contested crafting of the *Rockefeller Report on the Americas*. The chapter then telescopes on politically charged letters sent to Rockefeller in the aftermath of the mission. It argues that these represent an expansion of patronage petitions, whose long history within Latin American society dates back to the colonial era but which had been appropriated successfully by populist regimes during the installation of corporate statist regimes in countries like Brazil or Argentina. Last, it analyzes the letters as an indication of a missed opportunity for hemispheric aperture. The closing pages elaborate this conclusion by highlighting the multiple publics that encountered Rockefeller in 1969.

The Goodwill Mission as Transnational Barometer

Nelson Rockefeller's journeys represented the culmination of three decades of "goodwill missions" to Latin America by high-profile Americans. These tours were more elaborate than previous diplomatic travels, seeking to deploy mass spectacle, to manipulate media coverage, and to identify the visiting American celebrities as objects of cultural desire. These spectacles reached an early apogee during the Good Neighbor days of the Roosevelt administration but waned commensurate with declining U.S. interest in Latin America during the postwar era, only to rise again following Vice President Richard Nixon's ill-fated 1958 tour of South America. As I will suggest, these goodwill tours can thus be seen as a window into both the cultural facets of policy and the degree of diplomatic investment in the region.

Nelson Rockefeller helped oversee the rise of the goodwill tour as a critical component of Roosevelt's Good Neighbor Policy following his appointment as Coordinator of Inter-American Affairs (CIAA) in 1941.[9] Rockefeller adopted a model initiated in 1939 by John Royal, a vice president of NBC, who dispatched Arturo Toscanini and the NBC Orchestra to Brazil, Argentina, and Uruguay to counter a rise in Axis radio broadcasting that Royal had witnessed during a South American tour earlier that year.[10] The CIAA's policy has suggestively been labeled a "seductive imperialism" by Antônio Pedro Tota because of the confluence of popular culture, political propaganda, and product placement designed to further open South American markets at the expense of European manufacturers.[11] This began with the well-known visit of Walt Disney and a cohort of animators known as "El Grupo" to five South American countries. Their leisure trips to an Argentine *estancia*, to the Copacabana beach in Rio de Janeiro, and to Lake Titicaca resulted in the animated feature films *Saludos Amigos* (1942) and *The Three Caballeros* (1944), along with a plethora of propagandistic shorts advocating the Allied cause.[12] Other trips from the summer of 1941 included visits by Lincoln Kirstein's American Ballet Caravan, the Yale Glee Club, a Museum of Modern Art traveling exhibition, and Moe Berg, the former Chicago White Sox catcher, who used his Spanish to teach about the national pastime.[13] These tours had the desired effect of shoring up Allied support, as dramatically evidenced at the Rio de Janeiro Conference of January 1942, where all but two Latin American countries severed diplomatic relations with the Axis powers. The two countries that maintained formal ties, namely Argentina and Chile, promised to remain neutral in the conflict. By 1945, every Latin American nation had formally joined the Allies.

Though Eleanor Roosevelt famously visited the Caribbean, Central America, and northern South America at the height of the Allied push into Europe in March 1944, the CIAA's attention to cultural tours waned after successfully securing continental solidarity.[14] Such high-profile tours all but disappeared with the office's dissolution in 1946. Conventional fact-finding missions by secondary administration figures, which had minimal impact on foreign relations or cultural exchange, reappeared during the 1950s. Brazilian diplomats, for example, scoffed that the mundane policy recommendations offered by President Dwight D. Eisenhower's brother Milton, who visited ten countries in 1953, could have been written without setting foot in the region.[15] For many Latin Americans, especially students and social reformers, the ignominy deepened given the lack of U.S. financial aid to the region, the State Department's support of dictators in Nicaragua and Cuba, and the CIA's involvement in the overthrow of Jacobo Arbenz, the reformist president of Guatemala, in 1954.

A burgeoning anti-Americanism crystallized during Richard Nixon's 1958 tour of South America. The trip had been organized in conjunction with the election of Arturo Frondizi as president of Argentina, replacing the populist dictator Juan Domingo Perón, and was meant to convey U.S. commitment to democratic rule.[16] Nevertheless, left-leaning students viewed this message as disingenuous in view of ongoing U.S. intervention. Although the vice president gaily (and poorly) dribbled a soccer ball to amuse the crowds in Quito, small groups of protesters burned both Nixon and his wife, Pat, in effigy. Students at the Universidad de San Marcos in Lima even threw stones at the couple. The largest conflagration occurred in Caracas on May 13, where a crowd of approximately five hundred people met Nixon's plane with banners loudly proclaiming "Tricky Dick, go home!" and "Out, dog!" Once Nixon deplaned, protesters threw garbage and spat through the air, hitting the security detail and prompting the Americans to quickly retreat to their motorcade. After leaving the airport, a mob of some three hundred swarmed the streets in the working-class suburb of Catia, throwing rocks and beating Nixon's car with sticks, pipes, and fists. President Eisenhower was so startled that he ordered a naval flotilla to sail to Venezuela in case Nixon needed to be forcibly rescued, an ultimately unnecessary operation ironically dubbed "Poor Richard."[17]

The U.S. State Department publicly decried the violence as the work of communist agitators, yet privately acknowledged the minimal role these groups had played in the uncoordinated and virulent uproar.[18] This sparked a reassessment of hemispheric policy at the diplomatic and fiscal levels.[19] As early as May 16, Nixon privately warned the cabinet of the dangers of unmitigated support for Latin American dictatorships and recommended cultivating ties with nonoligarchical social sectors, including helping organize pro-U.S. student groups who could be "bought."[20] The administration paid lip service to this goal over the next several months by repeatedly announcing its commitment to democratically elected governments. Moreover, at the urging of President Juscelino Kubitschek of Brazil, Eisenhower entertained suggestions to redouble aid to combat the region's underdevelopment and sponsored the creation of the Inter-American Development Bank that August. Nevertheless, little changed in practice until after the Cuban Revolution, when Latin America once again became a critical priority.

A less heralded aspect of Eisenhower's new policy was the rekindling of the splashy goodwill mission. In 1960, the lame-duck president himself conducted a diplomatic tour to the region that began just a week after Cuba announced a trade agreement with the Soviet Union. The president's popularity as a war hero ensured a happy reception by enthusiastic crowds; however, he was shocked by the visible markers of poverty and the depth of the opposition to the United States. Latin American leaders uniformly rejected his entreaties for support of his anti-Castro policy while even an anticommunist student league from Chile repudiated U.S. inattention to regional development.[21] These evaluations finally prompted Eisenhower to act on the direct-aid proposals that had been raised the previous year and inspired his request, in July 1960, that Congress approve the creation of a Social Progress Trust Fund. The final legislation was revealed in September 1960, in time for a summit of the Organization of American States in Bogota—an action that highlights the importance the administration had come to place upon linking state visits to high-profile diplomatic initiatives.

John F. Kennedy quickly expanded Eisenhower's late-term support of development aid to Latin America with his signature initiative, the Alliance for Progress. Beginning at a Washington summit in March 1961, Kennedy offered soaring rhetoric, promising to dispel hemispheric poverty by injecting billions of dollars in development aid into Latin American economies. The Alliance was formally adopted that August at a summit at Punta del Este, Uruguay. It formed the backbone of inter-American cooperation during a decade in which $20 billion were apportioned for Latin American aid.

It would be beyond the scope of this chapter to offer a comprehensive analysis of the Alliance for Progress and its successes and failures; however, it is worth pausing to consider the structure of the program, as well as its intersection within a network of mediated narratives that would prove crucial to the course of Rockefeller's travails. Three elements regarding its structure and implementation deserve to be highlighted. The first concerns a core stipulation that aid would be dispersed only to projects that received matching funds. The second, a requirement that Latin American governments purchase U.S. goods with aid monies despite the potential availability of cheaper goods elsewhere, exacerbated the pressure on cash-strapped governments already facing extensive indebtedness. After 1964, this hurdle would be amplified through a third procedure known as "additionality," which mandated that aid recipients continue to purchase as many U.S. goods after receiving aid as they had beforehand and that U.S. vessels transport these materials.

The most dissonant aspect of the Alliance for Progress, however, stemmed not from these policy shortcomings but from ongoing U.S. interventions in Latin American affairs. Conflict with Cuba represented the most visible symbol of this phenomenon and provided a rallying point for anti-American sentiment. The embarrassing April 1961 Bay of Pigs incident sparked scores of protests across the region, which targeted visible symbols of U.S. hegemony while also articulating local dissatisfactions. For example, student mobs targeting a U.S. Cultural Institute in Morelia announced both their solidarity with Cuba and their support for the agrarian reform that had been institutionalized by former President Lázaro Cárdenas of Mexico, a prominent advocate of Castro and a critic of the current government.[22] Similarly, several leaders gathered at Punta del Este seriously agonized over Ernesto "Che" Guevara's warning that the Alliance for Progress represented a mask for imperial pretensions. These worries proved grounded as the Kennedy and Johnson administrations actively sabotaged democratically elected governments whose leftist reformism they viewed as too radical, such as those of Cheddi Jagan in Guyana, Juan Bosch in the Dominican Republic, and João Goulart in Brazil. Recent scholarship has echoed this interpretation, highlighting the chasm between the ideals of the Alliance for Progress and the continuation and expansion of hemispheric intervention as a critical reason for its eventual discrediting, along with diminishing interest in Latin America during the Johnson and Nixon administrations.[23]

In spite of the evident interventionist bent, however, scholars such as Stephen G. Rabe have puzzled over the mass adulation and persistent mystique that Kennedy inspired.[24] To be sure, the young president's allure in the hemisphere was largely a product of his soaring oratory, his Catholicism, and, eventually, his martyrdom. But Kennedy also took great care to cultivate his image abroad in a manner that had been missing from U.S. Latin American policy since the Good Neighbor years. Like Roosevelt, Kennedy skillfully deployed the media for this purpose, as evidenced by the actions of the U.S. Information Agency, which flooded the region with news stories, pamphlets, films, and even comic books featuring anticommunist students promoting nonviolent tactics to resolve disputes.[25] He also, however, reinvigorated the goodwill tour in the aftermath of the Bay of Pigs debacle.

This began in June 1961, when Adlai Stevenson, then the U.S. representative to the United Nations, crisscrossed the hemisphere to gather support and information in anticipation of the Punta del Este conference. Stevenson's celebrity as a perennial Democratic Party presidential candidate and his lack of involvement in the Bay of Pigs fiasco earlier that year softened the public face of the administration.[26] In December 1961, Kennedy followed his envoy to Puerto Rico, Venezuela, and Colombia, accompanied by his wife, who charmed the crowds in accent-free Spanish, garnering great cheers and providing a natural feature for local radio, TV, and film broadcasts. The same formula was repeated during a second visit in June and July 1962, this time to Mexico, and again in Costa Rica in March 1963. Following President Kennedy's assassination, his aura continued to dominate southern travels. This was partly a result of President Johnson's attention to domestic initiatives and the growing conflict in Vietnam, which delayed high-profile trips to Latin America until Senator Robert Kennedy visited the region in late 1965, during which time he made no secret of his opposition to the Vietnam War and the administration's support for the recent coup in the Dominican Republic. Though the Latin American political and economic elite appears to have chaffed under the senator's political agenda, popular accolades demonstrated the seductive power of another Kennedy visit. Several American publications highlighted the ensuing tension between Robert Kennedy and President Johnson, perhaps best encapsulated in a New York *World Telegram* cartoon depicting Johnson telling a serape- and sombrero-clad Kennedy, "They loved you. Ever think of running for office . . . down there?"[27]

While Johnson would himself travel three times to the region over the next two years, a lack of popular enthusiasm helped signal the decline of U.S. prestige in the hemisphere. His lengthy tour of Central America in the summer of 1968 presaged some of the most extensive setbacks for U.S. policy in the region and contributed to the legendary tumult of that year. These culminated in October, which brought both the coup d'état by Juan Velasco's Revolutionary Government of the Armed Forces in Peru and the disastrous massacre of Tlatelolco in Mexico City on the eve of the Olympics. Nixon successfully painted these events as symptoms of the failure of Democratic policy on his way to claiming the White House that November. Once elected, however, he was forced to find a solution to Latin American woes, a much thornier enterprise. This is where Rockefeller entered the picture.

A Presidential Mission among Goodwill Tours

Despite Nixon's repeated criticism of Democratic foreign policy during the election, his inaugural speech strikingly omitted specific references to international problems beyond Southeast Asia. This sparked critiques by Latin American leaders concerned that the Johnson administration's neglect of their concerns would continue under a politician best known regionally for his stormy 1958 debacle. Hopeful of arranging a diplomatic solution while also postponing the articulation of a fully fledged policy, Nixon sought the advice of Galo Plaza, the former Ecuadorian president and current secretary of the Organization of American States. Plaza, a longtime friend of Nelson Rockefeller, suggested that the New York governor would be a strong candidate to conduct a high-profile "listening tour" to elicit a new policy based on direct engagement with Latin American states, one that would move away from the stagnation of the Alliance for Progress without abandoning its core commitment to hemispheric unity and progress. Mindful of the success of recent celebrity visits by "heroes" like Eisenhower and the Kennedy brothers, Plaza suggested that Rockefeller's legacy from his time as CIAA would yield dividends. As the secretary put it, "his name is still magic."

Despite the tussle between Nixon and Rockefeller for the Republican nomination the previous year, the president heeded Plaza's advice and invited the governor to conduct a limited tour of critical Latin American countries to assess current sentiments.[28] Rockefeller quickly agreed. With his typical largesse, however, he suggested expanding the goodwill tour into a "presidential mission" that would take him to twenty-three Latin American and Caribbean countries to create a hemispheric gesture of solidarity. The administration balked at the extravagance; however, Rockefeller's promise to use his own funds to supplement the budget convinced cautious bureaucrats. Over the course of the next several months, the governor and his key aides Berent Freile and Jim Cannon organized a contingent of dozens of advisers spanning the American political spectrum, including members of the Brookings Institution, the State Department, the American Civil Liberties Union; business and financial leaders; the governor's staff; and former diplomats. Armed with the resources of both the State Department and the Rockefeller fortune, the four voyages undertaken in May and June 1969 promised to become the largest spectacle of American propaganda in the region since Walt Disney and El Grupo.

However, the old Rockefeller mystique carried less currency in 1969 than it would have ten or even five years earlier. Joseph Persico, then the governor's speechwriter, would later reflect that "his name was still magic to the oligarchies, the *latifundistas,* the conservative, U.S.-educated, old-family ruling classes in Latin America. But to the Latin left, his name was anathema."[29] This disrepute stemmed partially from a general rise in anti-Americanism over the course of the decade and from the fading memory of the public health initiatives of the Rockefeller Foundation that had received so much praise during the 1940s and 1950s.[30] For the new generation, Rockefeller meant Standard Oil and long-term U.S. imperial interests. This association crystallized in early 1969 as a result of a protracted conflict between the new military-revolutionary government of Peru under General Juan Velasco and the International Petroleum Company (IPC), a Canadian subsidiary of Standard Oil of New Jersey. This clash stemmed from a questionable lease IPC had negotiated to exploit the La Brea oil fields without paying local taxes, which had led to extended strife in the mid-1960s. In 1967, IPC and the Peruvian state reached a controversial accord by which La Brea would be returned to Peru, which would forfeit its claim to back taxes and grant further concessions to IPC for potential Amazonian deposits. IPC's reciprocal promise to buy crude oil drilled by the state proved controversial, as the published accord failed to note the price for this oil. The public rancor inspired by this oversight helped precipitate Velasco's October 1968 coup and continued into the next year, leading to a last-minute decision to rescind Peru's invitation to Governor Rockefeller, citing his family's connections to Standard Oil. The standoff in Peru inspired solidarity strikes by students, local opposition groups, and anti-American activists across the hemisphere, curtailing ambitions for the presidential mission.

The shift from diplomatic politesse to ritualistic public clashes can be illustrated by raw footage preserved in the Rockefeller Archive Center that documents Nelson Rockefeller's first trip to Mexico and Central America (from May 11 to May 19, 1968).[31] The film begins with a smiling Rockefeller accompanied by his wife, Happy, deplaning in Mexico City on a red carpet, where an eager crowd listened to the first of many speeches highlighting his desire to listen to Latin American concerns in order to report back to President Nixon. Further footage of Mexico features Happy's tour of a children's hospital, complete with folkloric dances by youngsters in peasant blouses, doubtlessly intended to provide local color for a future documentary or newsreel. The tarmac arrival is repeated for other capitals, but signs begin to pepper the crowds, protesting the arrival of the American contingent. By the time the mission moves on to Honduras, the documentary footage captures scenes of protesters on a highway burning tires and clashing with the local police. The subsequent arrivals at national airports reveal an expanded police presence protecting the governor, who is quickly shuttled into limousines that cart him to his meetings with dignitaries.

These images reflected growing tensions on the ground. Indeed, the first three countries visited proved relatively harmonious and even led Rockefeller to cable Nixon and Henry A. Kissinger, adviser to the president for national security affairs, to communicate the surprising "warmth of sentiment and enthusiasm" felt for the new administration.[32] Despite this promising start, the mission encountered a major hurdle in Honduras, where the police fatally shot a protesting student, whose memory would be invoked in the expanding clashes on subsequent stops. As the violence mounted during the second trip with further deaths in Quito and Bogota, Chile and Venezuela followed Peru's lead by cancelling Rockefeller's visit due to domestic security concerns. On the third trip, in early June, the military government in Brazil neutralized these fears by proactively arresting thousands of student and labor activists in Brasilia, Rio de Janeiro, and São Paulo to ensure an eerie calm. The Uruguayan government of President Jorge Pacheco, which had only just lifted a state of emergency precipitated by labor struggles in reaction to runaway inflation, opted to greet the American visitors in Punta del Este instead of the capital, due to renewed protests following the lifting of martial law in May 1969. In Argentina, militant activists detonated a series of bombs at the Minimax chain of grocery stores, which Rockefeller co-owned, to welcome the mission. Its arrival proved even more volatile, however, because it occurred at the same time as the *Cordobazo*, a conflagration in the industrial city of Córdoba in which auto workers allied with the student movement to stage an extended work stoppage that inflamed residual tensions nationwide over the Argentine military government.[33] The most notorious moment in the four-journey saga, however, happened on the last leg, in the Caribbean, when Rockefeller appeared arm in arm with the notorious Haitian dictator François "Papa Doc" Duvalier on a balcony in Port-au-Prince, a sight that helped inspire the Students for a Democratic Society (SDS) to greet the governor with a solidarity demonstration upon his return to Idlewild Airport (now John F. Kennedy Airport) in New York.

While ritualized confrontations in urban streets had long characterized goodwill tours, as discussed earlier, the Rockefeller mission eclipsed its predecessors as a transhemispheric media event. While the coverage of the trip deserves its own study, its general framework demonstrates a rapidly expanding attention to a spectacle of ambiguity and paradox that complicated the typical Manichean framework of Cold War schemas. The mostly positive reports on the first voyage shifted toward this ambiguous stance during the second voyage. To cite one example, Guayaquil's daily *El Universo* juxtaposed columns extolling Rockefeller's long record of service in Latin America with graphic accounts of the violence that had greeted his motorcade in Bogota, which would be echoed in the throwing of bricks and wounding of passersby the next day in Quito.[34] In June, as the trips took on a life of their own and transcontinental appeals for their cancellation proliferated, the sight of tires burning and police beating protesters on television sets across the United States accelerated criticism at home, as well. Nevertheless, Rockefeller soldiered on. Perhaps the absurdity was best encapsulated in a cartoon by the popular Argentine caricaturist Basurto, whose cartoon in the daily *Crónica* sarcastically noted Rockefeller's iconoclastic virtue of being willing to visit even his enemies.[35]

Rockefeller publicly dismissed these manifestations as nefarious acts of communist insurgents, going so far as to joke in the introduction to the report submitted to Nixon some months later that only the SDS happening at Idlewild had inspired real fear among his entourage.[36] Both he and his advisers qualified this statement in private. In a rambling and classified speech given to the Center for Inter-American Affairs in July 1969, for example, Rockefeller acknowledged the gravity of the situation. On the one hand, he maintained that there existed a defensible frustration with U.S. policy given the dissonance between the stated U.S. goal of hemispheric collaboration and the substantial bureaucratic barriers that hampered development programs. In particular, he cited the example of a Brazilian petrochemical executive who secured a French loan in three months after spending two years negotiating with the decentralized American government at a loss of $600,000.[37] On the other hand, Rockefeller continued to argue that communist agitators, who "could really get these kids hopped up," had manipulated this frustration.

Nevertheless, during a supreme moment of candor considering the violent situation in Uruguay, Rockefeller stumbled in his reproval of the opposition to President Jorge Pacheco, whose imposition of martial law had been roundly criticized and had made identifying the culprits virtually impossible:

It isn't just that they are out to get military dictatorships. They are out to destroy. I say "they," and if you ask me who "they" is [sic] I cannot tell you because at the moment I don't think anyone really knows which combination it is, as it is, and how it works.[38]

These frank words illuminate Rockefeller's uncertain and unsettled state. Moreover, they appear in the midst of an extended assessment of the hurdles the mission had faced and what the governor considered his unfair treatment at the hands of the press and the public. This includes a defense of his appearance on "Papa Doc" Duvalier's balcony, an attack on Fidel Castro's support for Velasco's Peruvian government, and, in a chilling anticipation of the U.S. backing of Operación Condor, an embrace of the region's new military dictators, whose genuine concern for the people "goes across the board, whether it's in Argentina or in Brazil or in Panama or in Peru."[39]

This confusion indelibly colored the drafting of the *Rockefeller Report on the Americas*. As early as the third trip, Rockefeller and his advisers admitted that the conflicts on the ground made reaching unanimity on policy issues particularly difficult. During a conference in Asunción, they therefore agreed to a procedure that would both enable consensus and afford a space for internal division.[40] Clifton Wharton, vice president of the Agricultural Development Council, first raised the issue by underscoring the dangers that internal divisions would be leaked to the press and therefore undercut the effectiveness of the report. He therefore suggested that the contingent focus on areas of consensus in the summary report and then either add footnotes regarding their individual points of disagreement or agree to draft individual reports in which they could raise their concerns about specific points in the summary.

This suggestion received general enthusiasm, though Rockefeller strongly disagreed with the idea of footnotes, which he felt would distract from the internal coherence of a summary report and invite skeptics to emphasize the points of difference, rather than the general recommendations.[41] Ensuing discussion endorsed the governor's position that individual or area reports would be preferable to footnotes, and the group eventually agreed that it would be preferable to share early impressions quickly. Leroy Wehrle, an economist and, at the time, a Fellow of Harvard's Institute of Politics, underscored the stakes:

I might say I could paint a certain type of painting, but I am only going to paint a tiny piece of that, and without knowing the over-all canvas, I can't paint because I don't know if we are talking about preferences for South America, North America or [the United Nations Conference on Trade and Development]. . . . It depends very much on what we want the world of the Seventies to be, and all of us have a world of the Seventies in our minds to try to create policies that would be fruitful.[42]

Wherle's somewhat idealistic gauntlet not only cemented a decision to share summary impressions and begin discussing these during the fourth trip but also initiated a broader conversation about the goals of the mission that would be developed in subsequent conferences in Haiti and in Seal Harbor, Maine, and at a weekend retreat at Kykuit, the Rockefeller family estate in the Hudson Valley.

It would be beyond the goals of this chapter to track this entire debate; however, it is critical to note that eventually the group agreed that the main thrust of the report would be to support the notion of hemispheric interdependence as had been articulated by Thomas Wolf as early as June 28.[43] This would be enshrined in the atavistic overtones of the first lines of the report: "We went to visit neighbors and found brothers." This reflection probably stemmed at least partially from Rockefeller's personal nostalgia for the Good Neighbor policy, which was a frequently cited trope during writing sessions. Indeed, the echoes of Roosevelt's initiative can be easily identified in the key policy recommendations of the *Rockefeller Report on the Americas*, which stressed multilateral decisions on economic and diplomatic policy, support for the "populist" Latin American military, and the creation of a cabinet-level post affirming the special relationship between the United States and Latin America that some scholars have posited was possibly designed for Rockefeller himself.

This traditionalist stance lauding the military and the oligarchy received round criticism because of its failure to adequately account for national difference and the severe cleavages that separated social groups such as the elite, students, the left, and the burgeoning middle sectors across Latin America. As had been the case with the technocratic reports of the 1950s, both Latin American and U.S. congressional figures noted that Rockefeller's predictable observations could have been penned without the expense and spectacle of the four journeys.[44] This possibility had been foreseen by some of the advisers on the trip, such as Jerome Levinson, whose initial reflections highlight the divergence between U.S. and Latin American goals and the dissonance between supporting military dictatorships such as the Brazilian government and the report's "desire for an inspirational, moral, and idealistic theme."[45] Nancy Maginnes, a Rockefeller aide who would later marry Henry Kissinger, similarly maintained that the theme of interdependence remained a flaccid platitude without attention to the many cultural and economic hurdles that limited cooperation as she and a fellow aide, Hugh Morrow, sharpened the final draft.[46]

These critiques continued following the report's release, of which Roy Wehrle's castigation in the foreign affairs review *Interplay* is probably the most developed. Wehrle focused on the question he had first raised in Asunción, namely the lack of specificity regarding U.S. goals for the region and the deficiencies of relying on paternalistic diplomacy that deploys outmoded recommendations based on ideological fixity, rather than employing a nimble response to shifting current conditions. He particularly criticized the overweening emphasis on military aid based upon the undocumented assumption that communist infiltration drove anti-American sentiment and justified supporting repressive regimes. Citing a colleague in Ecuador, he noted that, in spite of its failings, the Alliance for Progress had succeeded by opening the space for dialogue and alternative development strategies, such as rural cooperatives, which had been seen as communist prior to Kennedy's endorsement. Wehrle held that a similar possibility to encourage "reform and openness and change and development" had been subverted by the report's defensive tack and implicit embrace of stability over change.[47]

The implications of the statement concerned the very purpose of the listening tour, whose primary objective was, as Rockefeller monotonously intoned, to listen. As Wehrle maintained, the report ultimately demonstrated a deafness in which voices raised in opposition, discord, or even counterpoint were sullenly silenced by a smiling façade. And so a chance for an alternate world of the 1970s was lost. As I underscore in the next section, which highlights the petitions and correspondence sent to Rockefeller following the presidential mission, the loss is all the more palpable because of the sense of possibility that the mission did succeed in awakening, despite all the turmoil.

Politics and Publics: Correspondence, Patronage, and Mutable Lefts and Rights

As mentioned in the introduction, the Rockefeller presidential mission inspired a secondary round of communications that remained below the radar. Thousands of individuals across Latin America responded to the governor's desire "to listen" and acted accordingly, putting pen to paper in attempts to express their ideas, struggles, and dreams. By and large, the letters took the form of solicitations—the governor was, after all, the scion of one of the wealthiest families in the world—but they also represent attempts to communicate a personal opinion of international politics or of the U.S. role in the world or hopes for domestic reform in their homeland. As such, they not only demonstrate the potency of the Rockefeller name but also provide a window into popular understandings of the Cold War.

The epistolary record broadly conforms to clientelist patterns developed during the colonial period and nineteenth century, in which a petition represented a first step at establishing a grievance and conceivably advancing a cause or redressing a wrong. Frequently, such solicitations were sent to symbolic figures whose status was seen as a potential circumvention of local troubles. As Florencia Mallon has noted, as late as the 1860s indigenous groups in Mexico continued to petition the King of Spain to redress incursions on their land or water rights by abusive landowners.[48] This tradition continued into the twentieth century and was even exploited by leaders seeking to cement clientelist networks. The populist Juan Domingo Perón of Argentina, for example, organized epistolary campaigns in which Argentine workers noted their struggles and hopes for his new regime, dreams selectively granted to bolster Perón's image as a generous leader. Getúlio Vargas of Brazil similarly requested communiqués from his constituencies, leading to coordinated petitions, as in the case of workers from São Paulo who requested Vargas's aid to overcome daily struggles of poverty. In both these cases, petitioners appropriated and deployed official rhetoric in order to better their lot and, in the process, vie for direct political participation.[49]

The letters to Rockefeller ought to be considered in light of this tradition, whereby he represents a patron whose affirmation may reify an individual political judgment or enable entrepreneurial activity, provide personal services, facilitate emigration, or otherwise redress social wrongs. However, the unique nature of his persona as an emissary of the U.S. government at the height of the Cold War distinguishes these petitioners as agents attempting to actively engage and redefine international politics according to their local circumstances.

As such, they provide a distinctive insight into the patterns of positionalities by singular individuals seeking to both describe their current circumstances and frame themselves within this international rubric. Attention to the particular in rhetorical schemas and citations thus provides a rich source for understanding how this journey helped to crystallize individual attitudes to the global strife of the late 1960s.

In many cases, this framework can be considered to be deployed at least partially in order to better couch the ask, that is, to underscore the credentials of the individual seeking patronage, soliciting travel to the United States, petitioning for health care, or hoping for some form of financial remuneration. However, a similar rhetorical schema can be identified within those letters that only incidentally include a solicitation, pointedly avoid requests for financial or other patronage, or directly address Rockefeller's stated goal of listening to Latin American voices. Even among the obvious solicitations, therefore, these preambles or other framing devices must be considered serious indicators of popular perceptions of Cold War politics that express an individual's perception of his or her own place within global political processes. Consider, for example, the following samples that directly address the political tensions of the day:

November 20, 1969, Buenos Aires, Argentina. Alejandro Crivocapich, writing for the second time, alerts Governor Rockefeller of his disappointment at not having received a grant to purchase a car to start a taxi business. The rejection especially smarts as Crivocapich has been defending the American's recent visit to those "who looked down upon the tour."[50]

October 20, 1969, Juaseiro do Norte, Brazil. Antonio Pedro da Silva, a politician and journalist, whose livelihood comes from a small commercial establishment selling electric and domestic goods, writes of a dream to publish two books of poems, again hoping the Governor will help realize this goal and subsidize tuition for his 10 children. Though he appreciates his government's engagement with infrastructural development, he knows this is why they won't help him publish those 2,000 copies.[51]

May 19, 1969, La Plata, Argentina. Calvin Respress, an African American expatriate of some fifty-five years, pens a request to the Governor to fund a boxing school, one where severe exertion and discipline would stem the desire for rebellion amongst the youth of his adopted country.[52]

June 8, 1969, Medellín, Colombia. Jorge Humberto Alvarez, Cesar Darío Gómez, and Jorge Velez Arango—three students from the Centro de Estudios Superiores para el Desarrollo—write the governor of their displeasure with his recent journey to their homeland, given that the ailing Alliance for Progress is an *engañabobos* (snare for fools) that serves only to enable shady deals between governments. However, given the governor's repeated statements that his desire was to "listen" to the people of Latin America, they hope that he may contribute to the development of a sporting league they are developing for starving people, in order to give them some joy while moving them out of the cantinas and bars.[53]

Each of these four sample letters includes a request for direct aid and would have therefore received a standard rejection letter from Rockefeller's offices. At the same time, they demonstrate individual encounters with the mission and distinct forms of positioning. Crivocapich, for example, emphasizes his entrepreneurial spirit and his vigorous defense of the tour to detractors that he has encountered. Da Silva hopes to play upon the governor's noted artistic and educational philanthropy but also highlights his sympathy with the development projects sponsored by the Brazilian government. Respress, on the other hand, notes a shared national origin and the desire to calm the flames of rebellion in his adopted homeland by channeling rebellious youthful energy into sport. Perhaps the most interesting example, that of the students from Medellín, represents a confrontational jeremiad lambasting U.S. policy and the very spectacle of the mission, which is tempered by lingering doubt and hope for support for a football league for the region's poor.

This small sample thus demonstrates the variety of publics that sent letters to Governor Rockefeller, as well as the degree to which the tensions that had accompanied his trips continued to be played out and redefined in the pages of the correspondence. As these letters indicate, the majority of correspondents represented the political right or center and often had some education. They tended to situate their writing within a global framework that engaged three points of interest: the role of the United States in the world, local conditions, and the global Cold War.

Besides disowning the recent violence as the actions of a few radicals or communists, many of the letters commonly demonstrate some familiarity with U.S. history or politics. For example, there are several mentions of the recent moon landing, which had caused a great stir worldwide. More common, though, were platitudes concerning the great leadership that the United States in general had shown over the years and praise for Rockefeller's own ties to Latin America or the health campaigns of the Rockefeller Foundation. Such was the case with Aristides Beltrán Martínez, who wrote twice to the governor during that fateful year of 1969. The first, on the eve of the visit to Colombia, noted Beltran's great respect for Rockefeller, esteem that had led Beltran to name his son Nelson in honor of the American. Although Beltrán's request that the governor become young Nelson's godfather was denied by the ubiquitous Louise Boyer form letter, he sent a follow-up missive in November lamenting the rough treatment that the missions had met earlier in the year, correspondence likely inspired by the publication of the *Rockefeller Report* in

October.[54] Others linked Rockefeller to great mythic characters; for example, Osvaldo González Britez, writing from Vallenar, Chile, in July 1969, identified Rockefeller as a new Quixote engaging in an equally idealistic crusade.[55]

Establishing one's own credentials was a crucial part of this endeavor, particularly for those letters that featured requests for assistance or remuneration of some kind. The Gondra Alcorta family of Bella Vista, Argentina, for instance, pronounced itself ready to attack the student radicals with sticks if Rockefeller said the word.[56] Erasmito Casanova of Bogotá, writing in May 1969, cited his experience as a Korean War veteran in the fight against Communism.[57] While old soldiers and far-right extremists of this sort tended to cite their military experience, students showcased their knowledge of history or current events. In Córdoba, Clive Walter Allemandi, requesting a scholarship, referenced the words of Fernando Belaunde Terry at Punta del Este the previous year, noting that dollars of aid were insurance for the Cold War and threatening to solicit the Soviet embassy for funds should Rockefeller refuse him. Allemandi continued to expound upon the importance of saving Western culture as a whole, an endeavor in which he hoped to participate.[58]

Others took the opportunity to showcase their knowledge of contemporary affairs and to provide some of the advice that Rockefeller had purportedly come to Latin America to find. These often transformed into manifestos, at times numbering dozens of typewritten pages. These were written by university students, journalists, petty bureaucrats, lawyers, millenarian prophets, and even the mentally unbalanced. A. Caballero Diaz, for instance, penned an extensive discourse on the problem of ancestral resentment in Argentine history as an explanation for the current generational conflict, a surprisingly lucid text given its immediacy; it was written on June 29, 1969, while Rockefeller was still in Buenos Aires.[59] Enrique Cuellar Vargas of Bogotá wrote of the country's extended history of violence, noting that he himself had published on the matter but was unable to continue to do so as a result of the National Front's resentment discussions of *la Violencia*, which served as a plea for either financial remuneration or a letter to a foreign press asking that his writing be kept in the public view.[60] At times, these extended ruminations proved rather esoteric themselves, as was the case of Antonio de Almeida Brisido, who, on June 16, 1969, penned a twelve-page letter outlining a vast Masonic conspiracy that he had encountered in the course of his travels as a sailor with the Brazilian navy and several merchant vessels, a vast saga that included a series of assaults in port towns across the world, as well as betrayals by numerous women.[61] For this one, Boyer simply responded with the initials NAN—No answer necessary—a categorization usually reserved for repeat correspondents and the psychotic. On the other hand, the initials might have just as well been placed on all the letters, for not a single one made it past the walls of assistants designed to screen Rockefeller from just that which he had ostensibly come to find—the voice of the Latin American people.

Conclusion: Varying Publics in Latin America

Much of the recent literature regarding the Latin American Cold War has emphasized the need to move beyond the dichotomous frame that dominated political language during the conflict itself.[62] This challenge is inherently tied to a broader historiographical tendency to rethink the primacy of the nation-state as a frame of analysis and to emphasize patterns of interregional, international, and global engagement. As such, there has been greater attention to cultural facets of the Cold War through analysis of cinema or other modes of propaganda, anti-American sentiment, and, increasingly, the centrifugal forces at the heart of Latin American societies themselves.

This chapter seeks to add to this literature by focusing upon the U.S. goodwill tour as a critical component of the twentieth-century development of hemispheric relations. As I have argued, Nelson Rockefeller's presidential mission to Latin America represented the pinnacle of this midcentury phenomenon because of its sheer scale and the virulence of the passions it unleashed. I have also held that it represents an opportunity lost, not as a result of the violence that ensued but because of a failure to heed the subtleties of the voices that confronted the Rockefeller mission. This includes not only those of the protesters in the streets but also those of mission advisers, other state actors, and, above all, the anonymous individuals who solicited the governor's support in the aftermath of the journey. It is imperative that further studies not only of the Rockefeller mission but also of Cold War Latin America pay concrete attention to the distinct publics that responded to U.S. policies, cultural production, and spectacle.

In the case of the Rockefeller mission, there are at least three discrete groups of actors that engaged the governor. First, there is the Latin American state, represented by the multiple officers, bureaucrats, politicians, and businessmen who met with the broader entourage, whose advice appears to have been accepted piecemeal in accordance with broader administration goals. The second includes detractors in the street, mostly students and members of the counterculture and the left. While much more research needs to be done into these groups' engagement with Rockefeller, their public display of resistance not only echoed global tensions but also conformed to existing patterns of ritualistic violence that had been reserved for U.S. goodwill missions for at least the previous decade. Again, Rockefeller ignored the ritualistic and historic nature of this clash, aside from the odd reference to Nixon's 1958 trip or periodic laments regarding the passing of the Good Neighbor era. The third group that the mission encountered comprises a diverse array of individuals who relayed their perception of both Rockefeller and the United States through written correspondence. These direct appeals demonstrate an ambivalent view of the United States that echoes the broader tenets of the Cold War, yet frequently transcends its Manichean language. These letters ought to be regarded as displays of both local and hemispheric engagement by people seeking to situate themselves within the maelstrom of global politics, to transform their daily lives, or to emerge from poverty or other struggles. As such, they not only represent alternate voices but also capture the potential for aperture and dialogue that the mission supposedly sought to find. As such, I consider them representatives of what I term the "pliable center."

I deploy this terminology intentionally as a challenge to terms such as middle sectors, middle class, bourgeoisie, or petit bourgeoisie, each of which inherently prioritizes economic status. Authors such as David Parker, writing of white-collar workers in Lima, or Pablo Piccato, in his studies of honor, elites, and public spheres in Mexico, note the importance of establishing respectability in defining status in twentieth-century Latin America.[63] The murky nature of terms such as respectability, honor, patriotism, communism, and capitalism in the midst of the Cold War, however, politicized these divisions in a stark contrast, yet did not eliminate the essentially fluid nature of Latin American economic and social conditions. As a result, this "pliable center" represents a paradoxical amalgamation of social actors, including the wealthy and the impoverished, the educated and the illiterate, the young and the old, the urban and the rural—in short, it cuts across the grain of the social or cultural categories that are typically employed. Politics integrates these individuals but does not define them, as their ideological fixations tend to themselves fluctuate according to the situation. As such, they represent a fluid contingent loosely situated to the left of the state and to the right of the street.

Correspondence appears to have served their needs by offering a medium of expression that avoids the inflexibility of accords signed in ballrooms and boardrooms or shouted on the street. Instead, these essentially reflective and reflexive communiqués afforded the chance to detail ambivalence and paradoxical positionalities. As such, the frequent assertion of personal humility or poverty not only serves to assert one's honorable intentions and lamentable plight but also justifies a claim to a pliable center that subverts the Manichean dualisms with which the Cold War was fought. In writing to the *gringo patrón*, these correspondents thus attempted to continue a dialogue ostensibly started by Rockefeller, never realizing that both he and the Nixon administration would ultimately be shielded from exposure to their efforts—the grandiose listening tour notwithstanding.

Notes

The author would like to thank the Rockefeller Archive Center for its support for the research that resulted in this chapter, which was funded by two Rockefeller Archive Center Grant-in-Aids in 2008 and 2009.

1. Gustavo Borja Moncayo to Nelson Rockefeller (NAR), August 7, 1969, folder 218, box 27, Series E—Countries (Countries), Record Group 4—NAR Personal (NAR Personal), Nelson A. Rockefeller Papers (NAR Papers), Rockefeller Family Archives (RFA), Rockefeller Archive Center (RAC), Sleepy Hollow, NY. Orig.: "como le indico yo puedo trabajar en lo que usted me indique, ya que en los Estados Unidos todo el mundo trabaja, porque para mi, es el país ideal, donde todo el mundo es igual, en el sentido de trabajo."

2. Peter Bales, "Nelson Rockefeller and His Quest for Inter-American Unity" (PhD diss., State University of New York at Stony Brook, 1992). Materials on the mission are to be found in Subseries 8—Presidential Mission to Latin America (PMLA), Series O—Washington, DC (DC), NAR Personal, NAR Papers, RFA, RAC. Other relevant staff files not processed when Bales completed his dissertation include those of John Cannon, Ann Whitman, Hugh Morrow, and Dianne Van Wie.

3. *The Rocky Horror Picture Show*, Jim Sharman, director, 1975.

4. Gerald Colby with Charlotte Dennett, *Thy Will Be Done: The Conquest of the Amazon: Nelson Rockefeller and Evangelism in the Age of Oil* (New York: HarperCollins, 1995).

5. See the essays in Gilbert M. Joseph and Daniela Spenser, eds., *In from the Cold: Latin America's New Encounter with the Cold War* (Durham, NC: Duke University Press, 2008), and Gilbert M. Joseph, Catherine LeGrand, and Ricardo Donato Salvatore, eds., *Close Encounters of Empire: Writing the Cultural History of U.S.–Latin American Relations* (Durham, NC: Duke University Press, 1998).

6. See the introduction to Sandhya Rajendra Shukla and Heidi Tinsman, eds., *Imagining our Americas: Toward a Transnational Frame* (Durham, NC: Duke University Press, 2007).

7. Hal Brands, *Latin America's Cold War* (Cambridge, MA: Harvard University Press, 2010), 8.

8. On Rockefeller's personal involvement in postwar Latin American economic patronage, see especially Elizabeth A. Cobbs, *The Rich Neighbor Policy: Rockefeller and Kaiser in Brazil* (New Haven, CT: Yale University Press, 1992); Darlene Rivas, *Missionary Capitalist: Nelson Rockefeller in Venezuela* (Chapel Hill: University of North Carolina Press, 2002); and Bales, "Nelson Rockefeller and His Quest." On the Rockefeller Foundation, see Marcos Cueto, *Missionaries of Science: The Rockefeller Foundation*

and Latin America (Bloomington: Indiana University Press, 1994); Anne-Emanuelle Birn, "Revolution, the Scatological Way: The Rockefeller Foundation's Hookworm Campaign in 1920s Mexico," in *Disease in the History of Modern Latin America: From Malaria to AIDS*, ed. Diego Armus (Durham, NC: Duke University Press, 2003); and Anne Zulawski, *Unequal Cures: Public Health and Political Change in Bolivia, 1900–1950* (Durham, NC: Duke University Press, 2007).

9. On Rockefeller's appointment as CIAA, see Cary Reich, *The Life of Nelson A. Rockefeller: Worlds to Conquer, 1908–1958* (New York: Doubleday, 1996), 165–209. For a general history of the cultural programs of the Office of the CIAA, see Antônio Pedro Tota, *O imperialismo sedutor: Americanização do Brasil na época da Segunda Guerra* (São Paulo: Companhia das Letras, 2000).

10. Donald C. Meyer, "Toscanini and the Good Neighbor Policy: The NBC Orchestra's 1940 South American Tour," *American Music* 18, no. 3 (Autumn 2000): 233–56.

11. Tota, *O imperialismo sedutor*.

12. See J. B. Kaufman, *South of the Border with Disney: Walt Disney and the Good Neighbor Program, 1941–1948* (New York: Disney Editions, 2009); Dale Adams, "Saludos Amigos: Hollywood and FDR's Good Neighbor Policy," *Quarterly Review of Film and Video* 24 (2007): 289–95; and Tota, *O imperialismo*. See also Ariel Dorfman and Armand Mattelart, *How to Read Donald Duck: Imperialist Ideology in the Disney Comic* (New York: International General, 1991), regarding the broader importance of hemispheric policy to Disney films.

13. Reich, *The Life*, 215.

14. Rockefeller intended to have Orson Welles film a documentary featuring the real lives of Latin Americans, but the attempt was abandoned after preliminary shooting in 1942 due to artistic differences. See Adams, "Saludos Amigos," 289. Eleanor Roosevelt's "My Day" columns describing her impressions of this trip can be accessed online at http://www.gwu.edu/~erpapers/myday/.

15. "Inter-American Notes," *The Americas* 10, no. 2 (October 1953): 229–32; Stephen G. Rabe, *Eisenhower and Latin America: The Foreign Policy of Anticommunism* (Chapel Hill: University of North Carolina Press, 1988), 66.

16. Marvin R. Zahniser and W. Michael Weis, "A Diplomatic Pearl Harbor? Richard Nixon's Goodwill Mission to Latin America in 1958," *Diplomatic History* 13, no. 2 (Spring 1989): 163.

17. The best descriptions of this event can be found in Zahniser and Weis, "A Diplomatic Pearl Harbor," and in Alan L. McPherson, *Yankee No!: Anti-Americanism in U.S.–Latin American Relations* (Cambridge, MA: Harvard University Press, 2003), 21–31.

18. McPherson, *Yankee No!*, 30.

19. Zahniser and Weis, "A Diplomatic Pearl Harbor," 186–90; McPherson, *Yankee No!*, 33–36.

20. Zahniser and Weis, "A Diplomatic Pearl Harbor," 186; McPherson, *Yankee No!*, 36.

21. Rabe, *Eisenhower and Latin America*, 136–37.

22. Eric Zolov, "¡Cuba Sí, Yanquis No! The Sacking of the Instituto Cultural México/Norteamericano in Morelia, Michoacán, 1961," in *In from the Cold: Latin America's New Encounter with the Cold War*, ed. Gilbert M. Joseph and Daniela Spenser (Durham, NC: Duke University Press, 2008), 214–52.

23. See, for example, Stephen G. Rabe, *The Most Dangerous Area in the World: John F. Kennedy Confronts Communist Revolution in Latin America* (Chapel Hill: University of North Carolina Press, 1999), and Jeffrey F. Taffet, *Foreign Aid as Foreign Policy: The Alliance for Progress in Latin America* (New York, Routledge, 2007). For a general framework see also Peter H. Smith, *Talons of the Eagle: Latin America, the United States, and the World*, 3rd ed. (New York: Oxford University Press, 2007). These evaluations echo contemporary evaluations, of which the most important is probably Jerome I. Levinson and Juan de Onis, *The Alliance That Lost Its Way: A Critical Report on the Alliance for Progress* (Chicago: Quadrangle Books, 1970).

24. Rabe, *The Most Dangerous Area*, 1–2, 194.

25. Taffet, *Foreign Aid as Foreign Policy*, 44–45.

26. Ibid., 31.

27. Berent Friele to NAR, December 16, 1965, folder 181, box 17, Subseries I—General Files (General), Series 21.2—Hugh Morrow (HM), Series 15—Nelson A. Rockefeller Gubernatorial (NAR Gubernatorial), NAR Personal, NAR Papers, RFA, RAC.

28. Some scholars have also speculated that Nixon wanted his rival out of the country. See Colby and Dennett, *Thy Will Be Done*, and Taffet, *Foreign Aid as Foreign Policy*.

29. Joseph E. Persico, *The Imperial Rockefeller: A Political Biography* (New York: Simon and Schuster, 1982), 102.

30. See note 8 on the Rockefeller Foundation's activities in Latin America.

31. Film footage, Presidential Mission Trip 1, May 11–19, 1969, PMLA, DC, NAR Personal, NAR Papers, RFA, RAC.

32. NAR to Richard Nixon, May 14, 1969; NAR to Henry Kissinger, May 14, 1969, folder 98, box 12, Subseries 2—Latin American Mission (LA Mission), Series 7—James Cannon Files (JC Files), NAR Gubernatorial, RFA, RAC.

33. James P. Brennan, *The Labor Wars in Córdoba, 1955–1976: Ideology, Work, and Labor Politics in an Argentine Industrial Society* (Cambridge, MA: Harvard University Press, 1994).

34. "Visita de Nelson Rockefeller provoca nuevos brotes de violencia en ciudades colombianas" and "Desde 1937 N. Rockefeller labora tesoneramente por América Latina," *El Universo* (May 29, 1969), 13.

35. Basurto, "Visitas," *Crónica* (June 17, 1969), 1.

36. Nelson A. Rockefeller, *The Rockefeller Report on the Americas: The Official Report of a United States Presidential Mission for the Western Hemisphere* (Chicago: Quadrangle Books, 1969), 9.

37. "Address of Governor Nelson A. Rockefeller at the Center for Inter-American Affairs, July 21, 1969," p. 22, folder 997, box 122, PMLA, DC, NAR Personal, NAR Papers, RFA, RAC.

38. Ibid., p. 20.

39. Ibid., p 20. Operación Condor was a coordinated purging of leftist elements by South American militaries in the mid-1970s, particularly strong in the Southern Cone.

40. "Discussion between Governor Nelson A. Rockefeller and Advisers, American Embassy, Asunción, Paraguay, June 20, 1969," folder 991, box 121, PMLA, DC, NAR Personal, NAR Papers, RFA, RAC.

41. Ibid., pp. 4–5.

42. Ibid., p. 13.

43. Thomas H. Wolf, "A Declaration of Interdependence," ABC News, June 28, 1969, folder 121, box 14, LA Mission, JC Files, NAR Gubernatorial, NAR Papers, RFA, RAC.

44. Steven V. David to Ann Whitman, December 4, 1970, folder 288, box 27, General, HM, NAR Gubernatorial, NAR Personal, NAR Papers, RGA, RAC.

45. Jerome Levinson to NAR, June 22, 1969, folder 1198, box 149, PMLA, DC, NAR Personal, NAR Papers, RFA, RAC.

46. Nancy Maginnes to Hugh Morrow, n.d., folder 996, box 122, PMLA, DC, NAR Personal, NAR Papers, RFA, RAC.

47. Leroy Wehrle to NAR, January 13, 1970, folder 151, box 17, LA Mission, JC Files, NAR Gubernatorial, RFA, RAC.

48. Florencia E. Mallon, *Peasant and Nation: The Making of Postcolonial Mexico and Peru* (Berkeley: University of California Press, 1995.)

49. Eduardo Elena, "What the People Want: State Planning and Political Participation in Peronist Argentina, 1946–1955," *Journal of Latin American Studies* 37, no. 1 (2001): 81–108; Joel Wolfe, "'Father of the Poor' or 'Mother of the Rich'?: Getúlio Vargas, Industrial Workers, and Constructions of Class, Gender and Populism in Sao Paulo, 1930–1954," *Radical History Review* 58 (1994): 80–111.

50. Alejandro Crivocapich to NAR, November 20, 1969, folder 33, box 6, Countries, NAR Personal, NAR Papers, RFA, RAC. Orig.: "quienes veían con malos ojos esa gira."

51. Antonio Pedro Da Silva to NAR, October 20, 1969, folder 76, box 11, Countries, NAR Personal, NAR Papers, RFA, RAC.

52. Calvin Respress to NAR, May 19, 1969, folder 36, box 6, Countries, NAR Personal, NAR Papers, RFA, RAC.

53. Jorge Humberto Alvarez, Cesar Darío Gómez, and Jorge Velez Arango to NAR, June 8, 1969, folder 175, box 22, Countries, NAR Personal, NAR Papers, RFA, RAC.

54. Aristides Beltrán Martínez to NAR, May 5, 1969, folder 175, box 22, Countries, NAR Personal, NAR Papers, RFA, RAC.

55. Osvaldo González Britez to NAR, July 16, 1969, folder 156, box 20, Countries, NAR Personal, NAR Papers, RFA, RAC.

56. Gondra Alcorta family to NAR, n.d., folder 33, box 6, Countries, NAR Personal, NAR Papers, RFA, RAC.

57. Erasmito Casanova to NAR, May 13, 1970, folder 175, box 22, Countries, NAR Personal, NAR Papers, RFA, RAC.

58. Clive Walter Allemandi to NAR, August 22, 1969, folder 33, box 6, Countries, NAR Personal, NAR Papers, RFA, RAC.

59. A. Caballero Diaz to NAR, June 29, 1969, folder 34, box 4, Countries, NAR Personal, NAR Papers, RFA, RAC.

60. Enrique Cuellar Vargas to NAR, June 14, 1969, folder 175, box 22, Countries, NAR Personal, NAR Papers, RFA, RAC.

61. Antonio de Almeida Brisido to NAR, June 16, 1969, folder 70, box 10, Countries, NAR Personal, NAR Papers, RFA, RAC.

62. See the essays in Joseph and Spenser, *In from the Cold*, which build upon a broader historiographical tendency that reconsiders U.S.–Latin American relations and calls for a great attention to hemispheric approaches. For an introduction to these tenets see Joseph, LeGrand, and Salvatore, *Close Encounters of Empire*, and Shukla and Tinsman, *Imagining Our Americas*.

63. David S. Parker, *The Idea of the Middle Class: White-Collar Workers and Peruvian Society, 1900–1950* (University Park: Pennsylvania State University Press, 1998); Pablo Piccato, *The Tyranny of Opinion: Honor in the Construction of the Public Sphere* (Durham, NC: Duke University Press, 2010); Pablo Piccato, "Public Sphere in Latin America: A Map of the Historiography," *Social History* 35, no. 2 (May 2010): 165–92.

3

The Mexican Student
Movement of 1968

National Protest Movements in International and Transnational Contexts

SARA KATHERINE SANDERS

Viewed from the perspective of other developing nations, Mexico's 1968 student movement emerged from an era of stability at home and instability elsewhere in Latin America. The 1968 Summer Olympics bestowed international legitimacy on the Mexican state; by contrast, turmoil defined other parts of the Americas. The first Games hosted in a Latin American or Spanish-speaking country, the event was supposed to signal a reinvigoration of the "Mexican miracle," a period of high growth beginning in the 1940s that made Mexico's economy almost self-sufficient. Instead, the opening of the Games was abruptly disrupted by waves of lethal government-ordered violence against protesters assembled in the Plaza de las Tres Culturas—the Tlatelolco massacre—which revealed to the world that Mexico City, too, had been swept up in the same patterns of dissent and repression that were appearing in major urban centers on multiple continents. The "Spirit of Sixty-Eight" had arrived in Mexico, and, with it, the specter of state repression. How the protests started and their relationship to those broader trends in global dissident politics are issues that form the subject of this chapter.

Viewed closely and with hindsight, we can now see that, by the time of the 1968 Summer Games, Mexico had already traveled an increasingly ominous path with respect to its prospects for political and social stability. The postwar era, which soon became the Cold War era, started smoothly enough. Mexico's strong security ties to the United States, formalized by the 1947 Inter-American Treaty of Reciprocal Assistance, pledged its leaders to an openly anticommunist stance following the 1948 International Conference of American States, which resulted in the formation of the Organization of American States (OAS). This period of international calm was to be short lived. Following the June 25, 1950, outbreak of Cold War hostilities on the Korean peninsula, geopolitical conflict came to Mexico's doorstep in 1954 with the U.S.-led overthrow of Jacobo Arbenz's democratically elected government in Guatemala. Later, in the wake of the 1959 Cuban Revolution, U.S. attempts to consolidate control over Latin America intensified. With this intensification, however, also came a surge in student protests within Mexico targeting the state, U.S. business, and imperialism. The focus of student concern was national sovereignty—an issue that would come to define the movement in the moments leading up to, during, and after "Sixty-Eight."

As described in this chapter's account of student political concerns during the Sixty-Eight movement, subsequent events of a broadly international character and significance reinforced a sense among Mexican students that change in their own political system was not only possible but likely. The death of Ernesto "Che" Guevara, killed by U.S.-trained Bolivian soldiers on October 9, 1967, was followed by the assassinations of Martin Luther King Jr. (April 4, 1968) and Robert F. Kennedy (June 6, 1968). These momentous political events, coupled with reports of guerrilla violence in Chiapas, dominated the international news media and further sustained student perceptions that a breakdown in the status quo might be imminent. In fact, some students and citizen political dissidents hoped to effect or precipitate that very breakdown through direct political action. The mix of national and international precedent that they cited in defense of their confrontation with state authority—described in detail in this chapter—suggest that they thus believed themselves to be taking part in a worldwide struggle against a moribund and vulnerable political order and that their actions were linked to those of a broader, global dissident community beyond Mexico's borders.[1] As the movement that became Sixty-Eight gained momentum, students exchanged letters with and released press statements directed at other members of this global and radicalized student community. In some cases, they crossed international borders to make these connections in person.[2]

This heady brew of national concerns, coupled with international points of contact and even emulation, is difficult for contemporary historians to untangle. For many Mexican students and for the global news media of the day, belief in the global nature and significance of "the movement"—in other words, an emerging pattern of student-led calls for sweeping and immediate political change—made events in Mexico seem that much more exciting or significant and (for the students) aligned the protesters within an international community of the young and righteous. Yet, in the context of daily confrontations with the state, much of the political rhetoric espoused by students also focused on conditions and political narratives specific to Mexico. Student protesters invoked their own national history frequently in praising heroes like Benito Juárez and Emiliano Zapata as important precursors to their own activities or when they imagined connections between historical villains like Porfirio Díaz and the then-president who shared his last name, Gustavo Díaz Ordaz. Another key theme in the discourse of Mexico's Sixty-Eight was the need to protect constitutional rights; indeed, one of the most central critiques of Mexico's government was that its agents and officials routinely violated the national Constitution by ignoring the political rights of students (and other citizens) and denying them the right to freedom of speech and assembly, mainly through the threat of violence or imprisonment. It is possible to conclude, in other words, that, although the students who participated in Sixty-Eight believed themselves affected by international events and in the international nature of their politics and movement, their concerns, icons, and rhetoric were *also* irreducibly national—that is, focused on Mexico, its people, and its future.

Despite the combination of national and international "frames" for the mobilization, the transnational remains the crucial paradigm in recent scholarship on Sixty-Eight and the 1960s ("the Sixties") more broadly.[3] Given the frequency of movements that year, with protests in such places as the United States, France, Italy, Germany, England, Prague, Tokyo, China, and Mexico City, scholars have sought to find similarities among them. Indeed, global historian Jeremy Suri has argued that the 1960s "produced pressures for radical change across political parties, national boundaries, and distinct cultures."[4] Likewise, Carole Fink, Phillip Gassert, and Detlef Junker argue that "activists throughout the world operated as part of formal and informal networks of communication and collaboration. Thus, 1968 was a global phenomenon because of the actual and perceived cooperation among protest movements in different countries . . . [and] because the protagonists believed in a common cause."[5] Martin Klimke and Joachim Scharloth similarly assert the importance of transnational networks in Europe during 1968, arguing that they allowed for exchanges between student organizations throughout Europe that diffused both ideas and strategies. Moreover, such networks encouraged students to outline transnational solutions for global problems and to prepare a global revolutionary strategy that would result in the transformation of the Cold War system.[6] In his seminal work on 1968 and the Cold War, Suri asserts that the 1960s and 1968, in particular, should be understood as a moment of "global conjucture . . . [that] requires an international history that treats power as both multicultural and multidimensional."[7] More recently, Immanuel Wallerstein has publicly invoked the memory of the Sixties as a global-radical conjecture by comparing the Occupy Wall Street movement to the "lasting legacy" of the "uprising of 1968" worldwide.[8] These scholarly analyses echo the popular memory of 1968, the year that is said to have "rocked the world."[9]

Scholarship on Sixty-Eight in Mexico highlights both the national and the transnational nature of the movement and of the 1960s more generally. Eric Zolov offers an excellent analysis of pro-Cuba, anti-imperialist sentiment in Mexico during the early 1960s, connecting these public expressions to deeper concerns over Mexican politics.[10] His work on the impact of the 1968 student movement on U.S.-Mexican relations stresses the presence of internationalist symbols in Mexico's student movement in 1968, and his work on the Olympic Games that year further elucidates the international nature of representations of Mexico during this major international moment and how such representations were intended to contribute to the legitimacy of the state at home.[11] Such work is part of a more recent inclusion of Latin America and the Third World in analyses of the Cold War.[12] Despite more recent forays into the international components of Sixty-Eight, the literature on the movement remains firmly rooted in the national. The bulk of the literature examines the trajectory of the movement, its grievances and strategies, the response of the state, and the memories of its participants. More recent work examines the culture of the movement, paying particular attention to the gendered nature of the mobilization.[13]

New sources on the Mexican Sixty-Eight student movement reveal the global nature of protest in 1968, illuminating the concrete dimensions of its international connections and, more important, the deeply national nature of the movement.[14] Although Mexican students joined with others around the world, considering themselves the vanguard of an international protest, they nevertheless responded to local concerns. Indeed, their grievances focused on national politics and economics, as did their agenda for reform. Student discussion of international relations was used mostly as a commentary on

domestic politics, a way to critique Mexico's politicians for their failure to protect the country and its citizenry from foreign influence. Connections between
Mexican students and those elsewhere were largely mediated by the news media, and students consciously employed the media as a forum to voice their
grievances globally. While there was some foreign presence in Mexico during
the 1968 protest, this points less to activist ties promoting a global movement
or the coordinated spread of information and more to the spirit of curiosity and exploration that abounded in the Sixties. While the proliferation of
nongovernmental organizations and transnational advocacy networks is well
documented for the post–Cold War era, less is known about the transnational
relations that directly preceded them. Indeed, Mexico in 1968 was, in many
ways, a precursor of the movement to protect human rights in the aftermath
of the Dirty Wars of the 1970s, and it sheds lights on the limitations of such
networks and the circulation of knowledge and information through the late
1960s.[15] Given the limited flow of information between students in Mexico
and those elsewhere, the links between them were vague, a result of a perceived
compatibility based more on a shared identity of youth and a loose critique of
imperialism than on direct coordination of grievances, information, strategies,
and solutions.

The Movement

Typically considered a watershed event in contemporary Mexican history, the
events of 1968 exposed the moral bankruptcy of Mexico's ruling party, the
Partido Revolucionario Institucional (PRI), when it responded to the protest
with violence. The Mexican student movement began in July 1968 and rapidly
gained momentum. Drawing students from all over Mexico City and, at times,
from the provinces, the mobilization centered on the two largest schools of
higher education: the Universidad Autónoma de México (UNAM) and the
Instituto Politécnico Nacional (IPN). On October 2, police encircled protesting students in Mexico City's historic Plaza de las Tres Culturas, also known as
Tlatelolco, and opened fire, resulting in an estimated four hundred deaths and
more than two thousand arrests. Part of an ongoing campaign of violence, the
October 2 massacre generated such fear that the movement effectively ended.
The mobilization occurred in the months prior to the opening of the 1968
Olympic Games, which Mexico hosted in that year, a symbol of the economic
progress the country had achieved in the post–World War II period. The mas-
sacre occurred approximately two weeks before the opening of the Games.
    The student agenda brought together a range of ideologically diffuse posi-

tions. Ultimately, a petition of six points, created by the movement's leadership, the National Strike Committee (CNH), would define the movement. Functioning as its explicit agenda and formal list of demands, the petition included the following: (1) government abolition of its corps of *granaderos*, a tactical force whose violence had started the rebellion; (2) dismissal of police chiefs Luis Cueto Ramírez, Raúl Mendiolea, and Armando Frías, who had organized state repression against the movement; (3) identification of the government officials implicated in the bloodshed; (4) indemnification of the families of the dead and wounded in the aggression since June 23; (5) release of all political prisoners; and (6) abolition of articles 145 and 146 of the Penal Code, which pertained to "social dissolution" and had been used to justify the government's conduct.

The movement lasted only a few short months, spreading from the schools, throughout the city proper, and finally, although in more limited fashion, to the provinces. In many ways, it began as a response to the violence of the Mexican state. The mobilization found its origins in police attempts to maintain stability in light of the impending Olympic Games, when licensed protesters inadvertently met with rival soccer teams, brawling after a match. The riot corp, or *granaderos*, arrived, shutting down both protesters and soccer players. That night, they raided the offices of the Mexican Communist Party, and students began to protest shortly thereafter.

Throughout the first week of August, students organized, drawing on the existing structure of the educational system and already formed political parties. By August 6, the large-scale demonstrations had begun, with students and others congregating in the nation's center of power, the Zócalo, to publicly demand redress of their grievances and public dialogue with state representatives. The government's unwillingness to meet student demands or, indeed, to speak publicly about the student protests resulted in considerable frustration among participants and an increasing radicalization. By October 2, the massacre in Tlatelolco made the violence against the students markedly visible, forcing a deep reorganization of the movement as the majority of its leaders were imprisoned. While a new leadership emerged that sought to continue the movement, fear of state reprisals was pervasive, and participation fell dramatically. Eventually, leaders lifted the strike.

While the movement coalesced around its six-point agenda, it was nonetheless ideologically fluid, bringing together a diverse assortment of people and politics. Participants ranged from those with earlier experience in organized student politics to those who were swept up in the heady ideas of the period or who simply happened to be passing by at the moment of some political activity. Among the organizations most involved in the movement were the Mexican

Communist Party, Communist Youth, the National Center of Democratic Students, the Communist Spartacus League, the Maoists, and the Trotskyites. These groups, many of them with global ties and aspirations, certainly influenced the global leanings of the movement. Yet, while these groups were active, the movement was nonetheless composed of a more diverse participant base. The coordinating body of the movement, the CNH, was made up of student representatives, with three elected from each school, creating a central body of considerable ideological diversity. Student organizations sponsored by the government were also present throughout the movement, most notably the University Movement for Renovated Morals and the National Federation of Technical Students. These routinely came into conflict with student protesters.

Student leaders sought to form a movement that was broadly inclusive and to expand both the meaning of student politics and the types of people who could be incorporated into the movement. In doing so, they incorporated, among others, professors, instructors, parents and relatives, workers, *campesinos*, mothers and wives. Among the most active organizations was the Coalición de Profesores de Enseñanza Media y Superior Pro-libertades Democráticas (Coalition of Teachers of Secondary and Universities for Democratic Liberties), which drew its numbers from the faculties of the preparatory schools and universities. In short, while a "student" movement in name, the mobilization had a varied and diverse participant base.

When the student strike committees and the CNH officially formed, only two weeks into the movement, that is, between August 8 and 10, they began with elections in every school and faculty. From these, 210 representatives were elected, three from each of the seventy schools and faculties. Students from the UNAM, the IPN, the Normal School, and the National School of Agriculture at Chapingo participated, with the UNAM and the IPN forming the dominant presence in the movement.[16]

The movement was centered in Mexico City, but students received and sent ambassadors and letters of support from their colleagues in Veracruz, Sinaloa, Puebla, Tabasco, Morelos, Guadalajara, and Nuevo León. While the organization was largely student-led, it joined with workers and *campesinos*, who formed their own brigades or sent delegations to the demonstrations. In its short life span—approximately 120 days—the movement grew rapidly from a movement composed of students into a more diverse and inclusive mass movement for democratization.

Reflecting the broader postwar boom, the Mexican student protest developed in the context of considerable economic, demographic, and ideological transformation. Students came of age during the Mexican miracle, a period of modernization, economic growth, and dramatic demographic expansion.

During this period, more students entered higher education, perhaps disguising higher levels of unemployment, and the state consciously fostered a more diverse student body as policymakers sought to develop a skilled and ideologically aligned labor force. Along with these demographic and economic shifts, movement participants were part of a leftist resurgence in Latin American in the wake of the Cuban Revolution of 1959, as well as the Mexican mobilizations of the 1950s, '60s, and '70s, which drew on middle-class sectors dissatisfied with the state and the limitations of the Mexican Revolution, most notably the railway workers who mounted strikes in the late 1950s and the medical workers and students who did so in the 1960s.

Fears for the Nation: Patriotism and the Cold War in 1968

The international context, Cold War tensions, emerging understandings of development and imperialism, and student awareness of the actions of their international counterparts all played a key role in 1968. Yet these factors were understood as significant in specific relation to events and experiences in Mexico and used to condemn national politicians and policies. Thus, while international currents of change were important to students' framing of the movement, they paled in comparison to the importance of national concerns. Despite this, the two were deeply intertwined. Most prominently, students invoked Mexico's political past, particularly the War of Independence, the Revolution, and the midcentury movements for social change on the part of dissatisfied sectors of the middle class, namely protesting teachers, doctors, and railway workers. They grounded their movement in the politics and economics of Mexico, invoking the failure of the state to provide for the bottom strata, despite political promises to the contrary, and its violation of the Constitution. In short, they sought to criticize state officials and agents for their failure to adhere to their own regulations and to make good on their own political promises. In doing so, they condemned the Mexican state for its failure to follow through on the hard-fought gains of earlier generations, attempting to garner legitimacy for their own movement, which they saw as the continuation of those earlier mobilizations.

In their public protests and propaganda, students repeatedly drew on the most popular symbols of the Mexican nation-state. Invoking heroes such as "Hidalgo, Morelos, Juárez, Villa, Zapata, and many more," a speaker during a September demonstration rallied the crowd to the student cause by portraying movement participants as the inheritors and "true" representatives of these earlier movements. He asserted that these earlier leaders had "struggled for the liberty of the Mexican people, but liberty with justice and equality not . . . the freedom to exploit what is left, which is all of Mexico, and the equal opportunity to be exploiters."[17] In light of this, the speaker claimed that the mobilization honored its historical predecessors and their sacrifices for the country. In this way, he forged a populist argument in which he criticized elites, state and business alike, for exploiting the nation's resources to enrich themselves while large sectors of the population remained impoverished.

As students invoked Mexico's political history and its heroes, attempting to harness these potent national symbols to the cause of student protest, they stressed the historic importance of Mexican autonomy vis-à-vis other countries, particularly the United States, by invoking past movements that sought to liberate Mexico from outside influence. Among these, the War of Independence from Spain and the Revolution that expelled foreign businesses were the two most powerful symbols of modern national identity, and the students frequently referenced these events, rather than social upheavals in France or Prague. In doing so, they criticized the Mexican state for its failure to promote the general welfare of the Mexican citizenry, casting the government instead as exploiters of the people on whose behalf it presumably ruled. A student flier circulated in September of that year stated that student demands were supported by "our Mexican Constitution and not foreign ideologies as our abusive government maintains. Their actions demonstrate that the true agitators are misery, ignorance, and injustice. The true provocateurs are the repressive Corp of *Granaderos* that serve the oligarchy, the same exploiters who are actually in Power."[18] Indicative of the movement's nationalist rhetoric and pride in the country's past movements for change was a placard at an August demonstration that expressed the following sentiment concerning the Mexican government: "They violate our autonomy American style, we need to kick their asses Mexican style."[19]

As the participants articulated a stance that promoted Mexican development independent of foreign powers, they echoed historic calls to create a Mexico for Mexicans in which the nation's wealth went to the nation's people. Professor Herberto Castillo, a teacher and a movement leader, argued in a letter to the editor that "we also know that as long as we continue to give the nation's wealth to monopolistic North American interests the political interventions of our northern neighbor will continue to grow, and with that, the repression of the just aspirations of our people."[20] Castillo pointed to the global relations of power to make a nationalist claim on the resources of Mexico, arguing that they should "unmask" the North American interests at work in Mexico.

Movement participants invoked the historical belief that Mexican resources ought to be controlled by Mexicans. They linked the desire of foreign business to exploit Mexico's resources to a similarly exploitative Mexican bourgeoisie, seeing the two groups as allies within an international system of wealth. Early propaganda from the vocational schools asserted that the student conflict "should directly confront the reactionary forces of Mexico, allied with the international police of the United States against the advanced and democratic forces of our country."[21] These notions found continued expression throughout the movement. Indeed, a flier later that month claimed that business in Mexico was increasingly foreign owned: "look for a business . . . that is Mexican owned and see that you are unable to find one, even the French Fries are foreign owned." The author concluded that these economic practices were antithetical to the welfare of the Mexican population and that "there isn't a climate favorable to our own development . . . [and] the people of Mexico . . . don't participate in the decisions the government makes."[22]

The Cold War context made the presence of U.S. economic interests in Mexico appear particularly threatening to movement participants. To many, the existence of "North American monopolies" in Mexico were part of a grand strategy to make Mexico ever more financially and politically dependent upon the United States and, therefore, a pawn in the effort by its northern neighbor to counter international communism. Well aware of the expansionist nature of U.S. politics and of U.S. intervention in other parts of Latin America, movement participants considered the possibility that U.S. agents were operating in Mexico and saw this as a threat to national sovereignty. Professor Castillo, one of the dominant voices of the movement, argued that "for the CIA agents who have infiltrated Mexico it is not difficult—given the situation of tension that prevails in the country—to put arms in the hands of some Mexicans who perform terrorist acts that . . . benefit those who are interested in increasing the repression to SILENCE the people who have expressed their desires through the students."[23] In a similar way, students from Vocational School 5 argued that U.S. security forces were willing to depict the student movement as part of an international communist conspiracy in order to use it as an excuse for their involvement in Mexican politics. In a letter to the editor of the newspaper *El Día*, the student authors asserted that the CIA and the FBI "had predicted a great communist conspiracy and they had to prove its existence, regardless of the methods they used!"[24] The students from Vocational School 5 felt that the CIA and FBI viewed the advent of the mobilization as their opportunity and accused the movement's leaders of being involved in a global communist plot. Movement leaders, however, argued that the plot was hatched by the U.S. government with the complicity of the Mexican state. The students concluded that they had in fact done the security forces a favor "and should receive payment for our services, from the North American agencies!"[25]

This position gained particular resonance as a response to accusations of communism and international agitation. State officials and state-sponsored organizations leveled charges of foreign agitation and communism as a justification for repression, invoking the laws of social dissolution. Students expended considerable energy depicting themselves as loyal and patriotic Mexican citizens. To this end, a student from the UNAM's Faculty of Philosophy and Letters invoked the words of Francisco Madero: "The sacrifices do not matter if we reach our goal of creating a better country. A small group enriches itself at the cost of the suffering of the people." He argued that these sentiments, expressed in 1968, would paint him as an agitator, yet they were spoken by one of Mexico's greatest revolutionary leaders.[26]

Students encountered disapproval from both supporters and opponents of the movement for their use of international symbols, a reflection of tension between nationalist and internationalist political discourse. Following a mega-demonstration on August 26, a meeting took place in the Physics-Mathematics building of the IPN. Representatives of the Parents Association expressed their disapproval of the images of Che Guevara hoisted by students at the previous day's demonstration.[27] They declared that such images were unnecessary when Mexico boasted heroes such as Juárez and Hidalgo. The students replied that the image represented "the global student struggle to defend their rights."[28] Nonetheless, given that movement participants were roundly criticized for their use of international symbols of protest, the CNH quickly encouraged students to restrict themselves to national icons and figures. Indeed, as one placard at an August demonstration read: "If Juárez hadn't died, the *granaderos* would have killed him."[29]

International Youth Culture and Protest in 1968 Mexico

While the focus of the movement was largely on national concerns, students nonetheless believed themselves to be part of an international community of youthful protesters. Indeed, the movement originated in a moment of international solidarity with a demonstration in support of the Cuban Revolution. This community was fueled primarily by the media, cultural consumption, and partially shared experiences of postwar socioeconomic, political, and cultural change. Students exchanged letters and materials, held demonstrations in solidarity in their home countries, and read about one another in the news.

While the information and knowledge they held about their counterparts in foreign countries may have been vague and partial, it nonetheless contributed to the notion that change was sweeping the globe. This feeling of global connection was also fostered by the highly interrelated nature of politics and economics during the Cold War. In many ways, global integration was nothing new. Mexico was connected to the rest of the world from the colonial period to the present. Yet students articulated an understanding of global relations in which political and economic power was heavily wielded by the United States to the detriment of low-income countries. In short, they responded to the particularities of global relations, envisioning themselves as a global community in counterpoint to these dominant forces.

As part of a perceived global community, students in 1968 Mexico looked to their counterparts for strategy, inspiration, and affirmation, and, indeed, their gaze was returned. In their press releases, interviews, and speeches and at rallies, Mexican student protesters made reference to movements outside Mexico, particularly those throughout Latin America, the United States, and Europe. Many felt that it was the responsibility of students to bring about change, that they alone would be the harbingers of a total, national, and, perhaps, global transformation. At a meeting convened on the theme of "The Global Student Conflict," one participant identified the common problem as a world structure in which "the majority of the families of the world" suffer economically and in which all states function "within a system in which the people are always condemned, that is why the student body of the world has intervened to defeat this."[30]

Many participants located their critique in terms of global economic and political practice, pointing to an international power imbalance. Author and activist José Revueltas located the events of 1968 and the actions of students within a context of international relations. He claimed that "it would be an inane provincialism to believe that the rebellion of the Mexican youth in 1968 is separate from the outside world and war and isn't influenced by the dominant tone of relations between countries—small or large."[31] He argued that the world was divided between those who possessed nuclear energy and those who did not and that the threat of nuclear war and the war in Vietnam undergirded both national and international politics.

Students particularly targeted the United States in their criticisms of the global nature of politics, arguing that the United States sought to keep Mexico and all of Latin America mired in poverty. They asserted that the United States protected its economic interests by an aggressive foreign policy and highlighted the involvement of the CIA in Latin American politics. For many, the coup against President Arbenz of Guatemala and the numerous attempts against Cuba were central to the formation of their political consciousness. It was not a far jump to assume CIA presence throughout Latin America and in Mexico itself.

Yet the power of the United States was not seen as absolute, and many considered outside interests to be bound to national ones. Indeed, students pointed to a global system in which economic elites and politicians in Mexico and the United States colluded to maintain power. As one student phrased it, "the intervention of the Central Intelligence Agency, that has acted in complicity with the national bourgeoisie and the pseudo-revolutionary parties of the UNAM, as well as the structures of the Mexican Government," was responsible for the public aggression against the students.[32]

Given this belief in the interconnectedness of politics and economics, as well as global youthful protest, students sought to learn about their contemporaries in other countries. Not surprisingly, given the movement's roots in the educational system, students wanted to know more about the activities of others like themselves, and this was one of the primary mechanisms by which they believed themselves to be part of a global community, locating themselves within an international community of youth culture and international protest. For instance, at a meeting in the UNAM, one professor raised "the French movement" in which he had "the opportunity to be present." He urged those at the meeting to bear in mind the experiences in France, using them to help students formulate their activities in Mexico.[33] Other students joined their contemporaries in Sofia, Bulgaria, for the Ninth Annual Youth Festival and brought back stories of their experiences there.[34]

As the movement gained ground, professors and students alike began to organize conferences and seminars on the international dimensions of student protest. On August 9, 1968, in response to student demands, teachers organized a lecture series on the "roots of the movement, the attitudes of the repressive forces, the French movement of May and June, and the crime of social dissolution."[35] Only days later, students from the UNAM's Faculty of Law circulated fliers for a conference titled "Roots and Perspectives on the Student Movement in Mexico and Latin America" and that focused on the relationship among the student movements in Mexico, France, Italy, West Germany, Czechoslovakia, and Brazil. They connected these countries because of "the deformations and contradictions of the liberal world . . . similarly, they are a product of the discontent that pervades studious youth that cannot be turned into democratic channels, and will continue making its presence felt in the movements that are now completely democratic, and that may lead to future revolutions."[36]

One of the primary ways in which students thought themselves to be of an international community was through the media, especially the news press. The students believed that international journalists, there en masse for the Olympic Games, offered them a degree of protection from state repression, assuming that reports of violence would reach foreign audiences and that this would be sufficient to deter the state from extreme violence. In this they were wrong, and the majority of international newspapers circulated the very low casualty numbers reported by the state, leading to little international awareness of the Tlatelolco massacre. They also hoped that the news media would broadcast their message to a global student community and throughout the world. In their view, the presence of international journalists gave them a unique opportunity to go over the heads of their own country's journalists, whom they assumed to be in the pocket of the government, to reach the world. In a speech given on August 9, one student leader explained that, in regard to "the violence that they were victims of, the Mexican press has quieted the reality, in Europe and the United States, especially in the journals *Time, New York Times*, and *News Report*, they explain the reality of the events and that there have been deaths that now reach twenty one in number."[37] Similarly, at another demonstration, a student speaker asserted that there were "foreign correspondents present and they would tell the truth and expose Mexico's corrupted press."[38] Students consciously played on the international media to create the sense of a global community of youthful protesters.

Students assiduously courted foreign journalists, inviting them to demonstrations and press conferences with the hope of creating an international readership and audience for events in Mexico. Among the almost three thousand people at one October 1 demonstration at the UNAM were correspondents from the United States and England, including representatives from CBS and NBC, as well as representatives from the French and Tokyo press. They came with pencils and paper and also with their cameras to film the event. Moreover, the spectators included foreign athletes who were attending the Olympic Games.[39] At another demonstration, one leader highlighted the role of the international press, arguing that "the spilt blood will be washed with blood and that the foreign journalists invited to this demonstration promised to tell the world the truth and nothing more.[40] In fact, as the Olympics approached, student leaders held a press conference with the explicit aim of sending a message to the students of the world. Explaining the significance of the movement, they told the journalists who were present that the Mexican student movement had broken "thirty years of official demagogy" and that the students would struggle until "total triumph." They outlined their demands for public dialogue and told the press that these demands had been met by state agents with "bayonets and tanks."[41]

Students also encouraged foreigners to support their cause by designing propaganda specifically for them. As early as mid-August, protesters marched through the city holding placards with slogans such as "FOREIGNER: IN THIS PLACE THERE IS NO FREEDOM."[42] Similarly, on October 1, students plastered the UNAM's Faculty of Law with fliers in French, Russian, and English.[43] Days later, following on the heels of the October 2 massacre, students decided to create propaganda in a multiplicity of languages to "be distributed among the foreign athletes with the hope that they won't go to the Olympics and, in this way, discredit the Government before the world"—or so claimed state security agents.[44]

As part of an international community of righteous protesters, students used their demonstrations as a forum to oppose issues beyond Mexico and to comment on events abroad. While the vast majority of the rhetoric and analysis focused on issues of national concern, students also used their platform to relate events in Mexico to events in other countries. At an August 26 march, the overall message was one of change within Mexico. Yet protesters carried signs whose messages went beyond national boundaries. One student carried a placard that read, "The students of Mexico decry the invasion of Czechoslovakia and Vietnam. Long live liberty!" Others carried signs with photographs of Mao Zedong.[45] At a meeting in late September, one student argued for the "strategies used by Mao Zedong in his famous Cultural Revolution, which the students should make use of."[46] Students connected themselves intellectually with movements abroad, adopting some of their strategies and at times embracing their revolutionary heroes, such as Mao and Che. In doing so, they attempted to legitimate their actions through them, giving an international gloss to their own movement.

Transnational Networks in 1968 Mexico

The international nature of 1968 can largely be understood as composed of youths who learned from one another and shared in a series of simultaneous national protests. Students existed in a political, economic, and cultural system that was increasingly global, and many of them were subject to similar structural changes: the Cold War, the waning of the postwar economic boom, and a global youth culture fueled by new patterns of consumption. Taken together, these created a feeling of shared community. These ties were greatly influenced by the international media, whose presence in Mexico during the 1968 movement was extremely important. Although this community largely existed at the rhetorical level, the connections were at times direct. Students exchanged letters, wrote in support of one another to foreign governments, held solidarity protests, and even crossed borders to learn about movements elsewhere.

The international exchange of letters was a key way in which Mexican protesters, particularly student leaders, sought to legitimize their movement. When they gained a seal of approval from their foreign counterparts, they were sure to make it widely known. At a meeting in August 1968, those in charge stated that they were not only mobilizing students to protest in the Mexican states of Oaxaca, Morelos, and San Luis Potosí with the hope of achieving a national student strike but also corresponding with students abroad. Indeed, leaders claimed to have received letters of support from "France, China, Germany, and various countries in Latin America." These letters were generally addressed to the President of the Republic, informing him of foreign support for the students; at the same time, they were intended for broad public circulation.[47] Similarly, months later, another student from the UNAM declared that "some universities" abroad had denounced the Mexican government for its occupation of the UNAM's University City, holding a demonstration in France in support of the Mexican movement on October 1, 1968, only one day before the massacre that ended the movement. He outlined the plan: "In France in front of the Mexican Embassy, they held a demonstration of solidarity with the Mexican students." He furthermore declared that a similar demonstration was held in Finland and that the university community in Colombia had written a letter to the president condemning "the repression exercised against many parts of the Mexican society," as had students from Brazil, Uruguay, Argentina, Venezuela, Italy, Spain, France, and England.[48] He outlined plans for a protest on October 5 that would be international in nature, with rallies outside the embassies of the countries discussed.[49] Thus, while the existence of a global community was sometimes subjective, it was also realized through direct correspondence and demonstrations of cooperation.

Not only did the students exchange letters of support; they also traveled to other countries. While this was far less common, foreign students and radicals were present in small numbers during the Mexican protests. Indeed, Mexican police detained at least fifteen foreign youths, the majority of them students from the United States, during the 1968 protest. These visitors were of great interest to the state security agents, who sought to find evidence of outside agitation in order to justify state repression on the grounds of territorial integrity and to publicly delegitimize the movement. The Mexican police, fearing the presence of outside "agitators" and foreign spectators more broadly, was quick to detain the visitors.

Among the few examples of a foreign presence during the protest were the journalists who were clearly drawn to the protest, although perhaps they had not arrived in Mexico with the intention of covering them. Such was the case of a trio of Germans who made their way to the IPN'S Vocational 5 School with television cameras. Claiming to be at work on a project on the colonial charms of Mexico and the Olympics, they had applied to the proper channels for visas and permits during their stay and were indeed granted permission to film the city. Police detained them, and, upon interrogation, the German visitors asserted that they had had no interaction with the students, despite being in their school, and that, moreover, they had been unable to communicate with the students because they did not speak Spanish.[50] Similarly, a Chilean journalist employed by *The Voice of Mexico* was arrested at one of the earliest demonstrations in support of the Cuban Revolution. After interrogation, he signed a statement that he later renounced, claiming that he "was held without communication and threatened by Agents, who hit him in the stomach and put a pistol to his neck." The security report noted that he "was a card-carrying member of the Mexican Communist Youth."[51]

Other foreigners, all students, were in Mexico because of their leftist politics or experience with political protest in their home countries. One such student, hailing from the United States, had stopped in the country on her way to Cuba, where she planned to study Spanish. Once in Mexico, she joined the student protesters, and police detained her at a student meeting. The foreign student claimed to have learned of the meeting at the university by seeing propaganda around the city and decided to attend as she had "assisted various demonstrations in New York City, in which they had demanded an end to war."[52]

Similarly, Mexican police arrested twelve more foreign students, the bulk of them law students and their companions, all from the United States. Police detained these students, eight men and four women, when they joined with Mexican student protesters on their way to a public demonstration. Security officials claimed that the students from the United States were in contact with the Cuban Embassy and planned to leave for Cuba from Mexico. During the demonstration, according to the security reports, they distributed propaganda on behalf of the "Black Panthers and Black Power," although police also noted that all but one of the students were white.

The students ranged in age from twenty-three to twenty-eight years old, and the majority studied law, although a social worker and an undergraduate were arrested as well. Most were from California or New York. They had stopped in Mexico to obtain visas for Cuba, their ultimate destination. On arriving in Mexico City the visitors had learned of the movement and had gone to the UNAM, where they boarded a hijacked bus on its way to a demonstration at the IPN. One of the detained explained his situation to security agents with these words: "He says he's not a socialist but that he wanted, because of curiosity, to know Cuba and decided to make the trip and he went to the demonstration for the same reason." The security agents stated that the students distributed propaganda and carried a placard reading "The Redemption of the People will be All or Nothing."[53]

The law students detained in Mexico formed a delegation from the National Lawyers Guild that intended to visit Cuba, both as a challenge to the embargo and because of the deep interest of many of its members in the nature of the Revolution there. Numbering perhaps twenty participants, none of them Black Panthers, they passed through Mexico City on their way to Cuba. While waiting for their visas, the delegation learned of the detention of a group of Black Panthers in Mexico City who were also making their way to Cuba on a completely unrelated trip. Fearing for their safety because of the violence directed against the Panthers in the United States, the group from the Lawyers Guild immediately went to the U.S. Embassy to demand the release of the detained Panthers. Some members of this group then made their way to the UNAM, the protest in the Zócalo, and later returned to their hotel to find secret service agents awaiting them. These actions, rather than difficulties with the Cuban Embassy, were likely the cause of subsequent events.

That evening, the police detained those present at the demonstration, along with their colleagues who had not participated in the demonstration. They were interrogated throughout the night and eventually taken in pairs to a jail outside the city, where they were held for several days. Drawing on their experiences with organizing in the United States and uncertain of their release, the law students organized a hunger strike that soon gained them a call to the U.S. Embassy. They were placed on planes, asked never to return to Mexico, and sent back to the United States. One detainee described the period with these words: "It was a wild time. There was the sense of a worldwide movement, that major changes were happening. You could have imperialist powers such as the U.S. who it seemed would be rocked back on their heels."[54]

The discovery of two Guatemalans, perceived by state agents to be both communists and active in the student movement, created a flurry of state activity in October when they were detained on the first day of the month. Casting them as communist agitators, security officials exhibited deep concern over the potential of these international connections, using them in reports as a strong case for the international nature of the student protests or at least the potential for an international communist conspiracy within the protests. During interrogations, both Guatemalans claimed to have arrived in Mexico in August as political refugees and self-identified as "Trotskyite urban guerrillas." The security report details a confession from the Guatemalans that they, along with an economics student at the UNAM, had killed a soldier "to take his weapon, with the aim of using it for guerrillas in Guatemala." According to the report, their student ally, "who actually acts in the Mexican student movement," was the one who planned the assassination of the soldier: "He gave them a pistol with which to rob a car . . . an armory, and a bank." Linking the movement to international guerrilla movements, the interrogators determined that "they have intervened, along with their Mexican Trotskyite friends, in different student activities such as assemblies . . . telling them about guerrillas activities in Guatemala and the tactics of urban guerrillas."[55] The nature of these international connections between students in Mexico and leftists elsewhere generated considerable concern among state agents, yet there is little evidence for a coordinated international movement.

Conclusion

What emerges from these materials is a picture of 1968, not as a global moment born of a single protest repertoire but as a highly diverse moment of social mobilization based on discrete national concerns, as well as a shared mobilizing framework of "global" revolution. In one sense, increased prosperity and ties to global commerce created an internationalized consumer culture and news media through which Mexican students became aware of the political activities of their counterparts in other countries. While actual contact was almost wholly mediated by the news media, this sense of solidarity nonetheless provided a powerful tool of legitimization through which students in Mexico justified their demands for justice by pointing to similar rhetoric in Paris, Prague, and elsewhere and left a powerful legacy for greater transnational solidarity.

Without a doubt, such conclusions also speak to the emergence of a global anti-imperialist framework, although the understandings and practices of such a network certainly varied between "first-world" and "third-world" students, and the global nature of the critique was, at best, vague and broadly articulated. In Mexico, notions of a pan-Latin American identity and solidarity were fairly common, as was an understanding of global relations that pitted the interests of the United States against those of Mexico. Students drew on the international "spirit" of the moment, in their propaganda and in their letters to the editor; indeed, the idea that Mexican movement participants stood at the vanguard of international leftism and in solidarity with other radicals throughout the world first gained currency during the movement and remains one way in which participants understood the significance of the event. However, from an organizational perspective, links between Mexican students and other student groups were quite limited and, indeed, given state control of the media, the free circulation of information concerning the massacre and state violence severely curtailed. From the perspective of political mobilization, an assessment of the global nature of the 1968 student movement in Mexico requires moving beyond a shared "student"- or "youth culture"- centered view of transnational political community and toward other points of contact between student politics and rightful resistance, or contentious politics, elsewhere.[56]

Economic growth, a demographic boom, and the concurrent emergence of a transnational, youth-targeted consumer culture and news media constituted the key structural conditions of Mexico's Sixty-Eight. These processes reflected broader, global transformations. Perhaps most important was the unmatched growth of the post–World War II era, a period of economic boom throughout much of the Western world. However, by 1968, the first signs of the limits to growth were becoming visible. Eric Hobsbawn has noted that 1968 seemed to signal the "end of the feast."[57] The promises of economic growth had created greater expectations for many sectors of society, especially educated youth.[58] Growth was coupled with the postwar population explosion, leading to higher numbers of young people in all countries and resulting in the subsequent development of a youth consumer culture. These overlapped with growing urbanization, larger schools, greater access to higher education, and technological advances. A growing news media covered global events, familiarizing audiences not only with local news but also with events from abroad as protesters used the media to disseminate their messages.[59]

The subjective experience of transnational solidarity, or internationalist "spirit," was the primary framework through which former students have remembered the event, but new sources reveal that actual connections to national events were just as significant, forming the primary content of movement discourse. Indeed, manipulation of the symbols and history of the Mexican nation proved to be among the most potent strategies employed by movement participants. During the actual protests, activists from the United States and Guatemala joined the Mexican students' ranks—sometimes in prison—as opponents to U.S. imperialism in Latin America or protesters expressing a general interest in global leftist politics. These international supporters, although few in number, sustained students' enthusiasm for rightful resistance to the state, but they also highlight the degree to which the movement was tied to regional Cold War–era concerns. While Sixty-Eight was certainly a global moment, in many ways it was an intensely national moment. Students were concerned not only with the Mexican state's violation of its own Constitution but also with their own economic and political futures as Mexican citizens.

Ultimately, the Mexican movement should be understood within the context of Mexican midcentury economic, demographic, ideological, and cultural change, connecting it to earlier historical processes and events.[60] It was part of an ongoing revolt against the PRI and should be considered part, perhaps the most vibrant part, of a series of midcentury movements and consequent violent state repression. The participants in the Mexican mobilization ultimately accepted the logic of the developmentalist state. They too believed that Mexico should continue to grow and develop but argued that the gains should be shared more broadly. At heart, it was a national movement, premised on restoring constitutional rights and on the notion of equality among economic groups in relation to Mexican politics.

Notes

1. The noted international and transnational historian Akira Iriye also points to the international dimensions of national movements during the 1960s: "Self-consciousness about global community may have been a key aspect of international relations of the 1960s, a decade that is usually seen through such geopolitical dramas as the Cuban missile crisis, the Vietnam War and the Chinese-Soviet rift. . . . Precisely because the world's geopolitics appeared so volatile and dangerous, forces and movements that had desperately sought an alternative world order during the 1950s redoubled their efforts." See Akira Iriye, *Global Community: The Role of International Organizations in the Making of the Contemporary World* (Berkeley: University of California Press, 2002), 96–97.

2. In many ways, the conditions that gave rise to nationalism also fostered a sense of internationalism during the 1960s and 1968 in particular, if "internationalism" is meant to convey a feeling of simultaneity and discontent, both largely mediated by the press. I would argue that Benedict Anderson's framing of the rise of nationalism has some applicability to the rise of twentieth-century internationalism, as well. See Benedict Anderson, *Imagined Communities: Reflections on the Origins and Spread of Nationalism* (London: Verso, 1983).

3. Framing is used to mean "strategic efforts by groups of people to fashion shared understandings of the world of themselves that legitimate and motivate collective action." See Doug McAdam, John D. McCarthy, and Mayer N. Zald, "Introduction," in *Comparative Perspectives on Social Movements: Political Opportunities, Mobilizing Structures, and Cultural Framings*, ed. Doug McAdam, John D. McCarthy, and Mayer N. Zald (New York: Cambridge University Press, 1996), 6.

4. Jeremy Suri, *The Global Revolutions of 1968* (New York: Norton, 2007), xi.

5. Carole Fink, Phillipp Gassert, and Detlef Juriket, eds., *1968: The World Transformed* (New York: Cambridge University Press, 1998), 2. The focus of the authors on transnational ties within Europe may lend itself to greater connections than those found within the larger and less geographically dense Americas.

6. Martin Klimke and Joaquim Scharloth, *1968 in Europe: A History of Protest and Activism, 1956–1977* (New York: Palgrave MacMillan, 2008), 4. While Mexican students

may have participated in some of the events Klimke and Scharloth describe, such as the Annual Youth Festival in Bulgaria in 1968, there is little evidence of such exchange in 1968 Mexico. Rather, goals and strategies were much more national in nature, and pan-regional leftist networks were of greater significance than global youth networks.

7. Suri, *The Global Revolutions of 1968*, 262–63.

8. Immanuel Wallerstein, "The Fantastic Success of Occupy Wall Street," October 15, 2011, http://www.iwallerstein.com/fantastic-success-occupy-wall-street/.

9. Mark Kurlansky, *1968: The Year That Rocked the World* (New York: Random House, 2005). Other works that examine the transnational dimensions of 1968 include Paul Berman, *A Tale of Two Utopias: The Political Journey of the Generation of 1968* (New York: Norton, 1996); Robert V. Daniels, *Year of the Heroic Guerrilla: World Revolution and Counterrevolution in 1968* (Cambridge, MA: Harvard University Press, 1989); David Farber, ed., *The Sixties: From Memory to History* (Chapel Hill: University of North Carolina Press, 1994); Chris Harman, *The Fire Last Time: 1968 and After* (London: Bookmarks, 1988); Gerd-Rainer Horn and Padraic Kenney, eds., *Transnational Moments of Change: Europe 1945, 1968, 1989* (Lanham, MD: Rowman and Littlefield, 2004); and Jeremy Varon, *Bringing the War Home: The Weather Underground, the Red Army Faction, and Revolutionary Violence in the Sixties and Seventies* (Berkeley: University of California Press, 2004).

10. Eric Zolov, "Cuba Sí, Yanquis No!," in *In from the Cold: Latin America's New Encounter with the Cold War*, ed. Gilbert M. Joseph and Daniela Spenser (Durham, NC: Duke University Press, 2008), 214–52. His work on counterculture in Mexico points to the development of an international consumer culture. See Eric Zolov, *Refried Elvis: The Rise of the Mexican Counterculture* (Berkeley: University of California Press, 1999). For the development of rock music in Latin America, see Deborah Pacini Hernandez, Héctor Fernándes L'Hoeste, and Eric Zolov, eds., *Rockin' las Américas: The Global Politics of Rock in Latin/o America* (Pittsburgh: University of Pittsburgh Press, 2004).

11. Eric Zolov, "Toward an Analytical Framework for Assessing the Impact of the 1968 Student Movement on U.S.-Mexican Relations," *Journal of Iberian and Latin American Studies* 9, no. 2 (December 2003): 41–68; Eric Zolov, "Showcasing the 'Land of Tomorrow': Mexico and the 1968 Olympics," *The Americas* 61, no. 2 (October 2004): 159–88.

12. Among the most important of these new works are Odd Arne Westad, *The Global Cold War: Third World Interventions and the Making of Our Times* (New York: Cambridge University Press, 2006), and Gilbert M. Joseph and Daniela Spenser, eds., *In from the Cold: Latin America's New Encounter with the Cold War* (Durham, NC: Duke University Press, 2008).

13. Among the most significant works on Mexico's 1968 movement are Raúl Álvarez Garín, *La estela de Tlatelolco: Una reconstrucción histórica del Movimiento estudiantil del 68* (Mexico City: Editorial Itaca, 1998); Gilberto Guevara Niebla, *La democracia en la calle: Crónica del movimiento estudiantil mexicano* (Mexico City: Siglo Ventiuno Editores, 1988); Javier Mendoza Rojas, *Los conflictos de la UNAM en el siglo xx* (Mexico City: CESU-UNAM/Plaza y Valdés, 2001); and Ramón Ramírez, *El movimiento*

estudiantil de México (Julio/Diciembre de 1968) (Mexico City: Ediciones Era, 1969). More recent work includes Elaine Carey, *Plaza of Sacrifices: Gender, Power and Terror in 1968 Mexico* (Albuquerque: University of New Mexico Press, 2005); Deborah Cohen and Lessie Jo Frazier, "Defining the Space of Mexico '68: Heroic Masculinity in the Prison and 'Women' in the Streets," *Hispanic American Historical Review* 83, no. 4 (November 2003): 616–60; and Kevin Witherspoon, *Before the Eyes of the World: Mexico and the 1968 Olympic Games* (DeKalb: Northern Illinois University Press, 2008).

14. This chapter is based on a variety of sources, including state security records, newspapers, memoirs or testimonials, and interviews; state security records constitute the bulk of the source material. These sources, many of them daily reports on the movement—its participants, activities, and alleged beliefs—were, in turn, produced by a sophisticated intelligence-gathering apparatus that permeated virtually the entire organizational structure of student politics. In terms of its mandate and functions, the Dirección Federal de Seguridad (Directorate of Federal Security, DFS) was a government security agency responsible for preserving stability within Mexico and for protecting the state against subversion and terrorist threats. Its rationale was to build a portrait of the movement as an organized, violent, and underground coalition with antistate intent—in other words, to build an argument for state repression of the movement. Where possible, the DFS sources have been corroborated with other sources such as newspaper reports, journalistic articles, and movement publications in order to develop a more complete perspective on the events of the movement. For an overview of the DFS, see Sergio Aguayo Quezada, *La Charola: Una historia de los servicios de inteligencia en México* (Mexico City: Grijalbo, 2001).

15. While this is true for students and activists, the same cannot be said for state agents who were privy to extensive information. The National Security Archive demonstrates the extent of U.S. knowledge of events in Mexico in 1968 and, indeed, elsewhere throughout the Cold War.

16. Movement participant and chronicler Ramón Ramírez asserted that there were approximately 200,000 participants from the schools of Mexico City. Students from the UNAM accounted for 90,000, the IPN for 70,000, and the remainder came from the Normal Schools and the National School of Agriculture at Chapingo. See Ramírez, *El movimiento estudiantil de México*, 22.

17. Archivo General de la Nación (AGN), Dirección Federal de Seguridad (DFS), Exp. 11-4-68, Leg. 42, Hoja 207-217, September 25, 1968.

18. Ibid.

19. AGN, DFS, Exp. 11-4-68, Leg. 28, Hoja 1-15, August 13, 1968.

20. Centro de Estudios Sobre la Universidad (CESU), Universidad Nacional Autónoma de México (UNAM), Colecciónes Universitarios, Movimientos Estudiantil Mexicano, Dirección General de Información, box 53, folder 273, page 35, newspaper article, January 30, 1969.

21. AGN, DFS, Exp. 11-4-68, Leg. 26, Hoja 3-14, August, 1968.

22. AGN, DFS, Exp. 11-4-68, Leg. 33, Hoja 313-323, August 25, 1968.

23. CESU, UNAM, Colecciónes Universitarios, Movimientos Estudiantil Mexi-

cano, Dirección General de Información, box 53, folder 277, page 27, newspaper article, August 18, 1968.

24. CESU, UNAM, Colecciónes Universitarios, Movimientos Estudiantil Mexicano, Dirección General de Información, box 50, folder 253, page 4, newspaper article, August 11, 1968.

25. Ibid.

26. AGN, DFS, Exp. 11-4-68, Leg. 34, Hoja 331, August 27, 1968.

27. While Che Guevara was the most frequently invoked international hero, students also referenced Mao, Stalin, Trotsky, Gandhi, and Martin Luther King Jr.

28. AGN, DFS, Exp. 11-4-68, Leg. 34, Hoja 328-355, August 27, 1968.

29. AGN, DFS, Exp. 11-4-68, Leg. 35, Hoja 56-59, August 1968.

30. AGN, DFS, Exp. 11-4-69, Leg. 91, Hoja 79, n.d.

31. CESU, UNAM, Colecciónes Universitarios, Movimientos Estudiantil Mexicano, Dirección General de Información, box 53, folder 273, page 48, newspaper article, April 4, 1969.

32. AGN, DFS, Exp. 11-4-68, Leg. 33, Hoja 58, August 22, 1968.

33. AGN, DFS, Exp. 11-4-68, Leg. 27, Hoja 253, August 8, 1968.

34. AGN, DFS, Exp. 11-4-68, Leg. 31, Hoja 13, August 15, 1968.

35. AGN, DFS, Exp. 11-4-68, Leg. 28, Hoja 8, August 9, 1968. A similar conference was organized in 1968 on the theme "Global Student Conflict." See AGN, DFS, Exp. 11-4-69, Leg. 91, Hoja 79, n.d.

36. AGN, DFS, Exp. 11-4-68, Leg. 31, Hojas 6-8, August 15, 1968.

37. AGN, DFS, Exp. 11-4-68, Leg. 28, Hoja 5, August 9, 1968.

38. AGN, DFS, Exp. 11-4-68, Leg. 44, Hoja 1, n.d.

39. AGN, DFS, Exp. 11-4-68, Leg. 44, Hoja 118, October 1, 1968.

40. AGN, DFS, Exp. 11-4-68, Leg. 44, Hoja 3, n.d.

41. AGN, DFS, Exp. 11-4-68, Leg. 44, Hoja 117-125, October, 1 1968.

42. AGN, DFS, Exp. 11-4-68, Leg. 30, Hoja 3, August 13, 1968.

43. AGN, DFS, Exp. 11-4-68, Leg. 44, Hoja 123, October 1, 1968.

44. AGN, DFS, Exp. 11-4-68, Leg. 44, Hoja 281, October 4, 1968.

45. AGN, DFS, Exp. 11-4-68, Leg. 34, Hoja 328-355, August 27, 1968.

46. AGN, DFS, Exp. 11-4-68, Leg. 44, Hoja 117-125, October 1, 1968.

47. AGN, DFS, Exp. 11-4-68, Leg. 28, Hoja 8, August 9, 1968.

48. AGN, DFS, Exp. 11-4-68, Leg. 44, Hoja 121-122, October 1, 1968.

49. Ibid.

50. AGN, DFS, Exp. 11-4-68, Leg. 32, Hoja 237, August 20, 1968.

51. AGN, DFS, Exp. 11-4-68, Leg. 24, Hoja 135, July 29, 1968.

52. Ibid.

53. AGN, DFS, Exp. 11-4-68, Leg. 30, Hoja 13-14, August 13, 1968.

54. Barry Winograd, in conversation with the author, April 11, 2010.

55. AGN, DFS, Exp. 11-4-68, Leg. 44, Hoja 124-125, October 1, 1968.

56. Kristin Ross makes a similar argument for the student movement in France, asserting the breadth of the category of "student" and the class-based nature of

participants' grievances. While her examination focuses on France, she nonetheless makes clear the global implications of such a revolutionary critique. See Kristin Ross, *May '68 and Its Afterlives* (Chicago: University of Chicago Press, 2000).

57. Eric Hobsbawm, "1968—A Retrospective," *Marxism Today* 22, no. 5 (May 1978): 136. In *1968: The World Transformed*, Fink et al. argue that, between 1968 and 1973, a shift in the world economy became apparent, mostly notably marked by the oil shocks of 1973–74 that ended a quarter-century of growth in the West (7–8). For a further exploration of these themes, see Robert M. Collins, "Growth Liberalism in the Sixties: Great Societies at Home and Grand Designs Abroad," in *The Sixties: From Memory to History*, ed. David Farber (Chapel Hill: University of North Carolina Press, 1994), 11–44.

58. In *The Year of the Heroic Guerrilla*, Robert V. Daniels argued that revolutions are most likely to occur not when society is in a state of hopelessness but rather during periods of dynamic development during which social expectations rise. When groups fail to advance socially or economically, the result is outrage at the government or customs that prevent them from doing so.

59. For an exploration of media and the New Left, see Todd Gitlin, *The Whole World Is Watching: Mass Media and the Making and Unmaking of the New Left* (Berkeley: University of California Press, 2003).

60. Given the prior history of protests, the student movement of 1968 should be understood as part of a series of midcentury protests in Mexico, such as the Jaramillista movement in Morelos, the teachers' strikes throughout the 1950s and 1960s, the railroad workers' strikes of the late 1950s, and the doctors' strike of the mid-1960s. These movements all ended in state violence, deployed much as it was in 1968. For *campesinos*, see Christopher Boyer, *Becoming Campesinos: Politics, Identity, and Agrarian Struggle in Postrevolutionary Michoacán, 1920–1935* (Stanford: Stanford University Press, 2003), and Tanalís Padilla, *Rural Resistance in the Land of Zapata: The Jaramillista Movement and the Myth of the Pax Priísta, 1940–1962* (Durham, NC: Duke University Press, 2008). For the railway workers strike, see Antonio Alonso, *El movimiento ferrocarrilero en México, 1958–1959: De la conciliación a la lucha de clases* (Mexico City: Ediciones Era, 1972); Mario Gill, *Los ferrocarrileros* (Mexico City: Editorial Extemporáneos, 1971); and José Luis Reyna, "El conflicto ferrocarrilero: De la inmovilidad a la acción," vol. 22 of *Historia de la Revolución Mexicana* (Mexico City: Colegio de México, 1978). For teachers' movements, see Joe Foweraker, *Popular Mobilization in Mexico: The Teachers' Movement, 1977–87* (New York: Cambridge University Press, 1993); O'Neill Blacker-Hanson, "La Lucha Siege! (The Struggle Continues!): Teacher Activism in Guerrero and the Continuum of Democratic Struggle in Mexico" (PhD diss., University of Washington, 2005); and Aurora Loyo Brambila, *El movimiento magisterial de 1958 in México* (Mexico City: Ediciones Era, 1979). For the violence of the PRI, see Aguayo, *1968*; Aguayo, *La Charola*; Héctor Aguilar Camín and Lorenzo Meyer, *In the Shadow of the Mexican Revolution: Contemporary Mexican History, 1910–1989*, trans. Luis Alberto Fierro (Austin: University of Texas Press, 1993); Barry Carr, *La izquierda mexicana a través del siglo XX* (Mexico City: Ediciones Era, 1996); and Barry Carr, *Marxism and Communism in Twentieth-Century Mexico* (Lincoln: University of Nebraska Press, 1992).

Part II

Solidarity in Action

4

Cosmopolitans and Revolutionaries

Competing Visions of Transnationalism during the Boom in Latin America

RUSSELL COBB

In the novel and film *Memories of Underdevelopment* (*Memorias del subdesarrollo*), the protagonist, a bourgeois intellectual Habanero and would-be writer, reflects on the rapid changes taking place in Cuba in the early 1960s. "The Revolution," he says, "is the only complicated and serious thing that has occurred to the Cuban mind."[1] He finds himself stuck between two worlds and two ideologies: on the one hand, many business owners are fleeing the island, seeking exile in Florida, while, on the other hand, intellectuals are becoming more committed to the Revolution, participating in programs such as the National Literacy Campaign of 1961. The protagonist finds it impossible to either commit to the ideals of the Revolution or succumb to the crass materialism of the exiles. "All of them," he says, meaning both the Cuban bourgeoisie and Marxist revolutionaries, "are deluded. The counter-revolutionaries because they believe they can recuperate their comfortable ignorance; the revolutionaries because they believe they can get this country out of underdevelopment."[2] Forced to take sides—to be "within" or "outside" the Revolution, in Fidel Castro's famous words[3]—the protagonist withdraws from society during one of the most important episodes in the Cold War: the Cuban Missile Crisis of 1962. Although the author of the novel, Edmundo Desnoes, intended the novel as a critique of uncommitted intellectuals in the 1960s, he later found himself trapped in a dilemma similar to that of his protagonist and finally sought exile in Spain in 1979.

Like the protagonist of *Memories of Underdevelopment*, writers, artists, and intellectuals from across Latin America negotiated an increasingly polemical atmosphere following the Cuban Revolution of 1959. What makes this period especially interesting is that the revolution in the region's politics, stemming from Cuba, occurred simultaneously with the so-called Boom in Spanish American literature, when writers such as Gabriel García Márquez, Mario Vargas Llosa, and Carlos Fuentes began to circulate in what Pascale Casanova has called "international literary space," a space outside national boundaries that is governed by international publishers and awards such as the Nobel Prize for Literature.[4] The term "Boom," with its English etymology and its capitalist connotations, has always been a point of contention in Latin American literature, since the very term seems anathema to the socialist, anti-imperialist politics of its writers. The term first appeared in the Argentine newsweekly *Primera Plana* in the mid-1960s as part of that magazine's efforts to promote a new group of young Latin American writers.[5] Gabriel García Márquez appeared on the cover of *Primera Plana* in 1967, right after the publication of his instant best seller, *One Hundred Years of Solitude*.

The Boom, as Chilean writer José Donoso noted in his memoir, *The Boom in Spanish-American Literature*, was not so much a movement as it was a commercial phenomenon.[6] The main writers associated with the period had little in common stylistically. Some, like García Márquez, specialized in a Caribbean magical realism steeped in eroticism and exotica. Others, like Mario Vargas Llosa, examined Peruvian reality with exacting detail. The French-Argentine Julio Cortázar toyed with European avant-garde techniques of narration while creating literary collages that tipped their hat to popular culture referents. As Donoso notes, writers who did not enjoy the publishing success and prestige of the three writers mentioned often derided the Boom as a "mafia" centered on Carlos Fuentes, who was viewed as much as a celebrity as he was a serious literary figure. In the mid-1960s, Fuentes was a diplomat married to a movie star, Rita Macedo; he had a well-connected agent in New York City and kept apartments in Mexico City and Paris. There was much to envy in Fuentes's star power, and starving writers in Lima, Buenos Aires, and Santiago regarded him as a bourgeois sell-out to capitalism. The contentious nature of the Boom led

Donoso to write that the period had become a "carnival [of] hysteria, envy, and paranoia."[7] Indeed, to this day, personal rivalries and political divisions continue to prevent an even-handed assessment of the period. One of the core figures of the Boom, Mario Vargas Llosa, became one of the most vocal proponents of neoliberalism in Latin America during the 1980s, denouncing his erstwhile best friend, García Márquez, who remains a friend of Fidel Castro.[8]

Nevertheless, a reexamination of the publishing history and the critical reception of Boom writers of the 1960s reveals a larger conflict between competing visions of cosmopolitanism.[9] Although political commitment to some form of socialism united most members of the Boom and all—at least initially—supported the Cuban Revolution, the period grew increasingly contentious as the intellectual prestige and international commercial success of Boom writers grew during the 1960s. The Boom's success outside Latin America led Hernán Vidal, among others, to see the period not as the literary manifestation of political revolution but, rather, as its opposite. Boom literature, despite its authors' claims to the contrary, was a symptom of Latin American economic reality: dependency on the exportation of commodities to developed countries.[10] In the case of the Boom, the commodity for export was literature, and the consumer was the bourgeois reader in North America or Western Europe. The Boom, then, replicated liberal capitalism, and the cosmopolitanism of its authors worked against the revolutionary project.

This Marxist critique of the Boom has been applied to the period's most significant literary magazine, *Mundo Nuevo*, by María Eugenia Mudrovcic, who argued that the literary magazine promoted the ideals of the Alliance for Progress.[11] Jean Franco, in her history of Cold War cultural politics, *Decline and Fall of the Lettered City*, also dwells on the efforts of the CIA to co-opt Boom writing. This relatively recent turn in scholarship has upended the previous view that Boom writing represented the last phase of high literary modernism, a type of literature more concerned with the inner workings of language than with the outer workings of political systems. In effect, this revisionism represents a new paradigm for the relationship between culture—especially "high culture," such as avant-garde literature and art—and politics.[12] In its crudest form, this turn reduces overdetermining cultural texts by their political associations, without taking into account the way in which writers subverted or resisted some of the political ties that bound them during the Cold War.

In 1949, the CIA started to fund cultural projects that it thought might encourage the "noncommunist left," but its voice was drowned out by the Marxist intellectuals sponsored by the Soviet COMINFORM.[13] The CIA had a few intellectuals—the most important being the German refugee and polyglot Michael Josselson—to coordinate the various programs, but, for the most part, the beneficiaries did not know where the money came from. Stonor Saunders discovered that many artists and intellectuals who thought of themselves as untainted by politics were, in fact, deeply involved with the anticommunist activities of the CIA-funded Congress for Cultural Freedom, to name the most infamous example. Although scholars have rightly called into question claims of artistic autonomy from politics, I argue here that this view not only runs the risk of instrumentalizing the arts as propaganda but also neglects to account for the establishment of a cosmopolitanism in Latin American writing that sought to balance a completely unprecedented amount of international literary prestige with political commitments. In what follows, I hope to show that writers did not always function as the puppets of their political masters; rather, they found creative ways of establishing a cosmopolitan transnationalism that cannot be reduced to a political program. As I will show in the case of the literary magazine *Mundo Nuevo*, cosmopolitan writers like Emir Rodríguez Monegal and Carlos Fuentes constantly navigated the rough waters of Cold War politics, even when, as public intellectuals, they claimed to be above the fray. These writers constituted a rebirth of "rooted cosmopolitanism" in Cold War Latin America; they were not pure cosmopolitans like Jorge Luis Borges, but neither did they fit within the nationalist discourse of the Cuban Revolution.[14]

From the PEN Club to Casa de las Américas: In Search of Hemispheric Solidarity

When the Chilean poet Pablo Neruda appeared before the annual PEN Club Conference in June 1966, he defied two political orthodoxies that had lobbied to keep him out of New York City.[15] The U.S. State Department had routinely denied Neruda a visa to visit the United States. Neruda, as a member of the Communist Party and a vocal opponent of U.S. foreign policy in his poetry,[16] was consistently denied entry into the United States under the Walter-McCarran Act, a McCarthy-era law that banned "subversive" aliens. Neruda's case represented nothing special in this regard: most Latin American writers of note were leftists of some stripe or another, a fact that led the anticommunist intellectual Julián Gorkin to remark that the only way to affect the youth of Latin America in the 1960s would be to "constantly denounce the U.S. and sing the praises of Sartre and Pablo Neruda."[17] Neruda's natural allies in Cuba, however, also sought to keep him from appearing in New York. Prominent Cubans such as Alejo Carpentier and Nicolás Guillén had been invited along with Neruda to attend the PEN Club conference, but, at the last minute, the entire Cuban delegation turned down the invitation. Although the PEN Club served as an international organization without a stated political agenda, the Cubans saw the meeting as a threat to the continent-wide revolution at the heart of the Cuban project. They urged Neruda to join the boycott in an act of political solidarity against the United States, reasoning that any meeting in that country would violate the revolutionary project.

The Cubans had reason to suspect that Neruda would agree with them and join the boycott. During the 1950s, Neruda had used his status as one of Latin America's most visible public intellectuals to issue strident denunciations of U.S. policies, including its position on sovereignty for Puerto Rico and its intervention in Guatemala in 1954. However, as the Alliance for Progress had changed its rhetoric on Latin America in the 1960s, Neruda, too, had changed his. He refused to go along with the Cuban boycott of the PEN Club meeting in New York and agreed to sit at a roundtable with some notable anticommunists. He wrote of his decision in the Chilean press: "The PEN Club is the only international organization of writers and I feel very honored to be invited by Arthur Miller and the North American PEN Club. That writers communicate with one another, whatever their politics beliefs may be, signifies a triumph of intelligence and a defeat of the Cold War."[18]

When Neruda wrote the column in *Portal*, a group of Cuban writers reacted by publishing an "Open Letter to Pablo Neruda" ("Carta abierta a Pablo Neruda") in *Granma*, Cuba's leading newspaper and the official organ of the Communist Party.[19] The letter was reprinted in many left-leaning newspapers and magazines in Latin America, including *Marcha* in Uruguay, a publication that had a long history of polemics between Marxist writers and literary cosmopolitans. The position of the signatories to the "Open Letter" was strident in its view that cultural production could not be separated from the political reality of U.S. imperialism. Many of the Cuban writers who signed the letter were now firmly ensconced in the cultural establishment of the revolutionary government and saw any visit to the United States as a compromise with the neo-imperialist behemoth of the North. Neruda's visit, the authors claimed, would signal to the U.S. government that the Latin American revolutionary left could be tamed into a "peaceful coexistence" with the United States. They thought that Neruda, who denounced such neocolonialist entities as the United Fruit Company in his poetic work, should know that the divide between the imperialist North and the oppressed South could not be bridged by cultural exchanges and, indeed, that such exchanges represented a Trojan horse of imperialism. In the midst of the Vietnam War and militaristic interventions throughout Latin America, they wrote, Neruda's address to the PEN Club would amount to a betrayal of revolutionary principles. The letter, signed by the leading lights of the Cuban literary scene (including the future exile Edmundo Desnoes) warned that writers should be on a "state of alert . . . against Yankee imperialist penetration." Reformist efforts such as intellectual exchanges and education programs were especially dangerous since they represented "new instruments of domination and castration." The letter reproached Neruda for meeting with the U.S.-friendly Peruvian president, Fernando Belaúnde Terry, and sounded an alarm against "reformist"-minded U.S. policy:

We have to declare in the entire continent a state of alert against the new imperialist penetration in the world of culture, against Plan Camelot, against scholarships that convert our students into sell-outs or simple agents of imperialism, against certain shadowy offers of "support" for our universities, against the disguises of the Congress for Cultural Freedom, against magazines paid for by the CIA, against the conversion of our writers into monkeys of Yankee salons, against translations that, even if they guarantee a place in the catalogues of the great editorial houses, cannot guarantee a place in history for our people, nor a place in the history of humanity.[20]

While the writers of the letter made no distinction between U.S. cultural and foreign policy, the PEN Club offered a different paradigm—cultural cosmopolitanism—for the relationship between individual writers and their countries' governments. Neruda, the literary lion of Latin American communism, unexpectedly found himself embracing the PEN Club's liberal cosmopolitanism after the blistering attack in the press by the Cuban authors of the "Open Letter."

Arthur Miller, the PEN Club's president at the time, insisted that the organization's charter made a clear distinction between the work of the individual writer and his or her country's politics.[21] Miller, noting the Cuban boycott and the controversy over Neruda, emphasized this idea in his opening address on June 13. "None of us comes here as a representative of his country," Miller stated. "None of us is obliged to speak here as an apologist for his culture or his political system." Miller claimed that the PEN Club offered a "neutral ground, a kind of sanctuary," where writers could commune with one another and highlight the commonalities between all cultures.[22] Although one might accuse Miller of a naïve or rootless cosmopolitanism that erased cultural difference, he had personally suffered under McCarthyism and would not serve as a lackey of U.S. government agencies, as the Cubans implied.[23] Indeed, Miller embodied the sort of cultural cosmopolitanism that the Cubans now battled against; he may have been a "fellow traveler" in the eyes of right wing anti-communists such as Joseph McCarthy, but his stance for "cultural freedom" put him at odds with official cultural policy in Cuba, which supported literature and the arts only "within the Revolution," in Castro's famous words.

From the Cuban point of view, such a separation between literary production and state power was impossible. Cultural cosmopolitanism, for them, would be possible only after the political project of the Revolution triumphed. Writers, whether they admitted it or not, were part of a larger political system. This was a lesson the U.S. beat poet Allen Ginsberg learned the year before the PEN Club controversy, when Casa de las Américas invited him to judge a literary competition in Cuba. Ginsberg, like Miller, could have been an ally of Cuba in the United States. But Ginsberg, accustomed to shocking mainstream audiences stateside with homoerotic and drug-induced imagery, soon learned that Cuba was not the tolerant, socialist utopia he had envisioned. Ginsberg told the local media that the government should stop persecuting gays because homosexuality should be a communist ideal, since it fosters solidarity between men. He also told the Cubans that he found Ernesto "Che" Guevara "cute" and would like to have sex with him. Government authorities ordered Ginsberg to leave Cuba shortly thereafter.[24] Over the course of the 1960s, many artists and writers associated with the New Left in North America ventured to Cuba in search of an idealized, authentic revolution, only to return home disillusioned with the heavy-handed tactics the government used to control the cultural images emanating from the island.[25]

Although Fidel and Che, with their unkempt beards and military fatigues, appeared to embody the sort of antiauthoritarian cosmopolitan ethos the New Left dreamed of, the reality on the ground in Cuba rarely fit the ideal. In the film version in *Memories of Underdevelopment*, the U.S. playwright Jack Gelber appears as himself, questioning a panel of Latin American writers gathered to discuss the "fundamental contradictions of capitalism." Gelber interjects with a question in English: "Why is it that if the Cuban Revolution is a total revolution, they have to resort to an archaic form of discussion such as a roundtable and treat us to an impotent discussion of issues I'm well informed about and most of the people here are well informed about, when there could be another, more revolutionary way to reach an audience like this?"[26] Gelber had been, in fact, traveling in Cuba during the filming of *Memorias*. Shortly thereafter, he returned to the United States, where he produced a play, *The Cuban Thing*, that was boycotted by anti-Cuba activists. The threat of a bomb canceled future performances. Gelber's and Ginsberg's experiences typify the dilemma of the cosmopolitan New Left. Disaffected by the role of the United States in the Cold War and by a paranoid anticommunism at home, they traveled to Cuba, only to find an authoritarianism of a different sort. As Jean Franco has written in her overview of the Cold War in Latin America, "In my adult lifetime, Cuba has gone from representing the revolutionary vanguard to evoking nostalgia for the lost revolutionary ideal, exemplified . . . in the photographs of Che Guevara."[27]

To better understand how the Revolution, which initially breathed new life into the Latin American literary scene, could turn dogmatic and authoritarian, it is worthwhile to take a short detour to reexamine the formation of an official Cuban literary culture during the course of the 1960s. By the end of the decade, the Cuban cultural establishment of the Revolution had matured, passing through what the Cuban writer and critic Lisandro Otero classified as the five stages of the cultural revolution. During the second stage of the Revolution (1961–62), the "bewilderment" and wild experimentation of the first stage (1959–60) gave way to an "intensification of the class struggle."[28] At this moment, the Revolution also began to establish official institutions for culture, making it easier to control the political messages of artists and intellectuals. The most important institutions included the magazine and cultural clearinghouse Casa de las Américas (established in 1960), the Cuban Institute of Movie Art and Industry, or ICAIC (established in 1959), and the Union of Cuban Writers and Artists, or UNEAC (established in 1962). Initially, these organizations fostered the work of writers throughout Latin America by creating a system of governmental support that had been lacking in the region. Some writers, including the Colombian Gabriel García Márquez, worked as journalists for Cuba's new pan–Latin American press agency, Prensa Latina. By creating these official cultural institutions, the government directed Cuban culture without imposing a heavy-handed dictum of "socialist realism," which it never endorsed.

Casa de las Américas was perhaps the most ambitious of these new organizations. Its monthly magazine featured writing from the core members of the Boom—García Márquez, Cortázar, and Vargas Llosa—along with cutting-edge graphic design. As an institution housed in an old art deco theater in Vedado, it sponsored readings from a diverse range of Latin American writers. In its literary awards and publications, it also appeared tolerant of writers whose work did not appear to square neatly with revolutionary ideals. Many poets who had suffered censorship elsewhere in Latin American traveled to Cuba to find a cultural laboratory in full swing. Nevertheless, these institutions could foster creativity or work as a force for crushing dissent, as the UNEAC had attempted to do with its "Open Letter to Pablo Neruda." UNEAC had the power to determine who was in and who was out of favor with the government, and its attitudes seemed to shift all the time. The novelist José Lezama Lima, for example, was a member of a jury that awarded Heberto Padilla the UNEAC prize for poetry in 1968. Lezama Lima initially enjoyed prestige within the cultural bureaucracy, only to be cast as an outsider during the debate about Padilla's revolutionary bona fides. Lezama Lima's reputation was later rehabilitated in the 1980s, after his death, and the poet and novelist was eulogized in the 1994 film *Fresa y chocolate*.

By the late 1960s, literary magazines such as *Casa de las Américas* had abandoned their artistic experiments and, following the lead of Che Guevara, turned their attentions to Marxist praxis. As Franco notes, this was a time of didacticism, when writers and government officials both expected that art would serve the cause of the Revolution by enlightening "el pueblo" and galvanizing it into action. Those who resisted this new cultural model were "gusanos," or counterrevolutionaries.[29] By the end of the decade, the same institutions that had given support to writers and had been instrumental in creating a visible public space for literary creation were persecuting writers, culminating in the infamous Padilla Affair. In 1971, after Padilla had been awarded the UNEAC prize for poetry, critics attacked him in another magazine run by the military, *Verde Olivo*, for publishing counterrevolutionary and "pornographic" poetry. After a series of attacks and counterattacks, Padilla was forced to confess to his counterrevolutionary "crimes" against the state on live television. The confession was decried by writers and intellectuals across the globe and marked a definitive change in the perception of Cuba in the international literary imagination.[30]

In 1966, however, the literary Cold War battle lines were still shifting, and the Cubans' Neruda letter put cosmopolitan, left-leaning authors associated with the PEN Club—including Miller—in an awkward position. On the one hand, most—if not all—of these writers identified strongly with the transnational, continent-wide ambitions of the Cuban Revolution. Most of them opposed the 1965 U.S. intervention in the Dominican Republic and the war in Vietnam. The Cuban Revolution, after all, had privileged writers by creating a series of magazines—*Casa de las Américas*, most famously—and cultural initiatives that encouraged literary production in the public sphere. On the other hand, however, with writers' newfound visibility came the belief that they were to act "responsibly" and sublimate individual creativity to the will of the Revolution. Fidel Castro turned this position into official policy with his "Words to Intellectuals" in 1961 after the closing of the iconoclastic literary magazine *Lunes de Revolución*. Writers and intellectuals should be allowed complete freedom of form, Castro said, but content was a different issue. The content of a work of art should never be against the Revolution, Castro said, leaving the public to guess at what constituted counterrevolutionary content. "Within the Revolution, everything; outside the Revolution, nothing" were the speech's most famous words.[31] Interpretations of the speech are as diverse as Cuba itself, with many Cuban writers insisting that the speech aimed to be inclusive and others arguing that it represented a turn toward Soviet-style censorship.

Neruda, although sympathetic—committed, even—to the Cuban Revolution, was outraged by the Cubans' open letter, although he did not comment publicly lest his response initiate a feud. In a letter to his secretary and future biographer, Margarita Aguirre, Neruda wrote: "Music from Havana: cults, equivocations, alienations, hatred to my family . . . all of it seasoned with envy and literary crap. In addition, a blackmail: I can't respond without breaking solidarity."[32] Later, a similar coterie of writers published another letter in Cuba, inviting Neruda back to the island "to open a cultural front against the Yankees." Neruda declined and never returned to the island.[33] Meanwhile, the communist poet was to return to the United States in the early 1970s as a diplomat with the Salvador Allende regime. During that visit, he criticized U.S. policy toward Puerto Rico and gave readings of many of his poems from *Canto general* that opposed U.S. foreign policy.[34] Neruda's alienation from the Cuban bloc of writers did not, as it did for others, cause him to reevaluate his political convictions, but, as a Nobel laureate and celebrity in the United States, he could now be viewed as a cosmopolitan fixture in international literary space, not reducible to his communist affiliations.

Constructing a New Cosmopolitanism: The Congress for Cultural Freedom in Latin America in the 1960s

The significance of Neruda's participation in the PEN Club conference is further complicated by the reversal of tactics that the Congress for Cultural Freedom had undergone leading up the conference in 1966. The CCF, as is well known, was started as an anticommunist coalition of writers and artists who were indirectly subsidized by the CIA.[35] The CCF had no specific political agenda but sought to counteract what it saw as the moral high ground of anti-Americanism offered by the Soviet Union. Anticommunists feared that the Soviets were winning the Cold War by controlling the terms of the debate. As Thomas Braden, head of the CIA's International Organizations Division—the division that oversaw the CIA's relationship with the CCF—stated in a 1967 article in the *Saturday Evening Post*: "First, they [the communists] had stolen all the great words. Years later after I left the CIA, the late United Nations Ambassador Adlai Stevenson had told me how he had been outraged when delegates from underdeveloped countries, young men who had come to maturity during the cold war, assumed that anyone who was for 'Peace,'

'Freedom,' and 'Justice,' must also be for communism."[36] While it is debatable whether words like "peace," "freedom," and "justice" actually connoted communism in Latin America during the Cold War, they clearly did not represent U.S. foreign policy in the minds of young Latin American writers and intellectuals in the early 1950s, when the CCF was founded. The abandonment of the Good Neighbor Policy, CIA support for the overthrow of Jacobo Arbenz in Guatemala in 1954, and the anticommunist Declaration of Caracas in the same year all served to eviscerate whatever pro-U.S. sympathies existed among left-leaning intellectuals in Latin America.

In theory, then, the CCF would win back the hearts and minds of intellectuals by providing them space for artistic expression and free debate. In practice, however, the CCF's Latin American journal, *Cuadernos por la libertad de la cultura*, took a rather dogmatic stand against communists and "fellow travelers." Its editor, a former Spanish anarchist named Julián Gorkin, had been coldly received by leftist groups in Latin America in the early 1960s when he toured the region to promote the magazine. Most audiences received him coldly, but some were downright hostile. He wrote of a meeting in Peru where young communists threw tomatoes at him. He planned to get back at his enemies in *Cuadernos*: "Upon my return to Paris, I plan to publish a brochure about this whole affair which will prove most annoying to Neruda and the communists," he wrote.[37] John Hunt, a CCF member and CIA agent who worked closely with the CCF's Latin American initiatives, had campaigned against Neruda when word got out that the Chilean poet was being considered for a Nobel Prize in the early 1960s.[38] Only two years earlier, Hunt had helped publish a pamphlet by CCF activist René Tavernier called "Le cas Neruda" (1964), which presented the poet's political commitments to communism, including his "Canto a Stalingrado," in which he eulogized Joseph Stalin.[39] After the Cuban letter incident, however, Neruda was under attack by Cuban Marxists for dialoguing with U.S. writers, and the Cubans—not the Americans—were perceived as impinging on the poet's artistic freedom. As the decade progressed, the rigid anticommunism of the 1950s and early 1960s gave way to a liberalized attitude that was as much a product of the worldwide success of Latin American literature as it was an ideological change of heart. Meanwhile, Hunt, the CIA man who had tried to smear Neruda's reputation in 1964, approved of the new CCF journal *Mundo Nuevo*'s intention to publish Neruda's nonpolitical poetry in 1966.[40]

Dogmatic anticommunism, it must be stated, did not emanate solely from the CCF. In Argentina, *Sur*, the literary magazine of the influential patron and editor Victoria Ocampo, became increasingly polemical in its views toward Cuba and revolution in general over the course of the 1960s. Ocampo's influence on the cultural elite of Argentina can hardly be overstated: she was a patron of the arts, an influential editor, and a nexus for cosmopolitan intellectuals who ventured to Argentina. Ocampo had never been seduced—as many intellectuals were—by the figures of Fidel Castro and Che Guevara. In a special issue of *Sur* dedicated to Latin America, Humberto Piñera, a former professor at the University of Havana, attacked the Castro regime: "Freedom disappeared from Cuba as soon as Fidel Castro came to power."[41] This sort of antagonism toward the Cuban Revolution was rare among the Latin American intelligentsia in the first years after the Revolution, but it did serve to create a polarized climate that extended throughout the region.

Despite the protests of the Cubans, who worried about Neruda becoming a symbol of Alliance for Progress policy, Arthur Miller and the PEN Club managed to get a group waiver for a number of Latin American writers who had previously been denied visas. Among that group was Carlos Fuentes, who then found himself caught in the crossfire between U.S. anticommunism and Cuban efforts to silence writers who did not toe the line. Fuentes and Emir Rodríguez Monegal featured the proceedings of the meeting in *Mundo Nuevo*, which had replaced *Cuadernos* in 1966 as the CCF's primary Latin American magazine. Rodríguez Monegal was an Uruguayan critic and journalist who had much admired the *Sur* crowd while working as the culture critic for the left-of-center Uruguayan newspaper *Marcha*. He had become disaffected by political differences between himself and the more radical writers on *Marcha*'s staff, including Angel Rama.[42] Rodríguez Monegal had been introduced to the PEN Club in 1965, when Botsford and Hunt encouraged him to travel to Yugoslavia and vote against the Guatemalan writer Miguel Ángel Asturias, a candidate for president of the PEN Club. Now, as the founding editor of *Mundo Nuevo*, Rodríguez Monegal had to mediate between two ideological extremes in his attempt to promote cosmopolitan liberalism in the magazine's pages. Rodríguez Monegal published many documents relating to the 1966 PEN conference and repeated Fuentes's claim that, during the reunion, the writers had managed to effectively end the Cold War as it related to literature. In a sign of the times—when the Boom coincided with the Cold War—Fuentes wrote about the PEN Club meeting for the mass-market publication *Life en español*, a publication more likely to feature Hollywood gossip than literary news. The article, "The PEN Club against the Cold War," assessed the contemporary intellectual climate after Fuentes's meetings with Miller and Neruda: "The Uruguayan critic Emir Rodríguez Monegal observed that we are saying our last goodbyes to the dead Senator McCarthy. We could go a step further and affirm that the 34th International Congress of the PEN Club will be remembered as the burial of the Cold War in literature. At the Congress, the conviction that isolation and lack of communication between cultures only serves international tyranny triumphed."[43]

Fuentes did not proclaim the end of the Cold War per se; the conflict still existed in Europe, Vietnam, and elsewhere. What had been achieved, however, was a solidarity among intellectuals, a transnational demilitarized zone for literature. The meeting represented a victory for cosmopolitanism, for the idea that writers did, after all, have autonomy from the foreign policies of their home countries. Nevertheless, writers such as Fuentes still identified with the Left, only now, rather than being dismissed as "fellow travelers," they were known as the "noncommunist left," a group the CCF sought to cultivate. If the rhetorical strategy here was to "bury the Cold War" among writers by dismissing the Cuban protest of Neruda's visit, it also consisted in differentiating between official politics and cultural production. While *Casa de las Américas* constantly attacked U.S. imperialism in its pages, *Mundo Nuevo* tried to balance noncommunist leftist politics with sympathy toward U.S. culture, if not toward U.S. foreign policy. When news of "Project Camelot"—a CIA-hatched plan to infiltrate Chilean social science—surfaced in the press, *Mundo Nuevo* criticized the plan itself, as well as the "extreme left."

Meanwhile, Rodríguez Monegal also expanded the Boom by publishing gay writers, marginalized by both the Cuban Revolution and the more conventional and conservative literary magazines. In this sense, *Mundo Nuevo* constituted a radical break from the stuffy, elitist anticommunism found in many CCF publications. The erotic, baroque, and highly stylized prose of Cuban writers such as José Lezama Lima, Severo Sarduy, and Reinaldo Arenas found a vehicle in Rodríguez Monegal's magazine, a practice that reportedly infuriated the cultural bureaucrats of UNEAC, who had the last say on who and what was published on the island. Indeed, Arenas wrote to Rodríguez Monegal in 1967 telling the editor of the trouble he had faced as a result of publishing a fragment of his violent, sexual, and experimental novel *Celestino antes del alba* in *Mundo Nuevo*. The letter is worth quoting at length because it demonstrates the increasingly repressive atmosphere in Cuba on the one hand and Arenas's attempt to become a cosmopolitan on the other:

Because of the publication of a fragment of my novel, *Celestino antes del alba*, in your prestigious magazine, which I am profoundly grateful for, I have been threatened by officials of UNEAC and their police, to write a letter of protest that they, the directors of UNEAC, will publish in their periodical, *La Gaceta de Cuba*. At first, I refused to write the letter and then they, headed by Nicolás Guillén in person, fired me from the UNEAC, where I work, an expulsion that will result in me going to a forced labor camp and to jail. I then wrote a benign letter, but Guillén rejected it. He wanted something angry and aggressive. I then had to elect between writing another letter or going to prison. . . . I am not a political person. But I know that all they say about *Mundo Nuevo* is slander. . . . I want—without much hope—to one day be a free man.[44]

Arenas's plea to Rodríguez Monegal reflects not only the repressive situation of marginalized writers in Cuba but also a lack of awareness of the political stakes of literature during the period; even if we sympathize with Arenas's desire to be a "free man," his claim that the connections among the CCF, *Mundo Nuevo*, and the CIA led them to "slander" his work demonstrates a sort of disingenuousness that would make him a target of the Cuban cultural establishment until his death in 1990.

Rodríguez Monegal, however, chose to focus not on politics but on art, a decision that may have rankled CIA men like John Hunt and Michael Josselson. Their idea had been to scrap *Cuadernos* and replace it with a more self-consciously literary journal, a decision that helped fuel the Boom as a worldwide phenomenon. The magazine's inaugural "Presentación" demonstrates the avant-garde cosmopolitanism that would come to dominate each issue: "Latin America has an enormous responsibility at this moment in which man finds himself on the verge of a new world. Liberated from the most obvious colonial ties a century and a half ago, but still tied to economic and political servitude. . . . *Mundo Nuevo* aims to insert Latin American culture in a context that is at once international and contemporary. *Mundo Nuevo* aims to give voice to the almost inaudible voices across a continent and establish a dialogue that transcends the well-known limits of nationalisms, political parties, and more or less literary groups."[45] Rodríguez Monegal navigates between cosmopolitanism rooted in Latin America and a sort of vague leftism, acknowledging the continent's "economic and political servitude" while also attempting to construct an international audience for Latin American literature. Central to the magazine's ethos was the idea of the "independent intellectual," the writer who could see beyond the petty political struggles of nationalism. *Mundo Nuevo*'s featured article in the first issue was an interview with Fuentes called "La situación del escritor en América Latina." It is a sort of manifesto-interview, calling for a new reflection on the realities of the shifting cultural and political landscape in Latin America, taking seriously the penetration of Latin American literature into new markets in North America and Europe. In the interview, Fuentes argues that Latin American writers should abandon all orthodoxies, while looking for new inspiration in the explosion of mass culture.[46] Writers should embrace "camp" culture, rather than the tired clichés of regionalism or folklore. Thus, both Fuentes—the writer—and Rodríguez Monegal—the critic—construct a version of cosmopolitanism that retains much of the leftist critique of capitalism while still embracing what might be described as the birth of the postmodern. Indeed, when Rodríguez Monegal asks Fuentes about his latest "happening"—a photo shoot in his apartment—Fuentes responds, "There's an expressionist, violent, and baroque background that's also our connection to a world that has become violent, expressionist, and baroque. The modern manifestations of this are to be found in pop art and in camp, in Günter Grass and Norman Mailer, in Andy Warhol and Susan Sontag, in Joan Baez and Bob Dylan. This is the world that I really care about. This is the world that counts."[47]

Conclusion

Fuentes, much like Neruda, had begun his career as a writer defined by a national culture, publishing for a small, well-educated audience. By the time of the Boom, however, both writers had become celebrities whose statements on the political topics of the day made it into the headlines of the mainstream press. The best-seller success of García Márquez's *One Hundred Years of Solitude* in 1967, followed by Neruda's Nobel Prize for Literature in 1971, meant that Latin American writers were no longer—like the protagonist of *Memorias del subdesarrollo*—marginal figures in the political life of a particular country. Some of these writers continued to work with—or within—the confines of state-run cultural institutions, while others—such as Reinaldo Arenas and Heberto Padilla—became literally stateless, cosmopolitan outcasts in the one Cold War battle that seemingly has no end.

Other writers, however, became transnational public intellectuals whose battles did not merely reflect the larger context of the Cold War but also shaped the discursive contours of that conflict as it passed into the 1970s and beyond. Indeed, this might be the unique and most compelling feature of the Boom: it did not merely represent politics (as did the canonical dictator novels of the 1950s) but rather shaped the discourse in a public way. Thus, to this day, we see Hugo Chávez recounting his friendship with Fidel Castro by paraphrasing *One Hundred Years of Solitude* or giving Barack Obama a copy of *The Open Veins of Latin America*. Vargas Llosa abandoned his increasingly tenuous links to the cosmopolitan left in the 1970s, then recast himself as a conservative candidate for president of Peru in 1990. Vargas Llosa duels with Chávez on *CNN en español*, trading barbs and accusations. In Latin American literary production, reality is not just stranger than fiction—it sometimes is fiction.

Notes

1. Edmundo Desnoes, *Memorias del subdesarrollo* (Seville: Mono Azul Editora, 2006), 39.

2. Ibid., 39.

3. Fidel Castro, "Words to Intellectuals," Havana, June 30, 1961. See Castro Speech Database, http://lanic.utexas.edu/project/castro/db/1961/19610630.html.

4. Pascale Casanova, *The World Republic of Letters* (Cambridge, MA: Harvard University Press, 2007). While Casanova argues that international literary space is governed by its own rules, more or less outside politics, I argue that the two are related, at least in the context of 1960s Latin America.

5. Alfred J. MacAdam, "The Boom: A Retrospective: Interview with Emir Rodríguez Monegal," *Review* 33 (January 1984): 30–34.

6. José Donoso, *The Boom in Spanish-American Literature: A Personal History* (New York: Center for Inter-American Relations, 1977).

7. Ibid., 1.

8. The rivalry between García Márquez and Vargas Llosa exemplifies the ways in which intensely personal conflicts are often inextricable from politics. Vargas Llosa floored García Márquez with a punch after the latter supposedly made advances toward the former's wife.

9. Cosmopolitanism has a long and contentious history as a moral, political, and cultural ideal. As Kwame Anthony Appiah notes, cosmopolitanism is usually characterized by the belief in "world citizenship" that is—or should be—balanced by a respect for cultural differences. See Kwame Anthony Appiah, *Cosmopolitanism: Ethics in a World of Strangers* (New York: Norton, 2006).

10. Hernán Vidal, *Literatura hispanoamericana e ideologia liberal: Surgimiento y crisis* (Buenos Aires: Ediciones Hispamerica, 1976).

11. María Eugenia Mudrovcic, *Mundo Nuevo: Cultura y Guerra Fría en la década del 60* (Rosario, Arg.: Beatriz Viterbo, 1997).

12. The origins of this paradigm shift can be traced back to Serge Guilbaut's *How New York Stole the Idea of Modern Art* (1985). Looking back at the development of abstract expressionism in the United States in the postwar period, Guilbaut saw a hidden agenda at work. While others argued that abstract expressionism was a manifestation of pure art—color and form divorced from content—and pure freedom, Guilbaut saw networks of political patronage that used "artistic freedom" as a way to counter Soviet-style socialist realism. Likewise, Frances Stonor Saunders's *The Cultural Cold War: The CIA and the World of Arts and Letters* (New York: New Press, 2000) excavates a history of CIA intervention into literary magazines, art exhibitions, and music festivals.

13. Hugh Wilford, *The Mighty Wurlitzer: How the CIA Played America* (Cambridge, MA: Harvard University Press, 2008).

14. For an extensive discussion of "rooted cosmopolitanism," see Kwame Anthony Appiah, *The Ethics of Identity* (Princeton, NJ: Princeton University Press, 2005).

15. The PEN Club, founded in 1921 by British writers, originally stood for "Poets,

Essayists, and Novelists," but it has since evolved to defend and support journalists and other writers of nonfiction. It functions, in its words, "to engage with, and empower, societies and communities across cultures and languages, through reading and writing. We believe that writers can play a crucial role in changing and developing civil society." International PEN, "About us," http://www.internationalpen.org.uk/go/about-us.

16. Neruda's poem "United Fruit Co." was first published in the collection *Canto general*, a covert publication of the Chilean Communist Party, in Santiago, in 1950. Its title page bore a "false imprint," suggesting that the collection's place of publication was Mexico City.

17. Stonor Saunders, *The Cultural Cold War*, 347–48.

18. David Schidlowsky, *Pablo Neruda y su tiempo: Las furias y las penas*, vol. 2 (Santiago: RIL Editoras, 2008), 1156.

19. Ibid., 1166.

20. "Carta abierta a Pablo Neruda," *Casa de las Américas* 38 (1966): 131–35. The original, reproduced in many left-leaning periodicals in Latin America, reads: "Tenemos que declarar en todo el continente un estado de alerta: alerta contra la nueva penetración imperialista en el campo de la cultura, contra los planes Camelot, contra las becas que convierten a nuestros estudiantes en asalariados o simples agentes del imperialismo, contra ciertas tenebrosas 'ayudas' a nuestras universidades, contra los ropajes que asuma el Congreso por la libertad de la cultura, contra revistas pagadas por la CIA, contra la conversión de nuestros escritores en simios de salón y comparsas de coloquios yanquis, contra las traducciones que, si pueden garantizar un lugar en los catálogos de las grandes editoriales, no puedan garantizar un lugar en la historia de nuestros pueblos ni en la historia de la humanidad."

21. "Introduction," PEN American Center Archives, Princeton University, http://infoshare1.princeton.edu/libraries/firestone/rbsc/aids/pen.html.

22. Ibid.

23. Miller was briefly blacklisted by the House Un-American Activities Committee in 1956 for refusing to reveal the names of Communist Party members. His conviction on federal charges of contempt of Congress was overturned by a Court of Appeals in 1958.

24. See Rafael Ocasio, "Gays and the Cuban Revolution: The Case of Reinaldo Arenas," *Latin American Perspectives* 29, no. 2 (2002): 78–98.

25. See Van Gosse, *Where the Boys Are: Cuba, Cold War America and the Making of the New Left* (New York: Verso, 1993). Gosse links the Cuban Revolution to the political and cultural developments that came to characterize the New Left in the United States: a rejection of Democratic Party–style liberalism as well as Communist Party dogma; an embrace of "hipsterism," including jazz, beat poetry, and other countercultural movements; sexual liberation; and an emphasis on direct action or "participatory democracy," as opposed to traditional political campaigns and electioneering. The New Left, in other words, can be seen as an attempt to reconcile cultural cosmopolitanism with Marxist Revolution.

26. *Memorias del subdesarrollo*, online video, directed by Tomás Gutiérrez Alea (Havana, Cuba: ICAIC, 1968).

27. Jean Franco, *Decline and Fall of the Lettered City: Latin America in the Cold War* (Cambridge, MA: Harvard University Press, 2002), 108.

28. Lisandro Otero, "Notas sobre la funcionalidad de la cultura," *Casa de las Américas* 68 (1971): 94–110.

29. This turn affected many writers less well known than Neruda. Heberto Padilla, Virgilio Piñera, and José Lezama Lima were a few others who found themselves viewed suspiciously even though, ironically, they had been cosigners of the "Open Letter to Pablo Neruda." See Franco, *Decline and Fall of the Lettered City*.

30. See Heberto Padilla, *Fuera del juego* (Miami: Ediciones Universal, 1998), for the original work of poetry and the series of accusations, confessions, and protests that followed its publication.

31. Quoted in Seymour Menton, *Prose Fiction of the Cuban Revolution* (Austin: University of Texas Press, 1975), 11.

32. Schidlowsky, *Pablo Neruda y su tiempo*, 1171.

33. Ibid., 1178.

34. According to Julio Marzán, during a reading at Columbia University, Neruda read a poem denouncing Puerto Rican governor Muñoz Marín as a traitor to all of Latin America but chose not to read an even more political poem, "Puerto Rico, Puerto Pobre," since it would have run counter to his supposedly nonpolitical role as a diplomat. Julio Marzán, "Pablo Neruda's Dilemma," in *Pablo Neruda and the U.S. Culture Industry*, ed. Teresa Longo (New York: Routlege, 2002), 156–62.

35. See Stonor Saunders, *The Cultural Cold War*. The CIA set up a "triple pass" by which it gave money to nonprofits, which then gave money to the CCF, which published magazines and books.

36. Thomas Braden, "Why I'm Glad the CIA Is 'Immoral,'" *Saturday Evening Post* 240 (May 20, 1967), 12.

37. Julián Gorkin, memo to Michael Josselson, April 1958, series II, box 131, folder 3, International Association for Cultural Freedom (IACF) Collection, University of Chicago Special Collections Research Center.

38. Stonor Saunders, *The Cultural Cold War*, 350.

39. Ibid., 350–51.

40. *Mundo Nuevo* published some of Neruda's "nature" poetry but never published his overtly political poetry.

41. Quoted in John King, *Sur: A Study of the Argentine Literary Journal and Its Role in the Development of a Culture, 1931–1970* (Cambridge: Cambridge University Press, 1986), 182.

42. See Russell Cobb, "Our Men in Paris? *Mundo Nuevo*, the Cuban Revolution, and the Politics of Cultural Freedom" (PhD diss., University of Texas at Austin, 2007).

43. Emir Rodríguez Monegal, "El P.E.N. Club contra la guerra fría," *Mundo Nuevo* 5 (November 1966): 85–90. The original Spanish reads: "El crítico uruguayo Emir Rodríguez Monegal observó que estábamos diciendo el último adiós al difunto senador McCarthy. Cabría ir más lejos y afirmar que el XXXIV Congreso Internacional del P.E.N. Club será recordado como *el entierro de la guerra fría en la literatura* [my em-

phasis]. Allí triunfó la convicción práctica de que el aislamiento y la incomunicación culturales no sirven sino a la tirantez internacional, de la que son inservibles reliquias."

44. Emir Rodríguez Monegal, *Homenaje a Emir Rodríguez Monegal* (Montevideo: Ministerio de Educación y Cultura, 1987), 47. The original Spanish reads: "A raíz de la publicación de un fragmento de mi novela *Celestino antes del alba* en su prestigiosa revista, lo cual le agradezco profundamente, me he visto, sin embargo, conminado por los oficiales de la UNEAC y sus policías, a redactar una carta de protesta que ellos, los directores de la UNEAC publicarán inmediatamente en su periódico, *La Gaceta de Cuba*. Primero me negué a escribir la carta, y entonces ellos, encabezados por Nicolás Guillén en persona, me presentaron la expulsión de la UNEAC donde además trabajo, expulsión que significa ir a parar a un campo de trabajo forzado y desde luego la cárcel. Hice entonces una carta benigna. Pero el mismo Guillén la rechazó: quería algo agresivo y denunciante. Así pues tuve que elegir entre la redacción de la infame carta o la prisión . . . No soy un personaje político. Pero sé que todo lo que se dice contra *Mundo Nuevo* es una infamia . . . Espero, aunque sin mucha esperanza, ser algún día un hombre libre."

45. Emir Rodríguez Monegal, "Presentación," *Mundo Nuevo* 1 (July 1966): 4. The original Spanish reads: "América Latina tiene una enorme responsabilidad en esta hora en que el hombre se encuentra al borde de un mundo nuevo. Liberado de los más obvios lazos coloniales hace ya siglo y medio, pero todavía atada a servidumbres económicas y políticas. . . . El propósito de *Mundo Nuevo* es insertar la cultura latino-americana en un contexto que sea a la vez internacional y actual, que permita escuchar las voces casi inaudibles o dispersas de todo un continente y que establezca un diálogo que sobrepasa las conocidas limitaciones de nacionalismos, partidos políticos, capillas más o menos literarias."

46. Carlos Fuentes, "La situación del escritor en América Latina," *Mundo Nuevo* 1 (July 1966): 4–21.

47. Ibid., 8. The original Spanish reads: "[E]se fondo expresionista, violento y barroco que es, insisto, nuestro verdadero enchufe con un mundo que se ha vuelto violento, expresionista, y barroco y cuyas correspondencias actualmente son el *pop art* y el *camp*; son Günter Grass y Norman Mailer, y Andy Warhol y Susan Sontag, y Joan Baez y Bob Dylan, ¿verdad? Para mí éste es el mundo que cuenta, el mundo que me interesa realmente."

5

Transnational Concepts, Local Contexts

Solidarity at the Grassroots in Pinochet's Chile

ALISON J. BRUEY

In the Chile of dictator Augusto Pinochet, the concept and practice of solidarity offered an alternative type of citizenship in poor and working-class urban communities torn apart by repression, fear, and economic misery. Solidarity offered a sense of dignity and belonging in a dictatorial regime that was actively marginalizing entire sectors of the population. The propagation of the concept of solidarity was especially prominent in the underground organizing networks that crisscrossed Santiago's poor and working-class neighborhoods, or *poblaciones*, which bore the brunt of repression and economic crisis from 1973 to 1990. Solidarity was first advanced most forcefully by the Catholic Church and the left, both of which straddled the international/domestic divide and operated transnational networks that were key to their ability to continue functioning in Chile after the military coup. Solidarity, *solidaridad*, as an organizing concept and strategy under the dictatorship, was not spontaneous or "natural": it was developed, taught, learned, and actively constructed in *poblaciones* during the mid-1970s. It coexisted and intersected with but did not originate primarily in internationalist solidarity

120

movements or the left, the sectors that have received the most attention in studies of Latin American solidarity during this period.[1] In Chile, its strength derived from its roots in leftist and Catholic historical legacies that intertwined in popular-sector political culture. In the Chilean context, the concept of "solidarity" cannot be understood without taking into account both its Catholic and its leftist antecedents: it was the product of dynamic interaction between the two. In *poblaciones*, *solidaridad* became a central principle for the organizing work that united disparate social and political sectors and established a foundation for grassroots opposition to the regime.

Marching in Solidarity

On Good Friday 1980, a mass procession of *pobladores* (residents of *poblaciones*), Catholic clergy, and nuns marched to the General Cemetery's Patio 29, where the Pinochet regime was rumored to have buried assassinated political prisoners in anonymous graves.[2] The marchers enacted the traditional Vía Crucis (Stations of the Cross) en route to the cemetery. While the Vía Crucis was a traditional Catholic holy week activity, this one raised the authorities' ire because the marchers' banners targeted the dictatorship and its policies. The *pobladores* carried banners announcing, "Thou shall not kill!," "Cain, what have you done with your brother?," and "All that you have done unto the poor you have done unto me."[3] The banners reproduced biblical verse and rhetoric from the Medellín (1968) and Puebla (1979) Latin American Bishops' Conferences. Eyewitnesses reported that marchers chanted, "The pueblo whimpers in pain, come and save us" and "Justice, Truth, and Liberty: *Presente!*"[4]

The banners presented only religious themes, but, if the eyewitness report is correct, the chants included leftist refrains. Whether religious or secular, the marchers' messages appealed to humanistic ideals using internationally recognized values, religious texts, and symbolic figures, including the recently assassinated Salvadoran archbishop Oscar Romero. Thus, they appropriated symbolism that sidestepped and, in theory, transcended the military regime's definitions of appropriate social and political expression.[5] The denunciations reflect an alternative vision of society in which the state did not kill and in which the poor were not oppressed and marginalized. They also placed God, Jesus, and the Catholic Church on the side of the pueblo—and suggested that divine punishment would fall upon the state as it had upon Cain for murdering Abel ("Cain, what have you done with your brother?"). Thus, the protesters addressed the military rulers with language taken directly from the

Bible and the Catholic Church, both of which were traditionally accorded a moral and spiritual authority transcending that of any temporal nation-state. In doing so, the marchers placed themselves within another realm of human belonging, of "citizenship," that superseded the Chilean nation-state, placed *pobladores* on a level equal to that of the country's rulers, and challenged the dictatorship's repressive practices. The marchers levied a trenchant critique of the political situation, the economic model, and related structures of inequality through the use of transnational symbolism and text.

Despite the obvious criticism, the authorities allowed the procession to proceed, in part because they believed themselves defenders of Western and Christian values; therefore, the banners did not constitute a clearly actionable offense. Moreover, openly attacking a Catholic religious procession could reap negative consequences for the junta abroad, especially so soon after the murder of Archbishop Romero and in view of international sensitivity to the ongoing violence against the Catholic Church in Central America. The marchers—members of Popular Christian Communities—organizations that included leftists, nonleftists, Catholics, and "nonbelievers" (atheists and agnostics)—likely understood that, in this context, religious imagery was safer and potentially more effective than secular political references.[6]

March participants included *pobladores* of diverse political and religious beliefs who participated in Popular Christian Communities under the banner of "solidarity." Despite historical legacies of distrust between the Catholic hierarchy and the left, at the level of base militancy and popular religiosity the Church and the left were not mutually exclusive or always antagonistic. In the popular sectors, all parties of the left counted both "believers" and "nonbelievers" among their ranks, and not all Catholics understood their faith in a way that precluded militancy in Marxist parties. The Christian Left (IC), the Unitary Popular Action Movement (MAPU), and MAPU Obrero Campesino were Christian Marxist parties, and *doble militancia* (double militancy) in a party and in the Church was not uncommon.[7] The Movement of the Revolutionary Left (MIR), a Guevarist, secular New Left party established in 1965, did not require that its militants eschew religious beliefs and practices. The Socialist and Communist Parties were more critical of the Church's role in society. However, even the officially atheist Communist Party did not exclude practicing Catholics from its ranks. In the 1970s, it was the concept of solidarity that created a space for the persecuted left in Popular Christian Communities and related social organizations, where they worked alongside Catholics; opposition grassroots organizing coalesced around this nexus.

Solidarity in Marxist and Catholic Traditions

According to Cecilia Dockendorff and others, during the dictatorship, Chileans understood solidarity as "fundamentally associated with the problem of the violation of human rights and social inequity."[8] In hindsight, this is true of the period overall, but it tells us little about the provenance of these associations or what purposes the idea served in given contexts. "Solidarity" is a term commonly used by those who were involved in social and political organizations at the time and by those who study the period, but its development and use are not often placed into historical context, and its implications for sociopolitical organization are not closely examined. In postcoup Chile, the concept became a potent organizing tool in the *poblaciones* because it provided points of convergence between Catholic and leftist currents deeply rooted in popular-sector society.

On the international Marxist left, "solidarity" traditionally referred to unity among the industrial proletariat. According to Steinar Stjernø, Marx rarely used the word "solidarity" in his writings, but the term was common in nineteenth-century European social democratic and anarchist traditions. Stjernø cites social democrat Karl Kautsky, who "utilised *solidarity* both as a general concept, meaning the feeling of togetherness in general, as 'servants may have in the families in which they live,' and more particularly as the feeling of community that develops among workers when they recognize their common interests."[9] Citing Mikhail Bakunin, Stjernø argues that anarchists used the term "solidarity" as a concept in its own right and were interested in it primarily as a *practice*: "The first [step in achieving revolution] is by establishing, first in their own groups and then among all groups, a true fraternal solidarity, not just in words, but in action, not just for holidays, but in their daily life. Every member of the International must be able to feel that all other members are his brothers and be convinced of this in practice."[10]

Chile has a long tradition of leftist organizing that drew on international currents of thought but developed within the national context.[11] Historians disagree about when anarchism first arrived in Chile, but it is clear that socialism, anarchism, and the labor movement developed in close relation to one another.[12] In 1897, members of the ideologically diverse Centro Social Obrero and Agrupación Fraternal Obrera formed the Unión Socialista to "implant socialism in Chile."[13] Meanwhile, anarchist workers organized mutual assistance associations and "resistance societies" to promote strike activity, and, in northern Chile, workers formed *mancomunales* that organized workers by geographic locale. By 1919, socialists and anarchists ran ideologically pluralistic national worker federations. The socialists took over leadership of the Federación Obrera de Chile (FOCH, est. 1909), and the anarchists formed an International Workers of the World affiliate called the Obreros Industriales del Mundo.[14]

The Catholic Church also participated in turn-of-the-century labor ferment. The first national labor organization, the FOCH, formed under the auspices of conservative Catholics. Workers in FOCH member organizations were exposed to anarchist and socialist ideas, as well as to priests who followed the precepts of Pope Leo XIII's 1891 Encyclical on Capital and Labor, *Rerum novarum*,[15] which presents ideas echoed in later understandings of "solidarity": "[among the earliest Christians] those who were in better circumstances despoiled themselves of their possessions in order to relieve their brethren; whence 'neither was there any one needy among them.'"[16] Leo XIII supported the principle of private property, accepted social inequality as natural, and rejected Marxism and class struggle. Nevertheless, he praised unionization and sharply criticized capitalist exploitation and greed, laying theological groundwork that justified organizations like the FOCH. He argued that the "working classes" were "citizens by nature and by the same right as the rich."[17]

In turn-of-the-century Chile, anarchism's, socialism's, and Catholicism's respective utopias were irreconcilable, but cooperation on common, shorter-term goals such as unionization and social reform was possible because all three ideologies recognized the existence of severe socioeconomic inequality and class conflict, the exploitation and oppression at the heart of contemporary capitalism, and the need for social reform. Coexistence and dynamic interaction between leftist and Catholic organizations and ideals in the popular sectors continued throughout the twentieth century, and ideas about "solidarity" developed in this context.[18]

Within Catholic social doctrine, although the word "solidarity" was not officially used until 1961 (*Mater et Magistra*),[19] proponents of solidarity with the poor and working classes in postcoup Chile identified national Chilean-Catholic precursors dating to the mid-twentieth century. Arguably the most important figure was the Jesuit priest Alberto Hurtado Cruchaga (1901–52, canonized 2005), who laid the groundwork for later Chilean-Catholic understandings of "solidarity" by criticizing the traditional concept of Catholic charity: "[many are] willing to give alms but not to pay a just wage," he commented. "Catholics' social attitudes seem more oriented toward impeding the communist advance than de-proletarianizing the masses. There is no visible effort to achieve [or apply] the teachings of the Encyclicals; and even in the exposition of this doctrine [the Church] is too 'prudent' so as not to go against the ruling classes."[20] Hurtado's work among the poor and working class and his calls for social justice earned him the epithet of "communist" in midcentury Chile.[21]

Most immediately relevant to postcoup Chile were the documents produced at the 1968 Latin American Bishops' Conference in Medellín, where the Latin American hierarchy interpreted Vatican II for Latin America and declared that lack of solidarity leads to "the committing of serious sins, evident in the unjust structures which characterize the Latin American situation."[22] To profit from the unjust structures or to be complicit in their maintenance through act or apathy constituted sin; liberation from sin required active effort to change the unjust structures. Although conservative detractors may have seen in this theological interpretation an unholy amalgamation of Church doctrine and Marxist ideology, the bishops criticized both capitalism and Marxism as systems that "militate against the dignity of the human person," capitalism because it puts capital and profit before human well-being, Marxism because, "although it ideologically supports a kind of humanism, [it] is more concerned with collective man, and in practice becomes a totalitarian concentration of state power."[23]

If Vatican II and Medellín displeased conservative Latin American elites who feared a changing status quo, the emergent Liberation Theology of the late 1960s was beyond the pale. Liberation Theology recognized the value of Marxist analysis in understanding the modern world and posited a direct relationship between the worldly and spiritual realms, arguing that only profound structural change could bring about liberation and spiritual salvation. Gustavo Gutiérrez, one of the world's principal liberation theologians, proposed that Christian solidarity was meaningful insomuch as it constituted practice (praxis): "solidarity" meant joining *with* the oppressed in their struggle to "[conquer] their liberty."[24] His theory of solidarity critiqued and combined legacies of Catholic- and left-inspired activism among the poor and proposed a new approach for the contemporary context:[25]

Christian poverty makes no sense, then, except as a promise to be one with those suffering misery, in order to point out the evil that it represents. No one should "idealize" poverty; rather, one should hold it aloft as an evil, cry out against it, and strive to eliminate it. Through such a spirit of solidarity, we can alert the poor to the injustice of their situation. When Christ assumed the condition of poverty, He did so not to idealize it but to show love and solidarity with men and to redeem them from sin. Christian poverty, an expression of love, makes us one with those who are poor and protests against their poverty.[26]

The class-sensitive nature of Liberation Theology, which argued that the Bible "is to a great extent the expression of the faith and hope of the poor . . . [and] reveals to us a God who loves preferentially those whom the world passes over,"[27] was revolutionary and deeply meaningful to many in the popular sectors who struggled for better lives but had previously experienced the Catholic Church as yet another institutional pillar upholding the status quo.

Liberation Theology's proponents, although a minority in both international and Chilean Catholicism, had a significant effect on pastoral work in popular-sector Chile. During the late 1960s and early 1970s, many priests and nuns moved into *poblaciones* and rural communities in response to Vatican II and Medellín, some closing their missions in upper-class neighborhoods to answer the call to prioritize the poor.[28] During the Allende administration, a relatively small but dedicated and influential group of Chilean priests participated in the "Calama Experience" led by Dutch priest Juan Caminada, in an attempt to become part of the working class and build a new theology and church rooted in the popular sectors. Known as worker-priests (or worker-nuns), they moved to *poblaciones*, did not practice formal ministry, and lived on what they earned in working-class jobs in an attempt to shed their "bourgeois" ideologies and "seek forms of faith that emerge from the working-class world."[29]

In the coup's aftermath the Grupo Calama's foreign priests were expelled from Chile. The Chileans regrouped in Santiago, forming the semi-clandestine Equipo Misión Obrera (EMO, est. 1975) to organize Popular Christian Communities, assist the persecuted, and support opposition organization.[30] They collaborated actively with like-minded clergy and laypeople to protect the persecuted, reconstitute shredded social fabric, and carry out their pastoral mission. These priests and nuns were among the first Church personnel to put into practice what later came to be understood more broadly as "solidarity," by assisting persecuted leftists and their families regardless of the persecuted individuals' political or religious beliefs.[31]

The most visible use of the word "solidarity" in the immediate postcoup context referred to international solidarity. Chile Solidarity Committees appeared soon after the coup and expanded as leftist exiles fled to the "exterior" with news of atrocities. Committees operated in Canada, Mexico, Argentina, Costa Rica, Cuba, Peru, Colombia, Venezuela, Spain, France, the United States, East and West Germany, Italy, Sweden, the United Kingdom, the Soviet Union, and Algeria, among others.[32] In a clandestine press conference a month after the coup, Miguel Enríquez, leader of the Movimiento de Izquierda Revolucionaria (MIR), praised the outpouring of support from abroad: "International solidarity has been fundamental . . . of enormous help."[33] He called for continued international pressure on the regime. In 1976, upon her release from political prison, Gladys Díaz, a MIR militant, praised and critiqued the work of international solidarity networks: "International solidarity is very important to the resistance. Liberation, however, is the task of the people themselves. Once in a while one thinks that international solidarity alone might liberate our people. This is not correct. It could bring about the destabilization of the junta, but only the power of the people and its organizations can make the final overthrow possible."[34] International solidarity networks disseminated information about abuses, sought international condemnation of the regime, pressured for the release of political prisoners, and supported opposition organizations inside and outside Chile. However, as Díaz pointed out, international solidarity had its limits.

Within the country at the time of the coup, the word "solidarity" was perhaps already in circulation among worker-priests and worker-nuns in the *poblaciones* because of its centrality to the Medellín documents and Liberation Theology. The practice of what ultimately came to be called *solidaridad* initially arose in response to the human rights crisis in all its facets: physical, economic, political, and social. With the left under attack and the center and the right cooperating with the dictatorship, religious institutions were the best positioned to respond to the crisis. The histories of the most well-known human rights organizations in Chile, Comité de Cooperación para la Paz en Chile (COPACHI) and the Vicaría de la Solidaridad (Vicariate of Solidarity), which took over COPACHI's work in January 1976, are relatively well known. However, the dominant historical narrative elides the ecumenical and transnational nature of this early movement for the defense of human rights in Chile and the fundamental importance to this process of actors outside the Catholic Church.

The first human rights organization, the Comité Nacional de Ayuda a los Refugiados (CONAR), was established on October 3, 1973, organized and financed by the United Nations High Commissioner for Refugees in cooperation with the military regime and the Chilean Catholic, Methodist, Christian Orthodox, and Evangelical Lutheran Churches. The junta authorized CONAR because it wanted foreign political refugees to leave the country and sought to burnish its reputation with the gesture.[35] By February 28, 1974, CONAR had facilitated migration for 4,443 foreign refugees. It received support from the Red Cross, the International Commission on European Migrations, and the World Council of Churches (WCC), which pressured foreign governments to provide asylum.[36]

COPACHI was born of a WCC recommendation that a human rights organization be established for persecuted Chileans. Thus, COPACHI formed in early October 1973 at the instigation of Protestants, with WCC money and with the Chilean Catholic Church's cooperation.[37] The organization's leadership initially included leaders of the Chilean Catholic, Methodist, Lutheran, Methodist-Pentecostal, Christian Orthodox, Baptist, and Jewish communities. Most of the initial staff came from the leftist MAPU; a smaller number were nonreligious socialists and communists.[38] By 1974, the Baptist, Methodist-Pentecostal, and Christian Orthodox leaders withdrew under pressure from the regime and their respective congregations, and the regime later banned Lutheran Bishop Helmut Frenz from reentering Chile. When COPACHI closed, in December 1975, only the Methodist, Catholic, and Jewish leaders remained in the organization.[39] In December 1975, under intense pressure from Pinochet, Silva Henríquez disbanded COPACHI but immediately opened the Vicaría de la Solidaridad to continue its work. COPACHI was funded by the WCC and other Protestant organizations,[40] but, overall, between 1973 and 1979, most funding for Church-sponsored programs came from Western European and North American Catholic organizations, the West German government (Zentralstelle), and the U.S. government's Inter-American Foundation.[41]

Solidarity at the Grassroots

Despite international efforts, *pobladores* faced persecution and economic crisis without effective means of response. The regime targeted *poblaciones* for repression regardless of residents' politics, and the human repercussions overwhelmed religious personnel in the neighborhoods. Soon after the coup, *pobladores* organized themselves with the assistance of local religious personnel and leftist activists, primarily soup kitchens for children and unemployed people's groups.[42] These "social organizations" often operated on the grounds of neighborhood chapels or in other church-related space such as nuns' backyards. They received decisive support, protection, and encouragement from COPACHI and the Vicaría de la Solidaridad.

In late 1974, Auxiliary Bishop Fernando Ariztía reported that in the Western Zone of Santiago residents faced escalating unemployment, alcoholism, prostitution, and domestic strife. In the Barrancas Norte sector, one-third of children under the age of six were malnourished. Many unemployed workers, accustomed to providing for their families with their labor and wages, were loathe to seek material relief because they equated it with charity, which they found offensive. This reaction was frequent enough, and the economic misery severe enough, that, in a widely disseminated bulletin, Ariztía admonished readers to rethink their approach to assistance. He cited the example of a *poblador* who yelled at local activists, "I want work and not a plate of food for the little kid; I don't want charity!" Ariztía explained that confronting this issue "requires a profound delicacy so as not to wound he who has always lived from his work," and he chastised those with patronizing or complacent attitudes:

"Some people become enthused [when they hear about the soup kitchens] and say 'how lovely!,' but in truth what we should say is 'how sad, how lamentable that we've come to this.'" Ariztía proposed, instead, relationships of mutual respect and assistance based on "solidarity," which he defined as "sharing what one has, it indicates equality between people."[43] In June 1975, Juan Ignacio Gutiérrez de la Fuente, S.J., reminded readers of the influential Jesuit magazine *Mensaje* that "these types of solutions are 'patches,' that the root of extreme poverty, as the Church's Social Doctrine says, is in the structural order of society, and that this disordered order is precisely what must be transformed so that Chile becomes a country of brothers and not charity."[44]

A significant shift in attitudes about the provision of material assistance was under way in the Chilean Catholic Church. Paternalistic attitudes associated with traditional charity were now understood to be offensive and clashed with the idea of solidarity emerging in the context of cooperation in the *poblaciones* and COPACHI between Christians and the nonreligious left. The discursive and theoretical framework for this practice of solidarity derived from leftist tradition and Liberation Theology, but its roots in official Vatican social doctrine made it difficult for the regime to attack. In practice, the concept served a very concrete purpose: it referred to solidarity with the oppressed. In the mid-1970s, the most acutely oppressed were the impoverished—who were oppressed by unjust socioeconomic structures, now exacerbated by neoliberal structural adjustment measures—and victims of political repression. In other words, Catholics were called upon to act in solidarity with the poor *and* the persecuted left.

In 1975, amid ongoing repression and economic crisis, the word "solidarity" swept through popular-sector grassroots organizations. In this context, both leftist and Catholic concepts of "solidarity" converged to contradict the regime's politically and socially exclusive vision for society, as reflected in its repression and demonization of the left and others that might create obstacles to the neoliberal economic policies sowing misery in the *poblaciones*.[45] In July 1975, the cardinal and vicars of Santiago emitted a Pastoral Letter on the subject of solidarity. The Letter explained the doctrinal foundations of "solidarity" as a practice and provided guidelines for its implementation via Christian Base Communities and social organizations.[46]

A related educational pamphlet circulated in the *poblaciones*. It emphasized the difference between solidarity and charity, interspersing cartoons with character dialogue and quotes from the Pastoral Letter. Solidarity, it explained, "is mutual dependence between people that makes it so that some cannot be happy if the rest are not."[47] The fundamental difference between solidarity and charity was the difference between sharing and distributing: "The basis of

Solidarity is sharing, and not only sharing material things but also joy, pain, and enthusiasm. . . . Solidarity is not distributed like heating gas, rather it is shared with broad fraternal sensibility."[48] The idea of sharing represented a marked shift from traditional approaches to charity in which the privileged gave castoffs to the poor rather than systematically sharing the wealth. The negative connotation was clear: recipients of charity were themselves castoffs, not worthy of sharing equally in the wealth. In the *poblaciones*, where nobody had surplus to distribute, the focus on sharing was also a way to engage as many people as possible in mutual assistance to alleviate the effects of unemployment and repression. Children who ate at soup kitchens, for example, learned that they should find ways for the organization to provide for even more people.[49] Well-being, from this perspective, was not a zero-sum game: those with more—in this case, more access to food—were obliged to enable others to join them at the table. Thus, the concept of "solidarity" encapsulated a set of values and practices to help reverse the social atomization that was tearing communities apart. "Solidarity" meant working together to protect one another, solve collective problems, and build community. It also meant providing assistance where needed, regardless of political or religious differences.

This concept of solidarity went a step further, positing justice as its explicit goal and encompassing more than just church-sanctioned activity: "The duty of Solidarity does not stop with simply sharing with the needy. The struggle for Justice is also an authentic form of solidary love that can exist in the sphere of social and political conflict just as in the path of non-violent action and performance in the public opinion."[50] Solidarity, then, a desirable and "Christian" practice, was not confined to religious or apolitical pursuits. The reference to social and political conflict appears to be a veiled nod to the left, which undertook clandestine resistance and political organizing in extremely precarious conditions. It could also be interpreted as an invitation to the authorities, who understood themselves to be engaged in combat against international Marxism, to seek social and political justice, rather than the elimination and domination of their enemies. It could, of course, serve both purposes, but, given the audience for which it was written and the places in which it was meant to be distributed and discussed, this passage more likely represents recognition of the left and an invitation to *pobladores* who were afraid of, politically averse to, or distrustful of their leftist neighbors to attempt rapprochement.

The Church hierarchy recognized the de facto alliance unfolding in *poblaciones* and organizations like COPACHI, where Catholics and nonbeliever leftists cooperated to mend the social fabric destroyed by repression, economic crisis, and fear. The pamphlet further supplied points of convergence and "positive duties"[51] that facilitated rapprochement and cooperation between Catholics and the left on the ground: "Fulfill, above all else, the demands of justice, so as not to give as charitable help that which is owed for reasons of justice"; "Eliminate the causes and not only the effects of the evils"; and "Organize the assistance in such a way that those who receive it progressively liberate themselves from external dependency and become self-sufficient." The first two points constituted a call to end injustice by working to change the social, political, and economic structures that produce and sustain it. The last point called for the reconstitution of the social fabric and an independent, mobilized society. The implications of such a society for the continuation of the dictatorship were significant. The junta was already worried about lack of support and communication in the *poblaciones*, where it relied heavily on violence and coercive cooptation to maintain control.[52]

Illustrations in the pamphlet depicted Chile's heterogeneous popular sectors as a group with shared interests. In one, two characters discussed their respective *poblaciones*: "In my *población*," said Doña Nena, "and even with the difficulties we've had, the people remain hopeful." Nicanor responded, "You're telling me! I see it every day, Doña Nena!" To which Doña Nena replied, "Then the people in your *población* must be just like in mine . . . ! Shake [my hand], Nicanor!" Another illustration showed men, women, and children, some with patched clothing, one blind, another with a wounded arm, and another with a shackle and chain still trailing from his ankle, walking together toward a point off-page. The caption read, "Solidarity is received and offered by men, women, and children, emerging from it life and hope born of pain, that guides itself in search of a more just and fraternal society animated by the spirit of the Gospel."[53] This call for liberation through class solidarity and active struggle was clear to both Catholics and leftist "nonbelievers." It was also clear to the authorities, who might view it for what it was: a call to organization and action.

Although the junta proclaimed itself a defender of Western Christian civilization and although junta members were Catholic, the regime routinely attacked the Catholic Church, especially popular-sector Base Communities and related social organizations.[54] In addition to repression, there were other obstacles to solidarity. Some conservative Catholics disagreed with Vatican II and Medellín. Neighbors harbored political grudges that were difficult to overcome. Some Catholics feared or abhorred leftists and atheists, and some on the left found little use for the Catholic Church, viewing it as an historical agent of oppression. Conflicts unrelated to politics or religion, such as property disputes, could also thwart solidarity. To address such obstacles, the document emphasized the transcendent nature of the struggle: "Because these aren't words of today but of always."[55] It cited the Bible: "The Spirit of the Lord is upon me, for that which he consecrated me. He sent me to bring the good news to the poor. To announce to the captives their liberty. To return light to the blind and free the oppressed (Luke 4:18–19)." As one MIR militant who participated in a Popular Christian Community recalled:

I'd say that from the theological point of view this way of working was very interesting. It opened themes of the Old Testament . . . especially Exodus. The story of the liberation of the pueblo of Israel: that, definitively, was the pueblo in which we wanted to see ourselves, that served as a mirror for this pueblo subjected to oppression that wants to make a path to liberty and that in some way has Yahvé as an ally. . . . This theology "organized," which also constituted a very large effort in the sense that the community not only had the opportunity to see it and problematize it, to feel supported by the word of God, but also [to feel] supported by their own experience of community: to feel that you're not alone in the world, you're not a crazy person who got loose and that the dictatorship hasn't managed to recognize and eliminate, but that life had more meaning and could be constructed in other ways.[56]

The Chilean Catholic Church defended "universal" human rights, it provided refuge to the persecuted, and it supported organizations such as Popular Christian Communities that encouraged political pluralism, discussion, and solidarity. In doing so, it created a fragile but significant space for an "alternative" citizenship to take root, one linked to internationally recognized ideals and opposed in its diversity and values to the dictatorship's exclusionary practices and its attempts to form obedient, "apolitical" citizens.[57]

The Church's decision to couch its calls for social change in language that evoked internationally recognized, historically significant principles such as liberty, equality, and fraternity was strategic. These principles had roots in both secular and religious Western thought, and, in theory, they superseded discrete national contexts and temporal conflicts. This laid the groundwork for the broadest possible political and religious pluralism within the social organizations and Popular Christian Communities. The emphasis on the universality of the struggle for liberty and freedom from oppression provided a point of convergence with the ideals of the left, thus offering a common ground for cooperation between estranged secular and religious actors. It also extended a small umbrella of protection: activities inspired in transcendent, transnational ideals and carried out under the shelter of the "universal" (Catholic) Church were more difficult for the authorities to openly attack.

Leftist leaders recognized the importance of the social organizations and the Church's orientation toward the popular sectors. In September 1974, the MIR called for militants to work within community organizations to "activate [them] and make them function," to join the "extant, semi-legal organizations in our sectors" such as social organizations, and to form Resistance Committees to "organize and multiply the aforementioned tasks."[58] In a July 1975 document prepared in East Berlin and disseminated in Chile, the Popular Unity (UP) leadership in exile highlighted the importance of the Church's orientation toward the popular sectors. The UP leadership, particularly the Communist Party, commonly referred to the Pinochet regime as fascist. Therefore, the Chilean left and other regime opponents constituted a new generation of antifascist resistance in an ongoing, worldwide struggle against fascism dating from the 1930s.[59] The UP leadership viewed favorably the "expressions of solidarity developed in the worker and popular sectors to mitigate the effects of unemployment and hunger"—direct references to social organizations in the *poblaciones*. They called for the formation of a popular front against the regime that would be "much broader, politically, socially, and ideologically, than the Popular Unity" and that would incorporate "the humanist values of Christians, lay people and Marxists" and a "superior and true, honest and egalitarian ideological pluralism in relations between members."[60] They made a pointed call to Christians: "In this new patriotic, revolutionary and libratory enterprise, an active role corresponds to the Christian masses together with the rest of the pueblo's organizations. They have a place now and in the future of the struggle to bring down the Junta and establish a new society."[61] Inside Chile, at least one clandestine publication, *Pueblo Cristiano*, reprinted the document several months later. It exhorted readers to discuss the document and urged them to struggle against the dictatorship alongside the clandestine left, declaring that "unity in the face of a common enemy—the dictatorship—is the light that will illuminate the path of the oppressed in search of a better society."[62]

It is impossible to know how many people read these documents. However, rapprochement was occurring in the *poblaciones*. There, leftists approached local Catholic chapels and social organizations. Some did so upon orders from their respective parties to support the organizations, others because they required aid, and others because they found common cause. Juan, a communist militant, approached his *población*'s Popular Christian Community because it sought justice for the disappeared: "The banner of the disappeared was ours: most of them weren't Christians, they were communists and some MIR militants . . . so it was our banner of struggle and [the Christians] were welcome to take it up, but we were going to support that situation."[63] In the Popular Christian Community, he found political pluralism and freedom of expression and association unavailable elsewhere; it was a place where people could exercise rights the regime had banned: "In those times we'd meet, I remember, in a kind of religious service that were Catholic meetings, spiritual, as they say, but that combined [spirituality] with the social thing. We met in an old, run down house and we spoke of . . . prohibited things such as liberty and the rights of the pueblo, how to reorganize ourselves, and how to fight, and how to make [the authorities] feel that they had to respect us."[64] Rosa, a teenager from a communist-affiliated family, also found in the Christian Community a place of common cause and freedom of expression that drew her into further sociopolitical activity:

You know, that word, [solidarity], is very important. There they started to talk a lot about "solidarity." I heard it and heard it, I was fifteen, and there was a meeting for the Month of María, which is November 8 to December 8, so every evening the really Catholic people would meet, and those of us in the soup kitchens and youngsters who participated in the Church would go. . . . One week my mama was so sick that I went to stand in line [at the soup kitchen] with my sister, and she said, "we have to go," and I went, not very pleased. When I arrived I felt, one feels it in her heart, that she shares the feeling that the other is experiencing. And I've never forgotten that moment, because it was the moment in which I was capable of stating an opinion. I was about to cry, because I was terribly embarrassed to speak in public. . . . But afterward I felt such relief when I stated an opinion about what solidarity was, and I felt the other people's support: they shared my opinion and that made me feel good, as if I had done something positive.[65]

Rosa and Juan found in these organizations religious and political pluralism and freedom of expression and association—cornerstones of the democratic society that the regime had destroyed but that had not been forgotten.

Meanwhile, clergy and nuns encouraged Catholics to reach out to the oppressed, including those they might consider enemies. Priests used the parable of the Good Samaritan to explain solidarity as an integral part of moral ethics dating to ancient times:

A man was going down from Jerusalem to Jericho, when he fell into the hands of robbers. They stripped him of his clothes, beat him and went away, leaving him half dead. A priest happened to be going down the same road, and when he saw the man, he passed by on the other side. So too, a Levite, when he came to the place and saw him, passed by on the other side. But a Samaritan, as he traveled, came where the man was; and when he saw him, he took pity on him. He went to him and bandaged his wounds, pouring on oil and wine. Then he put the man on his own donkey, took him to an inn and took care of him. The next day he took out two silver coins and gave them to the innkeeper. "Look after him," he said, "and when I return, I will reimburse you for any extra expense you may have." "Which of these three do you think was a neighbor to the man who fell into the hands of robbers?" The expert in the law replied, "The one who had mercy on him." Jesus told him, "Go and do likewise." (Luke 10:30–37)[66]

The symbolism of the priest and the Levite avoiding the injured man was particularly relevant to the Chilean context. In Chile, the most well-positioned people within the government and economic system did not aid or assume responsibility for the victims of economic and political oppression; on the contrary, they were either agents of the oppression or complicit with it, and many benefited from it. The persecuted left and the poor of the *poblaciones* in mid-1970s Chile had no recourse to traditional state institutions of citizen participation and protection. Constitutional guarantees were suspended, the junta served as both legislature and executive, and the courts were complicit with the dictatorship. Economic policy was generated within a small circle of dogmatic, model-obsessed technocrats shielded from public opinion and protest as state security forces tortured and killed with impunity. In the Chilean context of Marxist-Christian relations, the "Samaritan" unexpectedly revealed himself as the injured man's metaphorical neighbor. It was the Samaritan's act of "establish[ing] this *experience* of the *face-to-face* with those robbed, injured, or abandoned *outside the path*" (emphasis in the original) that made the Samaritan "good" and constituted the act as one of "solidarity."[67]

Thus, everyone was encouraged to think twice about who their "neighbors" might be: were the poor's "neighbors" the military regime that expected them to stoically and silently bear the burden of neoliberal structural adjustment even as their children starved? Were the leftists' "neighbors" only other leftists, or perhaps also non-Marxist Catholics willing to act in solidarity with them? This theoretical and theological orientation counteracted to a certain extent the atmosphere of atomization, fear, and enmity that permeated society after the coup, and it provided a framework for the construction of a broad-based, pluralistic movement for change.

Clergy encouraged Catholics and nonreligious leftists alike to seek fundamental similarities, not just overlook differences in isolated emergency situations. In the newsletter *Cristo Dialogante*, produced by the Chilean Catholic Church's Secretariat for Nonbelievers, a priest who joined the Association of Family Members of the Disappeared on a hunger strike explained his experience of solidarity with nonreligious Marxists:

We were well aware that this call [for solidarity] did not come from the Catholic camp. It came from them, the Association of Family Members of the Disappeared of dominantly Marxist tendency. . . . We discovered in them a marvelous faith. They believe, in spite of their terrible experiences, they believe in mankind, they believe in humanity. They believe in the power of truth and justice. They believe in the efficacy of love and pain. They believe that there is something great for which one can give one's life and they feel the pleasure of the total gift. Isn't this really a religious faith, an "implicit Christianity" . . . ? . . . We all have faith that something or Someone is moving, and that the structures of vested interests and oppression should cede. Because solidarity will triumph and love is stronger than death.[68]

It was encounters and deliberate organizing work like this, frequently less dramatic than quotidian, that built solidarity networks and grassroots opposition in *poblaciones*. In these processes, we see international concepts decanted and adapted to local contexts and reprojected outward for very concrete purposes—in this case, to build opposition to the dictatorship.

Conclusion

One of the most important implications of the Chilean case is that, in the study of transnationalism, we cannot overlook local conditions and actors. Every member of a transnational network or movement, no matter how supranational and widespread, emerges from and acts within a local context or contexts that inform his or her political and cultural understandings, interpretations, and decisions. Most also remain physically rooted in particular locales, cultures, and sociopolitical contexts, even as they participate in movements that transcend national boundaries.[69] As the Chilean example shows, "solidarity" emerged from currents of leftist and Catholic thought that circulated at both the national and the international levels. However, while the concept of "solidarity" that emerged in the popular sectors in 1970s Chile drew upon this national and international history, it responded primarily to and was highly contingent upon the local context. The solidarity movement derived its strength from its local nature even as it coexisted and interacted with internationalist actors and networks, and it can be understood only by considering its leftist and Catholic antecedents in Chilean popular-sector religious tradition and political culture.

Points of convergence and common cause between the persecuted left and religious actors provided the foundation upon which the Chilean solidarity network was built. Specifically, it was the violation of civil and human rights, broadly defined to include physical integrity, political rights, and socioeconomic justice, that brought these sectors together. This national popular-sector solidarity movement did not originate in the internationalist solidarity movement, although it intersected and interacted with it. The solidarity network within Chilean *poblaciones* relied upon an intricate web of local activists who worked in league with others with ties to national and international organizations. The delicate balance of the local, national, and international, and the flow of people, information, funds, and goods along the various highways and byways of the Chile solidarity networks inside and outside the country deserve further research. Only by considering the local alongside the international can we reach a fuller understanding of transnational concepts such as "solidarity" and the movements associated with them.

Notes

I thank Pamela Zeiser, Elizabeth Quay Hutchinson, and Paul Carelli and my colleagues Brenda Elsey, Margaret Power, Eric Zolov, and Jessica Stites Mor on the panel "Transnationalism and the Citizen: Solidarity and Human Rights in Cold War Latin America," at the American Historical Association annual meeting in Boston, MA, January 6–9, 2011, for their comments and suggestions. I also thank the staff of Chile's Facultad Latinoamericana de Ciencias Sociales, Biblioteca San Ignacio, and Fundación de Documentación y Archivo de la Vicaría de la Solidaridad and the University of Florida's Latin American Collection for their assistance in Santiago and Gainesville. Cecilia Riveros and Sandie A. Stratton provided research assistance in Santiago and Jacksonville. This research was made possible by grants from Fulbright-Hays, the Mellon Foundation, Yale University, and the University of North Florida. My profound gratitude goes to the many *pobladores* and their allies who spoke with me about their experiences during the dictatorship.

1. See, for example, Fernando Camacho Padilla, *Suecia por Chile: Una historia visual del exilio y la solidaridad, 1970–1990* (Santiago: Editorial LOM, 2009); Fernando Camacho Padilla, *Una vida para Chile: La solidaridad y la comunidad chilena en Suecia 1970–2010* (Santiago: Editorial LOM, 2011); Anna-Karin Gauding, *Lazos solidarios: La cooperación sueca en Chile 1970–2010* (Santiago: Editorial LOM, 2011); James N. Green, *We Cannot Remain Silent: Opposition to the Brazilian Military Dictatorship in the United States* (Durham, NC: Duke University Press, 2010); and Jeffrey L. Gould, "Solidarity under Siege: The Latin American Left, 1968," *American Historical Review* 114, no. 2 (April 2009): 348–75.

2. Eyewitness accounts and media estimates place the size of this march at between 600 and 1,500 people. Mariano Puga, "Los Vía Crucis de las Comunidades Cristianas," in *Crónicas de una iglesia liberadora*, ed. José Aldunate Lyon, S.J., et al. (Santiago: LOM, 2000), 131; Sergio Cárdenas, testimonio oral, Santiago, Chile, November 11, 1993, cited in David Fernández, *La "Iglesia" que resistió a Pinochet* (Madrid: IEPALA, 1996), 314; "Vía Crucis: La pasión de Jesús, hoy," *Solidaridad* #90, 1a quincena abril 1980, 5.

3. Puga, "Los Vía Crucis de las Comunidades Cristianas," 132; Ana María Hoyl, *Por la vida* (Santiago: CESOC, 2003), 84; and "Vía Crucis: La pasión de Jesús, hoy," *Solidaridad* #90.

4. Puga, "Los Vía Crucis de las Comunidades Cristianas," 132; and "Vía Crucis: La pasión de Jesús, hoy," *Solidaridad* #90.

5. This appeal to "universal" symbolism that superseded the merely national is not

unique. See, for example, Marguerite Guzmán Bouvard, *Revolutionizing Motherhood: The Mothers of the Plaza de Mayo* (Wilmington, DE: Scholarly Resources Books, 2002).

6. In Chile, Christian Base Communities and Popular Christian Communities (a type of Christian Base Community) predated Pinochet's Chile, but they reached their organizational peak during the dictatorship, in the 1970s and early 1980s. Within the world of Christian Base Communities—which designates organizational structure, not theological or political orientation—some called themselves Popular Christian Communities. The latter were usually based in the popular sectors and followed Liberation Theology. "Popular" signified "the irruption of the poor into the church as a collective subject with its own identity. . . . They are not individuals who 'incorporate' themselves into an already-made church and become 'eclesialized,' [but] rather a believing and oppressed people who imprint traces of their own identity onto the church, thereby 'popularizing' the church." Fernando Castillo, "Comunidades Cristianas Populares: La Iglesia que nace desde los pobres," in *La Iglesia de los pobres en América Latina*, by Fernando Castillo et al. (Santiago: PEC/ECO-SEPADE, 1982), 88.

7. The MAPU and the IC split from the Christian Democrat Party (PDC) in 1969 and 1971 and the MAPU Obrero Campesino from the MAPU in 1973.

8. Cecilia Dockendorff, José Antonio Román Brugnoli, and María Alejandra Energici Sprovera, "La neoliberalización de la solidaridad en el Chile democrático: Una mirada comparativa sobre discursos solidarios en 1991 y 2006," *Latin American Research Review* 45, no. 1 (2010): 189.

9. Steiner Stjernø, *Solidarity in Europe: The History of an Idea* (New York: Cambridge University Press, 2009), 43–46, 48. Marx posited two types of what could be understood as solidarity: "unity" of the industrial proletariat under capitalism and the "ideal solidarity" or "Gemeinschaft" that would be achieved only in a communist society. Ibid.

10. Mikhail Bakunin, "Three Lectures to the Swiss Members of the International" (1871), in Stjernø, *Solidarity in Europe*, 57.

11. See, for example, Sergio Grez Toso, *Los anarquistas y el movimiento obrero: La alborada de "la Idea" en Chile, 1893–1915* (Santiago: Editorial LOM, 2007); Jorge Arrate and Eduardo Rojas, *Memoria de la Izquierda Chilena*, vol. 1, *1850–1970*, and vol. 2, *1970–2000* (Santiago: Javier Vergara Editor, 2003); and Pedro Naranjo, Mauricio Ahumada, Mario Garcés, and Julio Pinto, *Miguel Enríquez y el proyecto revolucionario en Chile: Discursos y documentos del Movimiento de Izquierda Revolucionaria, MIR* (Santiago: Editorial LOM, 2004).

12. Arrate and Rojas, *Memoria de la Izquierda Chilena, 1850–1970*, 97, 108. For a history of anarchism and the labor movement, see Grez Toso, *Los anarquistas y el movimiento obrero*, 2007. See also Arrate and Rojas, *Memoria de la Izquierda Chilena, 1850–1970*, 55–108; Gabriel Salazar and Julio Pinto, *Historia contemporánea de Chile*, vol. 1, *Estado, legitimidad, ciudadanía* (Santiago: Editorial LOM, 1999), 39–41; and Gabriel Salazar and Julio Pinto, *Historia Contemporánea de Chile*, vol. 2, *Actores, identidad y movimiento* (Santiago: Editorial LOM, 1999), 112–22. For urban labor history, see Peter de Shazo, *Urban Workers and Labor Unions in Chile, 1902–1927* (Madison: Uni-

versity of Wisconsin Press, 1983); Mario Garcés Durán, *Crisis social y motines populares en el 1900* (Santiago: ECO, 1991); Elizabeth Q. Hutchinson, *Labors Appropriate to Their Sex: Gender, Labor and Politics in Urban Chile, 1900–1930* (Durham, NC: Duke University Press, 2001); Peter Winn, *Weavers of Revolution: The Yarur Workers and Chile's Road to Socialism* (New York: Oxford University Press, 1989); Franck Gaudichaud, *Poder popular y cordones industriales: Testimonios sobre el movimiento popular urbano, 1970–1973* (Santiago: Editorial LOM, 2004); and Peter Winn, ed., *Victims of the Chilean Miracle: Workers and Neoliberalism in the Pinochet Era, 1973–2002* (Durham, NC: Duke University Press, 2004).

13. Arrate and Rojas, *Memoria de la Izquierda Chilena, 1850–1970*, 55–56, 58.

14. Ibid., 60–62.

15. Ibid., 62–63.

16. Pope Leo XIII, *Rerum novarum*, Encyclical on Capital and Labor, 1891.

17. Ibid.

18. The existence of a vigorous Catholic Workers Movement alongside Chile's heavily socialist- and communist-influenced labor organizations in the mid-twentieth century is one example.

19. Stjernø, *Solidarity in Europe*, 43–44.

20. Oscar Jiménez quoting Alberto Hurtado in Oscar Jiménez, S.J., "Alberto Hurtado, precursor de La Iglesia Liberadora," in *Crónicas de una iglesia liberadora*, ed. José Aldunate Lyon, S.J., et al. (Santiago: LOM, 2000), 14, 15.

21. Ibid., 15.

22. Medellín Documents, Latin American Bishops, "Justice" Article 2, September 6, 1968, http://www.shc.edu/theolibrary/resources/medjust.htm.

23. Medellín Documents, Latin American Bishops, "Justice," Article 10, September 6, 1968.

24. Gustavo Gutiérrez, "Theology of Liberation," in *Gustavo Gutiérrez: Essential Writings*, ed. James B. Nickoloff (New York: Orbis, 2000), 29.

25. I thank Elizabeth Hutchinson for this observation and for the quote from Gutiérrez that follows it. Elizabeth Q. Hutchinson, e-mail communication, January 11, 2011.

26. Gustavo Gutiérrez, "Notes for a Theology of Liberation (1970)," in *Liberation Theology at the Crossroads: Democracy or Revolution?*, ed. Paul E. Sigmund (New York: Oxford University Press, 1992), 212–13.

27. Gustavo Gutiérrez, "The God of Life" (1989), in *Gustavo Gutiérrez: Essential Writings*, ed. James B. Nickoloff (New York: Orbis, 2000), 63. "Preferential" meant priority, not exclusivity. James B. Nickoloff, "Introduction," in *Gustavo Gutiérrez: Essential Writings*, 13.

28. José Aldunate Lyon, S.J., *Un peregrino cuenta su historia* (Santiago: Ediciones Ignacianas, 2002), 106.

29. José Aldunate Lyon, S.J., "La experiencia Calama," in *Crónicas de una iglesia liberadora*, ed. José Aldunate Lyon, S.J., et al. (Santiago: LOM, 2000), 90; José Aldunate Lyon, S.J., "EMO: Presencia y acción en 25 años," in *Crónicas de una iglesia liberadora*,

ed. José Aldunate Lyon, S.J., et al. (Santiago: LOM, 2000), 95. The "Calama Experience" takes its name from the group's initial headquarters in Chile, although while some priests worked at the Chuquicamata mine near Calama, others took their project to other parts of Chile, for example Villa Nonguén in Concepción and Villa Francia in Santiago. Not all worker-priests and worker-nuns in Chile were of the Grupo Calama, and not all those who followed Liberation Theology were worker-priests and worker-nuns, but members of the Calama group, and later EMO, had a significant influence on pastoral work in Santiago throughout the 1970s and early 1980s, reaching particular strength in the western zone of the city under the auspices of Bishop Enrique Alvear.

30. Aldunate Lyon, *Un peregrine cuenta su historia*, 131, 134–35.

31. Roberto Bolton García, "El asilo contra la represión," in *Crónicas de una iglesia liberadora*, ed. José Aldunate Lyon, S.J., et al. (Santiago: LOM, 2000), 153; Cristián Precht Bañados, "Del Comité Pro Paz a la Vicaría de la Solidaridad," in *Seminario Iglesia y Derechos Humanos en Chile*, by Arzobispado de Santiago Fundación de Documentación y Archivo de la Vicaría de la Solidaridad (Santiago: LOM, 2002), 19.

32. Peter Johnson and Francisco Fonseca, *North American Congress on Latin America (NACLA) Archive of Latin Americana* (Wilmington, DE: Scholarly Resources, 1999); see also Luis Corvalán, *De lo vivido y lo peleado: Memorias* (Santiago: Editorial LOM, 1997). The NACLA archive is located at the University of Florida at Gainesville.

33. Conferencia de prensa de Miguel Enríquez, Santiago, October 8, 1973, reproduced in Naranjo et al., *Miguel Enríquez y el proyecto revolucionario en Chile*, 274.

34. Gladys Díaz, December 10, 1976, quoted in "Women in the Chilean Resistance" pamphlet, 1978, 18–19, located at the NACLA Archive of Latin Americana, files 244–46, roll 45. The interview first appeared in *Arbeiterkampf* (West Germany), December 13, 1976.

35. Helmut Frenz, *Mi vida chilena: Solidaridad con los oprimidos*, trans. Sonia Plaut (Santiago: Editorial LOM, 2006), 137, 152. Frenz was a bishop of the Evangelical Lutheran Church and president of CONAR. Under Allende, Chile had become a place of political asylum and refuge for leftists fleeing repression in their home countries (e.g., Brazil, which had been under a military dictatorship since 1964).

36. Ibid., 137–38; Common Front for Latin America (COFFLA) News Summary, no. 29, September 29, 1973, 1, in NACLA Archive of Latin Americana, files 254–56, roll 48. The WCC also pressured Pope Paul VI to respond more strongly to events in Chile, resulting in a WCC/Vatican/Red Cross delegation to pressure the junta to stop the repression. Ibid.

37. Fernando Ariztía, "El Comité de Cooperación para la Paz en Chile," in *Seminario Iglesia y Derechos Humanos en Chile*, by Arzobispado de Santiago Fundación de Documentación y Archivo de la Vicaría de la Solidaridad (Santiago: LOM, 2002), 13; Frenz, *Mi vida chilena*, 159; and Pamela Lowden, *Moral Opposition to Authoritarian Rule in Chile, 1973–1990* (Oxford: St. Anthony's Press, 1996), 32.

38. Brian H. Smith, *The Church and Politics in Chile: Challenges to Modern Catholicism* (Princeton, NJ: Princeton University Press, 1982), 334; Lowden, *Moral Opposition to Authoritarian Rule in Chile*, 33.

39. Mario I. Aguilar, *A Social History of the Catholic Church in Chile*, vol. 1, *The First Period of the Pinochet Government, 1973–1980* (Lewiston, NY: Edwin Mellen, 2004), 87; Lowden, *Moral Opposition to Authoritarian Rule in Chile*, 46; Frenz, *Mi vida chilena*, 245–67.

40. Frenz, *Mi vida chilena*, 165.

41. Smith, *The Church and Politics in Chile*, 325–27.

42. One of the first soup kitchens formed in *población* La Legua shortly after the coup. Interview, Anita, July 5, 2005. Unless otherwise noted, all interviews were conducted by the author.

43. Fernando Ariztía, "Algunas reflexiones sobre la solidaridad," *Boletín Zona Oeste del Arzobispado de Santiago*, no. 52–53 (November–December 1974), reproduced in *Mensaje*, no. 236 (January–February 1975): 46–49.

44. Juan Ignacio Gutiérrez de la Fuente, S.J., "De la emergencia a la solidaridad," *Mensaje*, no. 239 (June 1975): 311.

45. For a discussion of neoliberalism and repression of *pobladores*, see Alison J. Bruey, "Neoliberalism and Repression in *Poblaciones* of Santiago de Chile," *Stockholm Review of Latin American Studies*, no. 5 (September 2009): 17–27.

46. Arzobispado de Santiago-Vicaría de la Solidaridad, "Solidaridad: Lea y coménte la Pastoral de la Solidaridad," pamphlet, Fundación de Documentación y Archivo de la Vicaría de la Solidaridad, 1975. See also "La Iglesia hoy: Orientaciones pastorales para Chile," reproduced in *Mensaje*, no. 240 (July 1975): 325–30. The Vicaría de la Solidaridad's bimonthly news magazine (est. 1976) was titled *Solidaridad*.

47. Arzobispado de Santiago-Vicaría de la Solidaridad, "Solidaridad."

48. Ibid.

49. Gutiérrez de la Fuente, "De la emergencia a la solidaridad," 310.

50. Arzobispado de Santiago-Vicaría de la Solidaridad, "Solidaridad."

51. The document provides a framework for what Sally J. Scholz defines as "political solidarity": a "particular form of solidarity that carries self-imposed moral requirements" (36) understood as "a unity of individuals who have made a commitment to struggle for liberation" (21). Sally J. Scholz, *Political Solidarity* (University Park: Pennsylvania State University Press, 2008).

52. Actas de las Sesiones de la Honorable Junta de Gobierno (ADJ), Acta #39, 21/nov/73, 18:30h–13:00h, del 22/nov/73 desde las 11:20h, Sesión Secreta, pp. 1–2; and ADJ, Acta #143a, 1/ago/74, 16:10h–20:17h, Sesión Secreta, p. 4.

53. Arzobispado de Santiago-Vicaría de la Solidaridad, "Solidaridad."

54. Hoyl, *Por la vida*, 225–97.

55. Arzobispado de Santiago-Vicaría de la Solidaridad, "Solidaridad."

56. Interview, Mario, December 21, 2004.

57. Philip Oxhorn argues that the social organizations provided a place for grassroots democracy to take root, especially in the 1980s. However, he underestimates the importance of the left to this process. Philip Oxhorn, *Organizing Civil Society: The Popular Sectors and the Struggle for Democracy in Chile* (University Park: Pennsylvania State University Press, 1995).

58. "Manifiesto del Movimiento de Resistencia Popular al Pueblo de Chile," September 1974, reproduced in Naranjo et al., *Miguel Enríquez y el proyecto revolucionario en Chile*, 346.

59. The MIR disagreed with the characterization of the regime as fascist for reasons too extensive to discuss here.

60. "La Unidad Popular y las Tareas del Pueblo de Chile," Berlin, German Democratic Republic (RDA), July 27, 1975, Fondo Eugenio Ruíz-Tagle, Facultad Latinoamericana de Ciencias Sociales-Chile (FERT-FLACSO).

61. Ibid.

62. *Pueblo Cristiano*, Año 3, no. 5, Chile, January–February 1976, FERT-FLACSO.

63. Interview, CP Villa Francia, March 12, 2005.

64. Ibid.

65. Interview, Rosa, Juan C., Ana, October 24, 2003.

66. *The Holy Bible: New International Version* (Colorado Springs: International Bible Society, 1984).

67. Enrique Dussel, "From Fraternity to Solidarity: Toward a *Politics of Liberation*," trans. Michael Barber and Judd Smith Wright, *Journal of Social Philosophy* 38.1 (Spring 2007): 80, 84.

68. *Cristo Dialogante*, no. 8 (August 1978): 2–6.

69. For a provocative study of social movement culture, politics, and place, see Arturo Escobar, *Territories of Difference: Place, Movement, Life, Redes* (Durham, NC: Duke University Press, 2008). See also Green, *We Cannot Remain Silent*.

6

Cuba's Concept of "Internationalist Solidarity"

Political Discourse, South-South Cooperation with Angola, and the Molding of Transnational Identities

CHRISTINE HATZKY

The Cuban Revolution is usually associated with "international solidarity," particularly because of Cuba's numerous civil cooperation projects in Latin America realized over the past two decades. But the phenomenon as such, its ideological background, its development and transformation are largely unknown. Already in the first years after the revolution, the Cuban government developed a foreign policy that crossed continental boundaries, singular in Latin America and unique for a small, "Third World" Caribbean country. The Cuban government put "internationalist solidarity" into practice within transatlantic and even global dimensions in political, military, and civilian terms. This chapter examines the specific features of this concept of "internationalist solidarity" and explores its practical implementation under the polarized circumstances of the Cold War from the early 1960s in Africa, Latin America, and Asia. My research is based on an empirical study of Cuban civil cooperation with Angola between 1976 and 1991, through which the transformation of the practical experience of this concept can be traced.

The Cuban political and military intervention in the postcolonial conflict in Angola in favor of the allied Marxist Movimento Popular de Libertação de Angola (MPLA), or Popular Movement for the Liberation of Angola, was part of one of the biggest "proxy wars" of the Cold War era in Africa. Because of its extent and duration, it was also a hitherto unique example of a transatlantic, Latin American–African, South-South cooperation between two formerly colonized countries. With few exceptions, there exist now only ideologically polarized versions of political positions on the Cuban military commitment in Angola, and hardly anything is known about the approximately 370,000 Cuban soldiers who participated in the war in Angola. Even less information is available about the 50,000 civilians who worked in Angola as doctors, teachers, technicians, advisers, or construction workers in order to establish a health service, an educational system, and a new social infrastructure. All these civilians did nothing less than support the whole process of nation-building in postcolonial Angola. Taking as an example the cooperation in the field of education, I analyze its development and critically assess its practical implementation. I also raise the question of the extent to which the experience of large-scale civil involvement abroad resulted in a change of the meaning of internationalist solidarity after the end of the Cold War, as Cuban military and civil cooperation in Ethiopia and Nicaragua were carried out parallel to that in Angola.

The demands of the Cuban engagement in Angola took place under the influence of the historical changes and hardships from the colonial period to independence.[1] The Angolan MPLA government expected the Cuban government not only to provide military support to overcome the postcolonial conflict but also, ultimately, comprehensive help in building a new society. This led to a significant transformation of the purely political and military concept of internationalist solidarity. The principle of "help for self-help," which initially determined the Cuban development policy in Angola, had to be adapted to the dynamics of the political and military developments in Angola and therefore modified significantly.

The Cuban-Angolan cooperation relationship can be characterized as a bilateral interaction of two friendly governments and state institutions. However, it also encompassed a transnational plane of relations that went beyond states to involve civilians, the individuals who put the cooperation programs into practice. Therefore, I turn my attention to these Cuban participants, the so-called internationalists, and raise the questions of how they imbued the practical challenge of internationalist solidarity with individual concepts of duty and political commitment and to what extent they accepted their government's proposal of a transnational political identity associated with this cooperation in Angola. During the recruitment campaign for Angola, the Cuban government promoted a new transnational identity: the "Latin American–African" nation. This leads to the question of whether this officially crafted identity was merely political propaganda or whether the experience of thousands of civilians working in Angola led to the development of a new transnational "Latin American–African" identity. A further related question is that of a personal identification with the political aims of internationalist solidarity: what new constructs of identity and phenomena of self-perception or perception of the "other" emerged from this experience? In order to address these questions, I conducted one hundred interviews with eyewitnesses, former civilian participants in the program in Angola, and these form the basis of the discussion in this chapter.

Cold War, Cuban Internationalism, and the Concept of International Solidarity

The Cuban Revolution involved not only the experiment of a radical economic and social transformation but also the attempt to pursue a sovereign foreign policy of independent interests and aims regardless of the international polarization of the Cold War. With the victory of the 26th of July Movement (M-26-7) over the authoritarian government of Fulgencio Batista on January 1, 1959, the revolutionaries led by Fidel Castro Ruz aimed to extend the revolution to other parts of the world: they wanted to "internationalize" it. In the course of this internationally oriented revolutionary mission from 1975 on, Angola became the pivotal focus of Cuban foreign policy for the next decade and a half. Although the spread of the revolution on the Latin American continents was a more obvious goal from a historical, geographical, and cultural perspective, by the early 1960s, the Cuban government supported anticolonial movements and friendly postcolonial governments in Africa. Support for revolutionary movements in Latin America and even in Asia was not forgotten but complemented this new, far-reaching global political perspective, aimed at revolutionizing the three continents of Asia, Africa, and Latin America, the so-called Tricont in the jargon of the time.

As a result of the bloc formation in the Cold War and the antagonism between the two superpowers, the United States and the Soviet Union (with revolutionary Cuba in the cross fire), these major foreign-policy ambitions were subject to severe limitations from the beginning. Although the support for liberation movements in the struggle of the Tricont against the industrialized Western countries was an essential part of the new revolutionary ideology, the need to ensure the survival of the revolution in the face of open hostility from the U.S. government had set much of the tone of Cuban foreign-policy making.[2] The dramatic break with the United States in the early 1960s was followed by a rapprochement with the Soviet Union—though much more slowly and by no means without conflict. This balancing act between the two world powers determined the framework of Cuban foreign policy.[3]

The isolation of Cuba by the U.S. government was extended across the Americas as Cuba was excluded from the Organization of American States (OAS) in 1962. This restricted the immediate scope for internationalization of the revolution. With the exception of the Mexican government, all Latin American governments conformed to the instructions of U.S. foreign policy and broke off both diplomatic and trade relations with Cuba. The Cuban government—whose public reaction remained firm—responded by expanding its economic relations with the Soviet Union and with Eastern Bloc states. In doing so, however, it pursued a foreign policy that was unusual and remarkably self-confident for a small country. This policy was characterized by support for oppositional, nationalist, and left-wing liberation movements in Latin America. Initially, the Cuban government assisted guerrilla movements operating in Latin America—in Guatemala, Colombia, Peru, Venezuela, and Bolivia—challenging the international position of the Soviet Union, the leading power in the socialist camp, which promoted a "peaceful path" to socialism as part of its policy of peaceful coexistence with the United States.[4]

At a time of rapid decolonization in Africa in the early 1960s, the Cuban government established contacts with postcolonial African governments and provided practical support for anticolonial movements. In doing so, it followed the principle of supporting those liberation struggles with which it shared a common history of repression and resistance and those that defended their right of self-determination and national sovereignty.[5] The foreign policy considerations of the Cuban government may also have included the assumption that an involvement in Africa, far from the sphere of interests of the United States, would not provoke immediate increased hostilities against Cuba. The first contacts were made with the government of Ghana, which had gained independence in 1957 under the leadership of Kwame Nkrumah, and with the Algerian liberation movement Front de Libération Nationale (FLN), or National Liberation Front. The latter received Cuban military support in its struggle against French colonial rule and, in 1962, also received the first civilian aid from Cuba, which sent doctors to Algeria.[6]

The first milestone in setting the political framework for this policy of international solidarity was the Tricontinental Conference in Havana in January 1966. Eighty-two representatives of anticolonial movements and governments from Africa, Asia, and Latin America were present. Based on the example of the Cuban Revolution, the goal of the conference was to open new political perspectives to the Tricont countries and to extend the revolution to these "main areas of exploitation by imperialism."[7] An appeal was made to countries that had already liberated themselves from colonial rule and imperialism to support other liberation movements, an authentic expression of internationalist solidarity.[8] At this time, the Cuban government had already found several like-minded supporters among the politicians and leaders of anticolonial movements in Africa and Asia, especially those that had met at the conferences in Bandung in 1955 and in Cairo in 1957. In 1961, they had founded the Non-Aligned Movement in Belgrade under the chairmanship of the Yugoslav president, Josip Broz Tito. The only founding member country from Latin America was Cuba.[9]

This new strategy of internationalism and internationalist solidarity, developed primarily by Ernesto "Che" Guevara and Fidel Castro, was based on a long tradition of revolutionary ideologies of the nineteenth and twentieth centuries. To these ideas they added a Latin American and Cuban tradition of armed rebellion, as well as a volunteer ethic that is best characterized by Guevara's statement that "the impossible is realistic." From this perspective, internationalist solidarity meant the realization of a political utopia on a global scale.

The Marxist theoreticians and practitioners of the nineteenth and twentieth centuries had a decisive influence on the development of the concept of internationalism: the "proletarian internationalism" advocated by Karl Marx and Friedrich Engels in *The Communist Manifesto* in 1848, the call to the working class to overcome national borders and to carry on the class struggle together, in solidarity and internationally. The theories of the leading politician of the Russian Revolution, Vladimir Ilyich Lenin, were even more influential. Lenin defined imperialist rule as the highest form of capitalism and demanded that it be overcome by a revolution on a global scale. At Lenin's instigation, the organization of the Communist International, which included for the first time anticolonial movements, was founded as early as 1919 to lead this world revolution. In the view of Lenin's closest adviser, the theorist and revolutionary Leon Trotsky, the Russian Revolution had a chance of long-term survival only if it could develop permanently and succeed globally.

It was Trotsky's concept of "permanent revolution" that probably most influenced the Cuban vision of internationalism and international solidarity. This view seemed to have determined the global future of Cuba, intended to lead the revolution of the Tricont against the rich, industrialized countries of the northern hemisphere. Therefore, the solidarity proclaimed by this vision no longer was justified only by a common class situation but rather was based on the assumption of a common opposition to imperialism. A further source of inspiration for the ideological underpinning of this anti-imperialist South-North perspective developed by Castro and Guevara seems to have been the Chinese Revolution led by Mao Zedong. Its large-scale sociocultural experiments and the emphasis on the leading role of peasants in a revolutionary process provided a model for social restructuring in the Tricont countries.[10]

Other fundamental principles of internationalism and international solidarity were—from the Cuban revolutionaries' point of view—anchored in the political culture of the island, particularly the tradition of anti-imperialism that had existed since the struggle for independence. One of the most important agents of Marxist and anti-imperialist traditions in twentieth-century Cuba was the student leader and co-founder of the (first) Cuban Communist Party, Julio Antonio Mella (1903–1929). His radical nationalism and anti-imperialism, in particular his appeal for a "revolution against the dollar," were not only based on European and Russian theories. On the contrary, he was the first to combine anti-imperialist and social revolutionary convictions with the tradition of armed insurrection among the Latin American independence revolutions of the nineteenth century.[11] The convictions of the Cuban revolutionaries of the twentieth century firmly linked internationalism and internationalist solidarity to armed struggle.

For Mella—and for Castro, Guevara, and their fellows, the generation of the revolutionaries of 1959—José Martí (1853–95), the polymath and visionary intellectual leader of the Cuban independence struggle, was the most important inspiration. It was Martí's thought that united nationalism with a vision of a nation that encompassed the whole continent of Latin America, in opposition to the imperial ambitions of the United States, which Martí considered to be the greatest threat to the Latin American continent. As a result of his commitment to Cuban independence "with a pen and a machete," subsequent generations declared him the "apostle," the embodiment of *Cuba libre*, a free and independent Cuba. The Cuban revolutionaries who participated in Castro's M-26-7 consciously took their place in this tradition, calling themselves the "centenary generation," in reference to 1853, the year of Martí's birth. On the basis of Martí's ideas—which were not founded on a Marxist analysis of society—they declared all the "poor" and the "colonized" to be the subjects of the revolution. The Cuban version of internationalism and internationalist solidarity meant, in concrete terms, the fight of the global village against the metropolis. And, with his motto, "the fatherland is humanity," Martí furnished a justification for the calls for international solidarity with friendly movements and governments that emanated from Cuba.[12]

Adopting this point of view, in 1962, Guevara declared the solidarity of the Cuban Revolution with all the repressed peoples of the Earth. From this perspective, he conceived the revolution as part of a global struggle against colonialism, neocolonialism, and imperialism in which "every front was of vital importance":[13] every country that took up the fight against imperialism would be supported by Cuba, stated Guevara. His "message to the peoples of the world" of April 1967 was a call to wage "worldwide war on imperialism" and an appeal for the "creation of a second or third Vietnam in the world."[14] Guevara declared that the issue at stake was nothing less than "the sacred cause of the redemption of humankind."[15]

In the "Second Declaration of Havana," in 1962, Castro called upon the peoples of Latin America to follow the example of Cuba and to organize a revolution. He emphasized that the only acceptable strategy for true revolutionaries was armed struggle in the form of guerrilla movements.[16] Another attempt was Guevara's expedition to the former Belgian Congo, in 1965, the goal of which was the establishment of a revolutionary armed guerrilla front in Africa to fight against imperialism. Although this expedition as a whole was a failure, it was eventually to be the starting point for Cuban military support for the MPLA in the final phase of the colonial war ten years later, an outgrowth of the personal contacts established between Guevara and the Angolan anticolonial guerrilla movement.

The violent overthrow of the democratically elected socialist government of Salvador Allende in Chile in September 1973 put an end to the hopes that revolutions would soon take place in Latin America. This development led the Cuban government to redefine the aims of its foreign policy and of its internationalist solidarity. The resulting change from a policy of mere support for guerrilla and liberation movements to one of strengthening diplomatic relations with progressive, internationally recognized governments did not, however, mean a fundamental renunciation of the principles of internationalism. On the contrary, internationalism was anchored in the new Cuban Constitution of 1976 as the leitmotiv and political strategy of the future foreign policy of Cuba. Proletarian internationalism and militant solidarity formed the ideological basis; wars of national liberation and armed resistance to aggression were legitimized and elevated to principles of foreign policy.

Cuba and Angola: South-South Cooperation and Educational Transfer, 1976–1991

In its initial phase, cooperation with Angola was based on the principles of internationalist solidarity mentioned earlier and was directed toward political and military support of the MPLA. In connection with the reorientation of Cuban foreign policy in the early 1970s, Cuba's engagement in Angola marked another turning point, as the challenges encountered there made it obvious that internationalist solidarity could not consist only of political and military support. In order to stabilize the transformation of Angola, a much more comprehensive, organized, and coordinated civil assistance was required, a kind of "socialist development aid." Angola was indeed the scene of the first large-scale involvement of Cuban civilian development aid workers. Whereas, before 1975, trained civilians (especially doctors) had been sent to friendly Tricont countries only in small groups, in Angola, for the first time, thousands of specialists were employed in organized groups. Their work had a contractual basis, and their composition in terms of expertise was directed to the needs of Angola, ascertained and specified by bilateral contracts and commissions consisting of representatives of the Cuban and Angolan governments and ministries.

The civil cooperation with Angola was established in early 1976, with a time lag of several months after the start of the Cuban military cooperation, initiated at the request of the MPLA in late October 1975 with the dispatch of Cuban elite troops and thousands of reservists. Only the help of this extensive Cuban military force, backed by the financial and military support of the Soviet government, enabled the MPLA to achieve dominance over the rival independence movements of União Nacional para a Independência Total de Angola (National Union for the Total Independence of Angola), known as UNITA, and the Frente Nacional para a Libertação de Angola (National Front for the Liberation of Angola), or FNLA. This backing also made it possible for the MPLA to stop the advance of the South African intervention force. As a result, on November 11, 1975, in the capital city of Luanda, the MPLA, as the only victor, was able to proclaim the independence of Angola and announced the establishment of a socialist people's republic.[17] Nevertheless, the MPLA's triumph remained precarious, as in autumn 1975 it actually controlled little more than Luanda and the oil-producing enclave of Cabinda. In the following decades, the state territory still had to be conquered in political and military terms.

The ensuing postcolonial military conflict came to a provisional end in March 1976, when the common resistance of the Cuban forces and the military units of the MPLA forced the troops of the Zulu Force of the South

African Defence Force (SADF) to retreat toward South Africa.[18] However, the war against UNITA and the South African army did not end with this withdrawal. On the contrary, after the inauguration of Ronald Reagan as president of the United States, in 1981, ushering in a new epoch of firmly anticommunist policy, a further escalation of the war in Angola took place, as the U.S. government supported the apartheid regime in its struggle against the MPLA and provided military support and armaments to UNITA to transform it into an effective bastion against the "communist forces" in Southern Central Africa. However, the conflict in Angola was never determined only by the dynamics of the Cold War. The war between the MPLA and UNITA did not end with the agreed withdrawal of the Cuban forces and the South African army in the summer of 1991 but continued remorselessly and lasted until the death of Jonas Savimbi, the leader of UNITA, in 2002.

Turning back to the Cuban civil cooperation that started in 1976, I will examine now the concepts and considerations that formed the basis of the Cuban civil involvement, as well as its realization. The beginning of the civil cooperation in Angola was part of an overall political and military strategy for the consolidation of the MPLA government after independence, jointly planned with the MPLA. Far-reaching political and ideological accord and a trusting personal relationship between the Cuban and the Angolan political leaders were fundamental to this cooperation. After independence, the MPLA faced the problems of an acute shortage of trained personnel and a lack of know-how in all areas of the Angolan economy, administration, and society. This resulted above all from the fact that the Portuguese colonial government had never handed over state and government power or institutions and that there was no transitional phase between the colonial government and independence in Angola. Moreover, most of the settlers of Portuguese origin, who had performed all the central functions in colonial administration and in the economy, left Angola hurriedly between 1975 and 1976. In addition to the political and military conquest of Angolan territory from internal and external opponents, the MPLA thus also faced the challenge of establishing administrative structures across the country, carrying out measures to modernize the infrastructure, putting in place new education and health systems, and establishing social programs.

Along with support for the health sector and infrastructure development, the field of education was at the center of the Cuban-Angolan cooperation. Already in its declaration of independence, the MPLA government had announced the creation of a scheme of mass education, the establishment of a new school system to guarantee access to education to all Angolans, and a program to promote literacy as top priorities, because 85 percent of the Angolan population was illiterate in 1975.[19] The intention was to create a new, emancipatory education system as a contribution to overcoming the legacy of colonial rule, racism, discrimination, and paternalism in the minds of all Angolans and to educate them as "new men," considered a prerequisite for building a socialist society.[20] After the revolution in 1959, Cuba had faced similar problems to those in Angola: a large number of illiterate citizens and an acute shortage of trained personnel. Through a successful literacy campaign and the establishment of a comprehensive education system, these problems were eradicated in Cuba within a few years. In revolutionary Cuba, literacy and education had also been central elements in the integration of broad sectors of the society into the new revolutionary and national project, serving the government's purposes of politicization and mobilization. From the point of view of the Angolan educators, the transfer of these proven measures in education and education policy seemed especially desirable.[21]

The first measure of support by the Cuban government for the Angolan educational campaign was a pilot project initiated in February 1976 in the enclave of Cabinda. In autumn 1975, Cuban military units were stationed in Cabinda to help the MPLA armed forces to defend themselves against their opponents—and to secure the production of oil, which guaranteed the state income of the MPLA government. Because of the Cuban military support, in February 1976, Cabinda and Luanda were the only areas that were completely controlled by the MPLA and were also the only areas in which public infrastructure, including schools, was functioning. In all other provinces, schools had to remain closed because of the continued fighting.[22]

A group of twelve educators that reported from Cabinda to the Cuban armed forces carried out an appraisal of the educational situation in Angola and performed a small-scale trial of the conditions for implementing a national literacy campaign and a teacher-training program. The experience gained there was made available to the Angolan Ministry of Education (MED) in Luanda with the aim of applying it to the whole of Angola as the next step. Using the Cuban education system as a model, both Cuban and Angolan educators intended to create a framework for the implementation of the new education policy and for establishing educational structures across the country.[23] The pilot project in Cabinda embodied, in essence, the political and military strategy with which the Cuban government intended to continue its support for the MPLA in the future: sending small groups of specialists who, parallel to the military defense of the territory, assisted in establishing a state network of social services, for example in the field of health care and in education.[24] The aim of this operation was to provide "help for self-help," to educate and to train specialists, in order to create Angolan disseminators of knowledge.

The purpose was to enable the MPLA government to remedy Angola's lack of specialists in all fields as soon as possible. From the point of view of the Cuban government, this procedure had also the benefit of keeping the number of civilians engaged in Angola to a minimum.

This was also compatible with the Cuban military strategy, which was to withdraw Cuban troops from Angola as early as March 1976, as the Cuban government was not prepared for a long-term military engagement in Angola, despite friendly relations with the MPLA and the military and financial support of the Soviet Union.[25] When the MPLA government, under its first president, Agostinho Neto, realized the acute danger still presented by internal and external armed opponents in spring 1976, Neto once again turned to the Cuban leaders, requesting continued support for the Angolan military forces and the extension of the civil assistance.[26] The aim was to consolidate the power of the MPLA. This wish went against both plans for military withdrawal and the limitation of civil support to small groups of specialized cadres. Nevertheless, the Cuban government gave its assent and found a quick and pragmatic solution to the problem by calling on the reservists stationed in Angola to remain in the country and to provide reconstruction assistance by using their civilian skills. Approximately one thousand reservists responded immediately to this appeal.[27]

The signing of an extensive Framework Agreement on Economic, Scientific, and Technical Cooperation[28] between the two states in July 1976 legalized the cooperation for civil reconstruction that already existed de facto and created the institutional context for further cooperation. This was the decisive step in transforming what was initially a politically and ideologically motivated internationalist solidarity into a long-term South-South cooperation, a socialist development aid project. On the basis of this agreement, in the following months, several bilateral contracts that defined specific cooperation programs tailored to the needs of Angola were established in various fields. In accordance with the principle of "help for self-help," the agreements in the field of education gave priority to the training of Angolan teachers and the employment of Cuban advisers who helped to organize, structure, and implement the new education policy. For this purpose, Cuban advisers and educators were allocated to different departments of the Angolan Ministry of Education. With the assistance of these advisers, a comprehensive audit of the educational situation in Angola was carried out and used as a base-line measure to orient and guide the development of further cooperation programs.[29] Furthermore, Cuban advisers assisted their Angolan colleagues in implementing the literacy campaign; in creating new teaching curricula, materials, and plans; and in carrying out basic and further training programs for teachers. They also supported an organizational overhaul and restructuring of the national education system. In setting a strategy on matters of teaching, administration, and educational policy, they usually recommended the adoption of structures and content borrowed from the Cuban and the German Democratic educational systems.[30]

The establishment of this new mass education system turned out to be so popular among Angolans that, as early as summer 1977, the cooperation programs agreed upon were insufficient to cope with the elevated numbers of newly registered pupils, which grew to more than one million. The Angolan government therefore turned to the Cuban government once again, this time with a request that it send Cuban teachers for direct support in the classroom. The Cuban government again reacted positively to this request and sent brigades of hundreds of Cuban students, the Destacamento Pedagógico Internacionalista "Che Guevara" (DPI),[31] to work as teachers in Angola, and several hundred more young teachers arrived beginning in early 1978. This measure marked another decisive change in the original scheme of cooperation: the aim of providing "help for self-help" through specific advisers and training programs took a back seat as the cooperation program concentrated on compensating directly for the lack of Angolan teachers and educators by putting in place Cuban teachers who were responsible for maintaining schooling in almost all provinces of Angola. From 1978 to 1991, the focus of Cuban-Angolan educational cooperation was the direct employment of Cuban teachers in Angola.

As a further measure of support for the Angolan education system, in fall 1977, the Cuban government established the first boarding schools on the Cuban Isla de la Juventud (Isle of Youth), where several thousand Angolan students were educated in the following years. The start of the educational cooperation with Angola was the decisive impulse for setting up this international schooling center, which still exists today. Not only students from Angola were (and still are) educated there; the Isla de la Juventud schooling program also included the establishment of nationally based boarding schools for Asian, African, and Latin American students from states friendly to Cuba. In the 1970s and 1980s, the aim of these boarding schools was to supplement students' normal educational formation and their participation in specified qualification programs with revolutionary education intended to transform them into revolutionary cadres. The Isla de la Juventud school center was an important part of the ambitious internationalist solidarity policy of the Cuban government, which enabled it to take a vanguard position within the Tricont states, as this large-scale educational project was extremely suitable for the purposes of self-presentation and propaganda.[32]

The employment of Cuban teachers in Angolan schools increased continually until the 1982–83 school year and reached its peak in mid-1982, when there were two thousand educators in Angola. In 1982, Cubans made up almost 80 percent of all foreign teachers in Angola; the other 20 percent were mainly Portuguese, but there were also Soviet, Bulgarian, East German, and Vietnamese instructors.[33] Most of the Cuban teachers worked in primary and middle schools.[34] Because of the language difference between Spanish and Portuguese, they were assigned only from school year 6 and were used not to teach Portuguese but to offer instruction in mathematics, physics, biology, chemistry, and history, subjects for which Angolan educators regarded the linguistic shortcomings of the Cubans as less serious. The teachers and lecturers were sent to Angola for one or two years. According to Cuban and Angolan statistics, more than ten thousand teachers and lecturers were active in Angola in the period 1976 to 1991 in primary and secondary education, including universities.[35] For Cuban society, the large scale of the whole civil cooperation with Angola from 1977 on represented an enormous challenge, particularly as, in many fields, the specialists requested by Angola (especially teachers and doctors) were not available because of shortcomings in Cuba. The situation came to a head in the late 1970s and early 1980s, when Cuban soldiers and civilian helpers also had to be available for large-scale internationalist programs in Ethiopia and Nicaragua. For this reason, many Cuban students were appointed as teachers in Angola to make up for the shortage of personnel.

This large transatlantic civil cooperation program in Angola required careful organization and meticulous planning. For this reason, the cooperation was accompanied by a process of professionalization and institutionalization of specific structures in both countries. On the Cuban side, this was manifested in the establishment of new state organizations such as the Comité Estatal de Colaboración Económica (CECE), or State Committee for Economic Cooperation, as well as in the founding of specialized state enterprises such as Cubatécnica, which was responsible for the preparation, registration, and sending of specialists to Angola. Corresponding organizations and institutions were created in Angola. Cuba and Angola also established specific bilateral structures and communication mechanisms at the governmental and ministerial levels in both countries for the purposes of planning, coordinating, and implementing the cooperation agreements. From the late 1970s, the Cubans built up an administrative and supply structure for the Cuban civilians engaged in Angola, who worked independently from the Angolan authorities. Here the Cuban organizers of the cooperation program had recourse to the already existing military structures and bases in Angolan territory that had been established to supply food, transport, and medical care and extended them to serve civilians. This demonstrates not only the close connection between civil and military cooperation programs but also the need to protect Cuban civilians from military attacks by the opponents of the MPLA government.

A previously unknown special feature of the cooperation was its funding—at least for the civil part.[36] In the course of my research, I discovered that, in fact, the educational mission was in large part paid for by the Angolan government. Therefore, this cooperation can be characterized as a measure not entirely supported by the often-cited ideal of internationalist solidarity. Although the Cuban government continues to maintain that it "took away only the dead" from Angola,[37] the documents from the Angolan Ministry of Education tell a different story: they show that every Cuban specialist was paid according to his or her personal qualifications.[38] The payments took place on an interstate level—that is, the Angolan government transferred the monthly amount directly to the Cuban government.

This places the Cuban-Angolan cooperation in a completely different light and reveals the economic pragmatism inherent in it. It was thus also a relationship of economic exchange in which the Cuban government both supplied the support requested by the MPLA government and was able to increase its state revenue by "hiring out" its workforce. The fact that the Cuban government received payment from its Angolan counterpart is not reprehensible. After all, Cuba itself was continually struggling with economic and financial difficulties and would therefore not have been able to provide such a comprehensive support free of charge on its own. It would have been remarkable if no compensation had been made for such far-reaching support. However, a certain contradiction comes from the fact that civilian workers themselves hardly benefited from the payments. They received room and board, travel, and a modest salary for the support of their relatives who remained in Cuba, but, during their employment in Angola, they received only a monthly allowance of pocket money, worth the equivalent of approximately ten U.S. dollars, a sum that interviewed participants described as equivalent to one dinner in a restaurant, a pair of movie tickets, or a taxi ride. Interviews with participants in the educational cooperation program reveal that, in addition, these workers were never informed about these payments to the Cuban government and that they are still convinced that the motives of their government were altruistic and based on solidarity.

Because of these payments, the Angolan government had an increased interest in controlling the workings of the cooperation agreement, specifically in ensuring that the services promised were delivered in accordance with the bilateral agreements. Therefore, a complex system of negotiation and control was established, consisting of direct negotiations and agreements between the Angolan Ministry of Education and the Cuban civil administration that had been established to oversee education in Angola.

The Role of Cuban Civilians in the Angolan Educational System

What role did the Cuban civilians play in implementing the educational cooperation agreement in Angola, and how was it realized? The support of Cuban advisers in the Angolan Ministry of Education was essential in the early phase of the educational reform that sought to establish the new education system. The Cuban teachers who were involved from 1978 on in order to overcome the lack of local teachers played a fundamental part in realizing the educational reform at all levels of schooling, including higher education. In particular, Cubans were responsible for introducing and putting into practice new, modern, interactive methods of teaching and learning developed and tested in Cuba. This included elements of socialist education such as the so-called monitor system, in which specific attention was given to especially gifted pupils, and out-of-school learning, which was introduced through aptitude groups that familiarized pupils with future professions according to their talents. Last but not least, Cuban teachers ensured that the obsolete teaching methods of the colonial period were superseded in Angolan schools.

In comparison to the extremely limited number of Angolan teachers as well as all other foreign specialists employed in Angola after the country's independence, Cuban teachers had the advantage of being almost "universally" employable. Cubans who volunteered for work in Angola were committed to unconditional internationalist solidarity and had absolutely no influence over where and under what conditions they were deployed. They were sent where they were needed, to remote provinces or places of military conflict where Angolan teachers did not want to work or to places to which other foreign participants could not be sent because the Angolan state was unable to organize a method of meeting their basic needs there. Instead, the Cuban civil administration structure handled the protection and supplying of the Cuban civilians. In addition, all of the Cubans had undergone basic military training in Cuba and were able to defend themselves and even their pupils in case of emergency.

A further special feature of the Cuban-Angolan educational cooperation was that the civilian specialists worked on behalf of the Angolan MPLA government. In regions and provinces where the Angolan government and state had hardly any presence and where the political and military influence of its opponents was strong, the ideologically trained and politically committed Cuban teachers were the "civilian outposts" of the new government. They thus represented the new state, the new society, and the new system of rule. Through their teaching, usually highly motivated and innovative, they represented a positive symbol of the existence of a government that actually carried out its promise of a progressive education policy. The use of Cuban teachers therefore not only served to implement education reforms but also spread the new national project of the MPLA that aimed at the integration of the whole population.

This policy occasionally culminated in such paradoxical situations as the one that found Cuban teachers, despite their often inadequate knowledge of Portuguese, supporting the MPLA's instruction to accept Portuguese as the national language and to introduce it in Angolan schools.[39] They therefore acted in accordance with the MPLA's policy of assimilation through linguistic homogenization. The Cuban teachers can thus be characterized as agents of political, social, and cultural change that represented the aims of the MPLA both as substance and symbol. As "representatives" of the MPLA government, they assisted in penetrating, controlling, and administering the Angolan territory. Against the background of their own socialization in a nation-state with a functioning infrastructure and administration, as well as a countrywide network of social services, they performed an educational mission that included support for the process of building state and nation in Angola, intensifying and stabilizing the rule of the MPLA.

Set against this backdrop, however, is the sobering assessment of setbacks in building up the Angolan education system that could not be prevented by the presence of large numbers of Cuban teachers. In addition to the escalating political and military conflicts in the southern and central provinces of Angola, which had a drastic effect on the educational system after the 1981–82 school year, the severe shortage of trained Angolan teachers became even more acute. Between 1981 and 1984, 23.6 percent of Angolan teachers abandoned their profession due to low salaries and the lack of future prospects in the profession. As a consequence, students suffered and attendance dropped. The proportion of children of school age who attended school fell from 63.7 percent in 1980 to 37 percent in 1984.[40]

The step-by-step withdrawal of Cuban teachers from 1983 on, the result of the escalating military situation and the offensives of UNITA in cooperation with the South African army, revealed that the involvement and the "universal" availability of the Cubans were also responsible for the inadequate efforts of the Angolan Ministry of Education to train Angolan teachers. In an internal memorandum, the Angolan Ministry of Education gave a self-critical analysis of this situation, concluding that, because of the constant, low-cost, and convenient availability of Cuban teachers, it had become "lax" and had completely neglected to train its own specialists.[41] Not only had the original aim of providing "help for self-help" lost its central importance, but, moreover, the presence of Cuban specialists had in effect allowed the Angolans to avoid taking responsibility for developing their own education system. On the other hand, it was not only the war situation, the destruction of infrastructure, and the lack of communication structures that were to blame for this situation. The ministry itself was responsible for the fact that Angolan teachers continued to be paid very badly after independence, and the ministry's efforts to improve teacher training had largely failed because of the lack of guidelines, coordination, and suitable teaching curricula.[42]

The Cuban government's aims in assisting the MPLA to establish a socialist state by providing support in the field of education (and in all other civil sectors) had clearly not been achieved by the late 1980s. The MPLA government had introduced reforms that moved the country toward a market economy in the mid-1980s, while retaining the centralized and undemocratic state structures of the socialist era, which promoted an increase in corruption. Within the education system, this development led to "excessive centralization in the Ministry of Education" that was responsible for the inefficiency of the school system, according to an internal analysis of problems conducted by the Ministry itself in 1991.[43] A study of the Angolan education system carried out in 1989 by the United Nations Development Program (UNDP) blamed primarily the devastating effects of internal and external wars for having destroyed the basis of the Angolan economy and infrastructure. However, it also directed criticism at the content and implementation of Angola's education policy, which was based "on a completely false assessment of the economic and financial situation of the country."[44]

The "Latin American–African Nation": New Transnational Identities Resulting from Engagement in Angola?

The large-scale involvement of civilians in Angola would have been impossible without the willingness of the Cuban people to show solidarity and support for the internationalist aims of their government through their own personal efforts. Until the beginning of the operation in Angola, the demand for Cubans to take part in internationalist solidarity missions abroad was relatively low. From 1976 on, this changed fundamentally, as not only thousands of soldiers but also civilian helpers were required on very short notice. The Cuban government, and especially its head of state, Fidel Castro, initiated an extensive propaganda campaign in order to legitimize the huge military operation in Angola that began in October 1975 in both the national and the international arenas. Castro invented a shared tradition between Cuba and Angola, and, without further ado, he declared Cuba to be a "Latin American–African nation." He founded his arguments not only on the principles of internationalist solidarity but also, and especially, on the "blood relationship" between Cubans and Africans, attributable to their common colonial past. From this concept he derived antiracist principles that applied to all Cubans and asked them to defend the independence of Angola against attacks by the South African apartheid regime.[45]

Castro referred to the historical fact that more than one-third of the Cuban people were descendants of Africans. He emphasized that, of the ten to fifteen million Africans who are estimated to have reached America alive as a result of the transatlantic slave trade between the sixteenth and the nineteenth centuries, almost one million came to Cuba. The prosperity of the island in the nineteenth century, based on sugar production for the world market, Castro argued, was essentially achieved by African slave labor. Between 1868 and 1898, most of the slaves or their descendants joined the fight for independence against the Spanish colonial empire, not only as soldiers but also as renowned military leaders. Supporting the struggle for independence, they were able to attain their individual freedom. The war of independence held out the prospect of the abolition of slavery and the integration of blacks into a society that had defined itself as exclusively white.[46] In 1886, abolition was achieved but not, however, integration into the postemancipation society, even though the experiences of war had brought about a variety of black-white alliances.[47] For Castro, this extensive participation by slaves of African descent in Cuba's war of independence—and thus the implication of a "common" experience of war against colonialism—was a further justification for the moral duty of all Cubans, regardless of the color of their skin, to support the Angolan independence war as internationalists: every Cuban had the obligation to pay Cuba's historic "debt towards humanity" by means of personal sacrifice.[48]

The purpose of this recruitment strategy was to motivate the population to take part voluntarily, because only people with revolutionary, internationalist convictions were regarded as able to support the building of a socialist Angola. Because the population had to be convinced of the political necessity of this mission, propaganda concentrated on moral appeals to the revolutionary duty of the individual. Agreements made with Angola regarding payment were never publicly mentioned, nor was the fact that the engagement would take place in a war zone. This information was accorded secondary importance, and potential dangers were rarely mentioned. Decisive aspects of this propaganda were the emphasis on internationalist principles and the demands made on the "new man," a concept defined by Che Guevara. In order to be able to push the revolution forward and spread it worldwide, the "subjects of the revolution" had to be actively involved in processes of social transformation. A fundamental aspect of transformation was to educate Cubans to be "new men," obligated not only to participate in revolutionizing their own society but also to transcend borders on the principle of internationalist solidarity. According to the ideas of Guevara, this "new man" was characterized by an inherent, boundless readiness for sacrifice, a revolutionary altruism, and a willingness to undertake the permanent fulfillment of duties in the service of the revolution. The willingness to engage in internationalist work in the name of solidarity and humanitarianism now became a touchstone of individual revolutionary conviction. The "new man" conceived by Guevara was a mythical combination of revolutionary heroism and self-abnegation that Guevara himself embodied, and, after his death, he was elevated by the Castro regime to the status of a symbol of this "new man" that every Cuban should emulate.

The Destacamento Pedagógico Internacionalista "Che Guevara" (DPI), the brigade of students employed as teachers in Angola, represented the clearest link between the myth of Che and the operation in Angola. The purpose of these brigades, as requested by the Angolan government, was to overcome the shortage of trained Angolan teachers. However, to the Cuban government, the program was also a social experiment, an attempt to build a political and pedagogical elite of youth cadres who would be expected to prove their revolutionary commitment on an internationalist mission abroad and, if necessary, to substitute "pencils for weapons."[49] The operation of internationalist solidarity in Angola was intended to give young Cubans a "heroic" experience in order to consolidate their revolutionary convictions.[50] From the government's perspective, the educational mission in Angola was eminently suitable as a nursery for revolutionary cadres: in war-torn and underdeveloped Angola, the achievements of socialist Cuba would shine all the more brightly. For Cubans of African origin, above all, the accomplishments of a socially just, nonracist society would be made clear; the young people would perceive and experience the destructive effect of colonialism, capitalism, and imperialism on the Tricont countries.

On the other hand, the organizers of the student brigades also looked to the symbol of José Martí, the intellectual precursor of the Cuban independence, adopting his phrase "Every person who is born into the world has the right to education, and in return has the duty to contribute to the education of other people"[51] as the motto of the brigades. This statement also contained a moral obligation, one that was connected less to the historic debt evoked by Castro than to the fact that all Cubans, regardless of the color of their skin or their class, had profited from the achievements of the revolution by receiving the opportunity to have a free education. As these benefits were claimed as a matter of course, so was participation in the educational cooperation program in Angola expected as a matter of course: the mission gave this generation the opportunity to pay its "historic debt."

In view of the government propaganda and the official proposal of an identity as part of a "Latin American–African nation," which motivation was decisive for Cubans who volunteered for civilian work in Angola? There exist no studies about their individual reasons and motivations, either in or outside Cuba, but we can now shed light on some of the personal motives behind people's decision to participate in the internationalist solidarity mission in Angola on the basis of the biographical interviews that I have conducted with Cuban participants between 2004 and 2006 in Cuba, the United States, Portugal, and Angola.[52] All publications and films released in Cuba about the Angolan operation have without exception evinced a pronounced propagandistic character. According to these, all Cubans, following the tenets of internationalist solidarity, took part voluntarily and were motivated only by revolutionary beliefs. Doubts about this have been repeatedly expressed outside Cuba, but these were generally politically motivated statements made by critics of the Cuban government who were living in exile.[53]

The focus of the interviews that I carried out was therefore to ask about participants' individual, personal motives for taking part in a mission in an African war zone ten thousand kilometers away from home. My analysis of these interviews has led me to the conclusion that, beyond the official discourse, participants had a great variety of personal motives and expectations for volunteering for service in Angola. Alongside revolutionary and internationalist convictions, as well as a kind of "Che nostalgia," the variety of motives included a sense of duty, humanitarianism, curiosity, desire to travel abroad and for adventure, opportunity to gain freedom from the parental home, professional advancement, and the expectation of material benefits.[54]

Therefore, it can be inferred that, although the Cubans participated in this cooperation program initiated and guided by the policy of the Cuban state, the fact that the participants associated diverse individual motives and interests with their engagement undermined both the political aims and the interpretative authority of their government. Nevertheless, the official political discourse was relevant in all interview situations and was clearly reflected in the answers of the witnesses. Most of the interviewees who lived in Cuba mentioned the principle of internationalist solidarity and the fulfillment of revolutionary obligations as important motives. Castro's propaganda point that Cuba had a "historic debt to humanity" that could be redeemed in Angola also played an important role. Consciousness of being in "debt" and the obligation to repay this debt was, however, not as abstract as in the government propaganda but rather had much more concrete roots in most cases. In contrast to the propaganda, the duty to transmit the education that participants had received themselves after the revolution was perceived in extremely specific and personal terms. The social reforms implemented after the revolution, especially the reforms in education, had made social advancement possible, especially for many women, Cubans of African descent, and members of underprivileged classes. More than half of my interviewees stated that they owed their profession and social status to the educational programs of the revolution. Referring to Martí, they observed that the call to participate in the Angolan mission included the demand that they transmit the privileges of free education and social advancement to the Angolan people.[55] That's why many participants felt they had a duty to get involved in Angola.

Referring to Castro's claim of a "Latin American–African nation," I asked the interviewees whether this proposal of a transnational and transcultural identity had also motivated them to go to Angola. The answers represented a clear break with the official discourse and could not have been more unambiguous: regardless of whether or not my interviewees had African ancestry, the majority of them stated that they had no special personal connection to Africa or Angola. This negative answer was in some case even more vehement on the part of the Afro-Cuban interviewees. Almost no one wished to be identified with Africa and Angola. On the contrary, several interview partners clearly communicated to me that the arguments for a "Latin American–African nation" were, in their opinion, either a pure political fantasy or a skillful propaganda move by the government. Very few interviewees admitted that the search for their own roots on the African continent was one of their motives to go to Angola.

In fact, the question relating to a "Latin American–African" identity brought to light a quite different result: most interviewees admitted that they had actually known nothing at all about Africa when they received the call to join the civil cooperation in Angola. Before they went to Angola, their image of Africa was of a very faraway and alien place. According to their answers, their view of Africa was limited to a very small number of stereotypes—"wilderness," "people with a low level of culture," "jungle," and "wild animals" such as lions, giraffes, and snakes, and even "cannibals." In many cases, "Tarzan" was the most immediate association with Africa. For many responders, their first real or perceived connection to Africa and Angola was the first state visit to Cuba by President Agostinho Neto of Angola in July 1976.

If the search for their own roots in Africa was not a significant motivation for participants to sign up for the cooperation effort in Angola, what impression had the actual experience of staying in Angola made on them? Had it led to stronger identification with Africa and Angola or even a new transnational "Latin American–African" identity? An unambiguous result that emerged from analysis and assessment of the interviews with the "ordinary" Cuban participants in the program with regard to their identification, their self-perceptions, and their perceptions of the "other" was their sense of demarcation from Africa. After their return, most of them identified much more strongly with Cuba and the social achievements of the revolution, and most drew a clear line between Cuba and Angola, which they had perceived as socially and culturally "backward." This result is largely congruent with the findings of other historical, sociological, anthropological, and cultural studies concerned with transcultural encounters carried out in other contexts.[56] According to these findings, descriptions and representations of oneself often arise only after one is confronted with the "other," and encountering difference seems to stimulate a reflection about one's own self and experiences previously taken for granted. For the Cuban participants that I interviewed, their encounter with Angola led to a greater appreciation of what was perceived as their "own" culture, nation, or society.

In the specific case of the cooperation program with Angola, this is unsurprising for two reasons. First, the experience of violence in the war in Angola had a decisive influence on the everyday lives of the civilians during their time in Africa. Participants experienced a wide range of trauma, as well as excessive demands that arose from the work situation, resulting in cultural shock and reinforcing feelings of being alien. This made the social progress attained in Cuba after the revolution appear all the more beneficial. In light of their experiences in Angola, the participants had good reason to show a much greater appreciation of positively viewed aspects of their own society that, they believed, were completely lacking in Angolan society in conditions of war and upheaval. They mentioned, for example, female emancipation, social justice, a high standard of education, and comprehensive medical care. Moreover, the patriotism and the consciousness of national unity they attributed to the Cuban society seemed even more desirable than before as guarantors of peace and progress, in contrast to what they perceived regarding the situation in Angola, where society was seen to be ethnically and culturally fragmented.

Second, the spatial, social, and cultural separation of the Cuban program participants from the Angolan population seemed to have been significant in maintaining their personal distance from what they experienced and perceived about Angola. Partly for security reasons, the Cuban civilians spent the whole duration of their stay in what I refer to as "Cuban enclaves," spaces that were largely isolated from the Angolan population. This was not just a matter of geographically separate residential complexes; these were sociocultural spaces, defined by the Cuban civil administration structure in Angola, that corresponded to the political and social order dominant in Cuba. The resultant diverse mechanisms of inclusion and exclusion between Cubans and Angolans defined not only the status of the program participants within Angolan society but also their own perception of Angolan society, of the Angolans, and of what was perceived to be "Angolan." This continuous and carefully maintained intentional separation between Cubans and Angolans encouraged misunderstandings and feelings of otherness. This seems to be another reason why the two sides largely remained strangers to each other during the sixteen years of transatlantic cooperation.

Demarcation from what was perceived as "Angola" or "Angolan" led to a new definition of the participants' own identity as "Cubans" and to a stronger identification with the social and political achievements of the revolution: "When I arrived in Cuba, I saw them there in their country as Angolans, as Africans, but I felt much more Cuban, more content with my revolution, I was much happier to be here, . . . to find fulfillment here, because we are like that, we love our country."[57] Similar responses were given by almost all my interviewees to the question of whether they had identified more with Angola or with the African continent after their return to Cuba as a consequence of their experiences there. The only exception to this demarcation seemed to have been those Cubans who had decided to stay in Angola and to marry Angolans. During my research, I could not find out whether this was a frequent phenomenon. In Angola, I found only two or three Cubans who had remained, and my impression after interviewing them was that Angola was never considered to be a popular option for "flight" from Cuba.

The "fraternization" between Cubans and Angolans that was repeatedly described in official propaganda could not and did not take place. Cuban-Angolan cooperation did not lead to the emergence of a collective transatlantic "Latin American–African" identity. Therefore, there are grounds for the assumption that the development among the Cuban participants of a stronger identification with their Angolan counterparts was not merely desired by the government but that its absence seems to have been an instructive side effect intended to raise acceptance of the Cuban system through this experience of strong sociocultural contrasts. This raises the question of whether the foreign-policy image of Cuba as a "Latin American–African nation," enhanced though the cooperation with Angola, was nothing more than a symbolic "exported identity" to demonstrate the identification of the Cuban government with the liberation struggles of nonwhite populations around the globe. This opinion was asserted by both the exiled Cuban historian Alejandro de la Fuente and the social scientist Frank Taylor in their works on "race" and "national identity" in twentieth-century Cuba.[58] My own research demonstrates that a satisfactory and differentiated discussion of this question requires further empirical social-scientific and anthropological investigation into identity and phenomena of perception and belonging in contemporary Cuban society. The transnational and transatlantic experiences of hundreds of thousands of Cubans through internationalist solidarity cooperation efforts like that in Angola probably led to phenomena of social and cultural change, for example in the fields of religion and music, which possibly contributed to the construction of transatlantic identities. However, as of now there exists no profound examination able to allow more specific conclusions on this subject.

The findings of my investigations, by contrast, are much more clear-cut. Their experience in Angola influenced former participants to feel more "solidarity" as a result of their personal involvement in Africa and the sacrifices they had made. The mission in Angola lasted more than a decade and a half and involved the direct participation of about 10 percent of the Cuban population (the whole population was involved indirectly, as almost every Cuban had a family member or friend who was in Angola). This seems to have had, according to the statements made by my interview partners, an effect on Cubans' self-perceptions as members of a society characterized by the principles of solidarity and willing to commit themselves to support social improvement beyond national borders. In particular, the difficult circumstances under which most civilian participants had worked in Angola seemed to have strengthened this feeling of having lived "true solidarity" as well as having contributed to the improvement of the situation in Angola and having given proof of their own personal humanitarianism. At this point in the interview, my interview partners referred less to the official discourse of their government than to their personal sacrifices and the sacrifices that all the participants in the Angola mission had made. They also referred to the fallen soldiers and those civilians who had been killed in Angola, a total of 2,016 persons, according to official figures; the long separation from their families, from which all participants suffered; the often extremely difficult work situation with which they had to cope; and their selflessness. From their personal perspective, this sacrifice was justified, as, ultimately, they were in fact the ones who actually fulfilled the altruistic ideal of internationalist solidarity emphasized by the Cuban government, for which they received almost no reward.

Conclusion

A balance of the results of the cooperation program between Cuba and Angola to establish a postcolonial education system in Angola is necessarily ambiguous. On the one hand, the energetic support of Cuban participants made it possible to lay the foundations for a new national education system and the establishment of a nationwide network of educational institutions. However, the power struggle for and the conflict over material and ideal aims between the MPLA and UNITA, which continued with undiminished severity after the withdrawal of the Cubans until 2002, was a considerable handicap to all educational activities after 1991. In the face of the renewed outbreak of civil war, which forced millions of Angolans to flee and claimed the lives of hundreds of thousands, the modest progress that had been achieved by that time by the Cuban-Angolan cooperation was largely canceled out. On the other hand, Cuba's support of the Angolan education reform was an instrument in the Angolan government's effort to retain power, as the transfer of central elements of the Cuban education system ultimately supported the authoritarian and centralizing tendencies in the Angolan government apparatus, which gained strength after 1991. Here the Cuban teachers and educators played an ambivalent role: on one hand they were transcultural agents of innovative methods of teaching and learning; on the other hand they were also agents of a system of transfer between Cuba and Angola that contributed to the permanent consolidation of the rule of the MPLA government beyond the socialist period.

The specific experience of the cooperation with Angola imposed clear limits on the goal of internationalist solidarity. The original, purely political and military aims of the program purported to strengthen progressive governments and movements in the global struggle against the dominance of the industrialized countries of the Western hemisphere. The Cuban mission neither led to the establishment of a socialist society in Angola nor was successful in ending the internal armed conflict. However, the experiences of organizing a large-scale civilian aid cooperation, both personal and institutional, led to a professionalization and reorientation of all Cuban civil missions undertaken after 1991. From the 1990s on, Cuban civil missions were no longer guided by revolutionary aims but had only humanitarian goals. The professionalization especially proved its worth after 1990, when civilian aid missions provided by Cuban specialists in zones of crisis and catastrophe, now separated from ideological premises, became an important source of income for the state. After the end of the Cold War and the breakup of the Soviet Union, Russia's financial and economic subsidies, which were vital to the Cuban economy, were terminated, precipitating a long-lasting economic crisis for Cuba from which the country is only slowly recovering. Cuban civil aid workers received at least 10 percent of the revenue obtained for their involvement; the remaining income still goes to the state. This opportunity to earn additional income through civil aid programs abroad helped many Cuban families to survive the crisis that began in 1990 with the end of Soviet support.

The civil cooperation ventures operated by the Cuban government were and continue to be extremely successful thanks to their long experience and professional organization, which grew out of the experience in Angola. Their success is also based on the outstanding reputation the Cuban civil aid workers enjoy worldwide thanks to their wealth of experience, their professional qualifications, and their demonstrated commitment. Today they are in high demand and are employed by international development organizations such as UNESCO and WHO. Cuban civil cooperation projects abroad have therefore become an essential component of Cuba's international prestige—especially in Latin America and Africa. Cuba is regarded as a Third World nation that demonstrates solidarity and is willing to support other countries, despite its own developmental shortcomings.

Notes

This article is based on some of the findings of my second book, *Kubaner in Angola: Süd-Süd-Kooperation und Bildungstransfer 1976–1991* (Munich: Oldenburg Verlag, 2012). The project was carried out through numerous periods of field and archival research in Cuba, Angola, Portugal, and the United States between 2004 and 2006, all thanks to the support of a research grant from the Deutsche Forschungsgemeinschaft (German Research Council). Sources and information consisted not only of extensive archival material, particularly from Angolan archives, but also of 139 interviews with Cuban and Angolan witnesses. With the exception of interviews with persons in public life, the witnesses are made anonymous in the notes that follow by the use of only initials, rather than full names. The archival materials and ministry files from the Cuban Ministry of Education (MINED) and the Angolan Ministry of Education (MED) are not classified and are given with their full title for the purposes of unambiguous identification.

1. The extremely complex political and social situation of Angola before and after independence cannot be discussed in detail within the framework of this article. I therefore refer to several seminal historical, political, and social science studies that are concerned with various aspects of the process of decolonization, e.g., Patrick Chabal and Nuno Vidal, eds., *Angola: The Weight of History* (London: Hurst, 2007); Christine Messiant, *L'Angola postcolonial*, vol. 1, *Guerre et paix sans democratization* (Paris: Éditions Karthala, 2008); Christine Messiant, *L'Angola postcolonial*, vol. 2, *Sociologie politique d' une oléocratie* (Paris: Éditions Karthala, 2008); and David Birmingham, *Frontline Nationalism in Angola and Mozambique* (New York: Oxford University Press, 1992).

2. Marjorie Woodford Bray and Donald Bray, "Cuba, the Soviet Union and Third

World Struggle," in *Cuba: Twenty-Five Years of Revolution, 1959–1984*, ed. Sandor Halebsky and John M. Kirk (New York: Praeger, 1985), 352.

3. Louis Pérez Jr., *Cuba: Between Reform and Revolution* (New York: Oxford University Press, 1988), 375.

4. William M. LeoGrande, *Cuba's Policy in Africa, 1959–1980*, Policy Papers in International Affairs 13 (Berkeley: Institute of International Studies, University of California, 1980) 4–5.

5. Armando Entralgo et al., "Notas sobre la política exterior de Cuba en África" (unpublished working paper of the Centro de Estudios de Africa y Medio Oriente [CEAMO], Havana, March 1986), 10.

6. Piero Gleijeses, Jorge Risquet, and Fernando Remírez, eds., *Cuba y África: Historia común de lucha y sangre* (Havana: Editorial de Ciencias Sociales, 2007), 107; Piero Gleijeses, *Conflicting Missions: Havana, Washington, and Africa, 1959–1976* (Chapel Hill: University of North Carolina Press, 2002), 35–38.

7. Ernesto Che Guevara, *Ausgewählte Werke in Einzelausgaben*, vol. 6, *Der neue Mensch: Entwürfe für das Leben in der Zukunft*, 4th ed., ed. and trans. Horst-Eckart Gross (Bonn: Pahl-Rugenstein Nachfolger Verlag, 2003), 218.

8. Nelson Valdés, "Revolutionary Solidarity in Angola," in *Cuba in the World*, ed. Cole Blasier and Carmelo Mesa-Lago (Pittsburgh: University of Pittsburgh Press, 1979), 89.

9. Olga Nazario and Juan Benemelis, "Cuba's Relations with Africa: An Overview," in *Cuban Internationalism in Sub-Saharan Africa*, ed. Sergio Díaz-Briquets (Pittsburgh: Duquesne University Press, 1989), 13.

10. The parallels between the Cuban and Chinese Revolutions have not yet been studied thoroughly. Patrick Manning and Yinghong Cheng, "Revolution on Education: China and Cuba in Global Context, 1957–1976," *Journal of World History* 14.3 (2003): 359–91, undertook an effort to compare several phenomena and developments in the field of education in the two countries.

11. Christine Hatzky, *Julio Antonio Mella: Una biografía* (Santiago de Cuba: Editorial Oriente, 2008).

12. Limbania Jiménez Rodríguez, *Mujeres sin fronteras* (Havana: Editora Política, 2008), 12.

13. Guevara, *Der neue Mensch*, 152.

14. Ibid., 225.

15. Ibid., 228.

16. Ibid., 126–27.

17. The best and most detailed accounts to date of these first months of the Cuban military intervention in Angola are provided by Gleijeses, *Conflicting Missions*, and Edward George, *The Cuban Intervention in Angola, 1965–1991: From Che Guevara to Cuito Cuanavale* (London: Frank Cass, 2005), 60–94. For a Cuban perspective, see Marina Rey Cabrera, *La Guerra de Angola* (Havana: Editora Política, 1989).

18. The military units of the MPLA were called the Forças Armadas Populares para a Libertação de Angola (People's Armed Forces for the Liberation of Angola), or FAPLA.

19. Ministério da Informação, Angola, 11 de Novembre de 1975, Documentos da Independência, Edição do Ministério da Informação, Luanda (Ministry of Information, Angola, November 11, 1975, Documents of Independence, Edition of the Ministry of Information, Luanda), 15.

20. The aims of the education reform were given in 1977 in an MPLA statement of basic principles, "Princípios de base para a reformulação do sistema de educação e ensino na R.P.A." ("Basic Principles of the Reformulation of the Education System of the RPA [People's Republic of Angola]"), Luanda, 1978.

21. Interview, Angola 2006, No. 7, Luanda, January 27 and March 17, 2006 (Artur Pestana). Artur Carlos Maurício Pestana dos Santos ("Pepetela") is one of the leading contemporary Angolan writers. As deputy minister of education in Angola between 1977 and 1981 he was one of the architects of the education system. He implemented the new countrywide education policy along with the minister of education, Ambrôsio Lukoki. Pestana, who was born in 1941 in the Angolan coastal town of Benguela, has Portuguese and Brazilian ancestry. After completing his studies in sociology in Algiers, he joined the anticolonial struggle of the MPLA. In addition to his work as an author under the pseudonym "Pepetela," until the mid-1990s he taught sociology at the Agostinho Neto University in Luanda. After resigning from his office as deputy minister of education, he retired from active politics.

22. Interview, Angola 2006, No. 8, Luanda, February 1, 2006 (J. Z.).

23. This account of the beginning of educational cooperation is essentially based on the consistent testimony of participants in the pilot project and on a number of internal written records: interview, Angola 2006, No. 8, Luanda, February 1, 2006 (J. Z.); interview, Cuba 2006, No. 11, Havana, June 16, 2006 (S. L.); interview, Cuba 2006, No. 8, Havana, June 10, 2006 (R. P. F.); interview, Cuba 2006, No. 4, Havana, May 25 and 31, 2006 (L. N. J. R.); see also Cuban Ministry of Education (MINED), Memorias del Trabajo de la Colaboración Cubana en la República Popular de Angola 1976–1978 (Memories of the Cuban Cooperation in the People's Republic of Angola), MED Archive, 2–5.

24. Interview, Cuba 2006, No. 8, Havana, June 10, 2006 (R. P. F.).

25. For more details on this, see Jorge Risquet Valdés, "Prólogo a la Edición Cubana," in *Misiones en conflicto: La Habana, Washington y África; 1959–1976*, ed. Piero Gleijeses (Havana: Editorial de Ciencias Sociales, 2004), vii–lv, 513–15; Edward George, *The Cuban Intervention in Angola, 1965–1991* (London: Frank Cass, 2005), 105–7.

26. Risquet Valdés, "Prólogo a la Edición Cubana," xviii–xviv; Mabeko Tali and Jean Michel, *Dissidências e poder de estado: O MPLA perante si próprio (1962–1977)*, vol. 2, *1974–1977* (Luanda: Editorial Nzila, 2001), 2:232–33.

27. Risquet Valdés, "Prólogo a la Edición Cubana," xix.

28. *Jornal de Angola*, July 31, 1976, 2; *Bohemia*, no. 32, August 6, 1976, 55–56.

29. Acordo especial de Colaboração entre o Ministério da Educação da República Popular de Angola e o Ministério da Educação dar República de Cuba (Special Agreement of Cooperation between the Ministry of Education of the Peoples' Republic of Angola and the Ministry of Education of the Republic of Cuba), signed in Havana,

December 5, 1976, MED Archive; and Acordo especial de Colaboração entre o Ministério da Educação da República Popular de Angola e o Ministério da Educação Superior da República de Cuba (Special Agreement of Cooperation between the Ministry of Education of the People's Republic of Angola and the Ministry of Higher Education of the Republic of Cuba), signed in Havana, December 6, 1976, MED Archive.

30. MINED, Memorias del Trabajo de la Colaboración Cubana en la República Popular de Angola 1976–1978, MED Archive, 3–5.

31. Between 1978 and 1986, a total of 2,026 Cuban trainee teachers, most of whom were between seventeen and twenty-one years of age, were sent to Angola with these brigades. See Lidia Turner Martí et al., *Breve historia de un destacamento* (Havana: Editorial Pueblo y Educación, 1996), 30.

32. The great social experiment on the Isle of Youth comprised at times up to thirty-four national education centers for more than ten thousand students. The program of scholarships continued after 1991 and still exists today. According to information supplied by the Cuban Ministry for Higher Education (MES), in the years up to 2004, more than forty thousand students gained a school or higher educational qualification on the Isle of Youth or at other Cuban higher education institutions. According to this information, thirty thousand of them came from sub-Saharan Africa; of these, eight thousand were from Angola. All figures on foreign participants in the programs cannot be verified, but they can be taken as guideline figures to show the scale of the program. See Jiménez Rodríguez, *Mujeres sin fronteras*; Juan Colina la Rosa et al., "Estudiantes extranjeros en la Isla de la Juventud (1977–1996)" (unpublished manuscript, Ministerio para la Inversión Extranjera y la Colaboración Económica, Havana, 2004), 8–11; see also Hauke Dorsch, "Übergangsritus in Übersee? Zum Aufenthalt mosambikanischer Schüler and Studenten in Kuba," *Afrika Spectrum* 43 (February 2008): 225–44.

33. RPA, Secretaria do Estado da Cooperação, Comissão de avaliação da cooperação ao Cda. Ministro da Educação, Luanda, Circular No. 1/CACI/SEC/Maio de 1982, Assunto: Avaliação da cooperação (People's Republic of Angola, State Secretary of Cooperation, Commission of Evaluation of the Cooperation to the Ministry of Education, Luanda, Circular, May 1982, Affair: Evaluation of Cooperation), MED Archive.

34. RPA, MED/GICI/GII, Evaluação das cinco nacionalidades e categoría com a maior expressão (People's Republic of Angola, Ministry of Education, Department of International Cooperation, Evaluation of the Five Nationalities and Categories with Largest Representation), ca. 1985, MED Archive.

35. See Angel García Pérez Castañeda, "El internacionalismo de Cuba en la colaboración económica y científico-técnica: Esbozo histórico de un cuarto de siglo de la Revolución Socialista Cubana 1963–1988" (unpublished manuscript, Instituto de Historia de Cuba, Havana, n.d.), 242; Jiménez Rodríguez, *Mujeres sin fronteras*, 96. It is difficult to present exact data, as there is little detailed information available from Cuban authorities and the figures at my disposal were not always consistent. Nevertheless, I had access to enough statistical material from both the Cuban and the Angolan sides to be able to make relatively reliable statements. The available information makes

it clear that the cooperation with Angola was the biggest civil operation in the history of Cuba until 1991 and that cooperation in the field of education was the most important in quantitative terms.

36. To date, there is proof of this payment only for the cooperative effort in education, but the Angolan government probably also paid for all other areas of civil work. All the evidence available so far suggests that the Angolan government's payments for cooperation in education began in 1977 at the latest and continued until the withdrawal of the Cubans in 1991. This arrangement was agreed to in 1977 in a separate contract with the Cuban government; see Acordo especial sobre as Condições Gerais para a realização da Colaboração económica e científico-técnica entre o Governo da República Popular de Angola e o Governo da República de Cuba (Special Agreement of the General Conditions for the Realization of the Economic and Scientific-Technical Cooperation of the Government of the People's Republic of Angola and the Government of the Republic of Cuba), Luanda, November 5, 1977, MED Archive.

37. "Aniversario de la Misión Militar Cubana en Angola: Discurso pronunciado por el Comandante en Jefe Fidel Castro Ruz, en el acto conmemorativo por el aniversario 30 de la Misión Militar cubana en Angola y el aniversario 49 del desembarco del Granma, el 2 de diciembre de 2005," *Granma*, December 3, 2005, 1.

38. All the evidence available so far suggests that teachers were paid between US$860 and $960 per month, advisers US$1,100, and university lecturers up to US$1,140. In 1983, the monthly costs for the Cuban education mission amounted to US$1,355,836. See RPA, MED, GICI/GII ao Gabinete do Plano do MED, Confidencial, Oficial Circular No. 013/ GII/171/I/1983, Cálculo de custos de Força de Trabalho Estrangeira e incremento previsto para 1983/1984, Luanda aos 27 de Março 1983 (People's Republic of Angola, Ministry of Education, Department of International Cooperation to Cabinet of Planning, Confidential, Official Circular No. 013/GII/171/I/1983, Calculation of Costs of the Foreign Workforce and the Expected Increase in 1983/84, Luanda, March 27, 1983), 2, MED Archive.

39. The statement of principles of the new educational system (MPLA, "Princípios de base") mentioned the linguistic and cultural diversity of Angola only in connection with the backwardness of the country. The various African ethnic groups of Angola, which are generally divided into the larger groups of the Bakongo, Mbundu, Ovimbundu, Lunda-Kioko, Nhaneka, Ambó, Ngangela, and Herero, with their differing regional and local Bantu and Khoisan languages, were not taken into account in national education policy until the mid-1990s.

40. RPA, MED, Gabinete de Estudo para o Diagnóstico, Relatório de balanço do trabalho realizado pelo grupo de prognóstico do Ministério da Educação da República Popular de Angola do mês de Março ao mês de Junho de 1986 (People's Republic of Angola, Ministry of Education, Cabinet for the Study of Diagnosis, Budget Report of the Prognostic Group of the Ministry of Education of the RPA between March and June 1986), 5–6, 35–36, MED Archive.

41. RPA, MED, GICI/GII, Memorandum, Problemática da retirada da cooperação Cubana da RPA, Luanda aos 15 de Agosto de 1990 (People's Republic of Angola, Minis-

try of Education, Department of International Cooperation, Memorandum, Problem of the Withdrawal of the Cuban Cooperation in the RPA, Luanda, August 15, 1990), 1, MED Archive.

42. RPA, MED, Direcção Nacional do Ensino Médio e Pré-universitário, Relatório sobre a situação do Ensino Médio na R.P.A.—Período 1978–1982 (People's Republic of Angola, Ministry of Education, National Direction of Secondary and Higher Education: Report on the Situation of Secondary Education in the RPA, 1978–1982), 3–4, MED Archive.

43. RPA, MED, Mesa redonda sobre educação para todos (People's Republic of Angola, Ministry of Education, Round Table for Education for All), 1991, 1–2, MED Archive.

44. Programmea das Nações Unidas para o Desenvolvimento, Programmea dos voluntários das Nações Unidas, Projecto do Governo da República Popular de Angola (UNDP, Voluntary Program of the UN, Project of the Government of the People's Republic of Angola), 1989, 3, MED Archive.

45. Fidel Castro, *Discursos*, vol. 3 (Havana: Editorial de Ciencias Sociales, 1979), 149.

46. Ada Ferrer, *Insurgent Cuba: Race, Nation and Revolution, 1868–1898* (Chapel Hill: University of North Carolina Press, 1999).

47. Aline Helg, *Our Rightful Share: The Afro-Cuban Struggle for Equality, 1986–1912* (Chapel Hill: University of North Carolina Press, 1995).

48. Castro, *Discursos*, 3:238.

49. See Turner Martí, *Breve historia de un destacamento*, 3. See also Bárbara Elena Toledo Amador, "Concurso 'Angola en la memoria,' Una misión internacionalista en la República Popular de Angola con el nombre 'Che Guevara'" ("Competition 'Angola in Memory,' an Internationalist Mission in the People's Republic of Angola named 'Che Guevara'"), Guantánamo, 2002 (DPI 1, Lubango 1978–1979), archive of Casa de Angola, Havana, 13.

50. Interview, Cuba 2006, No. 14, Havana, September 21, 2006 (José Ramón Fernández, Cuban Minister of Education, 1970–90).

51. José Martí, *Obras Completas*, vol. 19 (Havana: Editorial de Ciencias Sociales, 1975), 375, cited in MINED, UJC, FEU, Destacamento Pedagógico Internacionalista "Che Guevara," Documento de Base (Ministry of Education [Cuba], Union of Young Communists [UJC], Federation of University Students [FEU], Internationalist Brigades of Students of Educational Theory "Che Guevara"), October 1977, 1, MINED Archive.

52. Ninety-five interviews with a total of 106 Cuban participants focused on the participants' biographies. Most of them were "ordinary" participants, a category in which I include Cubans who simply carried out their normal professions as teachers, university professors, doctors, technicians, engineers, construction workers, or embassy employees in Angola (eighty interviews with ninety-one persons). Among them were twelve persons who had also participated in military operations, either as soldiers or as reservists or in both a civil and a military role. The remaining interview partners were "experts," organizers, planners, or persons with political responsibility for the cooperative program.

53. Especially after the flight to Miami, in 1987, of Rafael del Pino, a Cuban general in Angola, and his public criticisms of the military operation, this became a public issue among Cuban exiles. But to date there exist no serious studies that could provide evidence for a forcible recruitment of Cuban civilians. In an essay published in 1989, Juan M. del Aguila, a Cuban social scientist in exile in the United States, made a tentative effort in this regard but was not able to furnish proof; see Juan M. del Aguila, "The Domestic Attitude toward Internationalism: Evidence from Emigré Interviews," in *Cuban Internationalism in Sub-Saharan Africa*, ed. Sergio Díaz-Briquets (Pittsburgh: Duquesne University Press, 1989), 140.

54. The interviews showed that the opportunity of working in Angola (and abroad in general) always aroused hopes of acquiring consumer goods that were scarce in Cuba in the 1970s and 1980s: electrical, kitchen, and household devices, transistor radios, cassette recorders, clothing, shoes, and toys.

55. Interview, Cuba 2006, No. 4, Havana, May 25 and 31, 2006 (L. N. J. R.).

56. For a survey of the state of research and the different approaches to researching intercultural communication, cultural transfers, and perceptions of otherness, see Hans-Jürgen Lüsebrink, *Interkulturelle Kommunikation: Interaktion, Fremdwahrnehmung, Kulturtransfer* (Stuttgart: J. B. Metzler, 2008); from a historical and non-European perspective, see also Jörg Baberowski, Hartmut Kaelble, and Jürgen Schriever, eds., *Selbstbilder und Fremdbilder: Repräsentation sozialer Ordnungen im Wandel* (Frankfurt: Campus Verlag, 2008).

57. Interview, Cuba 2004, No. 24, Santiago de Cuba, November 12, 2004 (I. C. M.).

58. Alejandro de la Fuente, *A Nation for All: Race, Inequality and Politics in Twentieth-Century Cuba* (Chapel Hill: University of North Carolina Press, 2001), 296; Frank Taylor, "Revolution, Race, and Some Aspects of Foreign Policy in Cuba since 1959," *Cuban Studies* 18 (1988): 19–41.

Part III

The Influence of Transnational Solidarity on Postnational Responsibilities

7

"As the World Is My Witness"

Transnational Chilean Solidarity and Popular Culture

BRENDA ELSEY

On November 21, 1973, the Chilean football (soccer) team lined up in the National Stadium without an opponent. Militarized police guarded the stands as the captain Francisco Valdés kicked the ball into an open net. That "goal" qualified Chile for the 1974 World Cup in West Germany. Their scheduled opponent, the Soviet Union, had refused to play in the stadium because of its use by the military junta as a torture and detention center. Two months earlier, on September 11, 1973, the armed forces had carried out a coup against the democratically elected government of Chile's Socialist president, Salvador Allende. The military junta that came to power, led by General Augusto Pinochet, launched a massive campaign of repression against supporters of Allende's government, including unionists, student leaders, and leftist political-party members. The Soviets' refusal to play cost them an opportunity to compete in the 1974 World Cup and allowed Chile to qualify. It was the first boycott of the World Cup in protest of human rights violations, though not the first time that an international sporting event would be used to channel global censure of a nation-state's domestic affairs.

The controversy surrounding the Chilean national football team highlights the critical role of popular culture in the struggle between the regime of Augusto Pinochet and its opponents.

A transnational solidarity movement emerged from the relationships among exile communities, international organizations, and opposition groups in Chile.[1] Even before the military coup of 1973, solidarity organizations had formed outside Chile in support of Allende's Popular Unity government.[2] For left-leaning activists, the election of a Socialist government was an exciting prospect. Following the coup, they founded hundreds of organizations, some in likely places such as Mexico and Sweden and others in less predictable places such as Egypt. Membership in these groups was remarkably varied and included exiles, student associations, leftist political parties, labor unions, peace groups, and religious congregations. Solidarity activists wrote petitions, placed refugees, raised funds, organized protests, and created news bulletins. By the 1980s, many solidarity groups had made an uneven transition from a Marxist, anti-imperialist agenda to a human rights platform based on universal respect for the dignity of the individual.[3] As a guiding ideology, human rights offered activists a powerful challenge to Cold War polarities. Moreover, this new platform appealed to those who sought to expand their work beyond national boundaries. Human rights bridged activists from divergent political traditions, largely in Europe and North America, including labor unions, Amnesty International, the Catholic Church, and the United Nations Commission for Refugees.[4] Frequently, these groups were more conservative than were supporters of the Popular Unity that founded solidarity groups. Yet, they found common ground in denouncing the military junta's use of torture, disappearances, and illegal detentions. Under the umbrella of human rights, different political positions came to represent different specializations within the movement, creating a de facto division of labor.[5]

Through the lens of popular culture, this chapter explores struggles between the Pinochet regime and solidarity activists outside Chile. Over the course of seventeen years, the momentum of the solidarity movement abroad fluctuated and frequently corresponded with the opposition in Chile. The durability of the dictatorship and Augusto Pinochet's personal concentration of power make it possible to study the solidarity movement over a significant time period. That the coup forced a government into exile meant the solidarity movement counted on a well-connected leadership in its earliest stages. Scholarly research that treats human rights in Chile tends to focus on formal institutions, memory, and personal narrative. Although less studied, cultural practices are powerful vehicles for the construction of political subjects, especially when traditional means of communication were censored. This chapter examines four emblematic moments to understand the relationship between popular culture and the transnational solidarity movement and its change over time. First, the chapter analyzes the 1974 World Cup in West Germany. It then moves on to the production of *arpilleras*, or appliquéd tapestries, from approximately 1979 to 1981. Next, it evaluates cultural committees and the subversive music magazine *La Bicicleta* during the mid-1980s. Finally, the focus shifts to the 1987 Miss Universe pageant.[6] In the last instance, the chapter chronicles the Pinochet regime's efforts to co-opt feminism, discredit the opposition, and promote neoliberal economic policies through an international spectacle.

Defining popular culture is difficult given that its social meanings shift radically over time and space. Raymond Williams famously identified "culture" and its subcategory "popular culture" among the most difficult concepts to define in the English language.[7] In the cases examined here, "popular culture" is treated as a set of expressive practices that reaches a wide audience. Thinking of culture as practice helps to clarify culture as something active that one does (rather than what one is or has). While popular culture is shaped by prevailing social structures, these practices rarely reflect, like a mirror, the society from which they emerge. Although there are not fixed delineations between "popular" and "high" culture, the former has fewer obstacles to participation and less status than the latter. While one may assume that cultural expressions are charged with political significance, scholars face a difficult task in analyzing the nature of that significance and the process through which it occurs. This endeavor has become even more challenging as popular culture transgresses borders quickly and often, especially as commodities, and takes on local meanings unintended by its "authors."

This chapter argues that popular culture and the solidarity movement intersected in four important ways. First, popular culture facilitated dialogue among activists, connecting people in disparate locations and from divergent class, language, and political backgrounds. The dictatorship also sought to harness popular culture; thus, it became a place for the opposition to confront the claims of Pinochet's regime. Second, popular culture offered an opportunity for solidarity activists to reach people not engaged with politics or unaware of what was transpiring in Chile. Cultural symbols were essential to fostering feelings of shared history that went beyond sympathy among activists divided by language, social class, generation, and ethnicity. A central part of solidarity work lies in the creation of symbols that can motivate a broad public. As the historian William Sewell has noted:

[Members of a semiotic community] need not agree in their moral or emotional evaluations of given symbols. The semiotic field they share may be recognized and used by groups and individuals locked in fierce enmity rather than bound by solidarity, or by people who feel relative indifference toward each other. The posited existence of cultural coherence says nothing about whether semiotic fields are big or small, shallow or deep, encompassing or specialized. It implies only that if meaning is to exist at all, there must be systematic relations among signs and a group of people who recognize those relations.[8]

In this way, activists found themselves in a struggle with supporters of the Pinochet regime to define the same cultural symbols and venues.

Third, popular culture became a subject of struggle between Pinochet and solidarity activists. By this I mean that activists fought against the inculcation of values promoted by the regime through interventions in culture, including consumerism, European development models, and traditional religious ideals of family and sex, which they saw as creating a cultural disposition toward authoritarianism. Finally, popular culture served as a creative space for activists to promote new political agendas, such as women's rights, within the solidarity movement, agendas that they found difficult to integrate into established institutions, such as the Chilean Socialist Party (in exile).

For at least twenty years, transnational methodologies and theories of globalization have been at the forefront of historical research agendas. Yet, for most scholars, the national context has remained the center of their analyses.[9] The subjects of transnational history have challenged traditional modes of documentation, such as government archives. In the context of the Cold War, scholars increasingly felt obligated to transcend national borders to understand power relations.[10] The mobility of global capital, geopolitical objectives of nation-states, and improved communications technology altered the scope of political subjectivity. The Chilean coup coincided with a historical moment in which international nongovernmental organizations were growing exponentially, partly a response to the heightened power of multinational corporations in the 1970s. Thomas Bender, among others, has pointed to the ways in which a consideration of these transnational activist networks changes our view of the Cold War period, from one of major power conflict to a more nuanced view of the impact of globalization and cultural flows on political history.[11] Although formal centers of power, such as the state, achieved control over important communication channels, such as television, the exchange and production of cultural materials was more difficult to control than ever. With new technology, cassette tapes, print media, and video became cheaper to produce and easier to transport across borders. Ultimately, solidarity activists seized these opportunities to challenge the dictatorship's narrative of success.

Sports and Early Solidarity

The history of Chile's participation in the 1974 World Cup match sheds light on the early stages of solidarity activity. The Soviet team's refusal to play in the Chilean National Stadium, described in the opening of this chapter, cost them the chance to compete in the World Cup tournament of 1974.[12] Initially, the Soviet delegation requested that the match be moved to another stadium, but the Chilean Football Federation refused. During weeks of deliberation over whether the match would take place, Pinochet accused the Soviet Union of using "mental tricks" to defeat the Chilean team. The Chilean sports magazine *Estadio* agreed that the Soviet Union's moral objection was a façade for "psychological warfare."[13] Few supported the Soviet boycott of Chile's National Stadium. The *Times* of London called the Soviet Union's protest "a painful abscess."[14] In part, skepticism of the Soviet Union's humanitarian goals influenced the public reaction. Furthermore, the lack of support from members of the Fédération Internationale de Football Association (FIFA) indicated that they viewed the military government as legitimate. Finally, and most important, it reflected the belief, shared by journalists, players, and fans, that football should remain "apolitical." At the request of the Soviets, FIFA sent representatives to investigate allegations of torture in the stadium. They reported that "inside the outer fencing everything appears to be normal and gardeners are working on their gardens."[15] It is difficult to imagine how FIFA concluded that conditions were suitable for prisoners held there. According to Rodrigo Rojas, held prisoner in the stadium, the visit of FIFA inspectors prompted military guards to cover evidence of torture and transfer prisoners to other detention centers.[16] FIFA officials dismissed objections to their findings, explaining, "We are not concerned with politics or what regimes are ruling a country."[17] This position buttressed what had become a standard discourse among the right-wing in Chile that conservative projects were moral, not political. On the contrary, they argued, leftists intervened in cultural spheres in order to politicize them.[18]

Solidarity groups in Western Europe, led by Chilean exiles and university students, saw the World Cup as an opportunity to protest the military regime. Following the September 1973 coup in Chile, West Berlin was a center of solidarity activity, spearheaded by the Chile Solidarity Committee, based in the Free University.[19] By the spring of 1974, activists had formed Chilean solidarity groups in twenty-six cities in West Germany.[20] The Solidarity Committee, composed of Germans and exiled Chileans, hoped to use the World Cup to connect with detainees and to draw public attention to their plight. According to one organizer, "We made the decision to fight any attempt of the Pinochet propagandists to celebrate the participation of the Chilean team as an act of glorification of the military junta. . . . Our actions were also meant to show our solidarity with the prisoners in the different camps and prisons of the junta. We were informed, for example, that a significant number of prisoners were allowed to watch the television transmissions of the matches showing the Chilean national team."[21] The Solidarity Committee decried human rights abuses, although its overarching goal was to see socialism restored in Chile. Activists realized the importance of national identity in the World Cup and wanted to avoid being characterized as "anti-Chilean." They frequently used the slogan "Chile Sí, Junta No!"[22]

Local history shaped the interactions among demonstrators, the West German authorities, and the Pinochet regime during the World Cup. The protesters frequently drew comparisons between Augusto Pinochet and Adolf Hitler. To underscore this point, activists changed the "ch" in Pinochet's name to a swastika on their banners. Local officials in West Germany touted heightened security for the Cup in light of the tragic events of the 1972 Olympics. During those games, terrorists from the Palestinian organization Black September assassinated eleven members of the Israeli Olympic delegation in Munich. These events loomed large in the security plans of the West German police for the 1974 World Cup. The police infiltrated solidarity groups and informed the Pinochet government of the planned protests. Thus, even before the tournament began, reports of the demonstrations appeared in *El Mercurio*, the most widely disseminated newspaper in Chile and a supporter of the regime. The paper announced that three thousand "extremists" would protest the match between West Germany and Chile.[23] At the behest of the Chilean delegation, West German police assigned a bodyguard to each Chilean player, housed the team apart from other delegations, and sent one thousand plain-clothed officers to their matches.

General Pinochet hoped that the World Cup would improve the image of his regime abroad and at home. In June 1974, he was in the process of consolidating his one-man rule. He sent the national team with a letter that reassured the world of Chile's "restoration."[24] A key member of the Chilean entourage was Alberto Mela, the new president of the National Association of Amateur Football (ANFA). Mela, an appointee of the new military government, was sent as proof of amateur clubs' support for the junta. Throughout the twentieth century, ANFA had maintained strong ties to unions and leftist political parties; because of their support for the Popular Unity government, many amateur football directors had suffered persecution and remained in prison, exile, or hiding by the time of the World Cup. In addition, exiled amateur players organized football tournaments in honor of Salvador Allende in Brussels, Mexico City, Montreal, and Rome.[25] Despite ANFA's official appearance at the World Cup, curfews, restrictions placed on public gatherings, and police raids of football fields dampened amateurs' enthusiasm for the tournament. Furthermore, reports of Marxist terrorist threats created a somber mood in the World Cup coverage, even among sportswriters.[26] Reports of threats to Chilean soccer players in West Germany bolstered both the regime's portrayal of its opponents as terrorists and its efforts to discredit solidarity activists. It is difficult to ascertain the severity or veracity of the threats to Chilean athletes, but they were the *only* mention of activities of solidarity groups in the mainstream Chilean press, which equated solidarity organizations with the Irish Republican Army and the Palestinian Liberation Organization.[27]

Once the World Cup began, solidarity groups picketed the matches, held workshops in libraries, and demonstrated at team press conferences. Although activists recalled being received positively, Chilean sports magazines reported that football crowds were hostile toward the protesters and referred to their posters obliquely as "offensive."[28] One writer claimed that spectators applauded when the West German police forced protesters to relinquish their signs. Chilean media carefully avoided descriptions of the protesters' criticisms. The West German authorities tried to subdue protesters by confiscating their posters and threatening to remove them from the matches. When crowds chanted, "Chile sí, junta no," a voice over the loudspeaker ordered them to refrain from shouting anything unrelated to sports. *El Mercurio* characterized the demonstrators as anti-Chilean and claimed that they celebrated goals scored against Chile. The most disruptive action occurred during Chile's final match against Australia, on June 22. Throughout the first half of the match, activists chanted and raised placards they had smuggled into the stadium. As the second half began, fifteen members of a group called "For Chile" ran onto the center of the football field and unfurled a very large banner that read "Chile Socialista," or Socialist Chile.[29] *El Mercurio* claimed that the group was well known for its violent attacks against the Chilean military but did not offer any details. Confronted with a unique situation, the Iranian referee decided not to stop the match to eject the protesters and looked on with curiosity. While the Chilean press claimed that the sixteen thousand attendees booed the protesters, those involved in the protest action recalled being greeted with cheers.[30] Contested memories of protests at sporting events, like those following athletes' Black Power salute at the 1968 Olympics, reflect disagreement over the politics expressed, as well as over the appropriate sites for political expression.

During the World Cup, Pinochet connected himself to the Chilean team whenever possible, incorporating mentions of the team into his speeches and publicizing his telephone calls to its captain, Francisco Valdés.[31] In a restrained press release following the first match, Pinochet expressed appreciation for the football players' defense of the nation's honor. His advisers must have convinced him to appear more effusive, because, in a press conference on the eve of the match against Australia, he predicted that Chile would win 4 to 0.[32] After his discussion of the World Cup, Pinochet went on to explain that the discovery of weapons in "clandestine Marxist workshops" would force him to prolong the military control of the government.[33] He implored Chileans to model themselves after their football stars. He drew an analogy between the accomplishments of the team and the Chilean people, who had "defeated extremism, insecurity, and drastically halted inflation."[34] Pinochet created a parallel image of Chile as an underdog in football and in the struggle against Marxism.

Chilean players at the World Cup found themselves at the center of international controversy over the military government. Solidarity activity was greatly responsible for keeping the issue at the center of public attention during the tournament. Journalists sought political commentary from Chilean players and also those from Uruguay, where a military coup had also ousted the civilian government. Solidarity groups were bewildered by the fact that Chilean players either refused to comment on the situation or defended the military. They speculated that the footballers had been threatened or brainwashed.[35] After several tense exchanges with journalists, Chilean players demanded $50 per interview, and Uruguayan stars followed suit, requesting $200.[36] These fees were unheard of, but the head of the Chilean football delegation, Antonio Martínez, defended the players. In particular, Martínez objected when a journalist asked about the workers' standard of living in Chile. The Chilean press implied that the most offensive questions pertained to the Soviet squad's boycott and the repression in Chile.[37] Although star players were under pressure to protect their income potential by remaining politically neutral, it is surprising that not one player spoke out about the repression in Chile. Even Carlos Caszely, whose family belonged to the Communist Party and had suffered persecution, continued to play dutifully for the Chilean national team.[38]

The experience of the 1974 World Cup highlighted the importance of control over football for the Pinochet regime, and, before the start of the 1975 season, Pinochet moved to consolidate his control over the sport.[39] News of this activity traveled fast among solidarity activists in Europe, who worried that football could bolster Pinochet's popularity. Following the coup, the military government banned elections in football clubs, mother's centers, unions, and other civic associations.[40] Government officials orchestrated the first such elections in 1975, one for the Miss Chile contest and the other for professional football's governing body, the Central Association. When it became clear to the Central Association that the junta had chosen its own candidate, the directorate objected that the military had banned elections in civic associations. Pinochet granted special permission for the election and claimed that, so long as the Association did not elect a member of the opposition, he would not interfere.[41] Father Gilberto Lizano, a sportswriter for *El Mercurio* and a supporter of the junta, nominated Arturo Gordan, the deputy director of the Carabineros (Chile's militarized police), for president of the association. Once Gordan was on the list, police officers and military personnel pressured club leaders throughout the country to vote for him. One club director reported to solidarity activists in Berlin that he had been forced to go to a police station in the middle of the night to vote for Gordan.[42] That activists obtained news of this sort demonstrates the strong communication between solidarity groups in West Germany and the opposition within Chile.

The 1974 World Cup was not an isolated event; rather, solidarity activists used other sports events as opportunities to contest the legitimacy of Pinochet and to call attention to the regime's abuse of human rights. Members of Casa Chile, a prominent center for Chilean exiles in Mexico City, protested at matches of visiting Chilean football clubs whenever they could afford to buy tickets.[43] Solidarity organizations in Sweden, led by exiled members of the Movimiento de Izquierda Revolucionaria (MIR), the Revolutionary Left Movement, organized activities in response to visits by the Chilean tennis team. On the eve of one visit in 1975, the Chilean Tennis Federation announced that its players had received death threats.[44] It denounced these violent attacks in the international press as examples of the terrorism practiced by the Chilean left, grouping hunger strikers in Sweden with would-be assassins as "bad patriots."[45] Captain Luis Ayala dismissed the accusations of solidarity groups, claiming that his team was the victim of their "psychological weapons."[46] As with the World Cup, threats to athletes abroad coincided with reports of the military regime's "discovery" of stockpiles of Soviet weapons.[47] Once again, mainstream journalists discredited the activities of the opposition in Sweden by invoking the nineteenth-century ideal of the sportsman as "apolitical." This position found official state support. For example, when Italian tennis authorities scheduled a match in Santiago despite opposition from solidarity groups, led by the organization Chile Democrático in Rome, the Italian government explained, "Our country is proud of the independence of its sports organizations from political controversy."[48] This characterization ignored Pinochet's maneuvers to parlay these appearances into public relations opportunities.[49]

At the same moment that the junta faced demonstrations at the 1974 World Cup, solidarity groups in the United States hoped to prevent members of the Chilean navy from playing football in their area. That summer, Pinochet sent the ship *Esmeralda* on a "goodwill" tour of the Pacific Ocean. To celebrate, the navy scheduled football matches between its team and its local counterparts, as well as with a group of Chilean expatriates that supported the military junta.[50] Solidarity groups in California, Oregon, and Washington organized campaigns to stop the ship from docking in their ports. In the aftermath of the coup, the ship had been used as a floating prison, where detainees had been subjected to rape and torture. The United Committee to Stop the Esmeralda in the San Francisco Bay Area explained to residents that football was significant because "during the September coup the military turned the National Football Stadium in Santiago into a concentration camp for thousands."[51] Protesters forced the matches to move from Orange Park in South San Francisco to Treasure Island, where naval security was tighter.[52] Particularly sensitive to the plight of women prisoners, the prostitutes' union, COYOTE (Call Off Your Old Tired Ethics), participated in the protests against the football matches. They went further, declaring a moratorium on sex with Chilean naval personnel. Margo St. James, the leader of COYOTE, explained her organization's connection to the solidarity activities, pointing out that sex workers suffered increased violence and repression under regimes without respect for human rights.[53] Years later, St. James recalled that the music of the folk singers Joan Baez and Holly Near had first drawn her attention to the situation in Chile.[54]

Solidarity activities in the realm of popular culture, such as the campaign against the *Esmeralda* visit, reflected the collaboration among anti-imperialists, feminists, religious groups, and gay rights activists, as well as conflicts. This co-operation occurred more frequently in ad hoc campaigns than around formal political events and institutions. In their solidarity work, participants educated one another about their respective struggles. However, with respect to sexuality and gender, the conflicts could be insurmountable. These dynamics were reflected in the Bay Area solidarity movement. Gay and lesbian activists who joined solidarity organizations met with hostility from some Chilean exiles who expressed homophobic attitudes and sexist ideas and who connected class struggle to heterosexual prowess. One activist, Margaret Power, recalled that a friend from the Bay Area solidarity movement was invited to join the Chilean MIR, only to be un-invited when he revealed that he was gay.[55] Gay rights organizations were repeatedly told to stay away from demonstrations when leaders felt they would alienate potential allies, such as the Filipino labor unions.[56] Despite these incidents, gay rights organizations such as the June 28th Union continued to support Chilean solidarity. In 1975, they held a fundraiser that featured a performance by a lesbian choral group and showed the film *Campamento*. A speech by the event organizer, James N. Green, drew attention to the common sources of repression, especially police brutality, experienced by gays and lesbians in Chile and in the United States.[57] Although these alliances were tense, activists recalled their interactions as fruitful.

Women and Solidarity in "Folk" Art

Throughout Latin America in the 1970s and 1980s, women led movements against authoritarian governments. The strong channels of communication established between women's organizations, especially in Europe, Latin America, and the United States, strengthened the transnational character of the solidarity movement. Women's organizations broadened the discourse of human rights through their attention to rape, domestic violence, and poverty. Furthermore, women activists called the public's attention to the dictatorship's widespread use of rape and sexual assault to terrorize prisoners.[58] During the 1980s, women solidarity activists in Chile integrated their organizations into regional and international human rights networks, hoping to use international law and pressure to hold the Pinochet regime accountable. Given the high profile of right-wing women who demanded the military overthrow of Allende's government, women's leadership in the solidarity movement challenged the dictatorship's claims to popularity among women.[59] Although many of these women did not identify as feminists, their activities carved new political spaces for women.[60]

Women activists skillfully mobilized popular culture in their struggle against the Pinochet regime. *Arpilleras*, appliquéd tapestries created by women involved with the Catholic Church's Vicariate of Solidarity, are perhaps the most recognized examples of such a practice. The Vicariate in Santiago served those experiencing hardship in a variety of ways, including the provision of legal aid, employment opportunities, and education.[61] Women and some men who met at the Vicariate formed the Association of Relatives of the Detained and Disappeared (AFDD hereafter) in 1974 in the hope of obtaining information on their missing relatives. They created novel cultural practices that served as political protest, therapy, and a source of economic sustenance. *Arpilleristas*, as the artists are known, criticized the dictatorship's human rights violations, frequently drawing upon their personal stories. Over the next ten years, *arpilleras* became so successful that the regime persecuted *arpilleristas* and commissioned counter-*arpilleras*.

The popularity of *arpilleras* came at a critical juncture for the opposition movement. The period between 1979 and 1982, which the historian Steve Stern has dubbed "Triumph: Official Chile," proved particularly difficult for solidarity organizations.[62] The economy stabilized during these years, and Augusto

Pinochet normalized relations with foreign countries and lending institutions in an effort to create a "softer" public face. Within the solidarity movement, many activists turned their attention to the victory of the Sandinista Army in Nicaragua, in 1980; with the election of Ronald Reagan as president of the United States, activists worried that the United States would mobilize against the left-wing government in Nicaragua. Also, those who had supported the Popular Unity government in Chile saw new possibilities to establish socialism under the Sandinistas.

The Pinochet regime continued to mobilize Cold War rhetoric in its cultural affairs, including the boycott of the 1980 Olympic Games in Moscow. Furthermore, it organized cultural exchanges with other countries under authoritarian governments, including a series of rugby matches with the South African team in 1982.[63] In addition, voters, through a plebiscite of dubious transparency, ratified the regime's changes to the Chilean constitution. Pinochet donned the traditional presidential sash and moved to the palace, La Moneda, to bolster his legitimacy. In this moment, solidarity organizations shifted away from the rhetoric of the Cold War, which focused on the imperialism of the United States and exploitation endemic to capitalism, to embrace a broader human rights agenda. In part, this reflected disillusionment with the Soviet Union. In addition, it was a product of the relationships between victims of authoritarian military regimes throughout the region, whose organizations were ideologically heterogeneous. While solidarity organizations continued to criticize Pinochet's free-market policies, they focused more on repression and less on class inequality than they had in the years immediately following the coup.

Arpilleras countered the dictatorship's discourse of order, success, and social peace, which it hoped to promote abroad.[64] Moreover, the *arpilleras* sparked the interest of both a younger generation of Chileans and activists abroad in solidarity work.[65] *Arpilleras* that depicted scenes of everyday life were a popular art form throughout the Andean region. Rejecting *arpilleras*'s traditionally cheerful content, artists in the Vicariate's workshop sewed heartbreaking scenes of arrests, loneliness, terror, and poverty. In their subject matter, form, and materials and through the collective nature of their production, *arpilleras* challenged traditional notions of "art." Frequently, artists sewed pockets onto the back of their work, which contained letters explaining their plight. Others incorporated pieces of their missing relative's clothing or a photograph.

News that *arpilleras* were being sold abroad reached the regime by the late 1970s. Police began confiscating *arpilleras* at airports throughout Chile and detained people who attempted to smuggle them out of the country.[66] By the early 1980s, Amnesty International selected *arpilleras* as their cover art in greeting cards and calendars. Furthermore, supportive academics in the United States and Europe brought *arpilleras* to universities. In Chile, *arpillera* workshops were the subject of the subversive play *Tres Marías y Una Rosa*, which opened in Santiago in 1979, and *arpillera* designs were used to decorate protest banners.[67] Thus, by the time of the mass protests against the dictatorship between 1982 and 1984, *arpilleras* had become a widely recognized symbol of the opposition.

In their cultural expressions, women of the AFDD drew upon and challenged ideologies of gender in their protests of human rights violations, as did their counterparts in Argentina and El Salvador. In addition to doing needlework, they also performed the national dance, the *cueca*. They did so without partners to underscore the regime's violence against their relatives. Their use of cultural practices associated with traditional gender roles highlighted the regime's destruction of the values it claimed to restore. Women activists walked a fine line between mobilizing gender roles to their advantage, especially around their role as "apolitical" mothers, sisters, and daughters, and being discounted on that basis. In an article in the *Baltimore Sun* in 1983, a writer compared the *arpillera* to Picasso's *Guernica* in their recording of atrocities. Yet, according to the article, "Unlike Picasso, however, the arpillera artist arrives at her style naively."[68] A more salient subject of analysis would have been the relationship between the art and the conditions of production. For example, the light weight of *arpilleras* facilitated their clandestine transport out of the country. Women produced the *arpilleras* together in workshops under constant surveillance by the government. The cost of the materials dictated the fabrics the *arpilleristas* used and highlighted the poverty they denounced. Solidarity activists abroad sold *arpilleras* at their events and served as interlocutors, explaining the messages in the work.[69] While specifically about the situation in Chile, *arpilleras* appealed to "universal" values such as the love of mothers for their children, the hope for peace, and the humiliation of poverty. Many drew upon Christian symbolism, including crosses, fish, doves, and lambs. Despite the success of *arpilleras*, solidarity organizations did not categorize them as art or *arpilleristas* as artists.

Arpilleras may not have caught the attention of art critics, but their popularity reverberated among the highest political circles. In 1980, CEMA, the organization of Mother's Centers run by Augusto Pinochet's wife, Lucía Hiriart, opened the Galería Artesanal. Located in an upscale part of Santiago, the Galería sold sanitized versions of popular artwork, including *arpilleras*.[70] CEMA encouraged artisans to think in terms of the export value of these "folkloric" pieces. In 1982, the General Services Administration (GSA) in Washington, D.C., decided to arrange an exhibition of the Vicariate's *arpilleras* in the corridors of the agency's building.[71] The Chilean government complained that supporting *arpilleristas* was equivalent to supporting communist guerrillas. The two governments reached a compromise that left the *arpilleras* on the walls but without the personal stories sewn into the back of the tapestry. The following November, Lucía Hiriart, the wife of General Pinochet, brought her own *arpilleras* to tea with Nancy Reagan, the wife of U.S. president Ronald Reagan. During her visit, Hiriart arranged a display of these happier *arpilleras* at Georgetown University.[72]

The demand for *arpilleras* reflected the strengthening ties between women's organizations in Latin America, Europe, and North America. In the previous decade, Chilean women exiles who prioritized a socialist agenda had clashed with feminists in North America, while North American feminists who attended international conferences were concerned with gender inequality, domestic abuse, and, to a lesser extent, lesbian rights. Venues like the International Year of the Woman Conference, the first in Mexico City in 1975 and the second in Copenhagen in 1980, revealed deep disagreements among women over these issues.[73] By the mid-1980s, some participants felt they had learned from their experiences and become sensitive to different perspectives.[74] Chilean women's organizations found common ground with one another and their counterparts abroad in an inclusive human rights agenda. This agenda placed the oppression of women, perpetrated by the state, as well as by male relatives in the home, at the center of human rights work. A certain sector of North American feminists recognized the impact of imperialism on women's lives. Groups such as Action for Women in Chile (AFWIC), based in New York City, brought a feminist perspective to human rights' activism. When asked why, as a solidarity group, AFWIC focused on women, it responded: "The same forces that promoted the coup in Chile and continue to benefit from the existence of military dictatorships throughout Latin America are responsible for the oppression of women, minorities and working people in the U.S. . . . Many feminist groups have not yet developed a clear understanding of the role of U.S. imperialism in the third world and especially in Latin America. At the same time, many anti-imperialist groups deal with the question of women's oppression in a very limited way, or not at all."[75] AWIC promoted *arpilleras* in its publications and emphasized their creation in a cooperative setting. The hope of economic empowerment for women through artistic ventures inspired further projects developed by international NGOs, including Oxfam.

During the 1980s, celebrations of International Women's Day were some of the most energetic political events in Chile. These events inspired women in the United States and Europe, sparking interest in solidarity organizations. Women activists used artistic expression to unite members who were divided by ideological differences. For example, leaders of women's organizations in Chile convened a mass assembly for International Women's Day 1983 in the Caupolicán Theater. After much debate, they decided to create an artistic festival that would bring together demands for democracy and women's rights.[76] One group of women suggested that each political party opposed to the dictatorship present its vision of a future democratic Chile, but this idea was rejected in favor of an artistic representation focused on the end of state torture, a return to democracy, and economic cooperation.

The use of theaters, stadiums, squares, streets, and museums by women's groups constituted an important step in claiming public space from the dictatorship. The historian Temma Kaplan has shown that women activists effectively created rituals in public spaces that shamed the regime into public discussions of repression.[77] By lifting shame from victims and placing it on the military, they also bolstered the solidarity movement. As Kaplan explains, "Shame undercuts solidarity by weakening the personal identity that ties people to their family and community."[78] For instance, throughout the twentieth century, football fans had shamed female spectators in the stadium, a bastion of male sociability and athletic prowess.[79] Then, in 1984, the group Women for Life smuggled protest signs into the National Stadium. Women for Life sought to create a public memory of the abuses that the dictatorship had perpetrated in the stadium and to place women in leadership roles during the transition to democracy.[80] Women activists spearheaded the efforts to include women's rights within formal human rights protocols, which culminated in the United Nations Convention on the Elimination of all Forms of Discrimination against Women, in 1979. The relationship between global and local struggles for women's rights was crucial in changing the approach of human rights organizations, such as Amnesty International, toward women.[81] Activists in New York registered surprise that "Chilean women have been a vanguard of struggle against the abuses of the junta."[82] Whereas solidarity activists in the 1970s had hoped to use the "women effect" in their campaign against torture, women's organizations succeeded in controlling their own "effect" by the 1980s.[83] This constituted an important shift that involved women's public performance and creative expression. Together with the Mothers of the Plaza de Mayo in Argentina, formed by women searching for their detained and disappeared relatives, Chilean activists strengthened the image of women as leaders in the struggle for democracy. As Rita Arditti wrote of women in Argentina, "They transformed themselves from 'traditional' women defined by their relationships with men (mothers, wives, daughters) into public protesters working on behalf of the whole society."[84] Part of this transformation in Chile and in Argentina involved the use personal effects, including clothing, handkerchiefs, and photographs of their missing loved ones, which broke down the division between public and private. Transnational women's organizations contributed to the dissemination of these messages. Widows of the regime's victims, including Hortensia Bussi (widow of Salvador Allende), Joan Jara (widow of Víctor Jara), and Isabel Letelier (widow of Orlando Letelier), traveled around the world building support for the solidarity movement. Although initially recognized for their relationship to their husbands, these women became independently known for their work on behalf of human rights.[85]

Resisting the Cultural Blackout

Popular culture figured prominently in the regime's plans to promote "traditional values." Thus, cultural practices were not only tools of the opposition but also subjects of the struggle against Pinochet. Cultural producers in the solidarity movement criticized consumerism, European development programs, individualism, and conservative attitudes toward family and sex, which they saw as creating a cultural disposition toward authoritarianism. The imprisonment, exile, and murder of artists were part of the dictatorship's efforts to eradicate cultural expressions it categorized as subversive. The military targeted art that celebrated working-class identity, indigenous culture, and collectivism or that adopted a critical stance toward commercial and foreign influences. The censorship of these practices became known as the "cultural blackout" and impacted television, newspapers, radio, cinema, and live performances. In the 1980s, the dictatorship poured money into the International Song Festival in Viña del Mar and supported artists, especially romantic balladeers who focused on personal rather than social struggles.[86] Furthermore, the state attacked literature, staging book burnings and placing a prohibitive 20 percent tax on independent publishing houses. The regime prohibited most live venues, making Chileans a captive audience for mainstream media. Television stations imported an unprecedented number of shows from the United States and Brazil. Furthermore, the government's close relationship to multinational corporations was evidenced in its promotion of brands and corporate symbols, though with varying degrees of success. For example, in 1980, the state installed a sculpture in downtown Santiago that strongly resembled the Renault automaker's trademark, but public ridicule led to its removal.[87]

Solidarity groups that worked outside Chile recognized that the control of cultural practices was integral to the regime's ability to mobilize consent. Furthermore, they viewed cultural organizations as essential to maintaining connections across national borders, reaching new audiences, and preserving noncommercial expressions. One activist, who had founded theater troupes in Mexico and Belgium, stressed the importance of cultural practices to solidarity work, explaining, "Members of these groups were amateurs and sacrificed enormously to sustain them. . . . In addition, membership was in constant flux because none of us lived off theater or music and the instability of work forced us to migrate to other cities."[88] After the coup, playwrights instituted a boycott, refusing to allow their work to be staged in Chile, and supported exiled artists. At times, this boycott produced unintended hardship, preventing theater troupes from performing anti-authoritarian pieces that might have been permitted as being of foreign origin.

Musical groups, especially those that played *nueva canción*, or the "new song" genre, were at the forefront of those who criticized the "cultural blackout." *Nueva canción* was politically charged from the outset of the dictatorship.[89] Prominent musicians of the genre, including Víctor Jara, supported Salvador Allende's presidential campaign.[90] They also played concerts in occupied factories to lift the spirits of workers. As a result, Pinochet canceled the folk category in the renowned International Song Festival, held in the Chilean coastal city Viña del Mar, between 1974 and 1980. Throughout the 1970s, musical groups supported the solidarity movement in a variety of ways, from providing financial support to exiled families to supporting armed resistance organizations. Based in the Parisian suburbs after the coup, the band Quilapayún, for example, played across the world and helped solidarity organizations raise money. U.S. folk musicians, including Joan Baez and Bob Dylan, performed concerts that provided organizations with their largest revenues. The musician Patricio Manns released his album *Songs of the People's Underground in Chile* to the Quebec-Chile Solidarity Committee in 1975 in order to fund the group's activities.[91] Within a few years, bootlegged copies of the album appeared in Chile and circulated throughout the Americas and Europe.

At times, Chilean musicians, artists, and writers in exile felt themselves misunderstood by solidarity activists and noted a tendency to exoticize their work in North America and Europe. Artists such as Quilapayún found that, despite *nueva canción*'s hybrid roots, audiences abroad identified it as an "authentic" indigenous cultural expression. Assumptions about the "primitive" nature of Latin America infused Andean music with an exotic Third Worldism.[92] This diverged from the origins of the genre. According to the ethnomusicologist Fernando Ríos, "Chilean middle-class university students looking for a way to musically identify with Amerindians but largely uninterested in Mapuche songs were instead attracted to Andean *kenas* and *charangos*, which easily complemented the standard Southern Cone folkloric-popular music lineup of acoustic guitars and *bombo* drums. *Nueva Canción* folklorists, after all, used modernist-cosmopolitan versions of rural indigenous instruments rather than the ones actually used at the time in Southern Andean highland villages."[93] Although some artists expressed discomfort with European interpretations of their work, others, such as the writer Soledad Bianchi, felt that Latin Americans in exile created a rich regional identity. Bianchi explained, "For the first time, in Europe, I feel deeply Latin American. What happens in Argentina hurts me as much as what happens in Chile."[94]

An association of musicians opposed to the dictatorship formed in the late 1970s and was conceived of as a transnational organization named the "Committee of Chilean Musicians." The committee, with members in Chile and abroad, denounced the regime's censorship of music and musical venues, as well as its promotion of foreign music.[95] Its members complained that Pinochet's regime was spending large sums on contracts with "mediocre" artists such as Sheena Easton for the International Song Festival. Easton, along with pop singers such as José Feliciano and John Denver, unwittingly became part of Pinochet's efforts to improve his regime's image abroad. The Committee complained, "As the cultural sector we take to the streets to say that the Festival of Viña is scandalous. Not only is it mediocre, but on top of that, millions of pesos are spent on it while people die of hunger and don't have anywhere to live. In the City of Viña itself and in Valparaiso, there is a high level of unemployment and lack of housing. And yet, they pay Sheena Easton seventy thousand dollars. Scandalous, right?"[96] Repression hampered efforts to promote local music, especially music with political messages. In 1980, twenty-two students from the Technical University were banished to Chiloé for organizing a solidarity concert.[97] In working-class neighborhoods, a few folk-music clubs, or *peñas*, re-emerged but faced police harassment. Part of the Committee's work involved the creation of a music archive that chronicled solidarity activities of musicians around the world. When the committee's leader, Jorge Narvaéz, received a dubbed cassette tape containing the music of the U.S. folk singer Holly Near, he explained, "This is very important to us, to get to know them and to create an archive, a library that will be available to Chilean artists."[98] The Committee focused on the improvement of "the human rights situation for artists and cultural workers."[99] The use of "human rights," rather than language that referred to class, revolution, or socialism, demonstrated a shift in the Chilean solidarity movement paralleled abroad.

The magazine *La Bicicleta* strengthened the relationships between musicians opposed to the dictatorship abroad and their counterparts within Chile. *La Bicicleta* was among the few Chilean opposition publications in the late 1970s and 1980s. It received a significant portion of its funding from solidarity groups abroad.[100] Its label as "cultural" rather than "political" enabled *La*

Bicicleta to escape permanent closure. Still, its writers and directors were jailed on several occasions, and the government interfered with the magazine's publication during the massive protests of 1984. *La Bicicleta,* written by and for young people, connected a new generation to the protest music of the 1960s. Yet, it also responded to the reality of young Chileans a decade after the coup. The magazine and its collaborators promoted the emergence of *canto nuevo,* a new musical genre. The label acknowledged the influence of *nueva canción* (both terms mean "new song"), as well as music from Uruguay, Argentina, and Cuba. Ricardo García, a record producer, explained that the need for a new label stemmed from the fact that *nueva canción* was in exile.[101] García described *canto nuevo* as more eclectic than *nueva canción,* especially in its incorporation of rock music.[102] It also differed from *nueva canción* in the subtlety of its politics and in the middle-class background of its audience. Many fans of *nueva canción* were also middle class, but artists had brought their music to land occupations, strikes, and union rallies. *La Bicicleta* kept readers informed on the performances of exiled musicians; therefore, the Popular Unity government and solidarity movement were frequently discussed. At the same time, the magazine promoted a new generation of Chilean musicians.[103] *Canto nuevo* chronicled the national protests of 1983–84, capturing a large audience abroad. This was facilitated by the advent of the tape cassette, which provided an easy medium by which to record, copy, and distribute music.

Canto nuevo artists explored tensions between the exile and the domestic experience of the dictatorship. In a song dedicated to Víctor Jara titled "Homenaje," Santiago del Nuevo Extremo sang, "Your life was your life. Mine, another story. And the world was the witness of those days. I want only to sing in the present and allow you to speak. But the words remain silent. And I don't want to lie. . . . My song was different from yours."[104] Artists formed close relationships with their counterparts in exile. For example, Hugo Moraga visited Ángel Parra, son of Violeta Parra, in Paris and recalled being very influenced by songs such as "Me gusta la democracia."[105] In it, Parra criticized electoral democracy in a society with class inequality. Parra implicated popular culture, especially professional football, in encouraging workers' exploitation.[106] Moraga pointed to the football club Colo Colo's support for the dictatorship as evidence that Parra had been right all along. Musicians in exile also connected to new political causes, such as the struggle against apartheid in South Africa. Members of the band Illapú explained, "The position of artists demands them to look for universals, that is to say, messages that are valid around the world."[107] Thus, one can observe an interesting tendency among musicians in the solidarity movement: they valued "folk" roots and local artists even as they sought to be a part of a global discourse of social justice.

Miss Universe and the Mainstream

Solidarity activists, adept at expressing their criticism through culture, faced a formidable opponent in the Pinochet regime. Beginning with the junta's appearance on television to announce its assumption of power, the military controlled mass media outlets. In the coming years, the Pinochet regime used television, newspapers, and radio to promote its policies and to encourage consumerism. Its repeal of laws that restricted commercial advertisements intensified corporate interest in television. Moreover, censorship, financial difficulties, and the fear of repression limited television programming. Imported content from the United States increased during the 1980s and shaped attitudes toward fashion, politics, and family life.[108] The subtle strategies of the dictatorship as it engineered mainstream culture contrasted with the efforts of solidarity activists, who sought to attract as much attention as possible. In most instances, the dictatorship capitalized on or controlled popular culture, rather than creating new practices. An illustrative example is the Miss Universe pageant of 1987, which took place in the last year of military rule mandated by the 1980 constitution. During intense political agitation, the pageant offered the dictatorship an opportunity to mobilize nationalism, project its legitimacy abroad, and showcase its achievements.[109] Held in Singapore, the luxurious set, costumes, and jewelry created a fantastical world where all nations prospered and competed under equal conditions. Commercials and product placement during the contest emphasized that freedoms could be won through consumption. Furthermore, beauty contests sent the message that women could advance through competition and manipulation of their appearance. Women's support was critical to Pinochet's success in the coming plebiscite, particularly given the international attention to the women leaders of human rights organizations.

Miss Chile, Cecilia Bolocco, won the Miss Universe pageant on May 27, 1987, to the delight of many Chileans. In a moment of international scrutiny over whether Pinochet would remain in power, Bolocco's victory was interpreted by supporters of the regime as proof of the country's success. Enzo Bolocco, Cecilia's father, claimed that his daughter's victory had silenced the critics of Chile, at home and abroad. In two parallel messages, Pinochet and his wife sent cables to congratulate Bolocco. The following day, Pinochet sent Minister Francisco Cuadra to visit the Bolocco home. Cuadra explained to the press that he "brought greetings from President Pinochet and the government as a whole, to the Bolocco family, expressing the enormous happiness that all Chileans felt in regard to Cecilia's enormous success in representing all Chilean women."[110] The mainstream press, especially *El Mercurio*, reported that

Bolocco's win had unified the nation. Photographs of Chileans, with the Chilean flag, chanting "Viva la mujer chilena" appeared in the major newspapers. *El Mercurio* described the festivities as "national euphoria." Many Chileans reported being moved to tears by Bolocco's victory.[111] For her part, Bolocco declared, "I have succeeded in unifying all Chileans."[112]

In their analysis of the pageant, journalists established Bolocco as representative of Chileans vis-à-vis other nations' contestants. Television reporters praised Bolocco's stoicism and confidence. One journalist observed, "She received congratulations with dignity, in contrast to the runner-up [Miss Italy], who began to cry before the results were announced."[113] A recurrent theme that connected interpretations of the Miss Universe contest to the rhetoric of the Pinochet regime was the intrinsic value of winning and being a winner. That victory justified everything else was at the heart of Pinochet's defense of the repression following the 1973 coup. Observers lauded Bolocco's "winning attitude." When asked how she won, Bolocco explained, "Because I am the best, I have personality, a pleasing physique, and, most importantly, I have the drive to win. I won because I deserved it."[114] The conservative ideologue Jaime Guzmán reacted to Bolocco's victory: "Generally, we Chileans lack a winning mentality . . . she has shown the opposite."[115] The popular singer Raúl "Florcito Matuda" Alarcón described Bolocco as a new type of Miss Chile, contrasting her with traditionally timid and self-effacing Chileans.[116] *El Mercurio* claimed that Chileans' "addiction" to "moral victories" was a psychological flaw that Bolocco had overcome.[117] Bolocco's friends and family repeatedly described her as having "the mentality of a winner."[118]

An instant celebrity, Cecilia Bolocco was likely surprised by the political questions asked by journalists. In interviews, she stated that young people needed to look forward, rather than dwell on past events. When asked her opinion of the pro-democracy demonstrations and student protests of 1987, Bolocco remarked, "I would like us to realize that there are many things we have to take as they come because we cannot change them. With aggression, shouting, and scandalous behavior, we gain absolutely nothing."[119] Bolocco's characterization of the opposition dovetailed with Pinochet's supporters, who framed human rights activists as obstacles to progress, anachronistic, and fixated on the past. Furthermore, Cecilia contrasted her own controlled appearance with the behavior of the opposition and diminished the gravity of the opposition's claims by referring to them as "scandalous." Upon her return to Chile in August 1987, Bolocco registered to vote but refused to tell reporters whether she favored Pinochet's continuation in power. However, she made her feelings clear regarding the opposition's public protests: "I believe . . . that all Chileans should do their part for the progress and tranquility of the country, without avoiding their responsibilities by blaming others for their problems."[120] Whether intentional or not, this rhetoric reinforced that of Pinochet's supporters who criticized the opposition for re-igniting divisions in Chile.

It would be difficult to overstate the media frenzy that surrounded the Miss Universe pageant of 1987. Throughout the year, Bolocco toured the world as a representative of Chile with corporate sponsors of the pageant.[121] Given the dramatic events in national politics, especially the University of Chile strike, it is not far-fetched to claim that major newspapers, magazines, and television stations intentionally avoided covering political stories in favor of pageant news. The pageant was re-televised; Bolocco graced the covers of magazines for months and was awarded the highest national honor, the medal of the heroes of Concepción. Occasionally, there were jokes that compared Miss Universe's term limit to Pinochet's attempts to stay in power indefinitely. These jabs trivialized the terror he had inspired among his victims. In one parody, a caricature of Pinochet (referred to as "El capítan general") remarked, "They should allow her to run for reelection in order to protect her crown."[122] Supporters of Pinochet mocked José Sanfuentes, leader of the Popular Democratic Movement, who suggested that Chile focus on a transition to democracy and human rights, rather than on Miss Universe.[123] Foreign Minister Jaime del Valle dismissed Sanfuentes, saying, "This is good news for anyone and everyone, for people of all ages and ideologies."[124] For human rights groups, the hyperbole must have been overwhelming when the minister of national defense, Patricio Carvajal, exclaimed, "Finally there is justice. . . . The Chilean women deserved this a long time ago."[125]

Catholicism constituted an important part of the narrative of the Miss Universe pageant as constructed by the Bolocco family, state officials, and journalists. Supporters and leaders of the military regime viewed what they termed "traditional" or pre-Vatican II Catholicism as foundational to Chilean nationalism. Beginning in the mid-1980s, the government had sought to erase its conflicts with the Vicariate of Solidarity over human rights. The beatification of Saint Teresa de los Andes and the visit of Pope John Paul II earlier in 1987, for example, provided Pinochet a showcase for his improved relationship with the Catholic Church. The Bolocco family's strong identification with the Catholic Church was a main theme of journalists. Cecilia's mother, Rose, attributed the victory to the divine intervention of her elder son, Rodrigo, who had died the previous year.[126] According to one journalist, "Two of Chileans' fatalist beliefs were laid to rest this year: That one of ours would never be raised to the altars and that we would never have a Miss Universe. The glories of Heaven and Earth seemed closed to them."[127] In interviews, Bolocco credited God with her recovery from a poor showing at the Miss South America contest.[128] Thus, the Miss Universe pageant represented a youthful version of femininity that maintained a Catholic and socially conservative foundation for gender roles.

In the 1987 pageant, the "national costume" portion of the contest at the opening of the show presented contestants in traditional outfits from their countries. The Chilean delegation selected a "national costume" for Cecilia Bolocco that was based on Mapuche dress. The use of a Mapuche-inspired outfit seems at odds with Pinochet's embrace of Western culture and his insistence on Chile's European heritage; yet it was in step with the government tourist board's marketing of "exotic" Easter Island and the "authentic" southern Indians in promotional material sent abroad. Bolocco's wildly exaggerated costume and jewelry, coupled with her European features, underscored her distance from Chile's indigenous communities. The costume reflected the government's freedom to exploit Mapuche culture and viewers' interest in it, while simultaneously undermining the Mapuches' struggle for recognition. The designer Marco Correa claimed that his costume was inspired by a nineteenth-century Cacique woman and explained that Cecilia's haughty air had brought the vision to his mind.[129] Correa's statement implied that dignified Indians were themselves relics of the past and disregarded the violent struggle between Mapuches and the state throughout the nineteenth century. Furthermore, the use of bits and pieces of Mapuche dress hampered efforts by Indians to control their own image in mainstream media. While solidarity groups such as the Musicians' Committee criticized the state's exploitation of indigenous culture, singling out the Ministry of Tourism, they failed to integrate indigenous artists into their organizations.

Beauty pageants borrowed elements of liberal feminism that stressed individual choice, careers, and civic freedoms. Yet Cecilia Bolocco represented freedoms that did not exist in an authoritarian state. In the coverage of Bolocco's win, the media sidestepped elements of her story that challenged traditional gender roles or provoked social commentary. Bolocco, like previous pageant participants of the 1980s, stressed that she belonged to a new class of women that combined professional and personal desires. During the interview segment of the pageant, hosted by Bob Barker, Bolocco explained her plans to launch an interior design business. Yet, rather than discuss her entrepreneurial spirit, the media harped on her feminine eye for beauty. When explaining her future plans, Bolocco told Barker that she would later go on to marry and have a family. While the message of heteronormativity pervaded the pageant, Bolocco added this aspiration almost as an afterthought. Contestants were forbidden to be married or to have had a child, yet the costumes defied any prudish mores regarding nudity. In terms of sexuality, women's magazines harped on Bolocco's sexy looks, especially what observers called her aggressive sensuality and forthrightness. Although Bolocco's "steady" boyfriend, Alejandro Lasen, held a press conference reassuring Chileans that their relationship was thriving despite the couple's geographical separation, he failed to mention that Bolocco had already rented an apartment in Beverly Hills, California. Finally, Chile's gay community embraced beauty pageants and disrupted any fixed notion of how to interpret their iconography.

Conclusion

Solidarity activists treated cultural practices as a field to contest the policies and ideology of the dictatorship, as a vehicle to strengthen the movement, and as a resource under siege by the "cultural blackout." An examination of popular culture provides a lens on the transition from a Marxist to a human rights agenda among solidarity activists. In 1974, solidarity activists at the World Cup believed that the defeat of the dictatorship would pave the way for socialism. By 1988, solidarity groups were more ideologically heterogeneous and focused on the return of democracy. Furthermore, they hoped for justice for the regime's victims, albeit with very different ideas of what that might entail. While it can elucidate many of the more quotidian and informal struggles between the dictatorship and the opposition, using popular culture as a lens marginalizes two important types of transnational solidarity activities—union boycotts and actions against multinational corporations. The most notorious example of the latter occurred when the U.S.-based Weather Underground bombed the headquarters of corporations involved in the overthrow of the Allende government. In conjunction with other organizations, the "weather people" carried out attacks on ITT in New York City (September 23, 1973), Anaconda Copper in Oakland (September 11, 1974), and Kennecott Copper in Salt Lake City (September 5, 1975).[130]

Trade union boycotts were an important part of early solidarity work, although recent literature has marginalized the initiatives of trade unions in human rights during the 1970s and 1980s.[131] For example, during Pinochet's trip to the Philippines in 1980, workers refused to service the Chilean presidential aircraft in Fiji.[132] In Scotland, Rolls-Royce jet engines gathered dust because the members of the Transport and General Workers' Union refused to load goods to and to unload those from Chile.[133] Before Prime Minister Margaret Thatcher attacked labor unions, the bulk of the British Solidarity organization came from their ranks.[134] As early as 1975, the British Longshoreman's Union formally petitioned the United Nations to condemn the junta's violations of the Universal Declaration of Human Rights. The diminished presence of organized labor in solidarity activity by early 1980 reflected its decreased power.[135] Thus, while popular culture shaped the solidarity movement, it hasn't recorded the whole of its history.

Confident of his popularity, Augusto Pinochet agreed to hold a plebiscite in 1988 on his next term, which he planned to last until 1997. The voters chose between "Sí" to support Pinochet's bid to remain in power and "No" to hold elections for parliament and president. Thousands of exiled Chileans returned, bringing their political experiences abroad to bear on the transition. Popular culture figured importantly in the "No" campaign, which chose the celebratory slogan "Joy is coming." Opponents of the dictatorship utilized songs, television commercials, and festivals as vehicles to mobilize supporters. Political analysts credited their use of popular culture with fostering the success of the "no" movement. After Pinochet's defeat, human rights advocates continued to utilize popular culture to memorialize victims of the regime and to punish the perpetrators of such abuses. After the end of the seventeen-year dictatorship, efforts to hold General Pinochet accountable became important to the expansion of universal jurisdiction to enforce human rights worldwide.[136]

From its inception, members of the Chilean solidarity movement identified popular culture as a terrain in which to contest the military dictatorship. Emerging in the 1970s, a transnational network of activists confronted the regime's legitimacy throughout the world. Public memorials to the Popular Unity government in Russia, Mozambique, Saudi Arabia, and Israel testify to the reach of their activities.[137] At times, ideological differences among activists caused tense confrontations. Popular culture, including theater, artistic exhibitions, and music concerts, provided venues where activists renewed their commitment to the cause and connected with new audiences. Cultural producers created a series of familiar codes that bridged linguistic, class, national, and political difference. In the 1970s and 1980s, feminist and gay rights activists broadened the agenda of solidarity groups to include issues hitherto considered "personal."

Organizations such as Action for Women in Chile viewed cultural practices as spaces where this intersection of personal and public oppression could be explored. Although solidarity activists did not succeed in dominating the mainstream media, they created a rich repertoire of alternative practices that challenged the image of success that the Pinochet regime sought to project. International condemnation threatened the diplomatic and economic relationships that Pinochet's government cultivated, ultimately culminating in his arrest in London, in 1998. Still, the neoliberal, consumerist, and socially conservative citizen, promoted by the regime in spectacles like the Miss Universe pageant, continues to shape Chilean political subjectivities.

Notes

I would like to thank Andrés Estefane, James N. Green, Elizabeth Hutchison, Thomas Miller Klubock, Jessica Stites Mor, Steven Volk, and the anonymous readers at the University of Wisconsin Press for their helpful suggestions on this chapter.

1. For a review of the literature on solidarity movements, see Van Gosse, "Unpacking the Vietnam Syndrome: The Coup in Chile and the Rise of Popular Anti-Interventionism," in *The World the Sixties Made: Politics and Culture in Recent America*, ed. Van Gosse and Richard Moser (Philadelphia: Temple University Press, 2003), 100–113; Margaret Power and Julie Charlip, "Introduction: On Solidarity," *Latin American Perspectives* 36 (2009): 3–9, José del Pozo, *Exiliados, Emigrados y retornados: Chilenos en América y Europa, 1973–2004* (Santiagao: RIL Editores, 2006); Julie Shayne, *They Used to Call Us Witches: Chilean Exiles, Culture, and Feminism* (Lanham, MD: Lexington Books, 2009); Steve Stern, *Battling for Hearts and Minds: Memory Struggles in Pinochet's Chile, 1973–1988* (Durham, NC: Duke University Press, 2006); and Mario Sznajder and Luis Roniger, "Exile Communities and Their Differential Institutional Dynamics: A Comparative Analysis of the Chilean and Uruguayan Political Diasporas," *Revista de Ciencia Política* 1 (2007): 43–66.

2. Actions against the coup in Brazil and against U.S. involvement in Vietnam laid the groundwork for coordinated efforts across the Americas. See James N. Green, *We Cannot Remain Silent: Opposition to the Brazilian Military Dictatorship in the United States* (Durham, NC: Duke University Press, 2010). Green also describes the importance of the coup in Chile for activists working in the United States.

3. For a review of the debates on the relationship between the human rights and neo-colonialism, see Anthony Pagden, "Human Rights, Natural Rights, and Europe's Imperial Legacy," *Political Theory* 31 (2003): 171–99.

4. See the archive of the North American Congress on Latin America (NACLA), located at the University of Florida at Gainesville, which is an invaluable resource. Its contents are detailed in Peter Johnson and Francisco Fonseca, *North American Congress on Latin America (NACLA) Archive of Latin Americana* (Wilmington, DE: Scholarly Resources, 1999).

5. Elizabeth Hutchison and Patricio Orellana, *El movimiento de derechos humanos en Chile, 1973–1990* (Santiago: Centro de Estudios Políticos Latinoamericanos Simón Bolívar, 1991).

6. Pierre Bourdieu, *The Logic of Practice*, trans. Richard Nice (Stanford: Stanford University Press, 1990).

7. Raymond Williams, *Keywords: A Vocabulary of Culture and Society* (New York: Oxford University Press, 1985).

8. William Sewell, *Logics of History: Social Theory and Social Transformation* (Chicago: University of Chicago Press, 2005)

9. "AHR Conversation: On Transnational History," *American Historical Review* 111, no. 5 (2006): 1441–65.

10. Gilbert M. Joseph, Catherine LeGrand, and Ricardo Donato Salvatore, eds.,

Close Encounters of Empire: Writing the Cultural History of U.S.-Latin American Relations (Durham, NC: Duke University Press, 1998).

11. Thomas Bender, ed., *Rethinking American History in a Global Age* (Berkeley: University of California, 2002).

12. Their participation would have been possible only if they defeated the Chilean squad; playing them was not enough.

13. *Estadio*, November 13, 1973, 54–56.

14. Geoffrey Green, "Chile May Yet Move the World Cup Match," *The Times* (London), November 12, 1973, 15.

15. Quoted in David Goldblatt, *The Ball Is Round: A Global History of Soccer* (New York: Riverhead Books, 2006), 609.

16. Rodrigo Rojas, *In the Hands of Chile's Hangmen: The Prison Experience of Rodrigo Rojas* (New York: New Outlook, 1975).

17. Alex Yannis, "Soccer Storm Brewing in Soviet Bloc," *New York Times*, November 4, 1973.

18. For the history of this debate in Chilean politics, see Brenda Elsey, *Citizens and Sportsmen: Fútbol and Politics in Twentieth-Century Chile* (Austin: University of Texas Press, 2011).

19. Personal communication, founders Professor Wolfgang Krashnaar, Hamburger Institut für Sozialforschung, October 8 and 15, 2009, and Stefan Saarbach, of Chile-Solidarität-Aktion, January 2010.

20. See, for example, *Chile Nachrichten* (Berlin), March 20, 1974.

21. Personal communication, Stefan Saarbach, January 19 and 21, 2010.

22. Wolfgang Kraushnaar, "'Chile Sí, Junta No!' Political Protests at the 1974 FIFA World Cup," trans. Toby Axelrod, *Eurozine*, July 8, 2008; personal communication, Professor Kraushnaar, October 8, 2009.

23. "Anticipan Clima Tenso para Chile," *El Mercurio*, June 6, 1974, 5.

24. The letter accompanied a pamphlet that the football representatives were instructed to distribute. *El Mercurio*, June 2, 1974, 35 (page number damaged). Unfortunately, I have not been able to locate a copy of the pamphlet and have found only references to its existence.

25. Chile Democrático, *Boletín Informativo* (Rome), June–July 1974; José del Pozo, "Las Organizaciones de Chilenos en Québec," in del Pozo, *Exiliados, Emigrados y Retornados*, 127–48; personal communication with Silvio Espinoza, e-mail, October 25, 2009.

26. Ramírez Banda, "'Dudas que Matan' en Equipos Sudamericanos," *El Mercurio*, June 1, 1974, 7. See also *El Mercurio*, June 1, 1974, which features a letter from Augusto Pinochet alongside news of the tournament.

27. *El Mercurio*, June 19, 1974, 6.

28. *El Mercurio*, June 15, 1974, 2.

29. "Berlin: Repudio a acto Antichileno," *El Mercurio*, June 23, 1974, 4.

30. Personal communication, Wolfgang Krashnaar, October 8, 2009, and Stefan Saarbach, January 21, 2010.

31. *El Mercurio*, June 19, 1974, 15.

32. *El Mercurio*, June 20, 1974, 1.

33. Ibid., 6.

34. Ibid.

35. Chile Democrático (Rome), *Boletín Informativo*, June–July 1974.

36. "Chilenos son criticados," *El Mercurio*, June 13, 1974, 4.

37. "Tenso enfrentamiento con la prensa tuvo selección Chilena," *El Mercurio*, June 12, 1974, 10.

38. Jorge Iturriaga, "Proletas, limpios, cobardes y burgueses: El fútbol en 1973," in *1973: La vida cotidiana de un año crucial*, ed. Claudio Rolle (Santiago: Planeta, 2003), 297–352.

39. *Chile Antifascista* (Berlin), May 1975, 2.

40. Peter Winn, ed., *Victims of the Chilean Miracle: Workers and Neoliberalism in the Pinochet Era* (Durham, NC: Duke University Press, 2004).

41. *Chile Antifascista* (Berlin), May 1975, 2.

42. Ibid.

43. On Casa Chile, see Claudia Rojas Mira, "La Casa Chile en México, 1973–1993," in del Pozo, *Exiliados*, 107–26; also, personal communication, Eliana Espinoza, September 16, 2009.

44. "Chile Davis Team to Go to Sweden," *New York Times*, September 13, 1975, 17.

45. "Chile irá a Suecia," *El Mercurio*, September 9, 1975, 1.

46. *El Mercurio*, September 10, 1975, 1.

47. *El Mercurio*, September 13, 1975. There is great controversy surrounding the veracity of the military's claims to have discovered stockpiled weapons. See Pamela Constable and Arturo Valenzuela, *A Nation of Enemies: Chile under Pinochet* (New York: Norton, 1991).

48. Ibid.

49. *El Mercurio*, September 14, 1975, 31. See the response in England to the Davis Cup controversy: *The Times* (London), September 10, 1975, 11.

50. Personal communication, Eric Leenson, January 18, 2011.

51. United Committee to Stop the Esmeralda, "Protests against Chilean Navy Visit to San Francisco Bay," North American Congress on Latin America (NACLA) Archive Latin Americana, file 118, roll 23.

52. Power, "The U.S. Movement in Solidarity with Chile in the 1970s," and United Committee to Stop the Esmeralda, "Protests Against Chilean Navy Visit to San Francisco Bay," NACLA Archive of Latin Americana, file 118, roll 23.

53. "San Francisco Prostitutes Boycott Chilean Navy," press release, June 17, 1974, NACLA Archive of Latin Americana, file 118, roll 23, Chile. Also, personal communication, Margo St. James, January 21, 2010.

54. Personal communication, Margo St. James, January 21, 2010.

55. Personal communication, Margaret Power, February 12, 2010. It should be remembered that a march for gay rights that took place in Santiago during 1972 was ridiculed by the pro-Allende *El Clarín* and was brusquely dispersed by the police. See Victor Hugo Robles, "History in the Making," *North American Congress on*

Latin America Archive of Latin Americana Report on the Americas 31 (1998): 36–44. James N. Green found that "Overtures by newly energized gay and lesbian activists toward radical nationalism and revolutionary organizations were mostly rebuffed." James N. Green, "(Homo)sexuality, Human Rights, and Revolution in Latin America," in *Human Rights and Revolutions*, 2nd ed., ed. Jeffrey N. Wasserstrom, Lynn Hunt, Marilyn B. Young, and Gregory Grandin (London: Rowman and Littlefield, 2007), 141.

56. Personal communication, James N. Green, January 24, 2011.

57. Ibid.

58. See NACLA Archive of Latin Americana (Chile Files).

59. Temma Kaplan, *Taking Back the Street: Women, Youth, and Direct Democracy* (Berkeley: University of California, 2004). For a historical view of the relationships among right-wing politics, the military, and women in Chile, see Margaret Power, *Right-Wing Women in Chile: Feminine Power and the Struggle against Allende, 1964–1973* (University Park: Penn State University Press, 2002).

60. Loreto Rebolledo, Teresa Valdés, Ximena Valdés, and Diana Veneros, "El movimiento social de mujeres: Memoria, acción colectiva y democratización en Chile en la segunda mitad del siglo XX," in *Memoria para un nuevo siglo*, ed. Mario Garcés et al. (Santiago: LOM, 2000), 213–29.

61. Stern, *Battling for Hearts and Minds*.

62. Ibid.

63. *The Times* (London), October 27, 1982, 22.

64. Marjorie Agosín, *Tapestries of Hope, Threads of Love: The Arpillera Movement in Chile* (Lanham, MD: Rowman and Littlefield, 2008); Julie Shayne and Jacqueline Adams, "Art in Social Movements: Shantytown Women's Protest in Pinochet's Chile," *Sociological Forum* 17 (2002): 21–56.

65. Stern, *Battling for Hearts and Minds*. See, for example, the story of Tanya R. For a discussion of *arpilleras*, see also Agosín, *Tapestries of Hope, Threads of Love*.

66. Agosín, *Tapestries of Hope, Threads of Love*.

67. Oscar Lepeley, "The *Cueca* of the Last Judgment: Politics of the Chilean Resistance in *Tres Marías y Una Rosa*," in *Imagination beyond a Nation*, ed. Eva Bueno and Terry Caesar (Pittsburgh: University of Pittsburgh Press, 1998), 142–66.

68. Henry Scarups, "Arpilleras Show Sad Images of Chilean Reality," *Baltimore Sun*, 1983, reprinted in *Chile Panorama* (published by Amnesty International), May–June 1984, 14.

69. Shayne and Adams, "Art in Social Movements."

70. Secretaría Nacional de la Mujer, *Amiga* (Chile), March 1980, 48.

71. *Chile Panorama*, May–June 1984.

72. Scarups, "Arpilleras Show Sad Images of Chilean Reality," 19.

73. See Jocelyn Olcott, "Cold War Conflicts and Cheap Cabaret: Sexual Politics at the 1975 United Nations International Women's Year Conference," *Gender and History* 22 (2010): 733–54.

74. Personal communication via telephone, Margo St. James, January 21, 2010.

75. "AFWIC Debates the 'Woman Question,'" *Action for Women in Chile* 2 (Summer 1978): 5.

76. Julie Shayne, *The Revolution Question: Feminisms in El Salvador, Chile, and Cuba* (New Brunswick, NJ: Rutgers University Press, 2004), 102.

77. Kaplan, *Taking Back the Streets*.

78. Ibid., 7.

79. Elsey, *Citizens and Sportsmen*.

80. Patricia Chuchryk, "From Dictatorship to Democracy: The Women's Movement in Chile," in *The Women's Movement in Latin America: Participation and Democracy*, ed. Jane Jacquette (Boulder, CO: Westview Press, 1994), 65–107; Shayne, *The Revolution Question*.

81. "The Charter of Santiago of Chile," NACLA Archive of Latin Americana, files 254–56, roll 48, did not specifically treat women in 1978. The "Convention on the Elimination of All Forms of Discrimination against Women," the international human rights treaty for women, was adopted the following year by the United Nations. Chile signed the convention in 1980, but it was not ratified until 1989, after Pinochet left power.

82. *Convergencia* (New York), October 1979, 19.

83. "Meeting at Amnesty International," March 28, 1977, NACLA Archive of Latin Americana, files 118–21, roll 23.

84. Rita Arditt, *Searching for Life: The Grandmothers of the Plaza de Mayo and the Disappeared Children of Argentina* (Berkeley: University of California Press, 1999), 97.

85. Scarups, "Arpilleras Show Sad Images of Chilean Reality," 14.

86. Victor Barberis, "Notas," *Arauco*, April 1982, 78.

87. American Friends Society Committee Report, "Few Glimmers Penetrate Chile's 'Cultural Blackout,'" NACLA Archive of Latin Americana, July 1980, files 246–48, roll 46.

88. Personal communication, anonymous source, October 23, 2009. This point is also established in Catherine Boyle, *Chilean Theater, 1973–1985: Marginality, Power, and Selfhood* (Rutherford, NJ: Farleigh Dickinson University Press, 1992), and in Grínor Rojo, "Teatro chileno bajo fascismo," *Araucaría* 22 (1983): 123–36.

89. For an overview of the genre, see Juan Pablo González and Claudio Rolle, *Historia social de la música popular en Chile, 1890–1950* (Santiago: Ediciones Universidad Católica de Chile, 2005); Nancy Morris, "Canto Porque Es Necesario Cantar: The New Song Movement in Chile, 1973–1983," *Latin American Research Review* 21, no. 2 (1986): 117–36; and Fernando Ríos, "La Flûte Indienne: The Early History of Andean Folkloric-Popular Music in France and Its Impact on Nueva Canción," *Latin American Music Review* 29 (2008): 145–81.

90. César Albornoz, "Cultura en la Unidad Popular: Porque esta vez no se trata de cambiar un presidente," in *Cuando hicimos historia: La experiencia de la Unidad Popular*, ed. Julio Pinto (Santiago: LOM, 2005), 147–76.

91. Comité de Solidarité Québec-Chili, "press release," April 17, 1975, NACLA Archive of Latin Americana, files 248–54, roll 47.

92. Ríos, "La Flûte Indienne."

93. Ibid., 173.

94. Manuel Alcides, "Haciendo Chile en el Exilio," *Apsi*, July 31–August 13, 1984, 48.

95. Comité de los Músicos Chilenos, *Chile: La Cultura Popular Resiste*, December 1978.

96. Mapocho Cultural Center, "Interview with Executive Secretary of Coordinador Cultural," and "Draft Transcript@Chile Alert," 5, NACLA Archive of Latin Americana, files 246–48, roll 46.

97. American Friends Society Committee Report, "Few Glimmers Penetrate Chile's 'Cultural Blackout.'"

98. Mapocho Cultural Center, "Interview with Executive Secretary of Coordinador Cultural," and "Draft Transcript@Chile Alert," 11.

99. Ibid., 1.

100. Claudio Pereda-Madrid, "Revista 'La Bicicleta: 30 años después," *La Nación*, September 28, 2008, n.p.

101. "El nuevo canto chileno: En la senda de Violeta: Entrevistas y canciones del canto nuevo," *La Bicicleta*, April–May 1981. For an earlier history of the label and *canto nuevo*, see Javier Osorio Fernández, "*La Bicicleta*, canto nuevo y las tramas musicales de la disidencia," *Contracorriente* 8 (2011): 255–86.

102. "Music Sparks Political Protests by Chilean Youth," *Chile Panorama*, June–August 1983, 10. For a more in-depth discussion of music performance in Chile during the dictatorship, see Gabriela Bravo and Cristián González Farfán, *Ecos del tiempo subterraneo: Las peñas en Santiago durante el régimen militar, 1973–1983* (Santiago: LOM Ediciones, 2009).

103. Alvaro Godoy, "Picoteo de música," *La Bicicleta*, May 1983.

104. Santiago del Nuevo Extremo, "Homenaje," *La Bicicleta*, October 1982, 19.

105. Rebeca Araya, "Ángel Parra: Vuelvo a Cada Rato," *La Bicicleta*, February 1984, 20.

106. Ibid., 24.

107. "Illapú," *La Bicicleta*, April–May 1981, 30.

108. Oscar Contardo and Macarena García, *La era ochentera: Tevé, pop y under en el Chile de los ochenta* (Santiago: Ediciones B Chile, 2005). An exception to the dominance of foreign imports was the tremendously popular show *Sábado Gigante*, which, despite host Mario Kreutzberger's declaration of neutrality, supported Pinochet. During a 1981 show, for instance, Kreutzberger made an on-air endorsement of the regime's privatization of pensions. For more information, see Mario Kreutzberger, *Don Francisco entre la espada y la TV* (Mexico City: Grijalbo, 2001). *Sábado Gigante* was so popular that it relocated, in 1986, to Miami, where it captured an even larger Spanish-speaking audience. Kreutzberger continues to broadcast the show.

109. Not all beauty pageants merely reinforce social hierarchies. See Karen Tice, "For Appearance's Sake: Beauty, Bodies, Spectacle, and Consumption," *Journal of Women's History* 18 (2006): 147–56.

110. "Chilena, Miss Universo," *El Mercurio*, May 27, 1987, A8.

111. *Paula*, ed. especial, June 1987.

112. *Paula*, June 1987.

113. *El Mercurio*, June 31, 1987, C12.

114. "Chilena, Miss Universo," *El Mercurio*, May 27, 1987, A8.

115. "Los famosos opinan: Por qué ganó," *Paula*, ed. especial, June 1987, 108.

116. *El Mercurio*, June 28, 1987, A10.

117. Pilar Molina, "Los Chilenos Número Uno en el mundo," *El Mercurio*, June 31, 1987, D7.

118. *El Mercurio*, June 29, 1987, C15.

119. *La Época*, October 3, 1987.

120. "Yo soy la belleza de la Mujer Chilena," *Cosas*, ed. extraordinario, August 1987, n.p.

121. As of yet, I have not found evidence that transnational solidarity activists protested Bolocco's appearances. This may be a result of the attention and energies directed toward Chile, given the return of exiles and the pending plebiscite.

122. Hernán Millas y Paz del Mar, "Miss Universo Cecilia," *Hoy*, June 1, 1987, 19.

123. *El Mercurio*, May 28, 1987, A10.

124. Ibid.

125. Ibid.

126. "Chilena, Miss Universo," *El Mercurio*, May 27, 1987, A8.

127. Hernán Millas y Paz del Mar, "Miss Universo Cecilia," 19.

128. *Paula*, ed. especial, June 1987, 19.

129. "Chilena, de la cabeza a los pies," *El Mercurio*, May 28, 1987, A4.

130. Weather Underground, "Weather Underground Organization Bombs Kenecott Corporation," NACLA Archives of Latin Americana, files 118–21, roll 23.

131. This is not the case in the United States, where leaders of the AFL-CIO actively participated in undermining labor union support for the Allende government, despite its professed concerns with democracy. Hobart Spalding, "U.S. and Latin American Labor: The Dynamics of Imperialist Control," *Latin American Perspectives* 3, no. 1 (1976): 45–69.

132. The incident prompted the resignation of Foreign Minister Hernán Cubillos; see "Scapegoat Found for Pinochet Fiasco," *The Times* (London), March 27, 1980, 10.

133. "Trade Union Stops Return of Jet Engines," *The Times* (London), June 10, 1978, 2.

134. Interview with Brian Nicholson, *America Insurrecta*, New York, September 1976. British trade unions reached out to fellow unionists in a way that undermined the nationalist discourse put forward by the Conservative government of Margaret Thatcher. For example, in 1981, Welsh miners offered housing and jobs to fifty Chileans. According to Brian Nicholson, leader of the British Longshoreman's Union and chairman of the British Solidarity campaign, the organization's membership included six million trade unionists and 250,000 members of churches and political groups.

135. Caroline Moorehead, "Amnesty and Unions Deplore Lifting of Chile Arms Embargo," *The Times* (London), July 25, 1980, 6. Thatcher quickly overturned the Labour Party's ban on the sale of arms to Chile.

136. Naomi Roht-Arriaza, *The Pinochet Effect: Transnational Justice in the Age of Human Rights* (Philadelphia: University of Pennsylvania Press, 2006).

137. Personal communication, Eliana Espinoza, Silvio Espinoza, and Mafalda Galdames, January 1, 2006 (Los Andes, Chile), and October 22, 2009.

8

The Politics of Refuge

Salvadoran Refugees and International Aid in Honduras

MOLLY TODD

A 1983 issue of *Refugees Magazine,* published by the United
Nations High Commissioner for Refugees (UNHCR), in-
cludes a photograph of a Salvadoran family resting after their arrival at a refugee reception center in Honduras. The young mother sits on the ground and
leans her head, hair tousled, against the wall behind her. Her feet, bare and
muddied, stretch out from under the hem of her torn dress. The father's shirt-
tails hang loose and gray as he wraps a blanket around one of his children. Two
toddler boys stare at the camera with sad and tired eyes; the smallest boy is on
the verge of tears. Behind them, a young girl buries her face in her hands. Her
sister watches her cry.[1]

Just a few months before this photograph appeared, a Honduran newspaper published an editorial cartoon depicting a refugee camp. In the center of
the drawing, a man kicks back in the shade of a palm tree. He sports a scraggly
beard, a beret, hefty boots, and a contented smile. On the sand next to him rest
a pistol, a rifle, and a bomb. A line of tents frames the sketch on one side, the
flaps of one tent open slightly to reveal boxes of war matériel hidden inside.[2]

These two images purport to represent the same group of people—
Salvadoran refugees in UNHCR-sponsored camps in Honduras. Yet they are

strikingly different. In one, refugees appear as desperate and helpless victims; in the other, they are rebels who are more than willing to use violence as a means to an end. Despite this difference, at their core, the two images are the same: they present the displaced as an anomaly, an aberration in the universally accepted "national order of things."[3] Whether victims or warriors, refugees are populations that must be managed and controlled. In short, they are problems to be solved.

These two images are quite representative of mainstream discourses about refugees in general. For much of the past fifty years, international policymakers, scholars, and humanitarian aid workers have tended to portray refugees not only as problems but as accessories to issues of *real* import: the roles of states in prompting or resolving refugee flows; the development of international law and norms relating to displaced populations and humanitarianism; and the mandates and behaviors of major organizations dedicated to protecting refugees, providing humanitarian aid, and promoting human rights. These approaches to the study of refugees stress "official" definitions and categorizations: who precisely is a legitimate refugee? To what rights and benefits is she or he entitled? As high-profile actors debate such questions in international policy circles and on the pages of scholarly journals, refugee bodies become sites of transnational struggle.

Perhaps ironically, displaced populations rarely, if ever, are party to these debates. Indeed, the high-profile participants tend to consider refugees incapable of meaningful engagement because their "judgment and reason ha[ve] been compromised by [their] experiences" of violence that typically accompany displacement. In other words, separation from their national communities renders refugees "no longer trustworthy as 'honest citizens.'"[4] Consequently, they must be managed, deciphered, and healed only by professionals.

This Central American case study turns the study of refugee crises on its head by allowing refugees to interpret and represent themselves and by placing their voices at the center of the debate. More specifically, it examines the case of Salvadoran *campesinos* who sought exile in Honduras during the dirty and civil wars of the 1970s through the early 1990s. Documentation produced in the refugee camps, oral history interviews, and internal records of the UNHCR reveal that, although excluded from official decision-making circles, refugees found alternative ways of entering conversations and affecting policy.

First, I outline the official debate by examining how Honduran and UN officials "imagined" the refugees and represented them before national and international publics. I then examine how refugees' own imaginings challenged official representations. This ground-up perspective offers crucial insights into how *campesino* refugees constructed political identities and how their transnational experiences influenced their understandings of themselves and their roles in Salvadoran affairs.

Imagining Refugees

By the 1970s, civil and dirty wars raged through much of Central America, prompting millions of people to leave their homes. Many of the displaced eked out a dangerous, clandestine existence in mountain ranges and jungles. Many others sought anonymity in urban centers. Still others trekked across international borders in search of refuge in other Central American nations, as well as in Mexico, the United States, Canada, and beyond. In El Salvador, as early as December 1981, more than one million people—approximately one-fifth of the country's total population—had been displaced by the civil war, which had officially begun only a year earlier. By the mid-1980s, some thirty thousand had crossed the international border into Honduras, where they settled in three major United Nations–sponsored refugee camps: Colomoncagua (sheltering around 8,400), San Antonio (approximately 1,500), and Mesa Grande (around 11,500), along with several smaller reception areas.[5] The majority of these refugees were *campesinos* from the northern fringes of El Salvador.

The Cold War context—and, more specifically, U.S. hegemony in the region—exacerbated local and regional problems. Fears that the Soviet Union would extend its communist empire into the American hemisphere prompted successive U.S. administrations to steadily increase their involvement in Latin American affairs. The 1959 Cuban Revolution, followed by the Sandinista overthrow of the Somoza dynasty in Nicaragua, in 1979, appeared to be proof positive of Soviet expansion. In light of these events and in an effort to counter other revolutionary movements, the United States poured billions of dollars of economic and military aid into Latin America. Under the leadership of President Ronald Reagan (1981–89), Central America became the "line in the sand" against Soviet-inspired communism, and Honduras became the staging ground for proxy wars in Nicaragua (via the Contras), as well as Guatemala and El Salvador (via government armed forces, along with extralegal vigilantes and death squads).

In this politically charged environment, refugee populations were not simply consequences of generalized violence; they were themselves sites of struggle. Throughout the 1980s, governments and international organizations—principally the UNHCR—debated endlessly about resource allocation and proposed solutions to the refugee crisis. They also argued about how to define a refugee, that is, whom to include in the refugee category. Of special concern was how to distinguish "legitimate victims" from other mobile populations, including insurgents and economic migrants. Each of the high-profile actors had different concerns about Salvadoran *campesinos* in Honduras, which led to differing definitions, policies, and procedures. Despite the differences, they shared a similar overarching goal: to contain Salvadoran refugees in space and time and, consequently, to depoliticize them and render them passive recipients of international aid.

Honduran government officials initially resisted granting formal recognition as refugees to the thousands of Salvadoran *campesinos* who had crossed the international border. This resistance was facilitated by the fact that Honduras was not a signatory to the United Nations Convention on Refugees (1951) or to its Protocol (1967) and, thus, was not bound by the definitions, rules, and regulations set forth within the documents. Beyond this, however, Honduran authorities had unique concerns about Salvadorans; despite the presence of tens of thousands of Guatemalans, Nicaraguans, and Haitians on Honduran soil at the same time, reactions to the Salvadorans were especially severe.

Such a response was, in large part, an outgrowth of the history of tense relations between the two nations. Indeed, tensions over regional economic balance, territorial claims, and migration policies had flared into a series of military skirmishes in the 1960s, which culminated in the 1969 Hundred-Hour War (also known as the Soccer War). In 1979, when large groups of Salvadorans first began entering Honduran territory in search of refuge from the violence raging at home, the two nations were still officially at war; they had never resumed diplomatic relations, even after military battles subsided a decade earlier.[6]

For Honduran officials, Salvadoran refugees personified many of the issues that had contributed to the 1969 war; they feared that the refugees would "turn into the friction point that will lead once again to an armed confrontation between the two countries."[7] For example, some believed that those crossing the border migrated for economic reasons. According to a government report, Salvadorans were "elements whose lives and properties are not at risk," who played the refugee role as "a method of getting into Honduras in order to make a new life in our territory. . . . They are people who came to Honduras already decided and convinced that they would remain living in the country."[8] In short, Honduran authorities did not want their nation to serve as an "escape valve" for a neighbor's overpopulation and related economic troubles.

Others feared far more sinister intentions. When Salvadorans began crossing into Honduras by the thousands, the international border dividing the two nations had yet to be fully demarcated. In fact, El Salvador and Honduras had been wrestling with each other about the borderline since achieving independence in the early 1800s. By 1979, progress had been made, but there were still several pockets of land in dispute. These territories, known as *bolsones*, represented nearly 420 square kilometers and approximately 20 percent of the borderline.[9] Salvadoran refugees often convened in areas adjacent to or even inside the disputed *bolsones*, which Honduran officials believed offered far too many options to Salvadoran forces. Concerns about territorial sovereignty, particularly with regard to the disputed *bolsones*, prompted the Honduran National Security Council to condemn Salvadoran refugees as an invasion force "endanger[ing] the country's national security."[10]

A related issue, but one that also moved beyond the shadow of the Hundred-Hour War, was the perception that, as Honduran colonel Flores Auceda put it, "there are only guerrillas living in the refugee camps."[11] Military authorities were especially adamant in arguing that *campesinos* who crossed the border maintained intimate connections with the Salvadoran insurgent forces of the Frente Farabundo Martí para la Liberación Nacional (Farabundo Martí National Liberation Front, or FMLN). Even if not combatants themselves, they were "connected to terrorist militants. Even a family relationship could indicate that they have a moral commitment that leads them to participate in such activity."[12] According to this perspective, Salvadoran guerrillas used the refugee camps as strategic sites to rest and recuperate from injuries; to recruit and train new soldiers; to produce boots, uniforms, and other items for combat; to broadcast propaganda from secret FMLN radio stations; and to transfer and store weapons and other supplies received from "communists" in Nicaragua, Cuba, and other Soviet allies.[13]

These economic, territorial, and political concerns prompted the Honduran government to distinguish Salvadorans from the other refugee groups in the country. Whereas the refugees from Nicaragua, Guatemala, and Haiti were "*non-national groups* that have no effect on the life of the country," Salvadorans constituted *a special, national group* that posed unique threats to the Honduran nation.[14] In light of this, the Honduran National Security Council insisted that officials "manage the situation in the most intelligent manner."[15] Toward this end—and to boost Honduras' international reputation—officials entered into formal negotiations with the UNHCR. In 1982, the two parties reached an agreement that "promised the containment and depoliticization of the refugee population."[16]

Per Honduran demands, Salvadorans were relocated away from the immediate vicinity of the border and held in "closed camps." This meant that military and political officials closely monitored all movements made by refugees: no one could enter or exit the refugee camps unless "duly authorized" by both national immigration officials and local military commanders; travel between the different camps and subcamps required a written pass, even when the distance was but a few hundred yards; and ever-changing curfews prohibited many things after hours, often including the use of lighting and any movement between tents. Other efforts to track and control the Salvadorans included the regular collection of census data from each of the camps and the stipulation that even emergency medical evacuations required military oversight and accompaniment. Moreover, officials declared it illegal for Salvadorans to attend schools in Honduras, participate in local markets, purchase land, or establish *colonizaciones rurales* (rural colonies or settlements). Persisting concerns that Salvadorans would use refugee status as a "foot in the door" for Honduran citizenship led the National Congress to rewrite the Constitution to further clarify Honduran citizenship requirements and to explicitly exclude children born to refugee parents.[17]

In their efforts to manage and control the refugee population, Honduran authorities received crucial assistance from the UNHCR. Although international representatives of this UN body often protested the more questionable control mechanisms (such as military patrols through refugee camps, detentions, and interrogations), they had limited jurisdiction given that Honduras was not signatory to the international agreements on refugees. Nonetheless, UNHCR's own approach paralleled that of the Honduran government in at least one fundamental way: the organization recognized only "pure victims" as legitimate refugees.

This narrow definition of "refugee" was closely linked to the UNHCR's organizational mandate. According to its 1950 founding document, "The work of the High Commissioner shall be of an entirely *non-political* character; it shall be *humanitarian* and social and shall relate, as a rule, to groups and categories of refugees."[18] Despite changes in world contexts over the ensuing thirty years and despite the multitude of experiences with refugees around the globe in those three decades, the UNHCR of the mid and late 1980s continued to proclaim itself a purely humanitarian organization. As Jean Pierre Hocké, High Commissioner from 1985 to 1989, explained, the international community takes "two parallel and simultaneous actions" to address refugee crises: "One is humanitarian, directed primarily towards alleviating human suffering and providing protection. The other is political, directed primarily towards attenuating the root causes and providing solutions. While UNHCR should concern itself with humanitarian action, it is the community of states which must undertake action in the political arena."[19] Hocké and the UNHCR, then, make a clear distinction between acts of humanitarianism and political acts. Whereas humanitarianism is the purview of the UNHCR and collaborating aid agencies, politics is the purview of states.

If the UNHCR was beyond politics, so too did it define refugees as such. Thus, as Salvadoran *campesinos* crossed into Honduras and *became* refugees, they *unbecame* everything else. They personified absence and loss—of home, livelihood, and civil and political rights. In others words, as one UNHCR official working with Salvadorans explained, "the refugees are victims."[20]

This victim label carried with it certain assumptions about the refugees' situation and behaviors. Officials from the UNHCR presumed, for example, that flight from El Salvador was due to circumstances beyond the *campesinos'* control. Chaos and desperation marked the crossing of the border, as *campesinos* fled with only their own physical survival in mind. A parallel assumption was that being without a home and without a state rendered them entirely dependent on the good will of their Honduran hosts and the international community, represented by the UNHCR.

In labeling the Salvadorans "victims," the UNHCR rendered them not only beyond the state and beyond politics but also outside of time. Their histories did not matter. And neither, in a way, did their present; their lives were on hold until the "best solution" of "voluntary repatriation" became possible.[21] Herein lies yet another assumption: that "return" was both possible and preferred. Yet, without addressing the back story—that is, the sociopolitical and economic roots that gave rise to people's decisions to move across the international border—voluntary repatriation meant little more than a return to the status quo ante.

The refugee-victim idealized by the UNHCR was, in short, dehistoricized and depoliticized. In light of such a narrow definition and given the pressures from the Honduran government, the UNHCR responded to nearly all kinds of organization and mobilization among the Salvadoran refugee population with punishment, including limitations on movement, curfews, and restrictions on resources and activities. As noted, the UNHCR also tolerated more direct and physical punishments meted out by Honduran and Salvadoran forces: military incursions into camps, the ransacking of refugee houses and offices, physical brutality, arrests, and deportations. For refugees who spoke out against such treatment or who mobilized in other, independent ways, the UNHCR struck from them the "refugee" label and replaced it with other labels carrying highly negative connotations: insurgent, communist, terrorist. Thus, once refugees mobilized—even via nonviolent routes—they were no longer victims; instead, they became delinquents, threats to order and security.

There can be no doubt that pressures from the Honduran government heavily influenced UNHCR procedures in the field. At the same time, the UNHCR—with its substantial financial, material, and human resources, as well as international legitimacy—had a considerable impact on the Honduran government's response to the Salvadoran *campesinos* on its soil. Although both parties' words and actions likely differed a great deal from what they would have preferred to say and do, they found common ground in sequestering Salvadorans in closed and isolated camps and silencing them. As a result, refugees existed as out-of-the-ordinary, exceptional beings, problems to be solved by states and the UNHCR.

Re-Imagining the Nation

Being a refugee and living in refugee camps, claimed the High Commissioner for Refugees, Jean Pierre Hocké, "crushes human dignity and reduces the human capacity for hope and regeneration."[22] A view from the ground—from the perspective of the refugees themselves—reveals a very different reality. The experiences and narratives of Salvadoran *campesinos* in Honduras illustrate that, although they had been victimized both at home and while in exile, pain and suffering alone did not define them. Moreover, Salvadoran refugees were interested not only in survival but also in improving their life circumstances and in prompting broader change. As they struggled in their endeavors, they continuously countered efforts by government and United Nations officials to remove their agency and decontextualize their experiences. Through their words and actions, refugees asserted themselves as participants in all realms of their life in exile, insisted on the relevance of historical and political contexts to their position as refugees, and emphasized their own relevance to the Salvadoran nation.

Salvadoran *campesinos* had considerable experience with marginalization and repression, as well as resistance to those patterns. They had long suffered the economic deprivations of life in El Salvador's northern *tierra olvidada* (forgotten land). The 1960s and 1970s brought the militarization of the border region, and by 1980 the "scorched earth" campaigns had begun. In response, *campesinos* acted of their own volition and joined with other societal actors to challenge economic structures by forming agricultural cooperatives and to stretch social and political boundaries through Christian base communities and human rights work. As violence dimmed the vibrancy of Salvadoran civil society mobilizations in the late 1970s and early 1980s, many *campesinos* left their communities for refugee camps across the international border. Life in exile in many ways continued in the same vein. In Honduras, they faced not only the physical and psychological effects of political violence and war; they also had to confront anti-Salvadoran propaganda, exclusion from "official" decision-making circles, military incursions into the refugee camps, arrests, tortures, executions, and deportations. In response, refugees organized and mobilized. Although many of their tactics shifted to address the new challenges they encountered in the refugee camps, the refugees also continued to keep the Salvadoran government in their sights.

Crucial to the refugees' efforts to assert their own authority and to maintain control over their surroundings in exile were the organizational structures they established in the camps. At Colomoncagua, San Antonio, and Mesa Grande, the largest and most populous of the UN-sponsored refugee camps, Salvadorans established entire systems of self-government. From the beginning, they used the geography of the camps to define several levels of administration. *Colonias* (neighborhoods) were groups of ten adjacent houses, and approximately ten *colonias* made up a subcamp. The one hundred or so refugees within each *colonia* then established committees to address their various needs, including construction, agricultural production, education, food preparation, health care, religious worship, security, and child care. With time, elected representatives from each of these work areas served on a *colonia*-wide coordinating committee. Each of these committees, in turn, elected one representative to serve on a subcamp coordinating committee. These subcamp committees then sent one member to the camp-wide coordinating committee. The refugees also established coordinating groups for each of the work areas (e.g., education, agricultural production), thus ensuring parity of services across the entire camp.

Documentation produced by refugees and international organizations reveals that coordination also occurred between the various camps in Honduras despite official efforts to isolate the Salvadorans. For example, representatives from Mesa Grande, Colomoncagua, and San Antonio worked together to produce *INFORESAL*, a cross-camp informational magazine complete with editorials, news stories, comics, and calendars of events. Representatives from each of the camps also orchestrated multiple mass protest actions, including letter-writing campaigns, sit-ins, and hunger strikes.

An important aspect of Salvadorans' organizing and mobilizing in exile was the building of alliances. They knew from prior experience that alliances could bring important benefits and advantages. Indeed, El Salvador saw extremely high levels of activism between the 1960s and early 1980s in large part because of the mobilization of "new social forces"—broad-based coalitions and partnerships that advocated progressive, yet often relatively moderate changes to the Salvadoran economic, political, labor, and land-tenure systems.[23] *Campesinos* participated in such forces from a variety of angles, including political parties, cooperatives, Christian base communities, and labor federations, to name just a few. Engagement in these forces sometimes led to benefits, including pay raises and improved working conditions on plantations, adjustments to land-rental rules that benefited tenants, and increased access to agricultural credit.

When *campesinos* began to abandon their war-ravaged communities, they established new alliances, joining with villagers from other areas of El Salvador, negotiating with FMLN combatants for safe passes through "liberated zones," and reaching agreements with rural Hondurans for temporary shelter and sometimes employment. And, in the refugee zones of Honduras, Salvadorans pointedly integrated international humanitarian aid workers and solidarity networks into their organizational efforts. Between the late 1970s and the mid-1990s, dozens of Honduran and international voluntary aid agencies assisted UNHCR and government officials with the Salvadoran refugees. Among them were the Comité Evangélico de Emergencia Nacional (Evangelical National Emergency Committee, or CEDEN), Caritas, World Vision, the Mennonite Central Committee, Concern, Catholic Relief Services, and Médecins sans Frontières (Doctors without Borders, or MSF). In addition, the refugee camps frequently hosted visitors from internationally known organizations such as Americas Watch and Amnesty International, members of national congresses, and representatives of local church and solidarity groups. With long-term workers and volunteers as well as short-term visitors, Salvadoran refugees were careful to detect and foster relations with groups and individuals with philosophies that paralleled their own, that is, toward the progressive end of the sociopolitical spectrum. These the refugees labeled *los internacionales* (the internationals); they were solidary witnesses, the allies in the refugees' various struggles, from short-term campaigns against relocation or in favor of repatriation to the ideal solution of peace and justice in El Salvador.

Internacionales offered significant resources, which Salvadorans put to good use. The very presence of *internacionales* in the camp, for example, increased the physical security of the refugees by curtailing the violence of security forces. "When [the *internacionales*] were there," explained one man, "they mistreated you, but they didn't kill you."[24]

Internacionales also provided another valuable resource: information. Aid personnel and visitors had access to media that were unavailable to refugees, including hand radios, telephones, faxes, and cables; not surprisingly, refugees frequently overheard information being passed through these media. In late 1981 and early 1982, for example, refugees in the La Virtud reception area learned via radio transmission that their compatriots in nearby villages had been forcefully relocated to the new UNHCR-sponsored camp at Mesa Grande. After the transfer of each group, the radios passed along "discouraging descriptions" of the new location, which spurred higher levels of resistance to official relocation efforts.[25]

Especially useful was information about international law. From *internacionales*, Salvadorans learned not only about their rights as refugees in light of international agreements such as the Geneva Convention and its Protocol; they also learned that it was the internationally sanctioned responsibility of the UNHCR to protect those rights and ensure the safety of refugees. The Salvadorans integrated such information into their communications. For example, in March 1988, the Coordinating Council of Refugees of the Mesa Grande, Colomoncagua, and San Antonio camps directed a communiqué to "the Salvadoran people, humanitarian organizations, churches and the international community" that included the following commentary:

We consider the UNHCR to be an organization delegated by the United Nations to guarantee and protect the lives and human rights of refugees. The UNHCR should—given the way the Government and military authorities behave and treat the refugees [and] understanding how we are disrespected in our lives and human rights—strengthen its presence and not passively accept any steps that reduce its protection role. . . . We Salvadoran refugees [demand] that the UNHCR does not passively accept the diminishment of its protection role and at the same time that it reinforces its presence in our camps 24 hours a day to fully comply with the role delegated to it by the United Nations.[26]

This passage illustrates how Salvadoran refugees learned to hold up the UN's refugee agency as "the *only* authority" in matters relating to safety and protection; throughout their time in exile, they pressured individual representatives, as well as the institution as a whole, to comply with its mandate.[27] In a similar vein, they frequently reminded the Honduran and Salvadoran governments of their duties and obligations.

In short, refugees used *internacionales* and the information they supplied as instruments and the humanitarian aid network as a space to make themselves visible, both as refugees and as Salvadorans. Responding to the peasant refugees' experiences and realities, *internacionales* spread testimonies, accounts, and denunciations across the globe and, in so doing, drummed up additional support for the refugees. *Internacionales'* firsthand observations added weight to the refugees' versions of events, which many audiences discounted on their own. (After one U.S. aid worker provided testimony about a military incursion into the La Virtud area in July 1981, a high-level UNHCR representative admitted to her, "It is so important that a North American witnessed it because this makes the testimony verifiable."[28]) Thus, international witnesses pushed the refugees' concerns and made them visible to higher levels of government and nongovernment agencies around the world. In a sort of "boomerang effect," pressures from these *internacionales* could lead to practical results; they could prompt the UNHCR to behave in ways agreeable to the refugees, by sending more protection officers, for example, or encouraging the Honduran military to soften curfews or lift bans on deliveries and travel.[29] The boomerang effect operated on a moral level as well, as international attention brought recognition and legitimacy to the refugees' demands.

Just as Salvadoran refugees mobilized these alliances and their own organizational structures to counter officials' imaginings of them as passive victims, so, too, did they struggle against the tendency to decontextualize their experiences. Testimonies and writings illustrate that, throughout their time in the Honduran camps, Salvadoran *campesinos* insisted on the relevance of political and historical contexts for their own circumstances as refugees. Indeed, their very exile, they argued, could not be understood without taking into consideration these broader contexts.

One of the refugees' primary concerns was U.S. involvement in Central American affairs. Newsletters, songs, and other documentation produced by refugees repeatedly critiqued both the Salvadoran and the Honduran governments' close relations with the United States. Particularly troublesome for the *campesinos* was the fact that the Salvadoran government had come to rely so exclusively upon the United States to boost its military and security forces. This had very real consequences for rural inhabitants. They knew firsthand the devastating capabilities of fighter jets, Huey helicopters, bombs, and other ammunition carrying U.S. insignia. They also were more than familiar with the harm inflicted by the Batallones de Infantería de Reacción Inmediata (Rapid Deployment Infantry Brigades, or BIRIs), elite forces created, trained, and equipped by the United States and which many peasants ranked alongside the death squads. *Campesinos* claimed that, although the armed forces had always been capable of savagery, U.S. involvement only perverted them further, causing ever more harm to the nation. "Our land of El Salvador," wrote one refugee poet, "has turned into a river / of the blood of the men / that Reagan ordered be assassinated."[30]

In a similar vein, refugees condemned the Honduran government's apparent subservience to the United States. Honduran willingness to allow the U.S. military to operate the Regional Military Training Center in Puerto Castillo, on the north coast of Honduras, was just one piece of evidence of the government's collaboration in U.S. regional strategy. Additional evidence was in Honduras' "disparate treatment of refugees fleeing the strongly anticommunist [Salvadoran government] on the one hand, and those fleeing the leftist government of Nicaragua on the other."[31] As noted, Honduran and UNHCR authorities concentrated Salvadorans in "closed" refugee camps. Nicaraguan refugees, in contrast, lived in "open" camps; they enjoyed freedom of movement and, thus, were able to work, attend school, and participate in markets and other events in nearby villages. Salvadorans noted this difference. They also noted that Nicaraguan camps in Honduras served as recruiting grounds and operational bases for the Contras, armed groups financed by the United States whose goal was to overthrow the Sandinista government. Perhaps needless to say, Salvadoran refugees considered this true hypocrisy. Why did the Honduran government continuously punish Salvadoran refugees for presumed (but never proved) armed opposition, while it allowed—and even facilitated—the Nicaraguan refugees' armed opposition? The answer, maintained the Salvadorans, was in the uneven alliance between Honduras and the United States.

Yet more proof of Honduran subservience to the United States was the oft-repeated effort to relocate Salvadoran refugees deeper into the Honduran interior. "The principal reason for the Relocation and Repression," announced an editorial in the refugee newsletter *Patria Nueva* (New Fatherland), "is to clean the border zone of Refugees and Honduran villagers because we are a bother to the involvement of the Honduran military in the Salvadoran conflict. All of this is part of the North American plan for direct intervention in our *patria*, which would bring as a consequence the lengthening of the war, affecting the Honduran *pueblo* as well, distancing the possibility for Peace in El Salvador and regionalizing the conflict."[32] With frequent commentary along these lines, Salvadorans placed themselves—and their very status as refugees—squarely within a Cold War context.

Just as Salvadorans placed themselves into broader political contexts, so, too, did they place their experiences within longer historical timelines. Many drew direct connections between their own experiences and those of their *campesino* counterparts of earlier eras. Struggles against exploitation were "in the beginning against the Spanish invaders" and then, after independence, "against the creole landowners and later against the coffee oligarchy."[33] The same exploitation that occurred during the nation's early years continued into the twentieth century; likewise, *campesinos* continued to struggle against it. A particularly vivid example of *campesino* mobilization—and the sometimes devastating consequences of struggle—occurred in January 1932, when tens of thousands of rural laborers launched a rebellion in the central and western regions of El Salvador. Armed with machetes, sticks, and a few rifles, they occupied several towns and a few isolated police posts and military barracks. According to most accounts, General Maximiliano Hernández Martínez, who had assumed the presidency just weeks earlier through a military coup d'état, responded swiftly and decisively; on his orders, the National Guard and local military and police forces marched through the countryside and systematically targeted all those suspected of participating in the rebellion. Although the military regained control of the region within a matter of days, eyewitnesses reported that indiscriminate killings of *campesinos* continued for weeks thereafter—especially in the heavily indigenous municipalities of the west. This "grotesque" revenge, for which President Martínez earned the nickname "El Brujo" (The Sorcerer), resulted in so many thousands dead that burial became impractical; fearing epidemics, the Salvadoran Department of Sanitation ordered the incineration of all corpses. In the end, an estimated thirty thousand perished—the vast majority of them *campesinos*.[34]

For Salvadorans exiled in Honduras, the civil war of the 1980s was in many ways an extension of both the struggle for independence and the events of the early 1930s. The desperate conditions imposed on Salvadoran *campesinos* through colonization and that drove so many thousands to revolt in the early 1900s continued to saddle the majority of the Salvadoran populace. Moreover, politicians regularly broke their own social and political promises, just as the military repeatedly dashed all hope and promise of fair elections and reform. For these reasons, mobilization continued within and between all sectors of Salvadoran society, and the military continued to rely on terror tactics to quell the unrest. The *campesinos'* status as refugees was proof positive of such tactics.

By putting themselves and their experiences into both historical and geopolitical contexts, Salvadoran refugees countered officials' tendency to decontextualize the refugee experience. In short, Salvadorans argued that war and exile were *not* extraordinary. Instead, they were quite ordinary, part of broader political and historical patterns.

As refugees insisted on the importance of context, so, too, did they assert their own relevance to the nation. That refugees continued to identify with their Salvadoran homeland is clear in their emphasis on their exile as temporary. To this end, Salvadorans nearly always employed the phrase *estar refugiado* rather than *ser refugiado*. Both phrases translate into English as "to be a refugee" or, literally, "to be refuged." In Spanish, however, *ser* denotes a permanent state of being, while *estar* is much more temporary or transient. The refugees' preference for the phrase *estar refugiado*, then, indicates their conception of exile as a temporary state of being. In a similar vein, refugee writings made repeated reference to *el retorno*, the ultimate return to their homeland. Indeed, Salvadoran refugees insisted on *retorno* not as a possibility but, rather, as an inevitability and focused much of their attention and energy toward that eventuality.

Further evidence that Salvadorans perceived exile as a temporary situation can be found in the fact that the vast majority did not reground themselves in Honduras. That is, they did not press for Honduran documentation, such as work visas, residency papers, or citizenship for their children born in the camps. Although Salvadorans initially recorded births and deaths in the civil registries of the Honduran towns nearest to their sites of refuge, the Honduran government prohibited this procedure by mid-1980. At that time, UNHCR representatives began keeping a separate registry, copies of which they delivered to the Salvadoran consulates nearest the refugee camps. It is telling that the refugees neither opposed this change in policy nor demanded that they be listed in the Honduran registries.[35] Similarly, most refugees did not actively seek resettlement outside the refugee camps, nor did they seek integration into Honduran communities or markets. In fact, Salvadorans actively opposed efforts to relocate them to a different region of Honduras where they ostensibly would have enjoyed greater freedom of movement, more land for farming, and better economic opportunities. Likewise, they resisted the involvement of Honduran government ministries in refugee camp operations and affairs despite the new resources and opportunities that officials promised to introduce.

That the Salvadorans did not wish to anchor themselves in Honduras did not mean that they did not identify with their spaces of exile. On the contrary, Salvadorans embraced their sites of exile. They did so, however, not as Honduran sites but, rather, as extensions of their homeland, El Salvador. Settling into an official, UNHCR-sponsored refugee camp meant claiming the space not only as belonging to them but also identifying it as specifically Salvadoran. Refugees insisted on flying the Salvadoran rather than Honduran flag; some named their spaces after important Salvadoran figures, including the slain Salvadoran archbishop Oscar Romero, who was especially beloved for his work on behalf of El Salvador's poor; others marked their territory as Salvadoran by carving *hecho por salvadoreños* (made by Salvadorans) into the drying cement of the foundations and walls of newly erected latrines and other infrastructure; and all observed Salvadoran Independence Day.

Through these various inscriptions, Salvadorans endowed their spaces of exile with critical personal meaning that, in turn, helped them to reestablish the boundaries of their community. As they took control over the definition and operation of the space, they further strengthened their own self-identification—now not only as members of a specific rural community of *campesinos* but also as a community of refugees, a community of Salvadoran citizens in exile. Furthermore, claiming a piece of Honduran territory as Salvadoran and associating it with important Salvadoran figures and dates sent a clear message to observers that they considered their sites of refuge to be extensions of their homeland. As such, they served as a kind of collective resistance to exile and the imposed identity of uprooted people without territory.

Just as they identified their spaces of exile as Salvadoran and defended them as such, so, too, did they define *themselves* as essentially Salvadoran. That is, in spite of their position outside national borders, they never stopped "being Salvadoran." As citizens of El Salvador, the refugees believed, they retained many legal rights in their native country: access to land and the right to vote in free and fair elections, to earn a living wage, and to organize, among others. Unfortunately, the country's governing elite had long denied *campesinos* these rights. Flight and exile offered incontrovertible evidence of this exclusion. But the denial of rights did not mean that the rights did not exist; indeed, the refugees believed them to be definite and real. They pointed to the Salvadoran Constitution and international human rights law as confirmation and demanded that Salvadoran leaders recognize these rights. Throughout their period of exile, then, Salvadoran *campesinos* wrestled not only with the Honduran government and the UNHCR but also with the Salvadoran government.

Salvadoran citizenship bestowed not only rights and freedoms but also certain duties and obligations. In the context of civil war, these duties became even more critical. The majority of Salvadoran refugees viewed the war as a necessary part of the transition to a "new dawn"—a time when leadership would be legitimate and peace, justice, and equality would reign. Active involvement in this process was a patriotic obligation expected of everyone—from university professors and the FMLN high command to factory workers and the poorest of *campesinos*. Refugees made clear that they not only were involved but were key contributors—even leaders—of the Salvadoran struggle. As early as 1982, refugees began referring to their unique role. "Conscious people are always needed to take charge of historic tasks," explained a document prepared by refugee teachers. "We do not want to waste time while we are refugees. . . . [We are] accomplishing something important and historic."[36]

The refugees' role in the national struggle was closely related to their status as refugees and their physical location outside the nation. In essence, by occupying fringe territory, they transformed themselves into a sort of nonviolent, civilian rearguard that defended the nation. From both sides of the border, they served as witnesses to the atrocities committed against El Salvador's poor majority. In testimonies presented to international aid workers, solidarity and human rights observation groups, and other visitors to the camps, *campesino* refugees provided detailed, firsthand evidence of the Salvadoran security forces' excesses: repression and harassment, torture, disappearances, and massacres. In addition, from their sites of refuge in Honduras, *campesinos* kept close vigil over El Salvador's northern region. Many military operations were visible from the refugee camps; these were tracked by the refugees and denounced before international audiences.

Through their writings, songs, theater sketches, sit-ins, marches, and other activities and protest actions, Salvadoran refugees worked to raise international awareness of the continued violence being inflicted upon their compatriots who remained in El Salvador. If the refugees' denunciations had the desired effect, then international observers would take action—for instance, by condemning the bombing of civilian-occupied territory before international assemblies at the United Nations or before state and national congresses—and northern El Salvador would be spared further destruction. Thus, Salvadoran refugees viewed the processes of witnessing and representing El Salvador as a direct contribution to the struggle for Salvadoran liberation.

Beyond witnessing and representing Salvadorans to world opinion, refugees in Honduras also saw themselves as agents of positive change. They considered their actions within the sphere of the refugee camps as preparation for El Salvador's "new dawn." Specific programs in the camps were preliberation reconstruction efforts and, therefore, *aportes a la lucha* (supportive action in the name of the national struggle). Refugees viewed their efforts in this light quite early in their exile, as illustrated by this excerpt from a poem written in 1983 by a group of refugees at the Mesa Grande camp:

We have already set the foundation
for a very solid consciousness,
at least in terms of everything that describes
our role as refugee.
Looking out over the border of the camps . . .
we learned more in depth
where our position really is
in the reconstruction of our country.
Can we reconstruct it here in Mesa Grande?
. . . Here—we agree—we can prepare ourselves
and many, yes, many have prepared ourselves well.[37]

As these lines indicate, many refugees considered their position in Honduras to be uniquely important because, in their sites of refuge, they began to "set the foundations" and prepare themselves for El Salvador's new dawn.

One of the ways they did so was through the camp workshops. Each of the refugee camps had a system of *talleres* (workshops) where refugees produced clothing and shoes, kitchen pots and utensils, and other needed items.[38] The *talleres* became a source of great pride for the refugees; they not only helped sustain the camp population but also taught skills that would be valuable in the eventual reconstruction of El Salvador. The refugee leadership even initiated a kind of lottery system that allowed almost everyone in the camps the opportunity to cycle through each of the workshops and to learn various skills and trades, including mechanical engineering, business administration and accounting, carpentry, shoemaking, tailoring, and crafts. The lottery itself stood as an example of things to come in the new El Salvador; according to the refugees, it was democracy in action.

Along with the system of *talleres*, refugees considered education to be a crucial and foundational task. Education not only contributed to personal liberation but also aided in collective liberation. In the words of Cristóbal, an adult student at Mesa Grande, literacy classes helped *campesinos* "discover the truth," which, in turn, helped inspire them to work toward and to "realize our dream." His "Poema dedicado a todos los refugiados" (Poem Dedicated to All Refugees) reflects this idea:

Since we have always wanted to escape exploitation
and that is what we will learn by studying with the literacy classes
we must study with determination while we are refugees
so that when we leave here we will not be the same terrorized people.
We must all insist on moving forward with this great literacy movement
to offer a contribution toward our liberation.[39]

From this perspective, education countered negative patterns of the past and established new, cooperative patterns. *Campesinos* would carry these new patterns with them into the future, and, upon their return to El Salvador, they would become the leaders and teachers that, as one source promised, "our pueblo will need so much."[40] In essence, then, academic efforts in the camps—from teachers and students alike—served as practice and preparation for the eventual homecoming. As such, they constituted both a personal and a patriotic duty.

On an even broader scale, the refugees viewed their overall camp organization in a similar light, as an important *aporte*. Many Salvadorans repeatedly emphasized the fact that, as refugees, they did not give in to *asistencialismo*, a term they adopted to describe passive acceptance of and reliance upon international aid. Rather, they embraced the collective way of life that was in many ways encouraged (or, perhaps, forced on them) by the very nature of the closed refugee camps. As described, they developed systems of self-government, with committees to address the needs of the community, from food storage and preparation to latrine cleaning and camp security, from news distribution and libraries to religious worship and child care. They held public assemblies, voted for representatives, negotiated with one another and with outsiders. They honed these organizational skills and, when necessary, revamped their structures to provide more efficient and effective service.[41] All of this they did with a dual purpose: first, to improve the quality of life in the camps and in the border region in general; and, second, to prepare for their eventual return to El Salvador. "The experiences with community management that we are acquiring here," explained a refugee document, "will serve us well when we return to El Salvador. There, we will have many duties of popular participation. That is why we should practice here our own participation and collective responsibility."[42] A Mesa Grande poet agreed: "What we are experiencing and learning here at Mesa Grande / we know that it will help us . . . / when we return to our country, because working [together, collectively] / we become better organized."[43] As these lines indicate, Salvadoran *campesinos* continued to view communal organization and collective labor as crucial steps toward a more promising and productive future in El Salvador.

If refugees imagined a new dawn for El Salvador and modeled the possibilities for that reformed nation through communal organization, education, and workshops, an even more influential *aporte* was to move back across the border and apply themselves on their home territory. By 1987, thousands had begun to plan the return journey. As one poet called to his compatriots:

Let us pack our suitcases
—with our abilities
—with our experience
—with our conscience
and carry them home
take to the pueblo that awaits us
everything we already have contributed from [exile]
to participate in the construction of our future.[44]

Between October 1987 and December 1989, at least six *retornos* (mass returns) occurred, involving some eighteen thousand Salvadoran refugees. Each of the *retornos* and the concomitant repopulations of rural villages was carefully planned and strategized by the refugees themselves. As a grassroots movement, the *retornos* further illustrate refugees' agency and capacity for nonviolent resistance.

Salvadorans prepared for the *retornos* in two stages. During the first, clandestine phase, they established organizational structures to formalize and carry forward a plan. As the plan solidified, they carried out a quiet public relations campaign to garner support and allies in El Salvador and in the international sphere. The amount of documentation generated by solidarity organizations can be used as one measure of the refugees' success in gaining allies in their endeavors. Public and private collections in the United States reveal a plethora of national and local organizations—including the SHARE Foundation, Catholic Relief Services, the American Friends Service Committee, the Lutheran

World Federation, and the National Council of Churches—that supported the Salvadoran grassroots repopulation movement. Numerous specialized support groups also appeared at this time, including the Going Home Interfaith Campaign and Voices on the Border.

In the second stage, the refugees and their international allies went public. They did so with a deliberately managed information campaign that staggered publicity so that the Salvadoran government was the last to learn of the refugees' plans. According to one *campesino* involved in the planning of the first *retorno* from Mesa Grande:

The thing was that we always had a secret information venue; we didn't give everything out at once. . . . More than anything, we publicized our plans internationally. . . . The UNHCR was not willing to negotiate given the conditions in El Salvador because the government then [of José Napoleón Duarte] wouldn't give the green light for us to return. . . . So that's why we hid—why we, um, publicized our information internationally. . . . We began the campaign outside and announced our return date—*before* giving it to the government. . . . So when we told [officials], we'd already publicized it abroad.[45]

Managing the information in this way ensured a wide base of support that forced all parties and the Salvadoran government in particular to take the refugees' demands seriously. An important component of this second stage was the pressure placed on officials by the refugees' international allies. The organizations noted earlier, along with their counterparts in other countries, promoted congressional resolutions, paid for advertisements, and sent letters and telegrams in support of the refugees' interests and demands. Members also raised funds for the returning families and ultimately sent delegations to El Salvador and Honduras to pressure for support prior to the *retornos*, as well as to accompany the returnees during the actual return journeys and repopulations.

During the months of negotiations that inevitably followed officials' receipt of the Salvadorans' announcement, refugees emphasized how their return to their "communities of origin" fit into broader contexts.[46] They argued that their return was a "legitimate right" in terms of international law and, in the same vein, that the Salvadoran government was "morally obligated" to accept and facilitate their repatriation.[47] They also parroted the rhetoric used by the new civilian president, José Napoleón Duarte (1984–89), who promised to end the work of death squads, submit the military to civilian authority, and support a "national dialogue."[48] Even if the refugees did not fully believe such promises, they consciously utilized the Duarte administration's self-styled democratic image as a tool to promote their own position in favor of return. Likewise, they linked their return to events occurring at the regional level. The first group to return from Mesa Grande, for example, emphasized the signing of the Central American Peace Plan, in August 1987, in Esquipulas, Guatemala. Organizers of the fourth *retorno* from Mesa Grande used a September 1988 follow-up meeting in a similar fashion: "[We] consider that the accords of the recent meeting of Central American Presidents in Tela, Honduras, open a climate of hope for all of Central America," they announced in their return platform. "These same agreements respect our voluntary decision to return to our country and call on the Salvadoran government and Armed Forces to commit themselves to not placing obstacles of any form or under any pretext against our arrival and our desire to remain in the repopulated areas of our choice."[49]

With such references, Salvadoran refugees demonstrated their agency on a number of levels. They were well aware of political developments at home in El Salvador, as well as regionally and internationally, and they used these details to their advantage. Moreover, by placing their *retornos* within these contexts, refugees not only boosted their justifications for return but also publicly associated their grassroots movement with peace efforts. Indeed, refugees frequently noted their intentions in this regard: "As Salvadorans we must help bring peace," declared one group from Mesa Grande. "We are peasants and the way we struggle to achieve peace is by planting our crops on our lands and demanding that our lives be respected."[50] Such rhetoric, particularly in light of the ongoing regional peace initiatives, made it difficult—and potentially very embarrassing—for the Duarte government to oppose the return of the refugees.

In the end, however, Salvadoran officials often characterized the *retornos* as "invasions." In a sense, this is true; despite resistance and outright opposition from Salvadoran government and military officials, *campesinos* succeeded in "conquering" not only physical sites of resettlement but also the more ethereal right to exist as civilians in a war zone. However, because *campesinos* (often literally) had to break through official resistance, they asserted their citizenship through what was, basically, a forced physical presence. Indeed, refugee committees in charge of the *retornos* billed the return home as a conquest; declarations of "Long live the conquest of our places of origin!" accompany many statements from the period.

From the perspective of the *campesino* refugees, *retorno* was an impressive victory. After years on the move and nearly a decade in exile, all the participants believed that going home was an important achievement. For many, the act also held great political significance, representing one more phase in a long struggle of resistance against an authoritarian regime. Rather than relying on the "hidden transcripts" and more clandestine forms of resistance of previous years, however, *campesinos* involved in the grassroots *retornos* challenged the Salvadoran regime directly and in multiple ways.[51] First, they rejected official repopulation programs. Statistics showed that upwards of 95 percent of refugees refused to sign on to government-sponsored repatriation projects, and interviews revealed a continued distrust of officials. "If we return to the government-controlled areas that [officials] proposed, do you know what will happen?" a man at the Colomoncagua refugee camp asked. "In a couple of months, all our projects will be destroyed by sabotage and harassment. We don't want to throw out nine years of work like that."[52] In a similar vein, refugees repudiated the Tripartite Commission process; spearheaded by the UNHCR, this commission brought together Honduran and Salvadoran officials to lay the groundwork for and to promote the voluntary repatriation of refugees.[53] Yet Salvadoran *campesinos* maintained that, because it was *tri*partite, it could not adequately represent refugee interests. So, instead of submitting to official whims, displaced *campesinos* developed their own independent process. In so doing, they challenged the Salvadoran government's authority over their individual bodies and their collective political body.

Another way that the *retornos* challenged the Salvadoran state was by insisting on a certain degree of autonomy. Platforms for return set forth a number of demands, including freedom from forced recruitment into the armed forces and the right to not maintain civil patrols. In the repopulated communities, moreover, *campesinos* continued to promote alternative social, political, and economic structures. And they did so with new vigor. No longer were community councils or cooperatives underground operations; with the continued support and accompaniment of international allies, *campesino* organizations were now fully public and intentionally high profile.

With such recognition, *campesinos* in repopulated communities put forth an alternative conception of the nation-state. Rather than simply profess liberty and equality for all, they sought to make such ideals a reality. Contrary to what their detractors claimed, they did not profess socialism or communism. Instead, they pursued a participatory social democracy—a democracy committed to the collective good. The returning *campesinos* intended to build such a system from the ground up. In the words of a refugee at Colomoncagua on the eve of the journey home, "We are returning to El Salvador even though the war continues because we want to forge [*impulsar*] democracy from inside."[54]

In a similar vein, many *campesino* refugees claimed that the *retornos* further altered the national social and political landscape by launching the peace process. Here it is important to recall that the apogee of the return and repopulation movement was between 1986 and 1990—before FMLN and government forces signed a peace accord and before they even began earnest negotiations.

In light of this, *campesinos* argue that they were leaders in the transition to a new El Salvador. From their sites of refuge, they posed political and moral challenges to the Salvadoran regime and worked to raise international awareness about the realities and consequences of civil war. The repopulation movement, moreover, did what the FMLN had been unable to do for years: break open the Salvadoran regime and force those in power to respond to popular demands. Among their many pressure points, returned refugees demanded that the Salvadoran government commit in earnest to a negotiated settlement to the war. Such a large civilian presence in the north, explained Norberto, meant "that the government was not going to soften . . . which compelled negotiations." Alejandro agreed: "The people's return . . . was a grain of sand of contribution to the peace process. . . . They saw those who achieved it, they saw the solidarity, they saw that the people were returning home and that they wanted peace and they didn't want war. There was, by example, a clear manifestation and this was a first step in starting the process."[55]

Conclusion: Displacement as Nonviolent Resistance

During the late 1970s and throughout the 1980s, the Salvadoran government and military applied counterinsurgency tactics not only to armed insurgents but also to civilians. Tens of thousands of *campesinos* from communities in the northern border region responded to these tactics by abandoning their homes, hiding in the mountains, and eventually crossing the international border into Honduras.

Although Honduran authorities eventually officially recognized the Salvadorans as refugees, they viewed the new arrivals with suspicion. Honduras's history of checkered relations with its southern neighbor, combined with the exigencies of the Cold War context, compelled authorities to restrict Salvadorans to closed camps under constant military surveillance. Honduran policies, moreover, prohibited many types of movement and activity. In a similar vein, all international aid coordinated by the UNHCR was contingent on the refugees' docility and, more specifically, their nonpolitical behavior. In essence, then, Honduran and UNHCR officials collaborated with each other—and with the Salvadoran government—to contain and depoliticize Salvadoran *campesinos*.

The *campesinos*, for their part, challenged all official efforts to control them. When the Salvadoran military brought its scorched-earth operations to the northern reaches of the country, *campesino* communities transformed physical mobility into a strategy not only of survival but also of resistance to a militarized, authoritarian regime. Likewise, as Honduran and UN officials sought to pacify and depoliticize them as refugees, the Salvadorans mobilized. By elaborating communal governance structures in the refugee camps, distributing newsletters, and coordinating protest actions, among other activities, they insisted on their own agency and asserted themselves as participants not only in all realms of their life in exile but also on the Salvadoran national scene.

Crucial to the refugees' mobilizations in exile were the alliances they fostered with progressive international solidarity workers and networks. Such alliances contributed to a shift in power dynamics on the ground in the refugee camps, as well as on the battlefields in El Salvador. International accompaniment, both during exile and in the subsequent processes of return and repopulation, offered *campesino* refugees new resources, which they activated in their struggles against the old (exclusion, repression, authoritarianism) and in favor of the new (equality, justice, democracy, peace). International scrutiny exhorted high-profile actors—namely government and UN officials and the FMLN—to recognize *campesinos* as active participants in the world around them.

As others strived for control over Salvadoran *campesinos*—often performing power through acts of violence—*campesinos* transformed their individual and political bodies into weapons. They retained as much control as possible over these bodies. They moved them to make political statements, they organized and collaborated with *internacionales* to gain short- and long-term benefits, and they maintained attachments to and engagement with their homeland even during nearly a decade of exile. As such, Salvadoran *campesino* refugees transformed displacement into a strategy of nonviolent resistance and a tool in the struggle for positive change.

This case study of organization and collective action among Salvadoran refugees has important implications for our understanding of humanitarian acts in 1980s Central America. Most markedly, it reveals how "official" representations of the displaced were incomplete at best and inaccurate at worst, often leading to negative repercussions for refugees; equating refugees with either armed rebels or apolitical victims led to restrictions on refugee's rights, including movement and freedom of expression. It is disturbing that the organizations that purported to uphold and safeguard the rights of the displaced vis-à-vis the sending nation also were responsible for withholding those very same rights. This, in turn, produced an environment ripe for dissent and protest. And herein lies another lesson of this case study: those who actively supported and defended the rights of refugees were not only from the North. The refugees' own organizations played a pivotal role in fomenting and directing an international effort.

Notes

The conclusions drawn in this article are primarily the result of research conducted in Central America, the United States, and Switzerland between 2002 and 2009. A Fulbright fellowship and grants from Augustana College helped to finance the research, and Thomas Todd and Julie Roy provided research assistance. Translations from the Spanish are mine unless otherwise noted. For the sake of privacy and safety, I have used pseudonyms for the *campesinos* I interviewed.

1. Annick Billard, "From El Salvador to Honduras: A Long Journey to Find a Safe Place," *Refugees Magazine* (May 1983): 7–8.

2. Cartoon by Roberto Williams (Rowi), published in *Diario La Prensa* (Honduras), February 5, 1982.

3. Liisa Malkki, "Refugees and Exile: From 'Refugee Studies' to the National Order of Things," *Annual Review of Anthropology* 24 (1995): 508.

4. Liisa Malkki, "National Geographic: The Rooting of Peoples and the Territorialization of National Identity among Scholars and Refugees," *Cultural Anthropology* 7, no. 1 (1992): 32.

5. These numbers, based on official UNHCR documentation, represent each camp's peak population. In addition, thousands of Salvadorans remained in the border towns throughout the 1980s. Because these *campesinos* were not officially recognized as refugees, they did not receive UN assistance, nor were they included in official statistics.

6. The two nations resumed relations after signing the U.S.-promoted Lima Treaty in 1980.

7. Honduras-Grupo de Expertos, "Antecedentes, análisis del problema, conclusiones, recomendaciones: Refugiados en Honduras," report ca. 1988, Anonymous, Central America records (hereafter cited as "private collection").

8. Honduras-Grupo de Expertos, "Antecendentes."

9. Centro de Documentación de Honduras, *Los refugiados en Honduras* (Tegucigalpa: Centro de Documentación de Honduras, 1982), 10.

10. "Acuerdo No. X," draft accord between Honduras and UNHCR, ca. 1985, private collection. Similar statements can be found throughout government sources.

11. Colonel Flores Auceda, in Leo Valladares Lanza, notes from meeting of the National Commission on Refugees (CONARE), May 9, 1984, private collection.

12. Francisco Merino in *Tiempo Nacional,* quoted in A. C. Zoller, "Summary of Report of International Delegation to Central America," Summer 1981, David Holiday, Americas Watch–El Salvador records (hereafter cited as AW).

13. Such accusations can be found throughout government documents from the period, with notes from CONARE meetings carrying particularly heavy charges.

14. Honduras-Grupo de Expertos, "Antecedentes" (my emphasis).

15. "Acuerdo No. X."

16. Kevin Hartigan, "Matching Humanitarian Norms with Cold, Hard Interests: The Making of Refugee Policies in Mexico and Honduras," *International Organization* 46, no. 3 (1992): 719.

17. I found interviews and Honduran government documents especially enlightening on these various efforts.

18. U.N. General Assembly Resolution 428 (V), Statute of the Office of the UNHCR, December 14, 1950 (my emphasis).

19. Gil Loescher and Laila Monahan, eds., *Refugees and International Relations* (Oxford: Clarendon Press, 1990), 47.

20. UNHCR, "Gracias al grupo de emergencia," *Refugiados*, July–August 1982, 9–10.

21. "Interview with Poul Hartling," *Refugees Magazine*, September 1982, 19.

22. Loescher and Monahan, *Refugees and International Relations*, 38.

23. I borrow the phrase "new social forces" from Aristide R. Zolberg, Astri Suhrke, and Sergio Aguayo, *Escape from Violence: Conflict and the Refugee Crisis in the Developing World* (New York: Oxford University Press, 1989), 208.

24. Norberto, interview by author, Chalatenango, El Salvador, February 22, 2003.

25. Yvonne Dilling, *In Search of Refuge* (Scottsdale, PA: Herald Press, 1984), 212.

26. Salvadoran Refugees in Honduras, Comité de Coordinación, communiqué, March 1988, records of the Center for Democracy in the Americas, Wisconsin State Historical Society, Madison (hereafter cited as CDA).

27. Quoted in Inter-Church Committee for Refugees (Canada), "Report and Recommendations to the United Nations High Commissioner for Refugees Regarding the Protection of Refugees and the Coordination of Material Assistance by the UNHCR in Honduras," September 1982, Centro de Documentación de Honduras, Tegucigalpa, Collection 2671 (emphasis in original).

28. Dilling, *In Search of Refuge*, 132.

29. Margaret Keck and Kathryn Sikkink develop the concept of "boomerang effect" in *Activists beyond Borders: Advocacy Networks in International Politics* (Ithaca, NY: Cornell University Press, 1998).

30. "Pueblo sin cabeza," in "Mesa Grande: Rescate cultural," collection of writings of Salvadoran refugees at Mesa Grande (1982–84), compiled by Gisela Ursula Heinrich, 1999, private collection. Commentary on U.S. military involvement can be found in many other songs and poems in this collection. Oral interviews from the 1980s and the postwar period are also replete with such references.

31. Lawyers Committee for International Human Rights, *Honduras: A Crisis on the Border, a Report on Salvadoran Refugees in Honduras* (New York: Lawyers Committee for International Human Rights, 1985), 11.

32. Salvadoran Refugees in Honduras, "Objetivo yanqui: Despoblar la frontera," *Patria Nueva* 3, no. 5 (1988), Beth Cagan and Steve Cagan, El Salvador records (hereafter cited as Cagan Papers).

33. Federación de Trabajadores del Campo, *Perspectiva histórica del movimiento*

campesino revolucionario en El Salvador, communiqué originally released in April 1977 (San Salvador: Ediciones Enero 32, 1979), 7–8.

34. Jenny Pearce opined that official revenge was "grotesque" in *Promised Land: Peasant Rebellion in Chalatenango, El Salvador* (London: Latin America Bureau, 1986), 85. The information about burials comes from William Stanley, *The Protection Racket State: Elite Politics, Military Extortion, and Civil War in El Salvador* (Philadelphia: Temple University Press, 1996), 42. The exact number of civilians killed during the Matanza, of course, will never be known. Estimates range anywhere from four thousand to more than fifty thousand. Thirty thousand has been the most commonly used figure.

35. After returning to El Salvador, however, many adults considered the children born in the refugee camps in Honduras to have dual citizenship, despite the fact that none of them had Honduran papers attesting to this.

36. Salvadoran refugees at Mesa Grande and Colomoncagua, "Manual para instructores populares," 1982, private collection.

37. "Refugiados," in "Mesa Grande: Rescate Cultural."

38. Interviews with former refugees and aid workers were most helpful in enabling me to understand the *talleres*. I am also grateful for conversations with Steve and Beth Cagan and Marc Rosenthal.

39. "Poema dedicado a todos los refugiados," in "Mesa Grande: Rescate cultural."

40. Salvadoran refugees, "Manual para instructores populares."

41. Beth Cagan and Steve Cagan describe one such overhaul at the Colomoncagua refugee camp during the later 1980s in *This Promised Land, El Salvador*.

42. Salvadoran refugees, "Manual para instructores populares."

43. "Refugiados," in "Mesa Grande: Rescate cultural."

44. Ibid.

45. Alejandro, interview by author, Chalatenango, El Salvador, July 27, 2003.

46. Although details of these negotiations fall beyond the purview of this chapter, it is worth noting that a key issue of debate was the location to which refugee groups would return. In the end, refugees returned to sites that they themselves had selected. The majority of these sites were in or close to previously depopulated northern communities; a few groups chose to venture further south. Although many returnees were not originally from their particular repopulation sites, they referred to the sites as their *comunidades de origen* (communities of origin). The choice of terminology was intentional: it highlighted that the return sites were selected by the refugees themselves and, therefore, distinguished them from the Salvadoran government's preferred sites for repatriation (which tended to be in southern export agriculture districts).

47. Salvadoran Refugees at Mesa Grande, Comité de Repoblación to President Duarte, April 4, 1987, AW.

48. For a scathing review of the "demonstration elections" that brought Duarte to power, see Noam Chomsky and Edward Herman, *Manufacturing Consent: The Political Economy of the Mass Media* (New York: Pantheon, 1988).

49. Salvadoran Refugees at Mesa Grande, Platform for fourth massive repatriation, August 12, 1989 (English translation), CDA.

50. Going Home Campaign, "Questions and Answers about the Mesa Grande Repatriation/Repopulation to El Salvador," August 23, 1982, CDA.

51. James C. Scott, *Domination and the Arts of Resistance: Hidden Transcripts* (New Haven, CT: Yale University Press, 1990).

52. Cagan and Cagan, *This Promised Land*, 143. For more details about government coercion and corruption in the handling of repopulation programs and aid, see Central American Refugee Center, *The Repopulation of Rural El Salvador* (Washington, DC: Central American Refugee Center, 1989); Beatrice Edwards and Gretta Tovar Siebentritt, *Places of Origin: The Repopulation of Rural El Salvador* (Boulder: Lynne Rienner, 1991); Elisabeth Jean Wood, "Civil War and Reconstruction: The Repopulation of Tenancingo," in *Landscapes of Struggle: Politics, Society, and Community in El Salvador*, ed. Aldo Lauria-Santiago and Leigh Binford (Pittsburgh: University of Pittsburgh Press, 2004), 126–46; and Elisabeth Jean Wood, *Insurgent Collective Action and Civil War in El Salvador* (Cambridge: Cambridge University Press, 2003), 135–47.

53. The Tripartite Commission first met in April 1986.

54. John Clifcorn, "Masivo retorno de salvadoreños," *Noticias Aliadas* (Peru) 27, no. 7 (1990): 3.

55. Alejandro, interview by author.

Epilogue

9

Desire and Revolution

Socialists and the Brazilian Gay Liberation Movement in the 1970s

JAMES N. GREEN

In 1993, as part of a graduate school exercise at ULCA, James N. Green wrote a "self-interview," reflecting on twenty years of participation in the struggle against authoritarianism and for gay rights across the Americas. In the early 1970s, while a member of a radical Quaker group, Green joined solidarity groups that advocated against torture and repression in Brazil and Chile. His quest to merge sexual and political identities was central to his activism in the United States and in Latin America. As this book was being realized, the editor approached Green and asked him to revisit this testimony to transnational solidarity and to reflect again on this history and specifically on how transnational activism played a role in the gay rights movement in Brazil. The original self-interview has been revised, edited, and reproduced as a narrative piece threaded through with new insights. It highlights the need for further scholarship related to sexual liberation movements in Latin America and their relationship to political change. Moreover, Green's experience sheds light on the complicated relationship between transnational social movements and political organizing.

❧

The year 1978 was an exhilarating time in Brazil. The air was heavy with the feeling of imminent political change. After a decade of harsh military rule,[1] everyone seemed to know that the demise of the generals' rule was approaching. Hundreds of thousands of metalworkers lay down their tools and struck against the government's regressive wage policies. Students filled the main streets of the states' capitals chanting: "Down with the dictatorship." Radios played previously censored songs that hit the top of the charts. Blacks, women, and even homosexuals began organizing, demanding to be heard.

During the long, tropical summer that ended 1978 and rang in 1979, I joined a dozen or so young students, office workers, bank clerks, and intellectuals in the city of São Paulo who met weekly. Rotating from apartment to apartment, sitting on the floor for lack of adequate furniture, we plotted the formation of the first homosexual rights organization in Brazil. Alternating between consciousness-raising and discussion groups, we debated the most recent antigay statements in the tabloids and coordinated a response from our newly founded group, Action Nucleus for Homosexual Rights. Every month, we poured over the new gay monthly publication *Lampião da Esquina*, produced by a collective of writers and intellectuals from Rio de Janeiro and São Paulo that declared itself a vehicle for discussion on sexuality, racial discrimination, the arts, ecology, and machismo.

This first wave of the Brazilian gay and lesbian liberation movement burst onto the national political scene in 1978–79 but then shrunk to a handful of groups five years later. During the mid to late 1980s, a cluster of people sustained the ideals of the movement while at the same time struggling to respond to the AIDS crisis.[2] In the 1990s, a new generation of activists emerged. Today, Brazil has one of the most dynamic LGBTQ movements in the world.

As a historian of Brazil and a leading participant in the most important Brazilian gay liberation organization during the movement's initial period, I had an insider's knowledge and access to sources that allowed me to write about various aspects of this history.[3] Yet I faced a challenge in narrating a history of that movement. How can a former leader of a social movement examine the events she or he helped shape with enough distance and circumspection to provide an adequate account of what took place? How do one's subjectivity and personal stake in recounting the past color interpretations? Academic protocol for historical articles written for peer-reviewed journals or edited collections usually demands "objective" distancing of the author from the subject, and the reader rarely gains an insight into the back story of why the author chose the topic or what his or her involvement in the subject may have been. The historical profession tends to disdain anthropological participant-observant narratives in which the author is positioned within the research endeavor. In writing this self-interview, I chose to articulate my role in the movement and to engage in a polemic with João Silvero Trevisan, another leading member, who had a starkly different vision about the directions that activism should take. Thus, my political perspectives clearly come to the foreground, and there is no pretense of hiding them behind a façade of distanced neutrality.

Raised as a Quaker, I was surrounded in my youth by people involved in social activism, especially in the civil rights and the peace movement. I started working against the Vietnam War when I was a junior in high school, in 1967, and continued through college, participating in all of the major antiwar mobilizations in Washington, D.C., in the late 1960s and early 1970s and also in local activities. Normally, Quakers and other pacifists who were called up in the draft performed an alternative service, such as working in a mental hospital for two years, instead of serving in the army. Like many of my young radical Quaker peers, I refused to do alternative service because I felt it was still a part of the military system. Although I turned in my draft card, I was never sent to jail for noncooperation because, a year later, the government changed the system and started drafting people by lottery. My number was high, and I didn't get called, but my torn-up draft card and letter to the government are likely in a file somewhere in Baltimore.

While in college, I spent the summer of 1971 in Cuernavaca, Mexico, learning Spanish at the Centro Intercultural de Documentación (CIDOC), which was founded by Ivan Illich, a former priest who was part of the progressive wing of the Catholic Church. CIDOC trained U.S. missionaries going to do work in Latin America. It was also something of an open university for progressive North Americans who wanted to learn about Latin America. There, I met left-wing Maryknoll missionaries en route to or from service in Guatemala and Chile, Americans who had gone to Cuba to learn more about that revolution, and others who had recently returned from Chile, where Salvador Allende, a Marxist, had been elected president with the support of a left-wing coalition. I also met socialists from different parts of Latin America, developed a more coherent critique of U.S. imperialism, and began to identify with the U.S. Marxist left. I came back to the States with a very romantic idea about revolution in Latin America.

In 1972, I finished college and joined a group of other young, radical Quakers in a rural commune in upstate New York. At the end of 1972, seven of us moved to Philadelphia and lived in an African American and Puerto Rican working-class neighborhood in North Philadelphia, just east of Temple University. Our plan was to study Latin America and to become involved in political action against U.S. involvement in the region. Our commune was linked to a larger radical Quaker movement in West Philadelphia called the Life Center, which promoted alternative lifestyles and nonviolent direct action.

I had gone to Mexico to learn Spanish because I sensed that the Vietnam War would soon end, and I had figured out that Latin America was where the U.S. government would engage in its next foreign intervention. My circle of activist friends shared a political viewpoint that Latin America had strategic importance to the United States, and we wanted to get involved in opposing the government's nefarious intentions. Of the seven people in the collective, one had done his alternative service in Bolivia and maintained deep connections to that country. The rest of us had some indirect interest in Latin America and were learning Spanish.

It was a tumultuous moment of my personal life. Although I had a girlfriend, over the course of the previous two years I slowly had accepted the fact that I had strong homosexual desires. Then, in early 1973, I finally came out. I desperately wanted to meet other gay people, and so a woman from the commune and I went to a meeting of the Gay Activist Alliance (GAA). The organization was planning a picket line in front of a gay bar that discriminated against lesbians, people of color, and transvestites. I immediately volunteered to join the protest even though I had never been inside a gay bar. Eventually, I found the GAA, with the exception of one or two people, too moderate and the membership little interested in the antiwar and civil rights movements, so I stopped going to meetings.

Within the commune, I ended up being the only person who pursued our original goal of getting involved in political action related to Latin America and participating in the transnational solidarity movement. I'm sure that my political motivations in part had to do with my feelings of being marginalized as a gay man and not conforming to normative gender roles. When growing up, I had always felt different and had identified with people who were oppressed or persecuted. It was a way of dealing with my own sense of isolation and loneliness.

In early 1973, at the same time that I was coming out to myself and to my friends, I contacted different Latin American–focused collectives on the East Coast. There were relatively few grassroots political organizations working on Latin America, and they were scattered throughout the country. I began doing work with some Brazilians and Americans in Washington, D.C., who had formed the Committee against Repression in Brazil (CARIB), in 1971, to denounce U.S. support for the dictatorship in Brazil and the torture of activists by the military. Marcos Arruda, a former Brazilian political prisoner who had been tortured by the regime, founded the group.[4] In 1971, he had managed to come to the United States, where his mother was living, and organized a protest against a visit by members of the Brazilian dictatorship to the Nixon White House. He and others then formed the Common Front on Latin America to broaden the work they had being doing on Brazil to include other countries, especially Argentina, Bolivia, and Chile.

At the time I didn't fully understand it, but, in the early 1970s, the left in the United States was collapsing. The antiwar movement had dissipated, and solidarity with Latin America was one of the few campaigns that kept the left's former momentum going. Chile became the new cause célèbre when, on September 11, 1973, the Chilean Armed Forces, led by General Augusto Pinochet, with the help of the Nixon administration and the CIA, overthrew the Allende government in Chile. The Chilean military arrested, tortured, and killed thousands of leftists. The coup d'état had a profound impact on me because Chile seemed to be a country where there could have been a peaceful transition to a more just society, and the experiment had failed. At the time, it seemed to confirm the idea that only armed struggle could successfully overthrow capitalism.

Overnight, people organized a demonstration in downtown Philadelphia, and we quickly set up a Chile Solidarity Committee that engaged in round-the-clock activities. Some months later, the ship *Esmeralda* docked in a port near Philadelphia for repairs. Immediately after the coup, the Chilean military had used this naval training vessel as a site to detain and torture an estimated one hundred political activists. The government then sent the ship on a world-wide mission to promote the new regime. We found out that its officers were invited to an event in the city, and so we prepared a public reception. When they came down the street en route to the event, a thousand people greeted them chanting "Chile sí, junta no!"

Those were very exciting moments for me in Philadelphia, but I felt isolated because I only had one left-wing gay friend, Jeff Escoffier. Although Jeff and I had organized a rather unsuccessful Marxist study group with a handful of gay men to see if we could figure out the relationship between gay oppression and Marxist theory, I met few people who shared my interests in the left and in gay and lesbian activism. During this period, I slowly came to the conclusion that capitalism was an exploitative system and socialism an alternative model for organizing society. I had traveled in Eastern Europe while I was in college, and I didn't like the bureaucratic nature of the societies there, but

I still considered myself a socialist. I had come out and was very relieved to accept my sexuality, but most leftist organizations, with the exception of the Democratic Socialists of America, the Socialist Workers' Party, and the Workers' World Party, were antigay. I didn't feel that I fit into the gay and lesbian movement because it didn't have an antiracist and anti-imperialist perspective. On the other hand, I never felt entirely at home in the solidarity movement. Although individuals were very nice to me, I felt that gays were not really accepted as equals. I simply couldn't reconcile my gay and my left identities.

Nonetheless, several Marxist groups tried to recruit me. Leftists invited me to open forums or discussed participation with me individually. Since the Socialist Workers' Party and the Workers' World Party had pro-gay positions, I was more open with them about being gay than I was with the Maoists and the Communist Party. I remained friendly but removed from the Socialist Workers' Party, largely because of the anti-Trotskyist sentiment that I picked up in the Chile Solidarity Committee from people in and around the Communist Party. I liked the pro-gay position of the Workers' World Party, but it didn't have an organized branch in Philadelphia at the time. I had discussions with the pro-Maoist Revolutionary Union, which later became the Revolutionary Communist Party, but I didn't like its position on homosexuality. The organization characterized it as a "product of bourgeois decadence." I remember a cute guy in their Philadelphia branch headquarters who told me that he had been gay, but, since he had joined the organization, he had realized that it was decadent and had given up his homosexuality. I sometimes wonder how long that lasted for him.

At first, leaders of the Young Workers' Liberation League, the youth section of the Communist Party, USA, tried to recruit me. Then, one Saturday evening, one of its members, also in the Chile solidarity movement, ran into me on Pine Street, a major gay cruising area in Philadelphia. I guess she figured out I was gay, because, after that night, I stopped receiving invitations to the group's meetings. I had also developed criticisms of the Communist Party's policies in the Soviet Union, Eastern Europe, and Latin America that made me reluctant to consider joining that organization.

In 1974, I had a bad experience with a segment of the left working on Latin America. I had applied to go to Cuba on the Venceremos Brigade and was turned down. The Venceremos Brigade was organized in 1969 by U.S. anti-imperialists who opposed the blockade of Cuba. Members of the Brigade did volunteer labor in Cuba for a couple of months. They helped cut sugar cane as a way of showing solidarity with the Cuban revolution, since the government had organized a countrywide mobilization to increase production. In 1971, at the First Congress on Education and Culture, the government had issued an official statement declaring homosexuality to be a pathological disorder. Some Brigade members who were in Cuba at the time protested, and a sector of the gay and lesbian movement in the United States spoke out against the Cuban government's policy. As a result, the Brigade carefully screened any gay or lesbian candidates who might in any way criticize the Cuban government's position on homosexuality. So, although I had an impeccable record as a solidarity activist, I was told that I was not suitable for the Brigade because I was "insensitive to people of color." Many years later, a second cousin, who was a member of the National Committee, admitted to me that it was because I was gay. When I heard that I had been screened out, I was very angry and hurt because I identified more with the left than with the gay community at the time. However, from that experience I developed a better understanding of the left's attitude toward homosexuality. I began to see that certain left currents were homophobic, others less so, and some not at all. Because of my experience with the Brigade in Philadelphia, I was also more hesitant to join a leftist party.

At the time most of the U.S. left thought that gay men were unstable, that they had weak emotional relationships, that they couldn't be trusted, that they would be vulnerable to telling secrets, and that they were flighty. Moreover, there was a pervasive notion circulating in the left at the time that romanticized revolutionary masculinity, which was predicated on a series of symbols and codes, represented by Ernesto "Che" Guevara, that idealized a cold, contained male who sacrificed for the cause. Gay men didn't fit into that model because they were seen as weak and effeminate, volatile, and not athletic, and, therefore, they couldn't possibly be revolutionaries. At the time, I observed that leftist women generally had to be masculine in order to assume positions of power. These hardened women also had to prove their femininity by showing they were capable of having sexual relationships with men. Some women I knew had a discreet personal life, and I don't know if they were lesbians or not. There were different standards for lesbians and for gay men.

Unable to find a political community in Philadelphia, I moved to California, assuming I might find more people like me. I eventually settled in the Bay Area in November 1974. Soon thereafter, I joined the San Francisco Chile Solidarity Committee. It was a welcoming group of people, in part because some of the most committed activists in the group prior to my arrival had been gay men. Several of them had done support work for the United Farm Workers (UFW), a rural union composed largely of Mexican and Filipino workers. While supporting the UFW, they had experienced incidences of homophobia and had confronted the leadership about it. A few of these same gay men later became involved in Nicaraguan solidarity work.

The San Francisco Chile Solidarity Committee was an eclectic group of people. By the time I became active in the group, the other gay men had moved on to other political activities, but I felt very much at home. Although the San Francisco Chile Solidarity Committee did not have a unified political perspective, one of the more influential people in the group was a woman who had been close to the Chilean revolutionary left group Movimento de la Izquierda Revolucionária (MIR). Others had never been to Chile but had been outraged by the brutality of the military regime and wanted to do something concrete to show support for the Chilean people.

In the Bay Area, the strongest solidarity group was Non-Intervention in Chile (NICH), which was based in Berkeley. NICH had considerable influence among Chile solidarity activists, and it generally supported MIR. The NICH newsletter highlighted information about the armed struggle and supported radical resistance to the Pinochet regime. When people in the solidarity movement discussed what had happened in Chile during the Popular Unity government led by Salvador Allende, NICH supporters usually disagreed with what they considered to be the reformist program and the errors of the Unidad Popular (UP) government. MIR and its supporters had a complex relationship with the UP, because, while they criticized its politics, they also tried to work with members and sympathizers of the Socialist and Communist Parties, which were the two main political forces within the Allende electoral coalition.

This tension was reflected in debates and other events organized at La Peña Restaurant and Cultural Center, a venue in Berkeley founded by NICH supporters as a location for solidarity activities. The organizers of La Peña sponsored concerts by the leading left-wing protest singers from Latin America, and they also held political events about the latest happenings in Chile. These meetings always provoked sharp debates among solidarity activists. For example, when Laura Allende, a former Socialist Party senator, political prisoner, and exile, traveled to the Bay Area in September 1975, she found herself in an awkward situation. Her son was a leader of MIR, but she supported the UP and was the sister of Salvador Allende. Most of the people who organized her tour supported MIR, but in her presentations she was a much more moderate leftist. There were ongoing underlining tensions among activists supporting different strategies for social change in Latin America.

At the same time that I was involved in Chile solidarity in San Francisco, I joined a group called the June 28th Union, named after the date of the 1969 Stonewall Rebellion in New York City, which marked the beginning of the modern gay and lesbian movement. The June 28th Union was a collective of twelve to fourteen men. Several of them had been in Students for a Democratic Society and supported the Prairie Fire Organizing Committee, which was the legal arm of the Weather Underground, or at least what remained of it.

They supported third-world struggles and antiracist campaigns in the United States. Within the group, we considered ourselves to be leftists or Marxists, but most of us had no set political ideology or affiliation.

The June 28th Union brought together gay leftists who raised questions about discrimination and homophobia and at the same time offered a left-wing program. Our meetings shifted between political discussions and activities within the Bay Area gay and lesbian community and among leftists. This was not an easy political balance to maintain. That year, for example, a coalition of left-wing groups vetoed our participation in a May Day activity organized in Oakland because of fears among some of the organizers that we might alienate or frighten off people they were trying to attract to the event.

Within the June 28th Union, members had the responsibility of organizing different public events. We decided that I should organize something about Chile on the second anniversary of the September 11 coup. We called the evening "Gay Solidarity with Chile." At the time, "gay" was still a code word for gays and lesbians and was not yet exclusively male-identified. The event was held in a community center between the Castro and the Haight-Ashbury district, very close to the center of gay life in the city. Approximately 300 to 350 people came to the event, which was considered a large turnout at the time. The evening featured a lesbian a capella group, gay and lesbian poets, a movie about organizing by MIR during the Allende government, and artwork by Lisa Kokin, a member of the Chile Solidarity Committee who displayed batik wall hangings about Chile and other third-world struggles.

The June 28th Union decided that I should give the keynote speech. In it, I argued that the lesbian and gay community in the United States should show solidarity with the Chilean resistance to the Pinochet regime. I didn't offer a very sophisticated political analysis, but I pointed out that, both in the United States and in Chile, gays and lesbians suffered police repression, and now the entire apparatus of the state was engaged in repressing unionists, leftists, and their supporters. At the time, we didn't have any direct contacts with gay men or lesbians in Chile and merely supposed that they were, indeed, suffering repression under the Pinochet regime. KPFA, the Pacifica-affiliated radio station, broadcast the event live. We raised about $1,000, which we gave to the "resistance," which really meant to MIR. It was an amazing event, an unheard-of articulation between the solidarity movement and the gay and lesbian community.

The exiled Chilean leftist organizations that worked with the solidarity movement in the Bay Area recruited several North Americans to their organizations. I knew this was happening and wanted very much to be asked to join. I was a *very* hard worker, and I didn't understand why I wasn't asked. Twenty years later, I discovered that several people had supported a proposal for me to be recruited to MIR, but members of MIR opposed it, arguing that the organization couldn't recruit queers. Although some of the Chilean members defended me, they were vetoed, and I was never asked to join. I had no idea at the time that this was taking place.

Soon after, in December 1975, I left San Francisco. A Brazilian friend and I traveled through Central America to Colombia. I got a job in a language school and stayed with a gay professor at the National Theater School who had lived in Cuba in the early 1960s. We discussed the idea of forming a gay group in Colombia, but we couldn't find other interested people. There was gay nightlife in Bogotá, but the people we approached thought it was impossible to organize something. They either were afraid of government repression or didn't think that others would be interested. In mid-1976, I went to Brazil, traveling through the Amazon and the North and Northeast. I ended up in São Paulo, which is the country's largest city and its political, cultural, industrial, and economic center. At the time, São Paulo was the main locus of the opposition to the dictatorship.

Before I arrived in São Paulo, in January 1977, João Silvéro Trevisan, a Brazilian whom I had met in Berkeley, had formed a gay consciousness-raising group. According to his account of what took place, it didn't last very long. Trevisan tells the story that most of the dozen or so participants in the group couldn't accept their homosexuality and even questioned whether or not they should have been discussing issues of sexuality instead of joining with other students and opponents of the regime to organize against the dictatorship. Trevisan is an important figure in the history of the Brazilian gay liberation movement. While a student in the late 1960s, he was involved in the Brazilian left. During the worst period of the dictatorship, he also directed an experimental, avant-garde film that was never shown due to government censorship. He then went into what he described as self-imposed exile, traveling through Latin America and living in the San Francisco Bay Area. He returned to Brazil in 1975 and published a collection of short stories, some with overt homoerotic themes, at a time when the military government censored books and films.

The political situation had changed dramatically in Brazil between 1976, when Trevisan organized the first consciousness-raising group, and a year later, when the movement got off the ground. Students began to demonstrate in the streets against the dictatorship. Human rights groups boldly denounced the excesses of the regime. Labor organizations protested the government's wage policies. Leftist political groups, including the pro-Soviet Brazilian Communist Party, Trotskyists, and other groups, secretly recruited workers and students to their ranks. The feeling that change was imminent also affected Brazilian gays and lesbians.

The qualitative transformations in the political situation inspired new mobilizations, and gay men and lesbians sensed that this presented new possibilities and opportunities. Even though this new political climate favored the emergence of a Brazilian gay and lesbian movement, one of the catalysts came from outside the country. In late 1977, Winston Leyland, the editor of the San Francisco–based publication *Gay Sunshine*, traveled to Rio de Janeiro and São Paulo to collect material for an anthology on gay Latin American literature. Trevisan and I met with him in São Paulo. He also met with a group of writers and intellectuals in Rio who decided to publish a gay monthly that was called *Lampião da Esquina*. The editorial board was made up of university professors, intellectuals, artists, and writers from Rio and São Paulo. Several of them, including Trevisan, had been involved in the left. In fact, *Lampião*'s managing editor had suffered discrimination in the Communist Party in the early 1960s because he was a homosexual.

Lampião was one of the "alternative" papers that came out in the late 1970s as government censorship loosened. The name *Lampião da Esquina* has a double meaning, "streetlamp on the corner" in reference to gay street life, and Lampião, a Robin Hood-type bandit figure who roamed the Brazilian Northeast in the early twentieth century. The editorial of the first issue published in April 1978 announced that *Lampião* would discuss sexuality, racial discrimination, the arts, ecology, and machismo. The editors also stated that they would support movements of homosexuals, women, Indians, blacks, and environmental activists. However, the thirty-eight issues that they published over the next two and a half years focused mostly on gay culture and the sexual liberation movement.

In May 1978, a month after the first issue of *Lampião* hit the newsstands, Trevisan, his boyfriend, and a handful of students and white-collar workers formed another group that they called Nucleo de Ação pelos Direitos dos Homossexuais (Action Nucleus for Homosexual Rights). It was a combination consciousness-raising circle and discussion group. As one of its first activities, the group debated the content of *Lampião* as each new issue came out. It also wrote an open letter to the Brazilian press protesting the negative portrayal of homosexuality in some of the city's tabloid scandal sheets.

I was out of the country, trying to obtain a visa to stay in Brazil, during the group's initial stages. When I returned, in September 1978, I immediately joined the group. At the same time, I began working with the editorial staff of *Versus*, another "alternative" monthly that had begun with a leftist, pan–Latin Americanist perspective. My boyfriend was an editor at *Versus*, although he was in the closet and afraid that his friends would reject him if they found out he was gay. I think that my boyfriend and I were initially attracted to each other because we were both leftists. Yet there was a constant strain on the relationship, because I wanted to be involved in both the gay movement and the left, whereas he thought that the gay group that was forming was filled with alienated, effeminate men. He wanted no part of it. Ever since I had come out, in 1973, I had tried to find a partner who was political, so I hoped that it was a matter of time for him to accept himself and support a political gay movement. Although we continued to have a tense relationship regarding gay activities, he opened the doors of the Brazilian left for me.

While my boyfriend was working at *Versus*, a majority of the editorial board joined the Convergência Socialista (Socialist Convergence, or CS), a Trotskyist organization that had semilegal status in this period of gradual liberalization during 1977 and 1978. I respected the CS's political organizing among Brazilian workers. Most members of the leftist groups that I knew in the United States were middle-class intellectuals who talked a lot about workers but did little to organize them. I also knew that, internationally, Trotskyism was the only leftist current that had actively participated in the gay and lesbian movement in the United States and Europe. Just as I had thought that there were likely to be gay socialists in San Francisco when I was isolated in Philadelphia, I guessed that there might be other open gays in the CS.

At the time, I also thought that the best way for me to work with the Brazilian left without being accused of being a CIA agent was as a very out gay man. It seemed too far-fetched that the U.S. government would recruit an open homosexual to infiltrate a Brazilian leftist organization. I also had the reference of my boyfriend, although he presented me not as his lover, just as a friend. The week I returned to Brazil in 1978, the military dictatorship ordered the arrest of all the members of the CS Central Committee and charged them with violating the National Security Act. I pitched in to help the organization by contacting Amnesty International. I remember arguing with my boyfriend that if anyone doubted my loyalty, all the more reason for him to come out and explain our relationship. He didn't agree, and several years later we broke up, partly because of these differences. Soon after beginning my work with *Versus* and the CS, I came out to the staff. I also coauthored an article on the new gay movement for the journal.

The core members of the gay group that Trevisan had organized knew that I supported the CS and that my lover was an editor of *Versus*. In fact, Trevisan and I discussed at length the relationship between CS and the gay movement. The leaders of the CS had been in a clandestine group called the Liga Operária (Workers' League), doing political work among industrial workers and students. When the government expanded the process of controlled liberalization in 1978, they decided to come above ground and take advantage of the new situation to recruit members. They founded the CS and organized a large public inaugural event. One of the participants in the meeting suggested that the issue of support for the rights of homosexuals be included in the group's program. It was unanimously included by a vote of the body. In an article published in *Lampião*, Trevisan sharply criticized the CS because the plank on gay rights had been an afterthought and not a part of the organization's initial proposal. I remember questioning Trevisan about why he spent his time criticizing the only leftist organization that had a positive position on homosexuality, instead of focusing his criticisms on those groups that had *no* position or were homophobic.

Although I heard that one or two gay men belonged to the CS, I didn't know them. So, I joined the Nucleo de Ação pelos Direitos dos Homossexuais and participated in its meetings beginning in September 1978. Around the same time, the military government released the leadership of the CS from jail and dropped charges against them. Soon thereafter, I approached one of the CS founders and asked about the possibility of forming a gay task force or working group within the organization to elaborate on the programmatic point in favor of the rights of homosexuals. She supported the idea and directed me to other gay men in the organization. Together, we created an internal education document about homosexuality as part of the CS's pre-Convention discussion. I authored most of the document that we finished in October 1979, titled "Theses for Homosexual Liberation." Following the Convention, we set up a working group composed of three members of the CS who wanted to participate in the gay movement, while continuing to hold periodic meetings with other gay and lesbian militants of the CS to talk about educating the membership about homophobia. We called ourselves the Homosexual Faction. It was like a gay and lesbian caucus. Eventually, almost two dozen members joined the gay and lesbian caucus. Within the CS, the response to our group ranged from indifference to enthusiastic support. Many members were proud that we were the only leftists that had a clear policy in favor of gay and lesbian rights. Others probably were hostile or didn't understand what we were doing but never said so publicly.

Some people in the movement knew about the internal organization of gays and lesbians in the CS. I never hid my political affiliation. I even distributed the document to members of the movement in São Paulo and organized a mini-discussion group with some of the more active members to explain the CS's analysis of how to build a gay and lesbian movement and possibly recruit them to the CS. I wasn't very successful, for several reasons. I think that many members of the movement had a hesitant attitude toward the CS, which was fueled by *Lampião*'s frequent attacks on the organization. This tension created a climate of hostility toward the left among a sector of the group. In addition, in 1978 and 1979, it was not at all clear how far the liberalization process would go. Many gays and lesbians probably felt that they were already taking risks by joining a homosexual organization. Some might not have wanted to be members of an organization whose central committee had been arrested the year before and charged with violating the National Security Act. The dictatorship also used the CS as a scapegoat, blaming it for having organized the strike wave of 1978–80. Joining a left group also meant more political work, more meetings, increased activities, or, in other words, a highly disciplined life. For a gay man or a lesbian who was dealing with coming out to family, friends, and society while participating in a gay organization for the first time, it was a big commitment.

Because of these factors, most of the gays and lesbians in the CS were first politicized and then came out. I have a theory that many gays and lesbians have sought out the left while in the closet as a way of coming to terms with their own homosexuality. Before I came out, I identified with the oppression of others because deep down inside I knew that society was oppressing me. I didn't have the courage to deal with my own homosexuality, so I fought for the rights of others until I developed the strength to accept myself. Many founders of gay and lesbian liberation movements throughout the world have been leftists. In the left, they gained the organizational experience and the political perspective that led them to understand the need to form a movement. However, I suspect that many of them initially joined the left as I did because they felt oppressed and dealt with it by fighting for other marginalized groups.

After the Nucleo de Ação pelos Direitos dos Homossexuais was founded, in May 1978, the group organized consciousness-raising groups along the lines of those run by the feminist movement in the United States. Subgroups met with facilitators and discussed topics such as coming out and sexism. Individuals would share their thoughts or experiences on the subject. The group also held general meetings and issued a few public statements about homophobia in the press. In the initial period, the group floundered for lack of a clear direction. It also faced the same kinds of problems that the gay and lesbian movement faced in the United States in the pre-Stonewall days, that is, before 1969. It was hard to find public meeting places, so people had to get together in someone's apartment. Although Brazil experienced the beginnings of a political liberalization, no one was fully confident that there wouldn't be more repression at some point. Some feared that their families would find out about their participation in the group or that they would lose their jobs if the group became too public. So we operated in a semi-clandestine fashion, much like the Mattachine Society and the Daughters of Bilitis did in the 1950s and early 1960s.[5]

In late 1978, the group decided that it needed to increase participation. No more than a dozen men and sometimes a lesbian friend of one of the members regularly attended meetings. As a result of an internal debate about how to broaden our appeal, we changed the group's name to SOMOS: Grupo de Afirmação Homossexual (WE ARE: Group of Homosexual Affirmation). Some members argued that the new name would pay homage to the Frente de Liberación Homosexual (FLH) of Argentina and its magazine, *Somos*. The FLH had been formed in 1971 as a coalition of several groups from Buenos Aires, one of which dated back to November 1969. The Front disbanded in mid-1976 after the military coup d'état. A former member of the FLH was living in São Paulo at the time and acted as an informal ambassador in exile, passing on information about the group to those members of the Brazilian movement interested in learning about the experiences of the Argentines in the early 1970s. At some point in the discussion, someone suggested that the new name include the word "gay" instead of "homosexual" because the latter term seemed cold and clinical. The group almost unanimously rejected the idea, arguing that using the word "gay" mimicked the movement in the United States. I agreed with that position because I thought the term "gay" was totally foreign to Brazilian culture.

Soon after SOMOS adopted its new name, the Student Association in the Social Science Department at the University of São Paulo invited the group to be part of a weeklong event to discuss new political movements. The panel included João Trevisan and Darcy Penteado, a noted artist, who were both members of *Lampião*'s editorial board, and three members of SOMOS. More than a hundred people attended. During the discussion period, several members of the audience complained that the Brazilian left was anti-gay. Representatives of pro-Soviet, pro-Albanian, and pro-Cuban organizations rebutted by arguing that, instead of fighting for specific issues that divided the left, people should unite in the general struggle against the dictatorship. Trevisan and others responded that the left was homophobic, and some leftists responded by criticizing the gay movement as irrelevant. Speaking from the audience at that meeting, I suggested that there was no contradiction between the fight against homophobia and oppression and the fight against the dictatorship. The discussion that night polarized into a caricature of the debate that would later split the movement.

The event at the University of São Paulo made SOMOS more widely known. We called a meeting several days later at the Catholic University

(Pontifícia Universidade Católica de São Paulo), and many new people, including quite a few lesbians, showed up and wanted to become members of the group. Whereas in 1978 no more than four women had spent some time in the organization, after February 1979 dozens of lesbians joined SOMOS. They quickly began to raise questions about machismo, gay misogyny, and sexism. Eventually, the lesbians in SOMOS formed their own autonomous group within the organization that they called Grupo de Ação Lésbica-Feminista (Lesbian-Feminist Action Group). There were tensions between the gay men and the lesbians within SOMOS, mostly because many new gay male members made sexist remarks. Most of the lesbians adopted a feminist perspective, and many of the men didn't understand what the women were arguing. Since I had considered myself a feminist since 1969, even before I became a Marxist or came out, I was one of the older members of SOMOS who criticized sexism in the group and made a point of defending the right of the women to organize separately. For most of the men, these feminist ideas were new and threatening, as was the idea of organizing autonomously.

While the formation of the Lesbian-Feminist Action Group within SOMOS was in part a result of the sexist discourse of many of SOMOS's male members, it was also a result of an increasing interest among lesbians in participating in the women's movement and in raising the issues of lesbians within a feminist context. By early 1980, most of the lesbians in SOMOS wanted to form a separate organization. They formalized their split in April of that year. A few women remained in SOMOS because they wanted to work in a mixed organization.

SOMOS's first ongoing political campaign was around the defense of *Lampião*. Since August 1978, the Brazilian government had tried to close down the paper. Four months after *Lampião* was founded, the police opened an inquiry in Rio de Janeiro and São Paulo, charging that the paper violated the Press Law by offending "public morality and propriety," which could have led to a year's imprisonment for those who worked for the paper. The police summoned *Lampião*'s editors to be fingerprinted and photographed in order to intimidate them. This action by the dictatorship was part of a larger strategy, discovered through a leaked government document, that revealed a plan to shut down the alternative press either through the use of the Press Law or through financial audits. The journalists' union denounced this government measure, and the Brazilian Press Association provided a lawyer free of charge to defend *Lampião*'s editors. At the time, SOMOS was somewhat without direction, so I proposed that we form a committee to defend *Lampião* and circulate a petition denouncing the military's action, a document to be signed by leading artists, intellectuals, and other opponents of the regime. My proposal was designed as much to have an impact on the government's actions as it was to get SOMOS's members into the mode of organizing political campaigns and forming alliances.

At the same time that I was participating in SOMOS, I was also active in the gay and lesbian group within the CS that met each week to have a political discussion and plan activities. When there were problems in the gay movement, I would go to an experienced person within the CS for advice. For example, the United Black Movement organized a march through downtown São Paulo to celebrate the National Day of Black Consciousness on November 20, 1979. The leadership of the CS suggested that we propose that SOMOS participate in the march since it was an important event and *Lampião* had been promoting the idea that gays should ally with women, blacks, and other minorities. (At the time, I rejected the word "minorities" and preferred to use the more cumbersome term "sectores oprimidos," or oppressed sectors, because I felt that the word "minorities" tended to marginalize gays, women, and blacks.) I took the idea to SOMOS, and everyone agreed it was a great proposal. I offered the CS's headquarters as a space to paint a banner, and members of SOMOS went there to design and make it. We organized a contingent of about twenty people and distributed a leaflet that expressed our solidarity with the United Black Movement and drew links between racism and sexism. We also carried a banner that read "Against Racial Discrimination, SOMOS: Group of Homosexual Affirmation." This was the first time that gays and lesbians demonstrated in the streets of Brazil. Like the campaign in defense of *Lampião*, it gave SOMOS members, many of whom had not participated in other political movements, the confidence to go public. My impression was that the members of the United Black Movement at the rally, amounting to no more than a hundred people, didn't quite understand who we were and passively accepted our participation in the event.

By late 1979, a half-dozen or so small groups had sprung up around the country, following the lead of SOMOS. In December, the editorial board of *Lampião*, which acted as a clearinghouse for these groups, called on them to send representatives to Rio de Janeiro to discuss the possibility of organizing a national meeting of homosexual groups. Those attending the meeting decided to hold the conference in São Paulo in April 1980, and SOMOS offered to host the event. About 150 people participated in the first two days of closed sessions of the National Meeting of Organized Homosexual Groups, hailing from eight groups that represented a total of about three hundred people. The third day, a public event drew a much larger crowd.

The meeting turned out to be the battleground for a controversy that had been brewing within the movement. Whereas in 1977 students had led the struggle against the regime through strikes and street mobilizations, the following year the Brazilian working class took center stage. More than 275,000 metalworkers in the greater São Paulo area brought production to a halt at plants owned by Ford, Pirelli, Mercedes-Benz, and Fiat, ending what had been hailed by the dictatorship as a decade of labor peace. The military recognized that it had to move fast to control the situation. The next month, the president announced new steps toward institutional reform and promised to speed up its promised "slow and gradual" return to democracy. The following year, more than three million workers went out on strike. Teachers, white-collar professionals, and public employees joined the metalworkers. Another massive strike wave shook the industrial suburbs of São Paulo in April 1980, but this time the government responded by taking over the metalworkers' union of São Bernardo do Campo, which had led the labor mobilizations. In response, strike leaders called for a May Day march and rally in São Bernardo, where the metalworkers' union was located, in support of the workers and against the regime.

At the opening session of the National Meeting of Organized Homosexual Groups, someone presented a motion expressing solidarity with the metalworkers' general strike. It passed unanimously, reflecting the widespread sympathy for the workers within Brazil at the time. Brazil had been under a dictatorship since 1964, and the opposition to the government had suffered very brutal repression between 1968 and 1977. The military targeted dissident workers, leftists, and intellectuals with a sophisticated and repressive apparatus. When students and later workers challenged the dictatorship, they showed not only that you could fight and win concessions from the government but that the democratic opening provided space for others to organize. In meetings of SOMOS, I argued that had there *not* been a harsh wave of repression in Brazil starting in late 1968, the gay liberation movement would have flourished as it had throughout Europe, the United States, Mexico, Argentina, and Puerto Rico. Gays and lesbians simply had no room to organize in such a climate in Brazil. It was such a simple argument, yet Trevisan and the anti-leftist sector of the movement criticized my analysis as a parroting of tired Marxist-Leninist rhetoric.

A more significant divergence within the movement arose when another motion was presented on the second day of deliberations. Someone proposed that the different groups represented at the Congress participate in the upcoming May Day demonstration. There was a messy and confusing debate, and the motion was defeated 54 to 53. Trevisan described the incident in a way that reflects the main arguments of the anti-leftist forces within the movement. His position is best reflected in this passage from *Perverts in Paradise*:

The most crucial moment and the one that best revealed the divergences in this first national congress was the vote on a motion that would oblige the whole gay movement to participate in the First of May celebrations in a football stadium in the industrial town of São Bernardo, near São Paulo. The group swollen and inspired by Trotskyists proposed an obligatory and unrestricted attendance. The opposing group wondered whether such a small number of homosexuals had the right to represent the movement and, consequently, the gay community. As an alternative, it proposed that there should be no obligation on groups, but rather a decision on the private or individual level. I was one of those who opposed compulsory attendance, horrified by the pocket leftists there. Furthermore, I knew that so-called "proletarian leadership" often hides every kind of demand and manipulation under its appeal for unity, and the only unity it accepts is that dictated by its central committee. I was also aware that behind the scenes the Trotskyists wanted to draw obvious benefits from the presence of homosexuals under their wing on May Day. In order to achieve this, they had been offering us for some time photocopying facilities and rooms in their headquarters where SOMOS activists could make banners and meet. It was clear that the very idea of autonomy of liberation movements was at stake. We did not want to be the vanguard of a dubious gay movement, much less to obey orders from a political party.[6]

Most of the left at the time was homophobic. Yet Trevisan and his supporters within the movement attacked the very sectors of the left that *participated* in the movement. If the CS thought that homosexuality was a product of bourgeois decadence or that gays and lesbians should abandon their own struggle to fight only against the dictatorship, why would it participate in the gay movement? Trevisan's interpretation of the left's activities influenced a whole circle of activists, yet his arguments ignore that there were only eight members of the CS at the National Meeting who had the right to vote. More than one hundred people expressed their opinion on the resolution. How had the left swollen the ranks of the meeting? Furthermore, the resolution called on the organizations to participate in the May Day march and rally. How could anyone possibly force people to participate against their will? If Trotskyists wanted to recruit new members, that would mean agreeing with the CS program and not simply marching in a May Day demonstration. If the Brazilian working class and the left were as homophobic as Trevisan and several editors of *Lampião* argued, defending the participation of homosexuals would have harmed their chances of influencing the labor movement.

According to his own writings, Trevisan wanted his vision of gay liberation to dominate the movement. He was a libertarian. He wanted the movement to operate on the basis of consensus, with the "rejection of leadership in order to avoid once against becoming the victims of spokespeople and interpreters."

He wanted an "authentically gay movement" without "outside influences." In practice, that meant that the editors of *Lampião*, who controlled a nationally distributed gay publication, had hegemonic influence over the movement. The paper published critiques of the CS month after month and yet refused to print an open letter to *Lampião* written by the Homosexual Faction in response, to cite but one example.

Although Trevisan criticized the rights of socialists to participate in the movement, he defended the rights of feminists. The women in SOMOS felt that the organization was not addressing the specific problems of lesbians. They thought that gay men's concerns dominated and that sexism made it difficult for them to function as equals. Over the course of 1979 and into 1980, they adopted a feminist program. While some men within SOMOS considered themselves to be feminist, including Trevisan and myself, the group had not adopted a feminist program or perspective even though the majority of lesbians within SOMOS were moving in that direction. According to Trevisan, socialists did not have the right to present their ideas, but feminists could. His notion of autonomy meant the exclusion of those with different political ideas who were also members of other organizations with which he didn't agree.

After the motion calling for the movement to participate in the May Day demonstration was narrowly defeated, on the third day of the Congress, there was a public rally in a São Paulo theater, attended by about eight hundred people. Representatives of the different organizations spoke and answered questions. It was a spirited meeting. Immediately thereafter, the majority of the membership of SOMOS met and decided to participate in the May Day activities. In order not to cause a split in the group, we decided not to use the name SOMOS, since a minority of the organization clearly opposed the idea. So, we formed an ad hoc group we called Homosexual Commission for May 1st and marched with two banners identifying the group and proclaiming, "Stop the intervention in the ABC Unions" and "Stop discrimination against homosexual workers." We prepared a leaflet signed by the commission that expressed solidarity with the striking metalworkers, linking their struggle with that of the oppressed: blacks, women, and homosexuals. We pointed to instances of the discrimination that gay men and lesbians suffered as workers and called on the unity of the working class to end such discrimination.

That day, I had no idea of the gravity of the events that were taking place as I met with other gays and lesbians in downtown São Paulo. Police blockades delayed all of the traffic to the march. We had taken a city bus, and I worried about whether we would ever get there and whether the crowd would jeer us. The May Day celebration in São Bernardo do Campo was held in a climate of repression. The military allowed the demonstrators to march through the streets of the city only at the last minute, while army helicopters flew overhead to disrupt the march. Nevertheless, more than 100,000 workers and supporters marched to Vila Euclides Stadium, where 50,000 applauded their arrival. Members of SOMOS, including some new activists who had joined as a result of the Congress and rally, as well as the Lesbian-Feminist Action Group, which was in the process of separating itself from SOMOS, marched in the gay and lesbian contingent. We were fifty strong. When we arrived at the stadium, we were roundly applauded.

I didn't interview those who cheered us as we entered the stadium to know their thoughts. I assume their response ranged from indifference and incredulity to support, if simply because of the novelty that "even queers are out in force today." Trevisan, who did not attend the May Day march, wrote, "They proudly paraded in front of thousands of left-wing unionists, students and intellectuals without realizing that they were there to present their good-conduct certificate and to ask for their superiors' blessing. Naturally they were approved in the form of applause. To me, however, this represented the beginning of the taming of the newly born gay movement, whose originality, if still crude, was being cut back before it had even flowered."[7]

The May Day demonstration was one of the most important days of my life because I felt that I finally had integrated two aspects of my being and had successfully led a small but important movement in that direction. I had helped other homosexuals understand that they did not exist in isolation from the rest of society and its problems, and I had been part of the first political interaction between gays and lesbians and ordinary working people in a positive climate. It was the first big step in the coming out process of the movement in Brazil, and it laid the foundation for a strategic alliance with the electoral left. It took a lot of courage for all of us to march, because we were facing a new unknown, and many of our fears may have been unfounded.

At a meeting held a couple of weeks later, the antileft faction split from SOMOS, accusing it of being totally under the control of the CS. The dissidents formed a group called Outra Coisa (Something Else). Ironically, there were still only three supporters of the CS in SOMOS. Although many of the members respected the CS and although more of the new members had been involved in the student movement and identified themselves as independent leftists, they didn't want to join a left-wing organization. *Lampião* played up the split and also accused SOMOS of being controlled by the CS. Because SOMOS had been the first gay rights organization and was certainly the largest one, the split had a demoralizing effect on the movement, especially among those who didn't really know what was going on. Yet SOMOS did not enter into a crisis. Only eight members left, while another forty remained in the group. A majority of those identified with the left or the labor movement in some way. The rest wanted to get on with what the group was all about, fighting homophobia and discrimination.

Several months after the split, the group unanimously passed a statement of principles. It held that SOMOS would not affiliate with any political party but that members of the organization were allowed to hold any political ideology and belong to any political party; in addition, the group would participate in any political demonstration it saw fit. I voted for this resolution because I believed that the group as a whole should remain independent but that supporters of political groups should have the right to participate in SOMOS and present their ideas as long as they did so democratically.

After the split, SOMOS organized a second anniversary celebration in May 1980 to lift everyone's spirits and to show Trevisan's camp that the group had life left in it. A big party was organized at a gay club. During the celebration, one of the members announced that the police had begun to round up gays, lesbians, transvestites, and prostitutes in downtown São Paulo. The head of a downtown police precinct had organized the dragnet to "clean up" the city, and he ordered the arrest of 1,500 people over the next month. SOMOS called an emergency meeting and invited the other groups in São Paulo to plan a response to the police actions. I decided not to attend the meeting because I had become a controversial figure, as some of the ex-SOMOS members held me personally responsible for the split. I was associated with the CS, and members of SOMOS were trying to convince people that the CS had *not* taken over the group.

The organizations held a demonstration, and SOMOS played a key role in it. On June 13, 1980, five hundred people gathered on the steps of the Municipal Theater to protest the police roundups. As a light rain began to fall, activists began calling for the removal of the police chief. They also shouted slogans urging the rally participants to march through the streets of São Paulo. Slowly the crowd moved through the downtown area, its numbers growing to almost one thousand. Carrying banners and chanting slogans such as "Down with repression, more love and desire," it was by far the largest political event of the Brazilian movement to that date. Most political observers agree that the demonstration was one of the reasons that the police raids and roundups ceased soon thereafter.

SOMOS began raising funds to rent a headquarters in downtown São Paulo. We became the first gay or lesbian group in Brazil to have a space that could hold one hundred or more people for meetings and for fund-raising parties. In October 1980, SOMOS received a threat from a right-wing group called the Cruzada Anti-Homossexualismo (Anti-Homosexual Crusade), which, in the style of other reactionary groups, such as the New Fatherland Phalanx, the Moral Brigade, and the Anti-Communist Commandos, sent the organization a letter threatening to "clean up the 'oil spot' of cheap perfume that is masculine prostitution . . . that prostitutes the Sacred Brazilian Family, weakening the foundations of the Nation." In protest, the group participated in another demonstration organized by the left in São Bernardo do Campo with the banner "Stop terrorist acts! SOMOS: Grupo de Afirmação Homossexual." Leftists, including the newly formed Workers' Party, had organized the event because the right had stepped up its activities against numerous organizations, including violent acts.

After a year of intensive activity, a meeting was held in Rio de Janeiro in December 1980 to plan a second national gathering. While representatives of sixteen groups attended, it became clear that the movement was still small, and the event never took place. Groups were not growing in membership, and there was widespread confusion about the direction of the movement. In part, I believe that the conflict within SOMOS demoralized the movement as a whole because SOMOS was seen as the vanguard, the leading organization. In São Paulo, four groups attempted to coordinate activities. In April 1981, the Lesbian-Feminist Action Group, SOMOS, the Homosexual Faction of the CS, and Alegria-Alegria (Happiness-Happiness), a friendly split-off from SOMOS, met at the University of São Paulo to discuss the movement's problems and to explore areas of common action.

Some members of SOMOS believed that the Workers' Party offered the potential to become the best political ally of the gay and lesbian movement. The Workers' Party was formed in 1979 as a result of a new law imposed on the Congress by the military dictatorship. The opposition political party, the Brazilian Democratic Movement, had been doing better in each successive election, even though the electoral laws were stacked against it. The generals feared that the opposition was getting too strong, so they passed the Party Reform Act, which permitted the formation of new parties. The regime intended to split up the opposition. The majority of the labor movement, leftists, and radical sectors of the Catholic Church formed the Workers' Party as an alternative to the other political parties that were being formed but that were dominated by sectors of the economic elite that opposed the dictatorship. Luiz Inácio da Silva, more popularly known as Lula, who headed the 1978–80 strike wave as the leader of the São Bernardo metalworkers' union, became the undisputed leader of the Workers' Party. Left-wing gay activists within the movement decided to raise the issue of rights for homosexuals within the Workers' Party. In a contingent organized as "Homosexual Militants Building the Workers' Party," members of SOMOS marched in a May Day parade in 1981 with banners that read, "Stop the discrimination against homosexual workers."

At the national convention of the Workers' Party held in September 1981, Lula announced that the Workers' Party would "not permit homosexuality to be treated as a sickness, and much less a case for the police in our party." He also stated that the Workers Party would "defend the respect that they deserve, calling on them to participate in the building of our society." This was an important declaration because it was the first time that a legal political party (the various leftist tendencies didn't have legal status) came out in support of gay and lesbian rights in Brazil. In the 1982 elections, the Workers' Party fielded eight gay candidates, including an incumbent, João Baptista Breda, who came out on national television. Although Breda lost reelection, the 1982 election was the first time that openly gay or lesbian candidates ran for public office in Brazil.

In July 1981, the editorial board of *Lampião* decided to close down the paper. The board reported that the circulation had dropped and that the community wasn't supporting the publication. Trevisan noted that the paper had become distant from the gay movement and repudiated activism. The editorial board of *Lampião* wanted to direct the movement through the newspaper, but, with the exception of Trevisan and Darcy Penteado, none of the editors became publicly active in any group. I remember proposing in 1979 or 1980 that every member of SOMOS pledge to sell ten copies of the paper. I saw it as a way of increasing the circulation of *Lampião* while encouraging SOMOS members to engage the gay community in a discussion of how the paper could serve the political movement. When I made the proposal, Trevisan and his supporters roundly criticized the idea as mimicking the left.

I could understand Trevisan's negative experiences with homophobic leftists in the 1970s on one level because I had experienced similar homophobia in the U.S. left. In fact, the Homosexual Faction of the Socialist Convergence published a booklet, *Homosexuality: From Oppression to Liberation*, that included interviews with the editors of the papers of the Communist Party, which was pro-Soviet; the October 8th Revolutionary Movement, which had been involved in urban guerrilla activities in the late 1960s and was pro-Cuban; and the Socialist Convergence. The October 8th Revolutionary Movement, which had some political influence at the time, clearly stated that homosexuality was a product of bourgeois decadence, whereas the Communist Party considered homosexuality a secondary question. So, one can understand the apprehension of gay leaders. However, the CS was a Trotskyist organization that criticized Stalinist regimes. Trevisan, for example, knew that the CS opposed the bureaucratic nature of Cuba and the Soviet Union. As far as he was concerned, the various factions of the left were one and the same.

Soon after the split in SOMOS, Trevisan sent me an open letter breaking off any personal friendship. He wrote, "For the good of our still fragile Homosexual Movement, I ask you to stay within the limits of your political organization, stop manipulating homosexual groups, and don't mix your sectarian 'socialist' beliefs with our legitimate struggle for sexual liberation and with our attempts for socio-cultural transformation based on our lives and not based on rules dictated from revolutionary manuals. . . . Let homosexuals speak for themselves without representatives and mediators of any tendency." I read this to mean either that he didn't consider me a homosexual or that for him I ceased to be gay when I became a socialist.

Activists looked to *Lampião* as a unifying force and as a publication that could provide leadership. When the editorial board attacked the CS and SOMOS, I believe it undermined the support it was receiving from the movement. I think that faithful readers thought that the movement was too small and precarious to sustain such divisions. For example, *Lampião* published an article denouncing Lula and the working class for not defending gay and lesbian rights, and then the Workers' Party came out in support of the right of homosexuals to organize. I think that activists didn't like the way it seemed that *Lampião* knew how to be critical only of others. In his book, Trevisan pointed out that one of the last issues of *Lampião* that focused on Cuba sold very poorly at the newsstands, while another about Carnival did quite well. He mentioned this as a reason why the paper folded. The readers weren't interested in politics. In a way, he was right. The majority of homosexuals were not political, and even the minority who were activists faced the overpowering weight of homophobia and a sexist society that depoliticized them. Their rejection by their families, peers, friends, the Church, and society in general created conditions that provoked a natural tendency to seek out other homosexuals and to band together to get support and to be able to express their sexuality freely. Frequently, gay men channel that need into going out, having a good time, and spending a lot of time looking for partners. That left little time for activism. Yet, even in a depoliticizing climate, after the First Meeting of Organized Homosexual Groups, a new generation came into SOMOS. Many were former student activists who were finally accepting their homosexuality. They brought with them a relatively positive attitude toward politics and helped sustain the organization after the split.

I'm very hesitant to draw any analogies between the U.S. and the Brazilian movements. However, if one looks at the history of the U.S. movement, it didn't begin with the 1969 Stonewall riots in New York City. The organized movement went back to 1950 with the founding of the Mattachine Society in Los Angles and to 1955 with the founding of the Daughters of Bilitis in San Francisco. They were small, marginal groups that represented an insignificant percentage of homosexuals. The social movements of the 1960s propelled the gay and lesbian movement into being, but there were at least twenty years of preparation and molecular changes that most gays and lesbians didn't even perceive were happening.

Unfortunately, because of the repressive Brazilian military dictatorship, which made organizing a risky business, gay and lesbian organizations didn't have a political space to develop prior to 1977. There could be no accumulation of experience, activists, and organizations. Yet there was a developing international movement. Brazilian gays and lesbians were aware of it and of the victories that it was achieving around the world. When the political conditions became propitious for groups to organize, they attempted to go from zero to a hundred in a single leap.

In 1981, only 200 to 250 people attended a demonstration in front of the Municipal Theater in São Paulo to commemorate the march, which had drawn 1,000 participants the previous year. It was clear that the movement in São Paulo was receding. One of the reasons was the exhaustion of many of the leading activists. By late 1981, for example, I was tired of doing political work in the gay movement because of all the pressures and problems that I had to confront as a left-wing leader. There was also the issue of the lack of leadership overall with the demise of *Lampião* and the inability of any one organization to win the confidence of the whole movement in order to bring groups together. There was no publication that could report on the news of the movement nationwide.

In 1982 and 1983, the mass movement in Brazil waned, as well. The labor movement lost the strikes of 1980 and faced massive layoffs of its membership. The Workers' Party did not do as well as many had hoped in the 1982 elections, obtaining only 8 percent of the votes. A severe economic recession and massive unemployment impacted the gay groups, whose members tended to be lower middle-class and white-collar workers, students, and the unemployed. Economic survival took precedence over political action. SOMOS tried to put out a monthly paper to fill the void left by the closing of *Lampião* but lacked the financial resources to sustain the project.

By late 1982, SOMOS's leadership had burned out, and the group folded in 1983. Only one or two organizations from this first period of the Brazilian gay liberation movement managed to sustain themselves. Grupo Gay da Bahia, led by Luiz Mott, an anthropologist at the University of Bahia, has survived until today and has done important work in advancing the cause of gay, lesbian, transsexual, and transgendered rights.

As I argued at the time, in my assessment, had Brazil not been under the domination of a military dictatorship in the late 1960s and the early 1970s, the Brazilian gay and lesbian movement would have developed somewhat earlier than it did. The political openings in Argentina from 1971 to 1976 provided the opportunity for a movement in that country, and there is no reason to believe that a comparable movement would not have coalesced in Brazil at that time had the political conditions been more favorable. Just as the gay liberation movement in the United States and Western Europe was impelled by the student, civil rights, feminist, and antiwar movements, so the belated Brazilian movement was encouraged by the organization of students, women, blacks, and laborers that struggled against the military dictatorship.

In my mind, the international gay movement had a direct impact on the Brazilian movement through the visit of gay activists from the United States and other countries and through the experiences of gay Brazilians who had lived abroad. SOMOS looked to Western Europe and to the United States for ideas and inspiration. Moreover, former activists from the Argentine FLH provided encouragement in the movement's first stage. My own experience as a gay activist in the United States was important in that I had the vision that a militant movement could evolve in Brazil. I remember that, during each new phase of the movement's development, I would point out in the meetings that we had just done something historical or monumental. I had lived in the United States and had repressed my sexual desires before Stonewall. The movement had transformed me. I believed that the same kind of transformation was possible in Brazil, and I tried to develop political strategies with that in mind. My experience as an organizer placed me in a unique position in the Brazilian movement. Many times I was respected as a leader because I projected a sense of confidence. I think that is what makes a good political leader—the ability to see far enough ahead to provide direction for a group and to inspire confidence that the impossible *is* possible.

In the United States and Western Europe, the New Left receded in the mid-1970s, and the gay and lesbian movement went through a corresponding change. Gay liberation organizations yielded to a plethora of community organizations, reformist political groups, and new service-oriented institutions. In Brazil, the impact of the first organizations waned, along with the general movement against the military regime, but there were few back-up organizations to replace them. This happened because, in Brazil, as in Argentina and other Latin American countries, there hadn't been a pre-gay liberation movement like the Mattachine Society or the Daughters of Bilitis to provide the accumulation of activists prior to 1969 who could assist the organizations that developed after 1969. In Brazil, SOMOS, *Lampião*, and other groups that were founded thereafter were both the pre-movement and the movement itself. When AIDS appeared in Brazil as a health crisis for the gay community, in 1983, many of the new groups founded to respond to the pandemic built upon the experiences of SOMOS and other groups as they tried to figure out how to organize homosexuals to respond to the disease. In fact, many AIDS activists had participated in the gay movement or in the left.

My dream had been to find a way to unite my political ideas as a socialist with the fight against the oppression I felt as a gay man. While I was able to do good work in San Francisco because I had found a community of left-wing activists who were openly gay socialists, their work seemed limited in its impact. I hadn't planned to help found the gay movement in Brazil when I began my trip down the Amazon River in August 1976. As events unfolded, I saw the possibility of linking two important movements in a way that over-came my own personal conflicts, and I did everything possible to see that the movement emerged with a progressive orientation and program. I struggled to get the sector of the left that I worked with to develop a clear pro-gay/lesbian program. Even though SOMOS and the left wing of the movement weren't able to sustain their activities, I believe that we set the stage and the tone for the emergence of an amazingly powerful movement that came thereafter.

Notes

I would like to thank Brenda Elsey for her outstanding editorial assistance in re-working and editing this "self-interview" into its current form.

1. In 1964, the Brazilian military overthrew the radical-populist government of João Goulart and initiated twenty-one years of authoritarian rule. Backed by the U.S. gov-ernment, the Brazilian generals outlawed opposition political parties, arrested leftist leaders, purged radical unions, and imposed tight controls over the press. From 1968 to 1973, the government carried out a campaign of state terrorism against the opposition, especially leftist organizations. Thousands were arrested and tortured. Faced with a strike wave in 1978, the Brazilian military accelerated a process of gradual liberalization that eventually returned the government to civil control and that included assurances that the generals involved in human rights violations would not face prosecution. For a comprehensive account of the military dictatorship, see Thomas E. Skidmore, *The Politics of Military Rule in Brazil, 1964–85* (New York: Oxford University Press, 1988).

2. In the late 1980s, Brazilian writers began to write the history of the Brazilian movement. The writer and one-time gay activist João S. Trevisan dedicated a chapter of his book, *Perverts in Paradise* (London: GMP, 1986), titled "Gay Politics and the Manipulation of Homosexuality," to the topic. The anthropologist Edward MacRae,

who conducted research for his doctoral dissertation while participating as a member of the country's first gay group, reworked that study into a book, *A construção da igualdade: Identidade sexual e política no Brasil da "abertura"* (Campinas: Unicamp, 1990). He has also published an article in English titled "Homosexual Identities in Transitional Brazilian Politics," in *The Making of Social Movements in Latin America: Identity, Strategy and Democracy*, ed. Arturo Escobar and Sonia E. Alvarez (Boulder, CO: Westview Press, 1992), 185–203.

3. For articles about the movement that I have written from different angles, see James N. Green, "The Emergence of the Brazilian Gay Liberation Movement: 1977–1981," *Latin American Perspectives* 21, no. 80 (Winter 1994): 38–55; "More Love and More Desire: The Building of the Brazilian Movement," in *The Global Emergence of Gay and Lesbian Politics: National Imprints of a Worldwide Movement*, ed. Barry Adam, Jan Willem Duyvendak, and André Krouwel (Philadelphia: Temple University Press, 1999), 91–109; "Desire and Militancy: Lesbians, Gays, and the Brazilian Workers' Party," in *Different Rainbow: Same-Sex Sexuality and Popular Struggles in the Third World*, ed. Peter Drucker (London: Gay Men's Press, 2000), 57–70; and "(Homo) sexuality, Human Rights, and Revolution in Latin America," in *Human Rights and Revolutions*, ed. Jeffrey N. Wasserstrom, Lynn Hunt, Marilyn B. Young, and Gregory Grandin (Boston: Rowman and Littlefield, 2007), 139–54.

4. For a compelling account of Marcos Arruda's arrest and ordeal, see Lina Penna Sattamini, *A Mother's Cry: A Memoir of Politics, Prison, and Torture under the Brazilian Military Dictatorship*, trans. Rex P. Nielson and James N. Green, introduction by James N. Green (Durham, NC: Duke University Press, 2010).

5. The Mattachine Society, formed in Los Angeles in 1950 by Henry Hay and other former members and supporters of the Communist Party, was the earliest post–World War II gay rights organization in the United States. The Daughters of Bilitis, the first lesbian rights organization in the United States, was founded in San Francisco in 1955.

6. Trevisan, *Perverts in Paradise*, 145–46.

7. Ibid., 147.

Selected Bibliography

Manuscript Collections

Archivo General de la Nación (AGN), Dirección Federal de Seguridad (DFS), Mexico City, Mexico

Centro de Estudios Sobre la Universidad (CESU), Universidad Nacional Autónoma de México (UNAM), Mexico City, Mexico

Documents Related to the Nationalist Party, Archivo General de Puerto Rico, San Juan, PR

Fondo Eugenio Ruíz-Tagle, Facultad Latinoamericana de Ciencias Sociales-Chile (FERT-FLACSO), Santiago, Chile

International Association for Cultural Freedom (IACF) Collection, University of Chicago Special Collections Research Center, Chicago, IL

Nelson A. Rockefeller Papers (NAR Papers), Rockefeller Family Archives, Rockefeller Archive Center, Sleepy Hollow, NY

Ralph T. Templin Papers, United Methodist Church Archives—GCAH, Madison, NJ

Ruth Reynolds Papers, Centro de Estudios Puertorriqueños (CEP), Hunter College, City University of New York, New York, NY

Vito Marcantonio Papers, New York Public Library, New York, NY

Books and Articles

Acosta-Lespier, Ivonne. "The Smith Act Goes to San Juan: *La Mordaza*, 1948–1957." In *Puerto Rico under Colonial Rule*, edited by Ramón Bosque-Pérez and José Javier Colón Morera, 59–65. Albany: State University of New York Press, 2006.

Adams, Dale. "Saludos Amigos: Hollywood and FDR's Good Neighbor Policy." *Quarterly Review of Film and Video* 24 (2007): 289–95.

Agosín, Marjorie. *Tapestries of Hope, Threads of Love: The Arpillera Movement in Chile.* Lanham, MD: Rowman and Littlefield, 2008.

Aguayo Quezada, Sergio. *1968: Los archivos de la violencia.* Mexico City: Reforma, 1998.

———. *La Charola: Una historia de los servicios de inteligencia en México*. Mexico City: Grijalbo, 2001.

Aguilar, Mario I. *A Social History of the Catholic Church in Chile*. Vol. 1, *The First Period of the Pinochet Government, 1973–1980*. Lewiston, NY: Edwin Mellen, 2004.

Aguilar Camín, Héctor, and Lorenzo Meyer. *In the Shadow of the Mexican Revolution: Contemporary Mexican History, 1910–1989*. Translated by Luis Alberto Fierro. Austin: University of Texas Press, 1993.

"AHR Conversation: On Transnational History." *American Historical Review* 111, no. 5 (2006): 1441–65.

Albizu Campos, Laura de. *Albizu Campos y la independencia de Puerto Rico*. Hato Ray, PR: Publicaciones Puertorriqueñas, 2007.

Albizu Campos, Pedro. *Escritos*. Edited by Laura Albizu-Campos Meneses and Mario A. Rodríguez León. Hato Rey, PR: Publicaciones Puertorriqueñas, 2007.

Albornoz, César. "Cultura en la Unidad Popular: Porque esta vez no se trata de cambiar un presidente." In *Cuando hicimos historia: La experiencia de la Unidad Popular*, edited by Julio Pinto, 147–76. Santiago: Editorial LOM, 2005.

Aldunate Lyon, José, S.J. "EMO: Presencia y acción en 25 años." In *Crónicas de una iglesia liberadora*, edited by José Aldunate Lyon, S.J., et al., 93–100. Santiago: LOM, 2000.

———. "La experiencia Calama." In *Crónicas de una iglesia liberadora*, edited by José Aldunate Lyon, S.J., et al., 89–92. Santiago: LOM, 2000.

———. *Un peregrino cuenta su historia*. Santiago: Ediciones Ignacianas, 2002.

Alonso, Antonio. *El movimiento ferrocarrilero en México, 1958–1959: De la conciliación a la lucha de clases*. Mexico City: Ediciones Era, 1972.

Álvarez Garín, Raúl. *La estela de Tlatelolco: Una reconstrucción histórica del Movimiento estudiantil del 68*. Mexico City: Itaca Editorial, 1998.

Anderson, Benedict. *Imagined Communities: Reflections on the Origins and Spread of Nationalism*. London: Verso, 1983.

Appadurai, Arjun. "Sovereignty without Territoriality: Notes for a Post-national Geography." In *The Geography of Identity*, edited by Patricia Yaeger, 337–50. Ann Arbor: University of Michigan Press, 1997.

Appiah, Kwame Anthony. *Cosmopolitanism: Ethics in a World of Strangers*. New York: Norton, 2006.

———. *The Ethics of Identity*. Princeton, NJ: Princeton University Press, 2005.

———. "Loyalty to Humanity." Reply to Martha Nussbaum's essay "Patriotism and Cosmopolitanism." *Boston Review* 19, no. 5 (October/November 1994): 10.

Arditti, Rita. *Searching for Life: The Grandmothers of the Plaza de Mayo and the Disappeared Children of Argentina*. Berkeley: University of California Press, 1999.

Ariztía, Fernando. "El Comité de Cooperación para la Paz en Chile." In *Seminario Iglesia y Derechos Humanos en Chile*, by Arzobispado de Santiago Fundación de Documentación y Archivo de la Vicaría de la Solidaridad, 11–18. Santiago: LOM, 2002.

Arrate, Jorge, and Eduardo Rojas. *Memoria de la Izquierda Chilena*. Vol. 1, *1850–1970*, and vol. 2, *1970–2000*. Santiago: Javier Vergara Editor, 2003.

Ayala, César J., and Rafael Bernabe. *Puerto Rico in the American Century: A History since 1898*. Chapel Hill: University of North Carolina Press, 2007.

Ayala Casás, César, and José Bolívar Fresneda. "The Cold War and the Second Expropriations of the Navy in Vieques." *Centro Journal* 18, no. 1 (Spring 2006): 10–35.

Baberowski, Jörg, Hartmut Kaelble, and Jürgen Schriever, eds. *Selbstbilder und Fremdbilder: Repräsentation sozialer Ordnungen im Wandel*. Frankfurt: Campus Verlag, 2008.

Bales, Peter. "Nelson Rockefeller and His Quest for Inter-American Unity." PhD diss., State University of New York at Stony Brook, 1992.

Bender, Thomas, ed. *Rethinking American History in a Global Age*. Berkeley: University of California Press, 2002.

Berman, Paul. *A Tale of Two Utopias: The Political Journey of the Generation of 1968*. New York: Norton, 1996.

Bethell, Leslie, and Ian Roxborough. *Latin America between the Second World War and the Cold War, 1944–1948*. Cambridge: Cambridge University Press, 1992.

Billard, Annick. "From El Salvador to Honduras: A Long Journey to Find a Safe Place." *Refugees Magazine* (May 1983): 7–8.

Birmingham, David. *Frontline Nationalism in Angola and Mozambique*. New York: Oxford University Press, 1992.

Birn, Anne-Emanuelle. "Revolution, the Scatological Way: The Rockefeller Foundation's Hookworm Campaign in 1920s Mexico." In *Disease in the History of Modern Latin America: From Malaria to AIDS*, edited by Diego Armus, 158–82. Durham, NC: Duke University Press, 2003.

Blacker-Hanson, O'Neill. "La Lucha Sigue! (The Struggle Continues!): Teacher Activism in Guerrero and the Continuum of Democratic Struggle in Mexico." PhD diss., University of Washington, 2005.

Bolton García, Roberto. "El asilo contra la represión." In *Crónicas de una iglesia liberadora*, edited by José Aldunate Lyon, S.J., et al., 151–54. Santiago: LOM, 2000.

Borstelmann, Thomas. *The Cold War and the Color Line: American Race Relations in the Global Arena*. Cambridge, MA: Harvard University Press, 2001.

Bourdieu, Pierre. *The Logic of Practice*. Translated by Richard Nice. Stanford: Stanford University Press, 1990.

Boyer, Christopher. *Becoming Campesinos: Politics, Identity, and Agrarian Struggle in Postrevolutionary Michoacán, 1920–1935*. Stanford: Stanford University Press, 2003.

Boyle, Catherine. *Chilean Theater, 1973–1985: Marginality, Power, and Selfhood*. Rutherford, NJ: Fairleigh Dickinson University Press, 1992.

Braden, Thomas. "Why I'm Glad the CIA Is 'Immoral.'" *Saturday Evening Post* 240 (May 20, 1967).

Brands, Hal. *Latin America's Cold War*. Cambridge, MA: Harvard University Press, 2010.

Bravo, Gabriela, and Cristián González Farfán. *Ecos del tiempo subterraneo: Las peñas en Santiago durante el régimen militar, 1973–1983*. Santiago: LOM Ediciones, 2009.

Brennan, James P. *The Labor Wars in Córdoba, 1955–1976: Ideology, Work, and Labor Politics in an Argentine Industrial Society.* Cambridge, MA: Harvard University Press, 1994.

Briggs, Laura. *Reproducing Empire: Race, Sex, Science, and U.S. Imperialism in Puerto Rico.* Berkeley: University of California Press, 2002.

Bruey, Alison J. "Neoliberalism and Repression in *Poblaciones* of Santiago de Chile." *Stockholm Review of Latin American Studies,* no. 5 (September 2009): 17–27.

Brysk, Alison. *The Politics of Human Rights in Argentina: Protest, Change, and Democratization.* Stanford: Stanford University Press, 1994.

Cagan, Beth, and Steve Cagan. *This Promised Land, El Salvador.* New Brunswick, NJ: Rutgers University Press, 1991.

Camacho Padilla, Fernando. *Suecia por Chile: Una historia visual del exilio y la solidaridad, 1970–1990.* Santiago: Editorial LOM, 2009.

———. *Una vida para Chile: La solidaridad y la comunidad chilena en Suecia 1970–2010.* Santiago: Editorial LOM, 2011.

Canales, Blanca. *La constitución es la revolución.* San Juan: Comité de Estudios Congreso Nacional Hostosiano, 1997.

Carey, Elaine. *Plaza of Sacrifices: Gender, Power, and Terror in 1968 Mexico.* Albuquerque: University of New Mexico Press, 2005.

Carr, Barry. *La izquierda mexicana a través del siglo XX.* Mexico City: Ediciones Era, 1996.

———. *Marxism and Communism in Twentieth-Century Mexico.* Lincoln: University of Nebraska Press, 1992.

"Carta abierta a Pablo Neruda." *Casa de las Américas* 38 (1966): 131–35.

Casanova, Pascale. *The World Republic of Letters.* Cambridge, MA: Harvard University Press, 2007.

Castillo, Fernando. "Comunidades Cristianas Populares: La Iglesia que nace desde los pobres." In *La Iglesia de los pobres en América Latina,* by Fernando Castillo et al., 81–105. Santiago: PEC/ECO-SEPADE, 1982.

Castro, Fidel. *Discursos.* Vol. 3. Havana: Editorial de Ciencias Sociales, 1979.

Central American Refugee Center. *The Repopulation of Rural El Salvador.* Washington, DC: Central American Refugee Center, 1989.

Centro de Documentación de Honduras. *Los refugiados en Honduras.* Tegucigalpa: Centro de Documentación de Honduras, 1982.

Chabal, Patrick, and Nuno Vidal, eds. *Angola: The Weight of History.* London: Hurst, 2007.

Chomsky, Noam, and Edward Herman. *Manufacturing Consent: The Political Economy of the Mass Media.* New York: Pantheon, 1988.

Chuchryk, Patricia. "From Dictatorship to Democracy: The Women's Movement in Chile." In *The Women's Movement in Latin America: Participation and Democracy,* edited by Jane Jacquette, 65–107. Boulder, CO: Westview Press, 1994.

Cobb, Russell. "Our Men in Paris? *Mundo Nuevo,* the Cuban Revolution, and the Politics of Cultural Freedom." PhD diss., University of Texas at Austin, 2007.

Cobbs, Elizabeth A. *The Rich Neighbor Policy: Rockefeller and Kaiser in Brazil.* New Haven, CT: Yale University Press, 1992.

Cohen, Deborah, and Lessie Jo Frazier. "Defining the Space of Mexico '68: Heroic Masculinity in the Prison and 'Women' in the Streets." *Hispanic American Historical Review* 83, no. 4 (November 2003): 616–60.

Colby, Gerald, with Charlotte Dennett. *Thy Will Be Done: The Conquest of the Amazon: Nelson Rockefeller and Evangelism in the Age of Oil.* New York: HarperCollins, 1995.

Collazo, Oscar. *Memorias de un patriota encarcelado.* San Juan: Fundación Francisco Manrique Cabrera, 2000.

Collins, Robert M. "Growth Liberalism in the Sixties: Great Societies at Home and Grand Designs Abroad." In *The Sixties: From Memory to History*, edited by David Farber, 11–44. Chapel Hill: University of North Carolina Press, 1994.

Constable, Pamela, and Arturo Valenzuela. *A Nation of Enemies: Chile under Pinochet.* New York: Norton, 1991.

Contardo, Oscar, and Macarena García. *La era ochentera: Tevé, pop y under en el Chile de los ochenta.* Santiago: Ediciones B Chile, 2005.

Coronil, Fernando. "Foreword." In *Close Encounters of Empire: Writing the Cultural History of U.S.–Latin American Relations*, edited by Gilbert M. Joseph, Catherine LeGrand, and Ricardo Salvatore, ix–xiii. Durham, NC: Duke University Press, 1998.

Corvalán, Luis. *De lo vivido y lo peleado: Memorias.* Santiago: Editorial LOM, 1997.

Cueto, Marcos. *Missionaries of Science: The Rockefeller Foundation and Latin America.* Bloomington: Indiana University Press, 1994.

Daniels, Robert V. *Year of the Heroic Guerrilla: World Revolution and Counterrevolution in 1968.* Cambridge, MA: Harvard University Press, 1989.

de la Fuente, Alejandro. *A Nation for All: Race, Inequality and Politics in Twentieth-Century Cuba.* Chapel Hill: University of North Carolina Press, 2001.

de Shazo, Peter. *Urban Workers and Labor Unions in Chile, 1902–1927.* Madison: University of Wisconsin Press, 1983.

del Aguila, Juan M. "The Domestic Attitude toward Internationalism: Evidence from Emigré Interviews." In *Cuban Internationalism in Sub-Saharan Africa*, edited by Sergio Díaz-Briquets, 124–43. Pittsburgh: Duquesne University Press, 1989.

del Pozo, José, ed. *Exiliados, emigrados y retornados: Chilenos en América y Europa, 1973–2004.* Santiago: RIL Ed, 2006.

Desnoes, Edmundo. *Memorias del subdesarrollo.* Seville: Mono Azul Editora, 2006.

Dilling, Yvonne. *In Search of Refuge.* Scottsdale, PA: Herald Press, 1984.

Dockendorff, Cecilia, José Antonio Román Brugnoli, and María Alejandra Energici Sprovera. "La neoliberalización de la solidaridad en el Chile democrático: Una mirada comparativa sobre discursos solidarios en 1991 y 2006." *Latin American Research Review* 45, no. 1 (2010): 189–202.

Donoso, José. *The Boom in Spanish-American Literature: A Personal History.* New York: Center for Inter-American Relations, 1977.

Dorfman, Ariel, and Armand Mattelart. *How to Read Donald Duck: Imperialist Ideology in the Disney Comic.* New York: International General, 1991.

Dorsch, Hauke. "Übergangsritus in Übersee? Zum Aufenthalt mosambikanischer Schüler and Studenten in Kuba." *Afrika Spectrum* 43 (February 2008): 225–44.

Duffy Burnett, Christina, and Burke Marshall, eds. *Foreign in a Domestic Sense*. Durham, NC: Duke University Press, 2001.

Dussel, Enrique. "From Fraternity to Solidarity: Toward a *Politics of Liberation*." *Journal of Social Philosophy* 38, no. 1 (Spring 2007): 73–92.

Edwards, Beatrice, and Gretta Tovar Siebentritt. *Places of Origin: The Repopulation of Rural El Salvador*. Boulder, CO: Lynne Rienner, 1991.

Elena, Eduardo. "What the People Want: State Planning and Political Participation in Peronist Argentina, 1946–1955." *Journal of Latin American Studies* 37, no. 1 (2001): 81–108.

Elsey, Brenda. *Citizens and Sportsmen: Fútbol and Politics in Twentieth-Century Chile*. Austin: University of Texas Press, 2011.

Escobar, Arturo. *Territories of Difference: Place, Movement, Life, Redes*. Durham, NC: Duke University Press, 2008.

Farber, David, ed. *The Sixties: From Memory to History*. Chapel Hill: University of North Carolina Press, 1994.

Fernández, David. *La "Iglesia" que resistió a Pinochet*. Madrid: IEPALA, 1996.

Ferrao, Luis Angel. *Pedro Albizu Campos y el nacionalismo puertorriqueño*. San Juan: Editorial Cultural, 1990.

Ferrer, Ada. *Insurgent Cuba: Race, Nation and Revolution, 1868–1898*. Chapel Hill: University of North Carolina Press, 1999.

Ferriera de Cassone, Florencia. *Claridad y el internacionalismo Americano*. Buenos Aires: Editorial Claridad, 1998.

Fink, Carole, Phillipp Gassert, and Detlef Juriket, eds. *1968: The World Transformed*. New York: Cambridge University Press, 1998.

Flynn, Jeffrey. "Human Rights, Transnational Solidarity, and Duties to the Global Poor." *Constellations* 16, no. 1 (2009): 59–77.

Foweraker, Joe. *Popular Mobilization in Mexico: The Teachers' Movement, 1977–87*. New York: Cambridge University Press, 1993.

Franco, Jean. *Decline and Fall of the Lettered City: Latin America in the Cold War*. Cambridge, MA: Harvard University Press, 2002.

Frazier, Lessie Jo. *Salt in the Sand: Memory, Violence, and the Nation-State in Chile: 1890 to the Present*. Durham, NC: Duke University Press, 2007.

Frenz, Helmut. *Mi vida chilena: Solidaridad con los oprimidos*. Translated by Sonia Plaut. Santiago: Editorial LOM, 2006.

Fuentes, Carlos. "La situación del escritor en América Latina." *Mundo Nuevo* 1 (July 1966): 4–21.

Garcés Durán, Mario. *Crisis social y motines populares en el 1900*. Santiago: ECO, 1991.

García Muñiz, Humberto. "Puerto Rico and the United States: The United Nations Role 1953–1975." *Revista Jurídica de la Universidad de Puerto Rico* 53, no. 1 (1984): 1–265.

Gaudichaud, Franck. *Poder popular y cordones industriales: Testimonios sobre el movimiento popular urbano, 1970–1973*. Santiago: Editorial LOM, 2004.

Gauding, Anna-Karin. *Lazos solidarios: La cooperación sueca en Chile 1970–2010*. Santiago: Editorial LOM, 2011.

George, Edward. *The Cuban Intervention in Angola, 1965–1991: From Che Guevara to Cuito Cuanavale*. London: Frank Cass, 2005.

Gill, Mario. *Los ferrocarrileros*. Mexico City: Editorial Extemporáneos, 1971.

Gilroy, Paul. *Postcolonial Melancholia*. London: Routledge, 2004.

Gitlin, Todd. *The Whole World Is Watching: Mass Media and the Making and Unmaking of the New Left*. Berkeley: University of California Press, 2003.

Gleijeses, Piero. *Conflicting Missions: Havana, Washington, and Africa, 1959–1976*. Chapel Hill: University of North Carolina Press, 2002.

———. *Shattered Hope: The Guatemalan Revolution and the United States, 1952–1954*. Princeton, NJ: Princeton University Press, 1991.

Gleijeses, Piero, Jorge Risquet, and Fernando Remírez, eds. *Cuba y África: Historia común de lucha y sangre*. Havana: Editorial de Ciencias Sociales, 2007.

Goldblatt, David. *The Ball Is Round: A Global History of Soccer*. New York: Riverhead Books, 2006.

González, Juan Pablo, and Claudio Rolle. *Historia social de la música popular en Chile, 1890–1950*. Santiago: Ediciones Universidad Católica de Chile, 2005.

Gosse, Van. "Unpacking the Vietnam Syndrome: The Coup in Chile and the Rise of Popular Anti- Interventionism." In *The World the Sixties Made: Politics and Culture in Recent America*, edited by Van Gosse and Richard Moser, 100–13. Philadelphia: Temple University Press, 2003.

———. *Where the Boys Are: Cuba, Cold War America and the Making of the New Left*. New York: Verso, 1993.

Gould, Carol C. "Transnational Solidarities." *Journal of Social Philosophy* 38, no. 1 (Spring 2007): 148–64.

Gould, Jeffrey L. "Solidarity under Siege: The Latin American Left, 1968." *American Historical Review* 114, no. 2 (April 2009): 348–75.

Grandin, Greg. *The Blood of Guatemala: A History of Race and Nation*. Durham, NC: Duke University Press, 2000.

———. "Human Rights and Empire's Embrace." In *Human Rights and Revolutions*, 2nd ed., edited by Jeffrey N. Wasserstrom, Lynn Hunt, Marilyn B. Young, and Gregory Grandin, 191–222. New York: Rowman and Littlefield, 2007.

———. "Off the Beach: The United States, Latin America, and the Cold War." In *A Companion to Post 1945 America*, edited by Jean-Christophe Agnew and Roy Rosenzweig, 426–45. Malden, MA: Blackwell, 2002.

Green, James N. "Desire and Militancy: Lesbians, Gays, and the Brazilian Workers' Party." In *Different Rainbow: Same-Sex Sexuality and Popular Struggles in the Third World*, edited by Peter Drucker, 57–70. London: Gay Men's Press, 2000.

———. "The Emergence of the Brazilian Gay Liberation Movement: 1977–1981." *Latin American Perspectives* 21, no. 80 (Winter 1994): 38–55.

———. "(Homo)sexuality, Human Rights, and Revolution in Latin America." In *Human Rights and Revolutions*, 2nd ed., edited by Jeffrey N. Wasserstrom, Lynn Hunt,

Marilyn B. Young, and Gregory Grandin, 139–54. New York: Rowman and Little-field, 2007.

———. "More Love and More Desire: The Building of the Brazilian Movement." In *The Global Emergence of Gay and Lesbian Politics: National Imprints of a Worldwide Movement*, edited by Barry Adam, Jan Willem Duyvendak, and André Krouwel, 91–109. Philadelphia: Temple University Press, 1999.

———. *We Cannot Remain Silent: Opposition to the Brazilian Military Dictatorship in the United States*. Durham, NC: Duke University Press, 2010.

Grez Toso, Sergio. *Los anarquistas y el movimiento obrero: La alborada de "la Idea" en Chile, 1893–1915*. Santiago: Editorial LOM, 2007.

Guevara, Ernesto Che. *Che Guevara Reader: Writings on Politics and Revolution*. Edited by David Deutschmann. North Melbourne, Australia: Ocean Press, 2003.

Guevara Niebla, Gilberto. *La democracia en la calle: Crónica del movimiento estudiantil mexicano*. Mexico City: Siglo Ventiuno Editores, 1988.

Guilbaut, Serge. *How New York Stole the Idea of Modern Art: Abstract Expressionism, Freedom, and the Cold War*. Chicago: University of Chicago Press, 1985.

Gutiérrez, Gustavo. "The God of Life." In *Gustavo Gutiérrez: Essential Writings*, edited by James B. Nickoloff, 60–64. New York: Orbis, 2000.

———. *Gustavo Gutiérrez: Essential Writings*. Edited by James B. Nickoloff. New York: Orbis, 2000.

———. "Notes for a Theology of Liberation (1970)." In *Liberation Theology at the Crossroads: Democracy or Revolution?*, edited by Paul E. Sigmund, 212–13. New York: Oxford University Press, 1992.

———. "Theology of Liberation." In *Gustavo Gutiérrez: Essential Writings*, edited by James B. Nickoloff, 28–30. New York: Orbis, 2000.

Guzmán Bouvard, Marguerite. *Revolutionizing Motherhood: The Mothers of the Plaza de Mayo*. Wilmington, DE: Scholarly Resources Books, 2002.

Habermas, Jürgen. "The Postnational Constellation and the Future of Democracy." In *The Postnational Constellation: Political Essays*, edited by Jürgen Habermas, 58–112. Cambridge, MA: MIT Press, 2001.

Harman, Chris. *The Fire Last Time: 1968 and After*. London: Bookmarks, 1988.

Hartigan, Kevin. "Matching Humanitarian Norms with Cold, Hard Interests: The Making of Refugee Policies in Mexico and Honduras." *International Organization* 46, no. 3 (1992): 709–30.

Hatzky, Christine. *Julio Antonio Mella: Una biografía*. Santiago de Cuba: Editorial Oriente, 2008.

———. *Kubaner in Angola. Süd-Süd-Kooperation und Bildungstransfer 1976–1991* (Munich: Oldenburg Verlag, 2012).

Helg, Aline. *Our Rightful Share: The Afro-Cuban Struggle for Equality, 1986–1912*. Chapel Hill: University of North Carolina Press, 1995.

Hite, Katherine. *When the Romance Ended: Leaders of the Chilean Left, 1968–1998*. New York: Columbia University Press, 2008.

Hobsbawm, Eric. "1968—A Retrospective." *Marxism Today* 22, no. 5 (May 1978): 130–36.

The Holy Bible: New International Version. Colorado Springs: International Bible Society, 1984.

Horn, Gerd-Rainer, and Padraic Kenney, eds. *Transnational Moments of Change: Europe 1945, 1968, 1989*. Lanham, MD: Rowman and Littlefield, 2004.

Hoyl, Ana María. *Por la vida*. Santiago: CESOC, 2003.

Hutchinson, Elizabeth Q. *Labors Appropriate to Their Sex: Gender, Labor and Politics in Urban Chile, 1900–1930*. Durham, NC: Duke University Press, 2001.

Hutchison, Elizabeth Q., and Patricio Orellana. *El movimiento de derechos humanos en Chile, 1973–1990*. Santiago: Centro de Estudios Políticos Latinoamericanos Simón Bolívar, 1991.

"Inter-American Notes." *The Americas* 10, no. 2 (October 1953): 229–32.

Iriye, Akira. *Global Community: The Role of International Organizations in the Making of the Contemporary World*. Berkeley: University of California Press, 2002.

Iturriaga, Jorge. "Proletas, limpios, cobardes y burgueses: El fútbol en 1973." In *1973: La vida cotidiana de un año crucial*, edited by Claudio Rolle, 197–352. Santiago: Planeta, 2003.

Jacobson, David. *Rights across Borders: Immigration and the Decline of Citizenship*. Baltimore, MD: Johns Hopkins University Press, 1996.

Jiménez, Oscar, S.J. "Alberto Hurtado, precursor de La Iglesia Liberadora." In *Crónicas de una iglesia liberadora*, edited by José Aldunate Lyon, S.J., et al., 13–20. Santiago: LOM, 2000.

Jiménez Rodríguez, Limbania. *Mujeres sin fronteras*. Havana: Editora Política, 2008.

Johnson, Peter, and Francisco Fonseca. *North American Congress on Latin America (NACLA) Archive of Latin Americana*. Wilmington, DE: Scholarly Resources, 1999.

Joseph, Gilbert M., Catherine LeGrand, and Ricardo Donato Salvatore, eds. *Close Encounters of Empire: Writing the Cultural History of U.S.–Latin American Relations*. Durham, NC: Duke University Press, 1998.

Joseph, Gilbert M., and Daniela Spenser, eds. *In from the Cold: Latin America's New Encounter with the Cold War*. Durham, NC: Duke University Press 2008.

Kaplan, Temma. *Taking Back the Street: Women, Youth, and Direct Democracy*. Berkeley: University of California Press, 2004.

Kaufman, J. B. *South of the Border with Disney: Walt Disney and the Good Neighbor Program, 1941–1948*. New York: Disney Editions, 2009.

Keck, Margaret, and Kathryn Skikink. *Activists without Borders: Advocacy Networks in International Politics*. Ithaca, NY: Cornell University Press, 1998.

Kelly, Patrick William. "'When the People Awake': The Transnational Solidarity Movement, the Pinochet Junta, and the Human Rights Movement of the 1970s." Lecture, University of Chicago Latin American History Seminar, March 19, 2009.

King, John. *Sur: A Study of the Argentine Literary Journal and Its Role in the Development of a Culture, 1931–1970*. Cambridge: Cambridge University Press, 1986.

Klimke, Martin, and Joaquim Scharloth. *1968 in Europe: A History of Protest and Activism, 1956–1977*. New York: Palgrave Macmillan, 2008.

Kreutzberger, Mario. *Don Francisco entre la espada y la TV*. Mexico City: Grijalbo, 2001.

Kurlansky, Mark. *1968: The Year That Rocked the World*. New York: Random House, 2005.

Landi, Oscar, et al. *Los derechos humanos como política: Encuentro realizado el 20 y 21 de Junio de 1984 en Santiago de Chile*. Buenos Aires: Ediciones La Aurora, 1985.

Lawyers Committee for International Human Rights. *Honduras: A Crisis on the Border, a Report on Salvadoran Refugees in Honduras*. New York: Lawyers Committee for International Human Rights, 1985.

LeoGrande, William M. *Cuba's Policy in Africa, 1959–1980*. Policy Papers in International Affairs 13. Berkeley: Institute of International Studies, University of California, 1980.

Lepeley, Oscar. "The *Cueca* of the Last Judgment: Politics of the Chilean Resistance in *Tres Marías y Una Rosa*." In *Imagination beyond a Nation*, edited by Eva Bueno and Terry Caesar, 142–66. Pittsburgh: University of Pittsburgh Press, 1998.

Lesgart, Cecilia. *Usos de la transición a la democracia; Ensayo, ciencia y política en la década del '80*. Rosario, Arg.: Homo Sapiens Ediciones, 2003.

Levinson, Jerome I., and Juan de Onis. *The Alliance That Lost Its Way: A Critical Report on the Alliance for Progress*. Chicago: Quadrangle Books, 1970.

Lewis, Gordon. *Puerto Rico: Freedom and Power in the Caribbean*. New York: Monthly Review, 1963.

Loescher, Gil, and Laila Monahan, eds. *Refugees and International Relations*. Oxford: Clarendon Press, 1990.

Lowden, Pamela. *Moral Opposition to Authoritarian Rule in Chile, 1973–1990*. Oxford: St. Anthony's Press, 1996.

Loyo Brambila, Aurora. *El movimiento magisterial de 1958 in México*. Mexico City: Ediciones Era, 1979.

Lüsebrink, Hans-Jürgen. *Interkulturelle Kommunikation: Interaktion, Fremdwahrnehmung, Kulturtransfer*. Stuttgart: J. B. Metzler, 2008.

MacAdam, Alfred J. "The Boom: A Retrospective: Interview with Emir Rodríguez Monegal." *Review* 33 (January 1984): 30–34.

MacRae, Edward. *A construção da igualdade: Identidade sexual e política no Brasil da "Abertura."* Campinas: Unicamp, 1990.

———. "Homosexual Identities in Transitional Brazilian Politics." In *The Making of Social Movements in Latin America: Identity, Strategy and Democracy*, edited by Arturo Escobar and Sonia E. Alvarez, 185–203. Boulder, CO: Westview Press, 1992.

Malkki, Liisa. "National Geographic: The Rooting of Peoples and the Territorialization of National Identity among Scholars and Refugees." *Cultural Anthropology* 7, no. 1 (1992): 24–44.

———. "Refugees and Exile: From 'Refugee Studies' to the National Order of Things." *Annual Review of Anthropology* 24 (1995): 495–523.

Mallon, Florencia E. *Peasant and Nation: The Making of Postcolonial Mexico and Peru*. Berkeley: University of California Press, 1995.

Manning, Patrick, and Yinghong Cheng. "Revolution on Education: China and Cuba in Global Context, 1957–1976." *Journal of World History* 14, no. 3 (2003): 359–91.

Marzán, Julio. "Pablo Neruda's Dilemma." In *Pablo Neruda and the U.S. Culture Industry*, edited by Teresa Longo, 156–62. New York: Routlege, 2002.

McAdam, Doug, John D. McCarthy, and Mayer N. Zald, eds. *Comparative Perspectives on Social Movements: Political Opportunities, Mobilizing Structures, and Cultural Framings*. New York: Cambridge University Press, 1996.

McCaffrey, Katherine T. *Military Power and Popular Protest: The U.S. Navy in Vieques, Puerto Rico*. New Brunswick, NJ: Rutgers University Press, 2002.

McPherson, Alan L. *Yankee No!: Anti-Americanism in U.S.–Latin American Relations*. Cambridge, MA: Harvard University Press, 2003.

Medina Ramírez, Ramón. *El movimiento libertador en la historia de Puerto Rico*. Vol. 1. San Juan: Imprenta Nacional, 1964.

Mendoza Rojas, Javier. *Los conflictos de la UNAM en el siglo XX*. Mexico City: CESU—UNAM/Plaza y Valdés, 2001.

Menton, Seymour. *Prose Fiction of the Cuban Revolution*. Austin: University of Texas Press, 1975.

Messiant, Christine. *L'Angola postcolonial*. Vol. 1, *Guerre et paix sans democratization*. Paris: Éditions Karthala, 2008.

———. *L'Angola postcolonial*. Vol. 2, *Sociologie politique d' une oléocratie*. Paris: Éditions Karthala, 2008.

Meyer, Donald C. "Toscanini and the Good Neighbor Policy: The NBC Orchestra's 1940 South American Tour." *American Music* 18, no. 3 (Autumn 2000): 233–56.

Morris, Nancy. "Canto Porque Es Necesario Cantar: The New Song Movement in Chile, 1973–1983." *Latin American Research Review* 21, no. 2 (1986): 117–36.

Moulian, Thomás. *La forja de ilusiones: El sistema de partidos, 1932–1973*. Santiago: ARCIS and FLACSO, 1993.

Mudrovcic, María Eugenia. *Mundo Nuevo: Cultura y Guerra Fría en la década del 60*. Rosario, Arg.: Beatriz Viterbo, 1997.

Naranjo, Pedro, Mauricio Ahumada, Mario Garcés, and Julio Pinto. *Miguel Enríquez y el proyecto revolucionario en Chile: Discursos y documentos del Movimiento de Izquierda Revolucionaria, MIR*. Santiago: Editorial LOM, 2004.

Nazario, Olga, and Juan Benemelis. "Cuba's Relations with Africa: An Overview." In *Cuban Internationalism in Sub-Saharan Africa*, edited by Sergio Díaz-Briquets, 13–28. Pittsburgh: Duquesne University Press, 1989.

Neruda, Pablo. *Canto general*. Santiago: Chilean Communist Party, 1950.

Nickoloff, James B. "Introduction." In *Gustavo Gutiérrez: Essential Writings*, edited by James B. Nickoloff, 1–22. New York: Orbis, 2000.

Nieves Falcón, Luis. *Un siglo de represión política*. San Juan: Optimática, 2009.

Ocasio, Rafael. "Gays and the Cuban Revolution: The Case of Reinaldo Arenas." *Latin American Perspectives* 29, no. 2 (2002): 78–98.

Olcott, Jocelyn. "Cold War Conflicts and Cheap Cabaret: Sexual Politics at the 1975 United Nations International Women's Year Conference." *Gender and History* 22 (2010): 733–54.

Olesen, Thomas. *International Zapatismo*. London: Zed Books, 2005.

Otero, Lisandro. "Notas sobre la funcionalidad de la cultura." *Casa de las Américas* 68 (1971): 94–110.

Oxhorn, Philip. *Organizing Civil Society: The Popular Sectors and the Struggle for Democracy in Chile.* University Park: Pennsylvania State University Press, 1995.

Pacini Hernandez, Deborah, Héctor Fernándes l'Hoeste, and Eric Zolov, eds. *Rockin' Las Américas: The Global Politics of Rock in Latin/o America.* Pittsburgh: University of Pittsburgh Press, 2004.

Padilla, Heberto. *Fuera del juego.* Miami: Ediciones Universal, 1998.

Padilla, Tanalís. *Rural Resistance in the Land of Zapata: The Jaramillista Movement and the Myth of the Pax Priísta, 1940–1962.* Durham, NC: Duke University Press, 2008

Padilla Pérez, Carlos. *Puerto Rico: Al rescate de su soberanía.* Buenos Aires: Publicaciones del Partida Nacionalista de Puerto Rico, 1958.

Pagden, Anthony. "Human Rights, Natural Rights, and Europe's Imperial Legacy." *Political Theory* 31 (2003): 171–99.

Palacios, Alfredo L. *Nuestra América y el imperialismo.* Buenos Aires: Editorial Palestra, 1961.

Paralitici, Ché. *Sentencia impuesta.* San Juan: Ediciones Puerto, 2004.

Parker, David S. *The Idea of the Middle Class: White-Collar Workers and Peruvian Society, 1900–1950.* University Park: Pennsylvania State University Press, 1998.

Pearce, Jenny. *Promised Land: Peasant Rebellion in Chalatenango, El Salvador.* London: Latin America Bureau, 1986.

Penna Sattamini, Lina. *A Mother's Cry: A Memoir of Politics, Prison, and Torture under the Brazilian Military Dictatorship.* Translated by Rex P. Nielson and James N. Green, introduction by James N. Green. Durham, NC: Duke University Press, 2010.

Pérez, Louis, Jr. *Cuba: Between Reform and Revolution.* New York: Oxford University Press, 1988.

Persico, Joseph E. *The Imperial Rockefeller: A Political Biography.* New York: Simon and Schuster, 1982.

Peterson, Spike V. "Whose Rights? A Critique of the 'Givens' in Human Rights Discourse." *Alternatives* 15, no. 3 (Summer 1990): 303–44.

Piccato, Pablo. "Public Sphere in Latin America: A Map of the Historiography." *Social History* 35, no. 2 (May 2010): 165–92.

———. *The Tyranny of Opinion: Honor in the Construction of the Public Sphere.* Durham, NC: Duke University Press, 2010.

Power, Margaret. *Right-Wing Women in Chile: Feminine Power and the Struggle against Allende, 1964–1973.* University Park: Pennsylvania State University Press, 2002.

———."The U.S. Movement in Solidarity with Chile in the 1970s." *Latin American Perspectives* 36, no. 6 (2009): 46–66.

Power, Margaret, and Julie Charlip. "Introduction: On Solidarity." *Latin American Perspectives* 36, no. 6 (2009): 3–9.

Precht Bañados, Christián. "Del Comité pro Paz a la Vicaría de la Solidaridad." In *Seminario iglesia y derechos humanos en Chile*, by Arzobispado de Santiago Fundación de Documentación y Archivo de la Vicaría de la Solidaridad. Santiago: Editorial LOM, 2002.

Puga, Mariano. "Los Vía Crucis de las Comunidades Cristianas." In *Crónicas de una iglesia liberadora*, edited by José Aldunate Lyon, S.J., et al., 131–36. Santiago: LOM, 2000.

Quataert, Jean. *Advocating Dignity: Human Rights Mobilizations in Global Politics.* Philadelphia: University of Pennsylvania Press, 2009.

Rabe, Stephen G. *Eisenhower and Latin America: The Foreign Policy of Anticommunism.* Chapel Hill: University of North Carolina Press, 1988.

———. *The Most Dangerous Area in the World: John F. Kennedy Confronts Communist Revolution in Latin America.* Chapel Hill: University of North Carolina Press, 1999.

Ramírez, Ramón. *El movimiento estudiantil de México (Julio/Diciembre de 1968).* Mexico City: Ediciones Era, 1969.

Rebolledo, Loreto, Teresa Valdés, Ximena Valdés, and Diana Veneros. "El movimiento social de mujeres: Memoria, acción colectiva y democratización en Chile en la segunda mitad del siglo XX." In *Memoria para un nuevo siglo*, edited by Mario Garcés et al., 213–29. Santiago: LOM, 2000.

Reich, Cary. *The Life of Nelson A. Rockefeller: Worlds to Conquer, 1908–1958.* New York: Doubleday, 1996.

Rey Cabrera, Marina. *La Guerra de Angola.* Havana: Editora Política, 1989.

Reyna, José Luis. "El conflicto ferrocarrilero: De la inmovilidad a la acción." Vol. 22 of *Historia de la Revolución Mexicana.* Mexico City: Colegio de México, 1978.

Ríos, Fernando. "La Flûte Indienne: The Early History of Andean Folkloric-Popular Music in France and Its Impact on Nueva Canción." *Latin American Music Review* 29 (2008): 145–81.

Rippe, Klaus Peter. "Diminishing Solidarity." *Ethical Theory and Moral Practice* 1, no. 3 (1998): 355–73.

Risquet Valdés, Jorge. "Prólogo a la Edición Cubana." In *Misiones en conflicto: La Habana, Washington y África; 1959–1976*, edited by Piero Gleijeses, i–xix. Havana: Editorial de Ciencias Sociales, 2004.

Rivas, Darlene. *Missionary Capitalist: Nelson Rockefeller in Venezuela.* Chapel Hill: University of North Carolina Press, 2002.

Rockefeller, Nelson A. *The Rockefeller Report on the Americas: The Official Report of a United States Presidential Mission for the Western Hemisphere.* Chicago: Quadrangle Books, 1969.

Rodríguez Monegal, Emir. "El P.E.N. Club contra la guerra fría." *Mundo Nuevo* 5 (November 1966): 85–90.

———. *Homenaje a Emir Rodríguez Monegal.* Montevideo: Ministerio de Educación y Cultura, 1987.

———. "Presentación." *Mundo Nuevo* 1 (July 1966): 4.

Roht-Arriaza, Naomi. *The Pinochet Effect: Transnational Justice in the Age of Human Rights.* Philadelphia: University of Pennsylvania Press, 2006.

Rojas, Rodrigo. *In the Hands of Chile's Hangmen: The Prison Experience of Rodrigo Rojas.* New York: New Outlook, 1975.

Rojo, Grínor. "Teatro chileno bajo fascismo." *Araucaría* 22 (1983): 123–36.

Roniger, Luis. "Human Rights Violations and the Reshaping of Collective Identities in Argentina, Chile and Uruguay." *Social Identities* 3, no. 2 (1997): 221–46.

Rosado, Marisa. *Las llamas de la aurora.* San Juan: Ediciones Puerto, 2006.

Rosemblatt, Karin. *Gendered Compromises: Political Cultures and the State in Chile, 1920–1950.* Chapel Hill: University of North Carolina Press, 2000.

Ross, Kristin. *May '68 and Its Afterlives.* Chicago: University of Chicago Press, 2000.

Salazar, Gabriel, and Julio Pinto. *Historia contemporánea de Chile.* Vol. 1, *Estado, legitimidad, ciudadanía.* Santiago: Editorial LOM, 1999.

———. *Historia Contemporánea de Chile.* Vol. 2, *Actores, identidad y movimiento.* Santiago: Editorial LOM, 1999.

Sassen, Saskia. *Territory, Authority, Rights.* Princeton, NJ: Princeton University Press, 2006.

Schidlowsky, David. *Pablo Neruda y su tiempo: Las furias y las penas.* Vol. 2. Santiago: RIL Editoras, 2008.

Schlesinger, Stephen, and Stephen Kinzer. *Bitter Fruit: The Story of the American Coup in Guatemala.* Cambridge, MA: Harvard University Press, 2005.

Scholz, Sally J. *Political Solidarity.* University Park: Pennsylvania State University Press, 2008.

Scott, James C. *Domination and the Arts of Resistance: Hidden Transcripts.* New Haven, CT: Yale University Press, 1990.

Seijo Bruno, Miñi. *La insurrección nacionalista en Puerto Rico, 1950.* Rio Piedras, PR: Editorial Edil, 1989.

Sewell, William. *Logics of History: Social Theory and Social Transformation.* Chicago: University of Chicago Press, 2005.

Shayne, Julie. *The Revolution Question: Feminisms in El Salvador, Chile, and Cuba.* New Brunswick, NJ: Rutgers University Press, 2004.

———. *They Used to Call Us Witches: Chilean Exiles, Culture, and Feminism.* Lanham, MD: Lexington Books, 2009.

Shayne, Julie, and Jacqueline Adams. "Art in Social Movements: Shantytown Women's Protest in Pinochet's Chile." *Sociological Forum* 17 (2002): 21–56.

Shukla, Sandhya Rajendra, and Heidi Tinsman, eds. *Imagining Our Americas: Toward a Transnational Frame.* Durham, NC: Duke University Press, 2007.

Sidaway, James. *Imagined Regional Communities: Integration and Sovereignty in the Global South.* New York: Routledge, 2002.

Skidmore, Thomas E. *The Politics of Military Rule in Brazil, 1964–85.* New York: Oxford University Press, 1988.

Smith, Brian H. *The Church and Politics in Chile: Challenges to Modern Catholicism.* Princeton, NJ: Princeton University Press, 1982.

Smith, Peter H. *Talons of the Eagle: Latin America, the United States, and the World.* 3rd ed. New York: Oxford University Press, 2007.

Spalding, Hobart. "U.S. and Latin American Labor: The Dynamics of Imperialist Control." *Latin American Perspectives* 3, no. 1 (1976): 45–69.

Spivak, Gayatri Chakravorty. *A Critique of Postcolonial Reason.* New York: Routledge, 1999.

Stanley, William. *The Protection Racket State: Elite Politics, Military Extortion, and Civil War in El Salvador*. Philadelphia: Temple University Press, 1996.

Stern, Steve. *Battling for Hearts and Minds: Memory Struggles in Pinochet's Chile, 1973–1988*. Durham, NC: Duke University Press, 2006.

Stjernø, Steiner. *Solidarity in Europe: The History of an Idea*. New York: Cambridge University Press, 2009.

Stonor Saunders, Frances. *The Cultural Cold War: The CIA and the World of Arts and Letters*. New York: New Press, 2000.

Suri, Jeremy. *The Global Revolutions of 1968*. New York: Norton, 2007.

Sznajder, Mario, and Luis Roniger. "Exile Communities and Their Differential Institutional Dynamics: A Comparative Analysis of the Chilean and Uruguayan Political Diasporas." *Revista de Ciencia Política* 1 (2007): 43–66.

Taffet, Jeffrey F. *Foreign Aid as Foreign Policy: The Alliance for Progress in Latin America*. New York: Routledge, 2007.

Tali, Mabeko, and Jean Michel. *Dissidências e poder de estado: O MPLA perante si próprio (1962–1977)*. Vol. 2, *1974–1977*. Luanda: Editorial Nzila, 2001.

Taylor, Frank. "Revolution, Race, and Some Aspects of Foreign Policy in Cuba since 1959." *Cuban Studies* 18 (1988): 19–41.

Tice, Karen. "For Appearance's Sake: Beauty, Bodies, Spectacle, and Consumption." *Journal of Women's History* 18 (2006): 147–56.

Tota, Antônio Pedro. *O imperialismo sedutor: A americanização do Brasil na época da Segunda Guerra*. São Paulo: Companhia das Letras, 2000.

Trevisan, João S. *Perverts in Paradise*. London: GMP, 1986.

Turner Martí, Lidia, et al. *Breve historia de un destacamento*. Havana: Editorial Pueblo y Educación, 1996.

Valdés, Nelson. "Revolutionary Solidarity in Angola." In *Cuba in the World*, edited by Cole Blasier and Carmelo Mesa-Lago, 87–117. Pittsburgh: University of Pittsburgh Press, 1979.

Varon, Jeremy. *Bringing the War Home: The Weather Underground, the Red Army Faction, and Revolutionary Violence in the Sixties and Seventies*. Berkeley: University of California Press, 2004.

Vidal, Hernán. *Literatura hispanoamericana e ideologia liberal: Surgimiento y crisis*. Buenos Aires: Ediciones Hispamerica, 1976.

Westad, Odd Arne. *The Global Cold War: Third World Interventions and the Making of Our Times*. Cambridge: Cambridge University Press, 2006.

Wilford, Hugh. *The Mighty Wurlitzer: How the CIA Played America*. Cambridge, MA: Harvard University Press, 2008.

Williams, Raymond. *Keywords: A Vocabulary of Culture and Society*. New York: Oxford University Press, 1985.

Winn, Peter. *Weavers of Revolution: The Yarur Workers and Chile's Road to Socialism*. New York: Oxford University Press, 1989.

———, ed. *Victims of the Chilean Miracle: Workers and Neoliberalism in the Pinochet Era, 1973–2002*. Durham, NC: Duke University Press, 2004.

Witherspoon, Kevin. *Before the Eyes of the World: Mexico and the 1968 Olympic Games.* DeKalb: Northern Illinois University Press, 2008.

Wolfe, Joel. "'Father of the Poor' or 'Mother of the Rich'?: Getúlio Vargas, Industrial Workers, and Constructions of Class, Gender and Populism in Sao Paulo, 1930–1954." *Radical History Review* 58 (1994): 80–111.

Wood, Elisabeth Jean. "Civil War and Reconstruction: The Repopulation of Tenancingo." In *Landscapes of Struggle: Politics, Society, and Community in El Salvador,* edited by Aldo Lauria-Santiago and Leigh Binford, 126–46. Pittsburgh: University of Pittsburgh Press, 2004.

———. *Insurgent Collective Action and Civil War in El Salvador.* Cambridge: Cambridge University Press, 2003.

Woodford Bray, Marjorie, and Donald Bray. "Cuba, the Soviet Union and Third World Struggle." In *Cuba: Twenty-Five Years of Revolution, 1959–1984,* edited by Sandor Halebsky and John M. Kirk, 352–71. Praeger: New York, 1985.

Zahniser, Marvin R., and W. Michael Weis. "A Diplomatic Pearl Harbor? Richard Nixon's Goodwill Mission to Latin America in 1958." *Diplomatic History* 13, no. 2 (Spring 1989): 163–90.

Zolberg, Astride R., Astri Suhrke, and Sergio Aguayo. *Escape from Violence: Conflict and the Refugee Crisis in the Developing World.* London: Oxford University Press, 1989.

Zolov, Eric. "Cuba Sí, Yanquis No!" In *In from the Cold: Latin America's New Encounter with the Cold War,* edited by Gilbert M. Joseph and Daniela Spenser, 214–52. Durham, NC: Duke University Press, 2008.

———. "Expanding Our Conceptual Horizons: The Shift from an Old to a New Left in Latin America." *Acontracorriente* 5, no. 2 (2008): 47–73.

———. *Refried Elvis: The Rise of the Mexican Counterculture.* Berkeley: University of California Press, 1999.

———. "Showcasing the 'Land of Tomorrow': Mexico and the 1968 Olympics." *The Americas* 61, no. 2 (October 2004): 159–88.

———. "Toward an Analytical Framework for Assessing the Impact of the 1968 Student Movement on U.S.-Mexican Relations." *Journal of Iberian and Latin American Studies* 9, no. 2 (December 2003): 41–68.

Zulawski, Anne. *Unequal Cures: Public Health and Political Change in Bolivia, 1900–1950.* Durham, NC: Duke University Press, 2007.

Contributors

ALISON J. BRUEY is an assistant professor of history at the University of North Florida. She received her PhD from Yale University. She is coauthor of the book *Tortura en poblaciones del Gran Santiago, 1973–1990* (2005) and author of articles on Cold War–era neoliberalism, repression, public housing, and popular protest. Her current projects include a book on human rights, neoliberalism, and grassroots activism in Chile and a study of political violence and social movements in Latin America.

ERNESTO CAPELLO is an associate professor of Latin American history at Macalester College. He received his PhD from the University of Texas at Austin and is the author of *City at the Center of the World: Space, History, and Modernity in Quito* (2011). He is presently working on two new book projects, one treating commemorative Franco-Ecuadorian cartographic exploration and a second concerning the transhemispheric identities that crystallized during Nelson Rockefeller's 1969 presidential mission to Latin America.

RUSSELL COBB is an assistant professor of Spanish and Latin American studies in the Department of Modern Languages and Cultural Studies at the University of Alberta. He holds a PhD in comparative literature from the University of Texas at Austin. His previous publications have examined the promotion of the Latin American boom in the United States and the rivalry between the literary magazines *Mundo Nuevo* and *Casa de las Américas*.

BRENDA ELSEY is an associate professor of history at Hofstra University in Long Island, New York. Her research focuses on the relationship between popular culture and politics. She is the author of several articles, including one in the *Journal of Social History*, and a full-length monograph on the history of soccer clubs in Chile, *Citizens and Sportsmen: Politics and Fútbol in Twentieth-Century Chile* (2011). Her next research project is on pan-Americanism and popular culture.

JAMES N. GREEN is a professor of Latin American history at Brown University and the author of *Beyond Carnival: Male Homosexuality in Twentieth-Century Brazil*

(1999) and *We Cannot Remain Silent: Opposition to the Brazilian Military Dictatorship in the United States* (2010). He is a past president of the Brazilian Studies Association (BRASA) and of the New England Council on Latin American Studies (NECLAS).

CHRISTINE HATZKY is a professor of Latin American and Caribbean history at Leibniz University in Hannover, Germany. She teaches and specializes in Mexico and Central America and in Cuba and the Caribbean, as well as Africa, especially the Portuguese-speaking countries. Her first book, *Julio Antonio Mella (1903–1929): Una biografía*, was about the Cuban student leader. Her second book, *Cubans in Angola: South-South Cooperation and Transfers of Knowledge* (2012), deals with the phenomenon of internationalist solidarity and civil cooperation between Cuba and Angola.

MARGARET POWER is a professor of history at the Illinois Institute of Technology. She is the author of *Right-Wing Women in Chile: Feminine Power and the Struggle against Allende* and coeditor of *Right-Wing Women around the World* and *New Perspectives on the Transnational Right*, in addition to numerous articles. She was a participant in the Chilean solidarity movement in the 1970s and continued her activism in the following decades around Puerto Rico. She is currently working on a project about the Puerto Rican Nationalist Party.

SARA KATHERINE SANDERS is a lecturer in history and in gender, women's, and sexuality studies at Grinnell College. She holds a PhD in history from the University of California at San Diego. She completed her dissertation, "The Dividing Line: Myth, Memory, and Experience in 1968 Mexico," as a visiting fellow at the University of Oxford International Gender Studies Centre. Her research focuses on student protests and politics in modern Mexico, transnational practices of citizen activists during the Cold War, and female radicals and radical movements in Latin America.

JESSICA STITES MOR is an assistant professor of history at the University of British Columbia, Okanagan. She was a research affiliate of the Instituto de Historia "Emilio Ravignani" of the Universidad de Buenos Aires from 2002 to 2007 and received her PhD from Yale University. She is coeditor with Claudia Feld of *El pasado que miramos: Memoria e imagen ante la historia reciente* (2009) and author of *Transition Cinema: Political Filmmaking and the Argentine Left since 1968* (2012).

MOLLY TODD is the author of *Beyond Displacement: Campesinos, Refugees, and Collective Action in the Salvadoran Civil War* (2010). She holds a PhD in history from the University of Wisconsin–Madison. She is the Mellon-Sawyer Postdoctoral Fellow at the University of Washington–Seattle and teaches at Augustana College (Illinois). Her new book project is a comparative study of forced displacement in Cold War Latin America.

Index

Acción Revolucionario Nacionalista Ecuatoriano (ARNE), 38
Action for Women in Chile (AFWIC), 190
Action Nucleus for Homosexual Rights (Nucleo de Ação pelos Direitos dos Homossexuais), 240, 249, 251, 252
AFDD (Association of Relatives of the Detained and Disappeared), 187, 189
Africa: anticolonial struggles in, 12, 23; apartheid in, 151, 160, 195; Cold War and, 12, 144; continent of, 163, 165; Cuba and, 147, 154, 160–66, 168; guerrillas in, 149; postcolonial governments in, 145–46; South Africa, 150, 151, 158, 160; Tricont countries and, 147
African American, 64, 242
AFWIC (Action for Women in Chile), 190
Agrupación Fraternal Obrera, 123
Aguirre, Margarita, 110
aid: Cuban civil, 147, 150, 153, 167–68; humanitarian, 210, 214, 218–19; international, 14, 212, 224, 226, 231; legal, 187; requests for, 49, 63, 65; U.S. financial, 52–54, 211; U.S. military, 50, 62, 211
AIDS, 240, 266
Alarcón, Raúl "Florcito Matuda," 197
Albizu Campos, Pedro, 42n7; assassination threat against, 30; death of, 39; incarceration of, 26, 31, 34, 40; Latin American solidarity and, 25, 33, 34; Nationalist Party and, 22, 25; pardon of,

39; poor health of, 34, 35, 37, 38; United Nations and, 27
Allende, Laura, 246
Allende, Salvador: Hortensia Bussi and, 192; Laura Allende and, 246; overthrow of, 149, 177, 200, 243; Pablo Neruda and, 110; presidential campaign of, 193; right-wing women and, 187; Socialist government of, 8, 9, 37, 126, 241, 247; solidarity organizations' support for, 178, 182, 246
Alliance for Progress: in the Boom, 103; changes to, 105; criticism of, 49, 55, 64; John F. Kennedy and, 54; Pablo Neruda and, 112; stagnation of, 57; structure of, 54
Amazon, 58, 248, 266; Amazonian deposits, 58
American Civil Liberties Union, 57
American Committee for the Independence of Puerto Rico, 35
American Friends Service Committee, 227
Americas Watch, 218
Amnesty International, 178, 188, 191, 218, 250
Anaconda Copper, 200
anarchism, 111, 123, 124
Anderson, Stewart, 49
ANFA (National Association of Amateur Football), 182, 183
Ángel Asturias, Miguel, 112

Angola: Agostinho Neto and, 163; apartheid in, 151, 160; Cuban civilians in, 145, 155–57, 159; Cuban involvement in, 13, 144–45, 149–51, 161–66, 168n17, 171–72n35; decolonization of, 168n1; education reform in, 152, 154, 158, 163, 167, 169n20, 169n21, 172n36, 172n39; FNLA in, 150; MED in, 152–53, 156–58; MPLA in, 144, 157; Portuguese in, 151, 158; proxy war in, 144; teachers in, 153–55, 157–59, 161, 171n31; UNDP in, 159; UNITA in, 150; war in, 160, 164, 167

anti-Americanism, 53–54, 57, 58, 62, 67, 110

anticolonialism: Che Guevara and, 149; communism and, 147; Cuban government and, 145–47, 149; language of, 5; Latin American solidarity and, 12, 22, 23; Luis Muñoz Marín and, 28; multiple meanings of, 12; Puerto Rico and, 12, 27, 39, 41; Tricontinental conference and, 147

anti-imperialism: Boom writers and, 102; Cuban Revolution and, 148, 244; feminist activists and, 190; gay and lesbian movement and, 244; global movement and, 28, 92; in Latin America, 15, 24, 26, 33, 36; Puerto Rican Nationalist Party and, 22–23, 27; solidarity activists, 178, 186; students and, 26, 77; U.S. and, 28, 32, 40

antiracism, 160, 244, 247

antiwar movement, 241, 242, 243, 265

aportes a la lucha, 225, 226, 227

Arbenz, Jacobo, 33, 53, 75, 111

Arenas, Reinaldo, 113–15

Argentina: Arturo Frondizi and, 53; Axis Powers and, 52; Carlos Padilla Pérez and, 36; Chile Solidarity Committee in, 126; Common Front on Latin America, 243; corporatist statist regime of, 51; FLH, 253; gay liberation in, 256, 265; Juan Domingo Perón, 63; militant activists in, 59; Nelson Rockefeller and, 51, 59, 60, 64, 66; protest music and, 195; Soledad Bianchi and, 194; student movements in, 38, 53, 89; support for Puerto Rico in, 26, 40, 46n71; *Sur*

magazine in, 111; University Federation of, 26; Victoria Ocampo and, 111–12; women's movements in, 189, 191

Argentine Asociación de Amigos pro Libertad de Puerto Rico, 21, 35

Ariztía, Fernando, 128–29

ARNE (Acción Revolucionario Nacionalista Ecuatoriano), 38

Arosemena Gómez, Otto, 36

arpilleras/arpilleristas, 179, 187–90

Arruda, Marcos, 243

Asia: European colonialism in, 23; international solidarity in, 144, 145, 147, 154; U.S. and, 56

asistencialismo, 226

Association of Family Members of the Disappeared, 135

Association of Relatives of the Detained and Disappeared (AFDD), 187, 189

Asunción, Paraguay, 60, 62

atheists, 122, 131

Auceda, Flores, 213

Australia, 183, 184

avant-garde, 102, 103, 114, 248

Ayala, Luis, 185

Baez, Joan, 115, 186, 193

Bakunin, Mikhail, 123

Baltimore Sun, 189

Baptista Breda, João, 262

Barby, William, 27

Basurto, 59

Batista, Fulgencio, 36, 145

Batallones de Infantería de Reacción Inmediata (BIRIs), 220

Bay of Pigs, 54, 55

Belaúnde Terry, Fernando, 66, 106

Belgian Congo, 149

Berg, Moe, 52

Berlin, 133, 181, 185

Bianchi, Soledad, 194

Bible, 122, 125, 131

BIRIs (Batallones de Infantería de Reacción Inmediata), 220

Black Panthers, 90–91

Black Power, 90, 183

Black September, 182

Blair House, 25, 30, 32, 38
Blest, Clotario, 37
Bogotá, Colombia, 54, 58, 59, 66, 248
Bolivar, Simón, 21
Bolivia, 37, 75, 146, 242–43
Bolocco, Cecilia, 196–200
Bolocco, Enzo, 196
bolsones, 213
bombo drums, 193
Boom generation of writers, 13, 102–3, 108, 112–15
Borges, Jorge Luis, 104
Borja Moncayo, Gustavo, 48
Bosch, Juan, 55
bourgeoisie, 28, 83, 86, 101, 244, 257, 262
boycotts: 1974 World Cup, 14, 177, 181, 184; 1980 Olympic Games, 188; *The Cuban Thing*, 107; PEN club, 105, 106; playwrights and, 193; union, 200
Boyer, Louise, 49, 65, 66
Braden, Thomas, 110
Brazil: gay and lesbian liberation in, 240, 248–49, 253, 255, 259–60, 264–66; human rights violations in, 239, 243; labor and, 63, 256, 264; the left in, 14, 250, 253, 257; military government of, 58, 62, 248, 262, 265, 266n1; the military in, 66; popular culture and, 52, 192, 249; the press in, 249, 254; transnational solidarity of, 14, 86, 89, 239, 243, 265; U.S. intervention in, 55; U.S. policy and, 52, 53, 60
Brazilian Democratic Movement, 261
British Longshoreman's Union, 200
British Solidarity Organization, 200
Brookings Institute, 57
Buenos Aires, Argentina, 9, 21, 37, 64, 66, 102, 253
Bussi, Hortensia, 192

Cabinda, Angola, 150, 152
"Calama Experience," 126, 139–40n29
California, 90, 200; San Francisco, 186, 245–46, 248–50, 264, 266; University of California, Berkeley, 246
Caminada, Juan, 126
"camp" culture, 114, 115

campesinos: education of, 226–27; in Honduras, 212, 215–16; mobilization of, 216–18, 220–21, 231; refugees as, 210–13, 223; *retornos* and, 229–30; rights of, 224; student movement and, 80; in the U.S., 220; violence toward, 221–22, 232
Canada, 27, 126, 211
Canales, Blanca, 30–31
Cancel Miranda, Rafael, 32
Cannon, Jim, 57
"Canto a Stalingrado," 111
Canto general (Neruda), 110, 117n16
canto nuevo, 195
Carabineros, 185
Caracas, Venezuela, 32, 53, 111
CARIB (Committee against Repression in Brazil), 243
Caribbean: Eleanor Roosevelt in, 52; Latin American solidarity in, 34; magical realism in, 102; Nelson Rockefeller touring in, 57, 59; U.S. Navy bases in, 27
Caritas, 218
Carpentier, Alejo, 104
Carter, Jimmy, 39
Carvajal, Patricio, 198
Casa Chile, 185
Casa de las Américas, 104, 107, 108, 109, 113
Castillo, Herberto, 82
Castro, Fidel: critique of, 112; and the Cuban Revolution, 102, 106, 145, 148, 161; Gabriel García Márquez and, 103; Hugo Chávez and, 115; influence of José Martí on, 148; Lázaro Cárdenas's support of, 55; Nelson Rockefeller and, 60; and the "new man," 161; policies of, 109; relations to the U.S., 54, 148; "Second Declaration of Havana," 149; strategy of international solidarity, 147; ties to Angola, 160; use of propaganda by, 159, 162–63; Victoria Ocampo and, 112
Caszely, Carlos, 184
Catholic Church: attacks on, 122, 131; Chilean Catholic Church, 127, 129, 132, 135; Communist Party and, 122; labor and, 124, 139n18, 261; the left and, 120–23, 129, 131; Liberation Theology of, 126; Miss Universe and, 198–99; Popular

Catholic Church (*continued*)
Christian Communities, 122, 126, 132; refugees and, 218, 227; social doctrine of, 124, 139; Vía Crucis, 122; Vicaría de la Solidaridad, 187
Catholic Relief Services, 218
Caupolicán Theater, 191
CBS, 87
CCF (Congress for Cultural Freedom), 104, 106, 110–14
CECE (Comité Estatal de Coloboración Económica), 155
CEDEN (Comité Evangélico de Emergencia Nacional), 218
Celestino antes del alba (Arenas), 113
Center for Inter-American Affairs, 60
Central America, 210, 211, 220, 229
Central American Peace Plan, 229
Central Association, 184–85
Centro de Estudios Superiores para el Desarrollo, 64
Centro Social Obrero, 123
charangos, 193
Chávez, Hugo, 115
China, 76, 89
China's Cultural Revolution, 88, 168n10
Chile: Action for Women in Chile, 190; anarchism in, 123–24; *arpilleristas* in, 187–90; and the Axis Powers, 5; Catholic Church in, 120, 124–29, 132, 135, 198; citizenship in, 122; Committee of Chilean Musicians, 194; Common Front on Latin America, 243; Communist Party in, 37; constitution of, 188; exiles from, 8, 181, 185, 186, 190, 201; "Gay Solidarity with Chile," 247; Grupo Calama, 126; human rights in, 14, 127, 132, 178, 194; indigenous communities in, 199; International Song Festival in, 193; *La Bicicleta*, 194–95; mainstream media in, 192; Maryknoll missionaries in, 241; military, 120, 177; MIR in, 246, 248; Miss Chile, 196–97; music in, 193; Popular Democratic Movement in, 198; postcoup, 123–26, 135, 178, 184, 197; "Project Camelot," 113; solidarity movement in, 14, 121, 123, 126, 136, 181, 186,

194, 201; solidarity with Puerto Rico, 37, 40; student protests in, 54; transnational solidarity with, 8–9, 126–27, 178, 181, 193; U.S. government and, 243; women solidarity activists in, 187, 190
Chile Democrático, 185
Chile Solidarity Committees, 126, 181, 193, 243–47
Chilean Football Federation, 181
Chilean military junta: and Christianity, 131, 133; civic associations and, 185; human rights under, 127, 135, 177, 178, 191, 200; international scrutiny of, 122; overthrow of, 127; *poblaciones* controlled by, 131; propaganda of, 182, 196; protests against, 182–83, 185, 243
Chilean National Football Team, 177–78, 181–82, 183–84
Chilean National Football Stadium, 177, 181, 183, 186, 191
Chilean Tennis Federation, 185
Christian Base Communities, 129, 131, 138n6, 216, 217
Christian Left (IC), 122, 138n7
CIAA (Coordinator of Inter-American Affairs), 52, 57
CIDOC (Centro Intercultural de Documentación), 241
citizenship: alternative forms of, 122, 132; economic, 10; global, 7, 11; human rights and, 6, 8; national, 7, 11, 14, 224; refugees and, 214, 223, 229; transnational solidarity and, 4, 5, 13, 16, 120
civil rights, 241, 242, 265
civil war: in Angola, 167; in El Salvador, 211, 222, 224, 231; in Honduras, 210
"closed camps," 213, 231
CNH (National Strike Committee), 79, 80, 84
CNN en español, 115
Coalición de Profesores de Enseñanza Media y Superior Pro-libertades Democráticas, 80
Collazo, Lydia, 35
Collazo, Oscar: arrest of, 35; assault on Blair House, 31–32; commutation of death penalty of, 33, 39; death penalty for, 32, 39; Griselio Torresola and, 31–32; first

degree murder conviction of, 32; hemispheric attention on, 38; Lydia Collazo and, 35; memoirs of, 30; as political prisoner, 39, 41; saving the life of, 25, 38, 39
Collazo, Rosa, 35, 39
Colo Colo, 195
Colombia, 55, 64–65, 89, 108, 126, 146, 248
Colombian National Front, 66
Colomoncagua refugee camp, 211, 217, 219, 230
colonialism: African, 144, 146; Carlos Padilla Pérez and, 36; European, 23, 114; Free Associated State, 30, 37; French, 147; global movement against, 25, 26, 149, 160; Latin American, 51, 85, 144, 157; legacy of, 152; neocolonialism, 105, 149; Pedro Albizu Campos and, 27; Portuguese, 151; Puerto Rican nationalists and, 23, 31, 32, 35, 40; Spanish, 21, 22, 26, 160; United Nations and, 28
colonizaciones rurales, 214
COMINFORM, 103
commercials, 196, 201
Committee against Repression in Brazil (CARIB), 243
Committee of Chilean Musicians, 194
Committee of Lawyers in Support of Puerto Rican Independence, 34
Common Front on Latin America, 243
communism: anticommunism, 107, 111, 112, 113; *campesinos* and, 230; Cold War and, 68, 111; Latin America and, 106, 111, 211; military regimes and, 18; Pablo Neruda and, 106, 111; student movements and, 83, 84; U.S. and, 27, 32, 83, 211
Communist International, 147
Communist Manifesto, The (Marx and Engels), 147
Communist Party: in Brazil, 248–49; in Chile, 32, 37, 122, 133, 184; in Costa Rica, 26; in Cuba, 105, 148; in Mexico, 79, 80; in Puerto Rico, 31; in the U.S., 244
Communist Spartacus League, 80
Communist Youth, 80, 90
CONAR (Comité Nacional de Ayuda a los Refugiados), 127, 140n35

Concern, 218
Confederation of Anti-Imperialist Students of America, 26
Congress for Cultural Freedom (CCF), 104, 106, 110–14
Congress on Education and Culture, 244
constitution: Chilean, 135, 188, 196; Cuban, 149; Honduran, 214; Mexican, 76, 81, 82, 93, 94; Puerto Rican, 29–30, 43n32; Salvadoran, 214
consumer culture, 92–93
consumerism, 180, 192, 196, 201
Contras, 211, 221
Coordination Council of Refugees, 219
Coordinator of Inter-American Affairs (CIAA), 52, 57
Copacabana beach, 52
COPACHI (Comité de Cooperación para la Paz en Chile), 127–30
Córdoba, Argentina, 59, 66
Cordobazo, 59
Correa, Marco, 199
Corretjer, Juan Antonio, 26
Cortázar, Julio, 102, 108
cosmopolitanism: anti-authoritarian ethos of , 107; the avant-garde and, 114; Boom writers and, 103; cultural, 106, 107, 117n25; humanism and, 7; intellectuals and, 104, 105, 110, 112, 113, 115, 116n9; in Latin America, 104, 114; PEN club and, 106, 113; solidarity and, 9, 104
Costa Rica: John F. Kennedy in, 55; Chile Solidarity Committee in, 126; the Communist Party in, 26
coup d'état: in Brazil, 253; in Chile, 9, 180, 243; in Dominican Republic, 56; in El Salvador, 221; in Guatemala, 85; in Peru, 56, 58; in Uruguay, 184
COYOTE (Call Off Your Old Tired Ethics), 186
Cristo Dialogante, 135
Crónica, 59
CS (Convergência Socialista), 250–52, 255, 257–63
Cuadernos por la libertad de la cultura, 111, 112, 114
Cuadra, Francisco, 196

Cuba: activism in, 90, 241, 244, 245; Alliance for Progress and, 54, 55; Angola and, 144, 145, 150–67, 171–72n35; anti-Cuban sentiments, 107, 112; civil aid workers, 167–68; civil cooperation, 144; constitution of 1976, 149; cultural establishment, 108, 114; "help for self-help," 144, 152–54, 158; House of Representatives and, 33; international aid to, 13, 145; literary culture in, 108–14; military, 144, 146, 149–50, 152–53, 155; Missile Crisis, 102; Organization of American States and, 146; PEN club and, 104, 105, 106, 107; politics of, 102; pro-Cuban sentiments, 77, 253, 262; Puerto Rico and, 26, 33, 34, 35; solidarity movements in, 34, 38; teachers, 154–55, 157–58, 167; Tricont countries and, 148; U.S. intervention in, 52, 53, 86, 146

Cuban-Angolan cooperation program, 144, 151, 153–57, 162, 165–67, 171–72n35

Cuban Association of Cancer, 35

Cuban Isla de la Juventud (Isle of Youth), 154, 171n32

Cuban National Junta for the Independence of Puerto Rico, 34

Cuban Revolution: Africa and, 145, 152, 161, 163–65; ambitions of, 109; antagonism toward, 112; anti-imperialist ideals of, 24, 101; Che Guevara and, 160–61; Cuban foreign policy and, 143, 146; culture and, 108–9; Fidel Castro and, 102, 106, 107, 109, 148; impact of U.S. policy on, 53, 75; and international solidarity, 84, 90–91, 103, 143, 145, 148–49; Latin American intellectuals and, 13, 102, 110; Organization of American States and, 146; popular culture and, 101, 107; Soviet expansion and, 211; Tricont countries and, 147–48; Venceremos Brigade in, 244; writers and, 105, 108, 109, 113

Cuban Thing, The (Gelber), 107

Cubatécnica, 155

cueca, 189

Cueto Ramírez, Luis, 79

"cultural blackout," 192, 193, 200

cultural practice, 4, 178, 187, 189, 192–93, 200, 201, 245–46

Czechoslovakia, 86, 88

Daughters of Bilitis, 253, 264, 265, 267n5

Daumy, Orlando, 35

death squads, 211, 220, 228

de Bernabe, Antonio Valero, 21, 29

Declaration of Caracas, 111

Decline and Fall of the Lettered City (Franco), 103

Del Valle, Jaime, 198

democracy: Brazil and, 256; Cold War and, 8; critique of, 25, 195; El Salvador and, 226, 230, 232; global, 16; Puerto Rico and, 24, 31, 34, 40; rights under, 5, 15; U.S. government, 23, 25, 27, 40; women's movements and, 191

Democratic Socialists of America, 244

Desnoes, Edmundo, 102, 106

Díaz, Gladys, 126–27

Díaz, Porfirio, 76

Díaz Ordaz, Gustavo, 76

dirty wars, 15, 78, 210–11

Disney, Walt, 52, 57

Dominican Republic, 25, 55–56, 109

Donoso, José, 102, 103

DPI (Destacamento Pedagógico Internacionalista "Che Guevara"), 154, 161

Duarte, José Napoleón, 228–29

Dussel, Enrique, 4, 15

Duvalier, François "Papa Doc," 59, 60

Dylan, Bob, 115, 193

Easter Island, 199

Eastern Bloc, 146

Ecuador, 36, 37, 38, 40, 48, 56

Ecuadorian Cámara de Diputados, 38

education system: Angolan, 152–54, 157–59, 166–67; Cuban, 152, 154, 167; German democratic, 154

Eisenhower, Dwight, 34, 53, 54, 57

Eisenhower, Milton, 52

elections: in Argentina, 53; in Brazil, 261, 262, 264; in Chile, 178, 184–85, 201; in El Salvador, 222, 224; in Mexico, 80; in Puerto Rico, 22, 29, 36; in the U.S., 56, 188

"El Grupo," 52, 57

El Salvador: activism, 217; atrocities, 220, 221, 224, 225; *campesinos*, 211, 216, 224, 230; civil war, 211; Honduras and, 212; "new dawn," 225, 227, 231; proxy wars in, 211; rebellion, 221; *retornos*, 227–30; U.S. and, 221; women's movement, 189. *See also* Salvadoran refugees

embassies: Cuban, 90–91; Mexican, 89; protests at, 89; Soviet, 66; U.S., 91

EMO (Equipo Misión Obrera), 126, 139–40n29

Engels, Friedrich, 147

England, 76, 87, 89

Enríquez, Miguel, 126

Escoffier, Jeff, 243

Esmeralda, 186, 243

Espeleta, Naldo, 35

Ethiopia, 144, 155

Europe: academics in, 189; Allied push into, 52; bourgeoisie in, 103; Chilean music in, 193; Cold War in, 113; Eastern, 243–44; gay and lesbian movement in, 250, 256, 265; human rights in, 178; Latin American literature in, 114; media in, 87; student movements in, 85; transnational solidarity networks in, 77, 181, 184; women's organizations in, 187, 190

Feliciano, José, 194

feminists: Brazilian, 254, 258–59, 261, 265; North American, 190, 252; scholars, 7; solidarity, 186, 187, 201

FIFA (Fédération Internationale de Football Association), 181

Figueroa Cordero, Andres, 39

Fiji, 200

Finland, 89

FLH (Frente de Liberación Homosexual), 253, 265

FLN (Front de Libération Nationale), 146

FMLN (Frente Farabundo Martí para la Liberación Nacional), 213, 218, 224, 230–32

FNLA (Frente Nacional para a Libertação de Angola), 150–51, 158, 160, 188, 195

FOCH (Federación Obrera de Chile), 124

Foraker Act, 22

Framework Agreement on Economic, Scientific and Technical Cooperation, 153

France, 60, 82, 86–87, 89, 102, 126, 147

Franco, Jean, 103, 107, 109

Free Associated State: legislative change and, 29; Luis Muñoz Marín and, 28, 29, 40; the Nationalist Party and, 30, 40; protests against, 22, 31, 37; Puerto Rico as a, 29; Puerto Rico's transition to, 25; the U.S. government and, 29, 40

Free University, 181

Freile, Berent, 57

Frenz, Helmut, 128, 140n35

Fresa y chocolate, 109

Fríaz, Armando, 79

Frondizi, Arturo, 53

Fuentes, Carlos, 102, 104, 112–15

GAA (Gay Activist Alliance), 242

Gag Law (Puerto Rico Law 53), 29, 31

García, Ricardo, 195

García Márquez, Gabriel, 13, 102, 103, 108, 115, 116n8

gay and lesbian: activists, 186, 243, 255, 259; community, 247; liberation movement, 240, 244–47, 250–52, 261, 264–65; militants, 251; organizations, 264; poets, 247; rights, 251, 262, 263

Gay Galbó, Enrique, 26

gay movement, 250–51, 253, 255–59, 262–66

gay rights, 14, 186, 201, 239, 251, 259

Gay Sunshine, 249

Gelber, Jack, 107

gender: human rights and, 10, 189; inequality, 190; roles, 189, 199, 242; solidarity movements and, 186; transgender, 265

General Cemetery's Patio 29, 121

Geneva Convention, 218

Georgetown University, 190

Germany, 76, 86, 89

Ghana, 146

Ginsberg, Allen, 107

globalization, 10, 180

Global North, 5, 25, 82, 105, 148, 232

Going Home Interfaith Campaign, 228

González Videla, Gabriel, 32

Good Friday March, 121
Good Neighbor Policy, 51, 52, 55, 61, 68, 111
Good Samaritan, 4, 134–35
Gordon, Arturo, 185
Gorkin, Julián, 104, 111
Goulart, João, 55, 266n1
granaderos, 79, 82, 84
Grass, Günter, 115
grassroots, 121–22, 129, 136, 141n57, 227–20, 242
Green, James N., 9, 14–15, 186, 239–40
Grupo de Ação Lésbica-Feminista (Lesbian
    Feminist Action Group), 254, 259, 261
Grupo Gay da Bahia, 264
GSA (General Services Administration), 189
Guatemala: activists from, 93; Central Ameri-
    can Peace Plan, 229; guerilla activity
    in, 92, 146; Jacobo Arbenz, 33, 53, 75,
    85, 111; Maryknoll missionaries in, 241;
    refugees from, 212–13; student move-
    ment activists, 91; support for Oscar
    Callazo from, 38; United Nations and,
    33; U.S. intervention in, 105, 111; U.S.
    proxy wars in, 211
Guernica (Picasso), 189
guerrillas: arpilleristas and, 190; in Chiapas,
    75; Cuban government and, 146, 149; in
    Guatemala, 92; refugee camps and, 213;
    urban, 91–92, 262
Guevara, Ernesto "Che": Allen Ginsberg and,
    107; Alliance for Progress, 55; anti-
    imperialist perspective, 148; death of, 75;
    expedition to the Belgian Congo, 149;
    images of, 84; international solidar-
    ity and, 147; José Martí as inspira-
    tion for, 148; Marxist praxis and, 109; "new
    man" 160–61; nostalgia for, 107, 162; as
    romanticized revolutionary masculin-
    ity, 245; ties to Angola, 149, 154; at the
    United Nations, 40; Victoria Ocampo
    and, 149
Guillén, Nicolás, 104, 113
Gutiérrez, Gustavo, 125
Gutiérrez de la Fuentes, Juan Ignacio, 129
Guyana, 55

Habermas, Jürgen, 9
Haiti, 25, 49, 59, 61, 212–13

Harvard University Institute of Politics, 61
Havana: Committee of Lawyers in Support
    of Puerto Rican Independence, 34;
    Juan Juarbe Juarbe in, 34; music from,
    110; Orlando Daumy in, 35; "Second
    Declaration of Havana," 149; Tricon-
    tinental conference in, 147; University
    of, 112
Henríquez, Silva, 128
Hiriart, Lucía, 189–90
Hobsbawn, Eric, 93
Hocké, Jean Pierre, 214, 216
"Homenaje," 195
homophobia, 245, 247, 251–53, 260, 262–63;
    attitudes of, 186; of the left, 245, 251,
    253, 257, 262
homosexuals: activism by, 240, 255, 258,
    263; AIDS and, 266; in Brazil, 240;
    Communist Party and, 244, 249, 262;
    in Cuba, 245; labor and, 256, 258–59,
    261–62; Lampião da Esquina, 249, 257,
    258; the left and, 245, 248, 250, 252, 257,
    262; persecution of, 107; the right and,
    260, 261, 263; rights of, 240, 249, 251,
    261; SOMOS, 253, 255, 261
Homosexual Commission for May 1st, 258
Homosexual Faction of the Socialist Conver-
    gence, 251, 258, 261, 262
Honduran National Security Council, 213
Honduras: authorities, 212, 214, 231; govern-
    ment, 212–15, 220–24; international
    aid in, 14; international border with
    El Salvador, 211, 212, 231; and Nelson
    Rockefeller, 49, 58; Nicaraguan refugee
    camps in, 221; refugee zones in, 218;
    Salvadoran refugees in, 209–12, 214–17,
    222–25; as staging ground for proxy
    wars, 211; UN convention on refugees
    and, 212; UNHCR and, 213; U.S.
    regional strategy and, 220–21
Hotel Quito, 49
Hull, Cordell, 26
human rights: in Chile, 14, 123, 127, 132, 136,
    177; in democracies, 5; global frame-
    works of, 4; laws for, 9, 224; in Mexico,
    78; nation-state and, 6; organizations
    for, 8, 196, 198, 201; refugees and, 210,

216, 219; recognition of, 8; transnational, 6, 8; transnational solidarity, 12, 15, 178, 182, 188, 200; Universal Declaration of, 200; in the U.S., 25, 40; violations of, 9, 185, 224; women's movements, 186–92
humanitarianism, 11, 161, 162, 166, 210, 214
Hundred-Hour War (Soccer War), 212, 213
Hunt, John, 111, 112, 114
Hurtado Cruchaga, Alberto, 124

ICAIC (Cuban Institute of Movie Art and Industry), 108
identity: Latin American, 36, 39, 92, 194; "Latin American–African," 145, 160–65; national, 82, 182; political, 13–14, 145, 239; refugees and, 223; sexual, 239; transregional, 24; working-class, 192
Idlewild Airport, 59
Illapú, 195
independence: Angolan, 144, 150–51, 157, 159–60; Antillean, 34; Cuban, 148, 160–61; Ghanaian, 146; Mexican, 21, 81–82; Salvadoran, 221–23; U.S. Declaration of, 6; wars of, 21, 48. *See also* Puerto Rican Independence
Independent Left Party, 37
indigenous, 7, 63, 192–94, 199, 222
INFORESAL, 217
Instituto Politécnico Nacional (IPN), 78, 80, 84, 90
Inter-American Development Bank, 53
Inter-American Foundation, 128
Inter-American Treaty of Reciprocal Assistance, 75
internacionales, 218, 219, 232
international border, 76, 211–12, 215–16, 231
International Commission on European Migration, 127
International Conference of American States, 75
internationalist solidarity: Angola and, 150, 159, 161, 167; Chile and, 120, 136; Cuba and, 143, 145, 147–49, 157, 161–62, 166; educational mission, 154, 156; practical application of, 144; South-South movement, 13, 153; Tricont countries and, 147

international law, 187, 210, 219, 228
International Organizations Division, 110
International Petroleum Company (IPC), 57, 58
international solidarity: in Chile, 126–27; in Mexico, 84; networks of, 232; Tricont conference for, 147
International Song Festival, Viña del Mar, 192–94
International Women's Day, 190, 191
International Workers of the World, 124
International Year of the Woman Conference, 190
IPC (International Petroleum Company), 57
Irish Republican Army, 183
Israel, 132, 182, 201; Olympic delegation from, 182
Italy, 76, 86, 89, 126, 197
ITT (International Telephone & Telegraph), 200

Jagan, Cheddi, 55
Jara, Joan, 192
Jara, Víctor, 192, 193, 195
Jayuya, Puerto Rico, 30–31
John Paul II, 198
Johnson, Lyndon, 55, 56
Jones Act, 22
Josselson, Michael, 103, 114
Juan Velasco's Revolutionary Government of the Armed Forces, 56, 60
Juárez, Benito, 76, 81, 84
Juaseiro de Norte, Brazil, 54
June 28th Union, 186, 246, 247
Junta Nacional Cubana pro Independencia de Puerto Rico, 26
Junta Revolucionaria, 26, 42–43n18

kenas, 193
Kennecott Copper, 200
Kennedy, John F., 54–57, 59, 62
Kennedy, Robert F., 56, 57, 75
King, Martin Luther, Jr., 75
Kissinger, Henry A., 58, 62
Kokin, Lisa, 247
Kubitschek, Juscelino, 53

La Bicicleta, 179, 194–95
labor: activists, 58; Catholic Church and, 124; charity, 128; collective, 227; forced, 113; labor force, 81; the left and, 37; militancy, 24; movements, 59, 123, 256–57, 260–61, 264; National Party and, 23; organizations, 124, 248; rural, 221; slave, 160; solidarity, 201, 217; unions, 178, 186, 200, 208n131; volunteer, 244
La Brea Oil Fields, Peru, 57, 58
Lampião da Esquina, 14, 240, 249–55, 257–59, 262–66
Lasen, Alejandro, 200
"La situación del escritor en América Latina" (Fuentes), 114
"Latin American–African," 13, 144–45, 159–60, 162–65
Latin American Bishops' Conference, 121, 125
La Virtud, 218, 219
Lebrón, Lolita, 32, 43n51
"Le cas Neruda" (Tavernier), 111
Lenin, Vladimir Ilyich, 147
Leo XIII, 124
lesbians: activism of, 245, 253–54, 259, 261; as artists, 186, 247; discrimination against, 242, 245, 258; as police, 260; rights for, 190, 265
Letelier, Isabel, 192
Levinson, Jerome, 62
Leyland, Winston, 249
Lezama Lima, José, 108, 113, 118n29
liberalization, 250, 251, 252
Liberation Theology, 125–27, 129, 138n6, 139–40n29
Life Center, 242
Life en español, 112
Liga Operária, 250
Lima, Peru, 53, 68, 102
Lincoln Kirstein's American Ballet Caravan, 52
Lizano, Gilberto, 185
Luanda, 150, 152
Lugo, Estanislao, 31
Lula (Luiz Inácio da Silva), 261, 262, 263
Luna, Rito D., 35
Luna Yépez, Jorge, 37–38
Lutheran World Federation, 227–28

M-26-7 (26th of July Movement), 145, 148
Macedo, Rita, 102
machismo, 240, 249, 254
Madero, Francisco, 84
magical realism, 102
Maginnes, Nancy, 62
Mailer, Norman, 115
mancomunales, 123
Manns, Patricio, 193
Maoists, 80, 244
MAPU (Unitary Popular Action Movement), 122, 127, 138n7
Mapuche, 193, 199
MAPU Obrero Campesino, 122, 138n7
Marcha, 105, 112
Marinello Vidaurreta, Juan, 26
Martí, José: as "the Apostle of Antillean Independence," 34; centenary of the birth of, 34; "the fatherland is humanity," 149; ideals of, 34; as revolutionary inspiration, 148, 161, 163; U.S. imperialism and, 148
Martínez, Antonio, 184
Martínez, Maximiliano Hernández "El Brujo," 221, 222
Marx, Karl, 123, 147
Marxism: Christianity and, 122, 125, 129, 133; class struggle and, 124; as critique/analysis, 103, 125, 148; Cuban, 111; gay and lesbian activism and, 243, 244, 254; ideology of, 125, 138n9; intellectuals and, 103, 105, 147; Julio Antonio Mella, 148; MPLA and, 144; praxis, 109; revolutionaries, 101; Salvador Allende, 241; solidarity groups and, 178, 200; terrorists, 183–84
Maryknoll missionaries, 241
Mater et Magistra, 124
Mattachine Society, 253, 264, 265, 267n5
May Day march, 247, 256–59, 261
McCarthy, Joe, 104, 106, 112
MED (Ministry of Education), 152–53, 156–59, 168n
Medellín, Colombia, 64, 65, 121, 125–27, 131
media: control of, 93; coverage, 51, 93; Cuban, 107; international, 75–78, 87–88, 92, 218; mainstream, 192, 196, 199, 201;

student movement and, 84, 87; transhemispheric, 59; use of, 55, 180
"Me gusta la democracia" (Parra), 195
Mella, Julio Antonio, 148
Memories of Underdevelopment (Memorias del subdesarrollo), 101, 102, 107
Mendiolea, Raúl, 79
Meneses de Albizu, Laura, 35, 45n66
Mennonite Central Committee, 218
Mensaje, 129
Mesa Grande refugee camp, 211, 217–19, 225–29
metalworkers, 240, 256, 258, 261
"Mexican miracle," 74, 80
Mexican Revolution, 81, 82
Mexican student movement: 1968 Olympics and, 77, 79, 87; anti-U.S. sentiment and, 75, 85–86; Che Guevara and, 84; CIA and, 83, 86; CNH and, 80, 84; Communist Party and, 80; direct political action and, 75; emergence of, 74; global nature of movement, 76, 68, 81, 84–92, 97–98n56; government relations with, 79, 96n14; historical construction of, 12, 98n60; IPN and, 78; the media and, 97; Mexican miracle and, 80; Mexican nationalism and, 75, 76, 81–82; police and, 79, 90–91; pro-Cuban sentiment of, 77; six-point agenda of, 79; Tlatelolco massacre, 56, 74, 78, 79, 87; UNAM and, 78, 86, 88–89; urban guerrillas and, 91–92; use of propaganda by, 81, 83, 88; Vocational School 5, 83
Mexican War of Independence, 81–82
Mexico, 75, 80; 1968 Summer Olympics in, 75, 78; Antonio Valero de Bernabe and, 21; CIA presence in, 86; Communist Party, 79, 90; Constitution, 76, 81, 82, 93, 94; dirty wars in, 78; foreign ownership in, 83; gay liberation in, 256; government of, 82, 86, 89, 146; independence of, 21; José Vasconcelos of, 38; Lázaro Cárdenas and, 55; media in, 87–88; "Mexican miracle," 74, 80; nation-state of, 81–83, 93; North American interest in, 82; pan–Latin American identity, 92; Pedro Albizu Campos

visits, 25; police in, 89–90; pro-Cuba sentiment in, 77; resources of, 82–83; Revolution, 81, 82; "Spirit of Sixty-Eight," 74, 77, 78, 93; transnational solidarity in, 26, 38, 89–91, 126, 178; UFW and, 245; UNAM and, 78, 89; at the United Nations, 33; U.S. relations with, 77, 83, 85–86, 92
Mexico City, Mexico: activism in, 9, 76; amateur football tournaments in, 183; Carlos Fuentes and, 102; Casa Chile in, 185; detention of Black Panthers in, 91; International Year of the Woman Conference held in, 190; massacre of Tlatelolco in, 56, 74; Rockefeller visits to, 58; student movement in, 78, 80, 90
Mielke, Thelma, 28, 43n27
Ministerio de Industrias y Comercio, 48
Ministers of Foreign Relations of the American Republics, 34
MIR (Movement of the Revolutionary Left), 37, 122, 126, 132–33, 138, 142n59, 185–86, 246–48
Miss Chile, 184, 196, 197
Miss Universe, 179, 196–201
Moraga, Hugo, 195
Morelos, Mexico, 80, 89
Morrow, Hugh, 62
Mothers of the Plaza de Mayo, 191
Mott, Luiz, 264
MPLA (Movimento Popular de Libertação de Angola), 144, 149–53, 155–59, 167, 168n18
MSF (Médecins sans Frontières), 218
Mudrovcic, María Eugenia, 103
multinational corporations, 10, 180, 192, 200
Mundo Nuevo, 103, 104, 111–14, 118n40
Municipal Theater, 260, 264
Museum of Modern Art, 52

Narváez, Jorge, 194
National Association of Amateur Football (ANFA), 182, 183
National Center of Democratic Students, 80
National Council of Churches, 228
National Federation of Technical Students, 80
National Lawyers Guild, 91

National Literary Campaign (Cuba), 152
National Meeting of Organized Homosexual Groups, 255, 256, 257
National Security Act, 250, 252
National School of Agriculture, 80
National Theater School, 248
nation-state: construction of, 158; critiques of, 4–8, 67, 122; human rights and, 10; imperialist ambitions of, 15; refugees, 230; symbols of, 81;
NBC, 52, 87
Near, Holly, 186, 194
neoliberalism: economics and, 6, 129, 179, 201; poverty and, 129, 135; proponents of, 104
Neruda, Pablo: the Boom generation and, 13; CCF and, 111; Nobel Prize, 102, 111, 115; "Open Letter to Pablo Neruda," 105, 106, 108, 110; PEN club and, 104, 106, 110, 112; U.S. visit, 105, 112–13
Neto, Agostinho, 153, 163
"new dawn," 224, 225, 227
New Left, 14, 17, 107, 117n25, 122, 265
"new man," 160, 161
New York: activists in, 90, 191; Carlos Fuentes and, 102; Governor Nelson A. Rockefeller of, 12, 48, 56; Idlewild Airport in, 59; ITT in, 200; Junta Revolucionaria in, 26; New York Times in, 87; Pablo Neruda in, 104–5; Puerto Rican Nationalist Party members and, 31; Stonewall rebellion/riots, 246, 264; World Telegram in, 56
Nicaragua: Cuban cooperation with, 144, 155; dictators in, 52; leftist government in, 220; proxy wars in, 211; refugees from, 212–13, 220–21; Sandinista Army in, 188; solidarity work in, 245; Somoza dynasty in, 211; support for Salvadoran guerrillas from, 213
NICH (Non-Intervention in Chile), 246
Nixon, Pat, 53
Nixon, Richard: administration of, 12, 55, 69, 243; Galo Plaza and, 56–57; hemispheric policy of, 53, 55, 68; Pat Nixon and, 53; "Poor Richard" operation, 53; Rockefeller presidential tours and, 49,

57–59; tour of South America, 51, 53, 68; White House of, 243
Nkrumah, Kwame, 146
Nobel Prize, 102, 111, 115
Non-Aligned Movement, 147
nongovernmental organizations (NGOs), 5, 9, 78, 180
nonviolent resistance, 227, 232
Normal School, 80
North America: Catholic Church and, 128; economic interests of, 82, 83; human rights and, 178; literature and, 103, 105, 107, 114; Puerto Rico and, 22, 26, 35, 38; Salvadoran refugees and, 219, 221; women's rights in, 178
Nucleo de Ação pelos Direitos dos Homossexuais (Action Nucleus for Homosexual Rights), 240, 249, 251, 252
nueva canción, 193, 195

Oakland, 200, 247
OAS (Organization of American States): Cuba's exclusion from, 146; formation of, 75; Galo Plaza and, 56; Gustavo Borja Mocayo and, 48; meeting in Caracas, 32; presentation of case for Puerto Rico to, 34; summit of, 54
Obama, Barack, 115
Ocampo, Victoria, 111–12
Occupy Wall Street, 77
October 8th Revolutionary Movement, 262
Olympics, 56, 74, 87–88, 90, 182–83
One Hundred Years of Solitude (García Márquez), 102, 115
"Open Letter to Pablo Neruda" ("Carta abierta a Pablo Neruda"), 105, 106, 108, 110, 117n20
Open Veins of Latin America, The (Galeano), 115
Operación Condor, 60, 72n39
Otero, Lisandro, 108
Outra Coisa (Something Else), 259
Oxfam, 190

Pacheco, Jorge, 59, 60
Padilla, Heberto, 108, 109, 115, 118n29, 118n30
Padilla Pérez, Carlos, 21, 36

Palestinian Liberation Organization, 183
Panama, 60
pan–Latin American, 92, 108, 249
Paris, France, 92, 102, 111, 195
Parra, Ángel, 195
Party Reform Act, 261
Patria Nueva, 221
PEN club, 116–17n15; 1966 conference,
    104, 110, 112; Allen Ginsberg and, 107;
    Arthur Miller and, 106, 112; boycott of,
    105, 106, 109; Carlos Fuentes and, 112;
    Pablo Neruda and, 104–6, 110
Penteado, Darcy, 253, 262
Perón, Juan Domingo, 53, 63
Persico, Joseph, 57
Peru: coup d'état, 56; Fernando Belaúnde
    Terry, 106; guerrilla movements in, 146;
    IPC in, 57; Latin American solidarity
    in, 26, 38, 58, 126
Perverts in Paradise (Trevisan), 256
Philadelphia, 14, 242–45, 250
Philippines, 200
Piñera, Humberto, 112
Piñera, Virgilio, 118n29
Piñero, Jesús, 28, 41n2
Pinochet, Augusto: 1974 World Cup and,
    181–85; 1980 Olympic boycott and, 188;
    COPACHI and, 128; defeat of, 201;
    economy, 187–88; Good Friday protest,
    121; military junta, 177, 243; Miss Chile
    and, 184, 196; Miss Universe and,
    196–99; popular culture and, 178–80,
    188, 193–94; solidarity movements
    against, 13, 120, 178, 182, 246–47; trade
    unions and, 200; UP leadership and, 133;
    women's rights under, 179, 187, 196, 201
Plan Camelot, 106, 113
Plaza, Galo, 48–49, 56–57, 74, 78
Plaza de las Tres Culturas, 74, 78
plebiscite, 188, 196, 201
poblaciones: Catholic Church and, 126–27,
    130, 133; charity in, 129–30; Liberation
    Theology in, 126; solidarity and, 120–21,
    123, 129, 136; UP leadership and, 133
police: brutality, 186; in Chile, 177, 185, 188;
    in El Salvador, 221; gay and lesbian
    community and, 247, 254, 258, 260,
        262; harassment by, 113, 194; in Hon-
    duras; in Mexico, 79, 89, 90; protestors
    and, 59, 78, 89–91; in Puerto Rico, 23,
    31; in the U.S., 83; in West Germany,
    182, 183
Popular Christian Communities, 122, 126,
    132–33, 138n6
Port-au-Prince, Haiti, 59
poverty, 5, 54, 63, 68, 85, 125, 129, 187–89
Prague, 76, 82, 92
Prairie Fire Organizing Committee, 246
Presbyterian Hospital in San Juan, 38
Press Law, 254
Prio Socarrás, Carlos, 33
propaganda: American, 57; anti-Salvadoran,
    216; the arts as, 104, 116n12; Black
    Panthers, 90; Cuba's use of, 159, 160,
    162–65; educational projects as, 154;
    FMLN, 213; Mexican students' use of,
    81, 83, 88, 90–92; modes of, 67; politi-
    cal, 52, 145
prostitutes, 186, 260, 261
"proxy wars," 13, 144, 211
political community, 3–7, 93, 245
political organizing, 4, 11, 123, 130, 240, 242,
    250, 263
political prisoners: calls for release of, 25, 34,
    79, 127; international solidarity with,
    39, 127; under the Pinochet regime, 121;
    of the Puerto Rican Nationalist Party,
    23, 24, 26, 40, 41
popular culture: Boom writers and, 102; in
    Chile, 178–79, 201; defining, 179; hu-
    man rights and, 13–14; imperialism and,
    52; Pinochet regime and, 180, 187, 192,
    196, 200–201; transnational solidarity
    and, 186, 195, 200–201
Popular Democratic Movement, 198
Popular Democratic Party (PPD): Luis
    Muñoz Marín as leader of, 28; relations
    with the U.S., 25, 29, 40; United Na-
    tions and, 33
postcolonialism: African governments and,
    145–46; in Angola, 144, 166; Cuban
    government and, 144, 145; military
    conflicts and, 150; nation-state and, 7;
    scholars of, 7, 10, 50

Power, Margaret, 12, 14, 186

Pro-Maoist Revolutionary Union, 244

Public Law 600, 29

Puebla, Mexico, 80, 121

Pueblo Cristiano, 133

Puerto Rican independence: Argentinian support of, 35; Costa Rican support of, 26; Cuban support of, 26, 34; Latin American solidarity with, 23, 24, 25–26, 33, 36–37, 40; Luis Muñoz Marín and, 28; movement, 22, 30, 38, 41; Nationalist Party and, 22, 24, 43n32; United Nations and, 28; U.S. and, 26, 28, 31

Puerto Rican Independence Party (PIP), 31, 42n13

Puerto Rican Insular Government, 29

Puerto Rican Nationalist Party, 41n4; anticolonial sentiment of, 23, 17, 28; Blair House and, 30; Latin American solidarity and, 12, 22, 39; members of, 21, 23, 26; political prisoners of, 24, 26, 34–38, 42n11

Puerto Rico: anticolonialist movement within, 12, 21, 28; citizenship, 41n2; Foraker Act, 22; Gag Law, 29; Independence Party, 31, 42n13; John F. Kennedy in, 55; Jones Act, 22; Latin American solidarity and, 23, 24, 26, 33–40; Pablo Neruda and, 105, 110, 118n34; political prisoners, 24; Popular Democratic Party, 25, 28; Republic of, 31; United Nations and, 28, 33, 36; and U.S. colonialism, 22–32, 40, 44n34, 55. *See also* Free Associated State; Puerto Rican Nationalist Party

Punta del Este, Uruguay, 54, 55, 59, 66

Quaker, 14, 239, 241, 242

Quilapayún, 193

Quito, Ecuador, 48, 49, 53, 58, 59

Rama, Angel, 112

Reagan, Ronald, 151, 188, 190, 211, 220

Reagan, Nancy, 190

Red Cross, 127

refugees: in Chile 127; in Honduras, 209–14, 218, 220, 225, 231; human rights and, 178; international witnesses for, 218–19; political, 91; problematization of, 210–11; solidarity for, 4, 178

Regional Military Training Center, 220

Renault, 192

Republic of Puerto Rico, 31, 34

Rerum novarum, 124

revolutionary cadres, 153, 154, 161

Revueltas, José, 85

Reynolds, Ruth, 35

rhetoric: cold war, 24, 188; Marxist-Leninist, 256; national, 76, 82, 88; of Pinochet, 188, 197, 198; political, 63, 76; U.S., 54, 105; use of, 63, 64, 92, 121, 228

Rio de Janeiro, Brazil, 52, 58, 240, 249, 254–55, 261

Rockefeller, Happy, 58

Rockefeller, Nelson A.: the Alliance for Progress and, 54; Archive Center, 50, 58; as CIAA, 56–57; communist agitators and, 59–60; with François "Papa Doc" Duvalier, 59; Galo Plaza and, 48, 56; Good Neighbor policy and, 52, 61, 68; Jorge Pacheco and, 60; letters of solicitation to, 13, 48–49, 51, 62–67; Minimax chain bombings, 59; Nancy Maginnes and, 62; protests against, 58–59; Richard Nixon and, 56–58; Rockefeller Foundation and, 51, 57, 65; *Rockefeller Report on the Americas*, 49, 51, 60, 61, 65; Standard Oil and, 57–58; ties to Latin America, 51, 65

Rockefeller Archive Center, 50, 58

Rockefeller Report on the Americas, 49, 51, 60, 61, 65

"Rocky Horror Road Show," 50

Rodríguez Monegal, Emir, 104, 111–15

Roig de Leuchsenring, Emilio, 26, 34, 42–43n18

Rojas, Rodrigo, 181

Rolls Royce, 200

Romero, Oscar, 121–22, 223

Roosevelt, Eleanor, 52

Roosevelt, Franklin Delano: Albizu Campos and, 26; Good Neighbor policy of, 51, 52, 61; use of the media by, 55

Roosevelt Roads Naval Base, 27

Rosado, Isabel, 34
Royal, John, 52

SADF (South African Defence Force), 151, 158
St. James, Margo, 186
Saludos Amigos, 52
Salvadoran forces, 213, 215, 224, 229, 230, 231
Salvadoran government: anticommunist, 220;
    campesinos and, 224, 228–31; refugees
    and, 217, 219, 228, 231; U.S. and, 220
Salvadoran Independence Day, 223
Salvadoran refugees: activism of, 216–17,
    223–25, 232; cultural construction of,
    14, 209–10, 214–15, 220–22; disputed
    territory and, 213, 221; Honduran
    officials and, 212–13; images of, 209;
    internacionales and, 218; as *retornos*, 222,
    227–29, 235n46; UNHCR and, 218–19,
    223, 233n5. *See also specific refugee camps*
San Antonio refugee camp, 211, 217, 219
San Francisco, 186, 245–46, 248–50, 264, 266
San Juan, Puerto Rico: attack of governor's
    palace in, 31; Cuban congressional mis-
    sion to, 33; La Princesa jail in, 36; Lions
    Club in, 27; nationalist party member-
    ship in, 23; Presbyterian Hospital in, 38;
    San Luis Potosí, Mexico, and, 89
Sandinista, 188, 211, 221
Sanfuentes, José, 198
Santiago, Chile: *arpilleras* of, 188–89; Chilean
    solidarity groups and, 185; Christian-
    ity in, 129, 187; Grupo Calama, 126;
    National Football Stadium in, 186;
    working-class neighborhoods of, 12, 120,
    128; writers in, 102
Santiago del Nuevo Extremo, 195
São Bernardo do Campo, Brazil, 256, 257,
    258, 261
São Paulo, Brazil: arrests in, 58, 260; FLH
    and, 253; gay and lesbian movement
    in, 240, 248, 251, 255, 258, 260–61, 264;
    labor and, 63, 256–57; Municipal The-
    ater in, 260, 264; police in, 258, 260;
    Pontifícia Universidade Católica de São
    Paulo, 254; University of, 253, 261
Sarduy, Severo, 113
Savimbi, Jonas, 151

"scorched earth" campaigns, 216
Scotland, 200
Seal Harbor, Maine, 61
"Second Declaration of Havana," 149
Secretariat for Nonbelievers, 135
Selective Service cards, 31
semiotics, 179, 180
sexism, 245, 247, 251, 252, 253, 254–55, 258
sexuality, 186, 199, 240, 244, 248–49, 263
sexual liberation, 14, 239, 249, 251, 263
SHARE Foundation, 227
social movements, 5–6, 9–11, 15–16, 142n69,
    240, 264
Social Progress Trust Fund, 54
socialism: Boom writers and, 103; *campesinos*
    and, 230; capitalism and, 243; in Chile,
    123, 124, 182, 188; labor movement and,
    123; Nationalist Party and, 22; solidarity
    and, 9, 194, 200; in Soviet Union, 146
Socialist Party, 37, 180, 246
Socialist Workers' Party, 244, 261–64
Sofia, Bulgaria, 86
solidarity activism: the arts and, 193, 194; Latin
    American left and, 9; Pinochet regime
    and, 179–80, 196; popular culture and,
    181, 186, 196; in West Berlin, 181, 183;
    women's movement, 186, 187, 189, 191
solidarity activists: Chile and, 246; Mexico
    and, 178; Pinochet regime and, 178–80,
    183–84, 187, 196; popular culture and,
    185, 189, 193, 200; transnational, 185
SOMOS: Grupo de Afirmação Homossexual,
    14, 253–63
Somoza dynasty, 211
Songs of the People's Underground in Chile,
    193
soup kitchens, 128–30, 134
South Africa, 150, 151, 158, 160
South-South solidarity, 11–13, 16, 144, 153
Soviet Union: allies of, 213; anti-
    Americanism, 110, 211; boycott of the
    1974 World Cup, 14, 177, 181, 184;
    Cold War and, 66, 145, 146, 167, 211;
    COMINFORM and, 103; Communist
    Party and, 244, 248, 262; Cuba and, 146,
    150, 153, 155, 168, 263; international trade
    and, 53, 146; solidarity and, 126, 188

Spain: former colonies of, 22; king of, 63; Mexican War of Independence from, 82; protests in, 38, 89, 126
Spanish-American War, 22, 29
Stalin, Joseph, 111
Standard Oil, 57, 58
Stevenson, Adlai, 110
Stonewall Rebellion, 246, 252, 264, 265
strikes: in Brazil, 252, 256, 261, 264; in Chile, 123, 135, 195, 198; hunger, 91, 135, 195, 198; in Mexico, 79–81, 89, 91; solidarity, 58
students: Angolan, 154, 158; anti-American sentiments of, 52, 53, 54, 65; Brazilian, 240, 246, 248–51, 255–56, 263–65; brigades, 161; *campesinos*, 226; Chilean, 177, 178, 193, 194, 197; Cuban, 148, 154, 155; Honduran, 58; labor and, 59; Nelson Rockefeller and, 49, 64, 65, 66, 67; Peruvian, 58; pro-American, 53; pro-Cuban, 55; Puerto Rican, 26, 37, 38; social actors, 5; U.S. and, 52. *See also* Mexican Student Movement
Students for a Democratic Society, 59, 246
Sur, 111–12
Sweden, 126, 178, 185
symbols: art as, 189; Christian, 122, 135, 189; cultural, 179–80; international, 77, 84, 121, 192; national, 78, 81–82, 93, 165; Puerto Rico as, 29, 40; revolutionary figures as, 161, 245; teachers as, 158; of U.S. intervention, 29, 40, 54

talleres, 225–26
Tarud, Rafael, 37
Tavernier, René, 111
Technical University (Chile), 194
television: Cuba and, 109; "cultural blackout" and, 192; gay candidates on, 262; international media, 59, 90; Miss Universe and, 197–98; U.S. and, 59
Thatcher, Margaret, 200, 208n134
"Theses for Homosexual Liberation" (Green et al.), 251
Third National Conference of Socialist Youth, 37
Third World: anti-imperialism and, 92; Cold War and, 77; Cuba and, 143, 168; June

28th Union and, 247; Latin America as, 193; solidarities, 11; struggles, 247; U.S. imperialism and, 190
Three Caballeros, The, 52
Tito, Josip Broz, 147
Tlatelolco massacre, 56, 74, 78, 79, 87
Tokyo, Japan, 76, 87
Torresola, Griselio, 31–32
Toscanini, Arturo, 52
transnationalism: 3, 5, 7, 10, 13, 50; activism and, 4, 5, 8, 13, 78, 180, 194, 201, 239; advocacy of, 4, 9, 78; gay rights and, 15, 239; human rights and, 12, 14, 127, 132; intellectuals and, 104, 113, 115; Latin American, 5, 8, 11, 15, 51; networks and, 5, 9, 77, 120, 136, 180; NGOs and, 5; scholarship and, 50, 76, 180; women's organizations and, 194
transnational solidarity campaigns: in Brazil, 239, 242; in Chile, 178, 179, 200, 208n121; local and, 4, 5, 11, 15, 16; in Mexico, 92, 93
Tres Marías y Una Rosa, 189
Trevisan, João Silvero, 241, 248–51, 253, 256–60, 262–63
Tricont, 145–48, 150, 154, 161
Tripartite Commission, 230
"Triumph: Official Chile," 187
Trotsky, Leon, 147
Truman, Harry: Blair House and, 25, 32, 38; Jesús Piñero and, 28; Oscar Collazo and, 38; Public Law 600, 29
Truman Doctrine, 32

UFW (United Farm Workers), 245
UNAM (Universidad Autónoma de México), 78, 80, 86–89, 90–92
UNDP (United Nations Development Program), 159
UNEAC (Union of Cuban Writers and Artists), 108, 109, 113
UNESCO (United Nations Educational, Scientific and Cultural Organization), 168
UNHCR (United Nations High Commission of Refugees): Honduras and, 213–16, 218, 220; human rights and, 219; international aid and, 231; organiza-

tional mandate, 214; *Refugee Magazine*, 220, 223; Salvadoran refugee crises, 211, 215, 218–19; sponsored refugee camps, 209–10, 218; Tripartite Commission, 230

unionization, 124

unions: boycotts, 200; journalists, 254; labor, 178, 186, 200, 208n131; left-wing, 259; metalworker, 256, 261; prostitute, 186; rallies, 195; rural, 245; trade, 200, 208n134; worker, 38, 177

Unión Socialista, 123

UNITA (União Nacional para a Independência Total de Angola), 144, 146, 149–50, 152–53

United Committee to Stop the Esmeralda, 186

United Fruit Company, 105

United Nations: charter of, 28, 36, 45n57; Che Guevara at, 40; Conference on Trade and Development, 61; "Convention on the Elimination of all Forms of Discrimination against Women," 191, 206n81; Development Program, 159; High Commission for Refugees, 127, 178, 188, 191, 209, 212, 214, 219; international awareness and, 225; officials for, 210, 232; petitions to, 38, 200; Puerto Rican Nationalist Party and, 27, 28, 32; sponsored refugee camps (*see* United Nations–sponsored refugee camps); U.S. involvement in, 33, 55

United Nations–sponsored refugee camps: "closed camps," 213, 216, 231; Colomoncagua, 211, 217, 219, 230; coordinating committees, 217; curfews at, 214, 215, 220; Mesa Grande, 211, 217–19, 225–29, 234n30; military incursions into, 215; San Antonio, 211, 217, 219; *talleres* in, 225–26

United States: anti-American sentiment, 21–22, 54, 82, 85; attacks on, 27, 32; colonialism, 22, 25, 29, 40; communism and, 12, 75, 104, 110, 151; economic interests, 83, 85; gay and lesbian movement, 14, 239, 245, 247, 252, 265, 267n5; as global power, 27, 65, 85, 86; "goodwill

tours" in Latin America, 51–53, 55, 57, 59, 67–68, 186; hegemony, 40, 50, 54, 211; imperialist ambitions, 15, 105, 148, 188; interventions in Latin America, 8, 24, 32, 83, 188; Latin American relations with, 40, 61, 211, 220, 242; media, 59, 87; political prisoners, 34, 38; popular culture, 107, 192, 196; transnational activism, 76, 85, 89–91, 93, 185, 239, 243, 250; Truman Doctrine, 32; security forces, 75, 83, 220, 221; United Nations and, 27–28, 33; women's movement in, 187, 190, 252. *See also* U.S. colonialism; U.S. Congress; U.S. foreign policy; U.S. government; U.S. imperialism; U.S. intervention; U.S. policy

Universal Declaration of Human Rights, 200

Universidad Autónoma de México (UNAM), 78, 80, 86–89, 90–92

Universidad de San Marcos, 53

University Alliance of Montevideo, 38

University Federation of Argentina, 26

University Movement for Renovated Morals, 80

University of Bahia, 264

University of California, Berkeley, 246

University of Chile, 198

University of Havana, 112

UP (Popular Unity), 133, 178, 182, 188, 195, 246

Uruguay: music in, 195; Nelson Rockefeller and, 52, 59–60; Puerto Rican independence and, 26, 39; student solidarity for Mexico in, 89; summit in Punta del Este, 54; University Alliance of Montevideo, 38; World Cup football team, 184

Uruguayan Group for the Freedom of Puerto Rico, 39

U.S. colonialism: Free Associated State, 29; Luis Muñoz Marín, 29; Puerto Rico and, 22, 24, 28–30, 41; World War II and, 24

U.S. Congress: attack of, 32, 36, 39; Nelson Rockefeller and, 62; Puerto Rico and, 22, 25, 29

U.S. Cultural Institute, 55

U.S. foreign policy: Cuba and, 146; in Latin America, 12, 42n9, 111, 156; opposition to, 104, 110, 185; Truman Doctrine, 32

U.S. government: anticommunist policy, 151; Brazil and, 250; Cuba and, 106, 146; Inter-American Foundation, 128; interventions, 31, 33, 242; Latin American left and, 105; Luis Muñoz Marín and, 29, 40, 41n2; Mexico and, 83; Nelson Rockefeller and, 63; Puerto Rico and, 23, 24, 26, 27, 28, 35

U.S. imperialism: in Cuba, 105–6, 148–49; feminist organizations and, 190; in Latin America, 10, 39, 50, 93, 241; in Mexico, 81, 91; opposition to, 15, 25, 55, 75, 78; in Puerto Rico, 22, 32–33, 41; solidarity organizations and, 186, 188; Tricont countries and, 147–48, 161; United Nations and, 27

U.S. Information Agency, 55

U.S. intervention: Alliance for Progress, 54–55; anticolonialist movements and, 12; CIA and, 86; in the Dominican Republic, 109; in Guatemala, 105; in Latin America, 105, 242; in Mexico, 82–83; responses to, 6; transnational solidarity and, 8

U.S. National Guard, 31

U.S. Navy, 27; naval bases in Puerto Rico, 27

U.S. policy: critique of, 65, 110, 50; dissonance in, 60; in Latin America, 24, 55; "reformist"-minded, 106; setbacks for, 56

U.S. State Department, 29, 52, 53, 57, 104

Valdés, Francisco, 177, 183
Vargas, Getúlio, 63
Vargas Llosa, Mario, 102, 103, 108, 115, 116n8
Varona, Enrique José, 26, 42n18
Vasconcelos, José, 38
Vatican II, 125–26, 131, 198
Velasco, Juan, 56–58, 60
Venceremos Brigade, 244
Venezuela, 32, 53, 55, 58, 59, 126, 146
Verde Olivo, 109
Versus, 249, 250

Vicaría de la Solidaridad (Vicariate of Solidarity), 127–28, 187–89, 198
Vietnam: Che Guevara and, 149; Cold War and, 113; Mexican solidarity with, 88; teachers in Angola, 155; Vietnam War, 12, 56, 85, 105, 109, 241–42
Vieques Naval Base, 27
Vila Euclides Stadium, 259
Villa, Francisco (Pancho), 81
Vocational School 5, 83
Voice of Mexico, The, 90
Voices on the Border, 228
"voluntary repatriation," 215, 218, 228, 230

Walter-McCarran Act, 104
Warhol, Andy, 115
Washington, DC: antiwar mobilizations in, 241; Blair House and, 30; CARIB and, 243; democratic ideals and, 27; diplomats in, 38; GSA and, 189; Harry Truman in, 38; hypocrisy in, 25; John F. Kennedy in, 54; Lydia Collazo detained in, 35; politicians in, 25; Puerto Rico and, 28, 29, 32; solidarity groups in, 186
WCC (World Council of Churches), 127, 128, 140n36
Weather Underground, 200
Wehrle, Leroy, 61–62
Western hemisphere, 17, 39, 40, 167
West Germany, 126, 177, 179, 181–85
Wharton, Clifton, 60
WHO (World Health Organization), 168
women: activists, 187, 189, 190, 191; movements led by, 187; organizations for, 187, 190, 191, 192; rights of, 180, 191
Women for Life, 191
"Words to Intellectuals" (Castro), 109
worker-nuns, 126,127, 139–40n29
worker-priests, 126, 127, 139–40n29
Workers' World Party, 244
working class: art by, 192, 194; Christianity and, 124, 126; Communist Manifesto and, 147; communities of, 13, 53, 120, 194, 242; homophobia of, 257; mobilization of, 256; rights of, 124
World Cup, 1974: ANFA and, 182–83; boycott of, 15, 177; Chilean participation

in, 181, 182, 184; Pinochet regime and, 182–85, 200; protests of, 181, 183
World Organization of Freedom, 37
World Telegram, 55
World Vision, 218, 227
World War II: post-WWII, 24, 78, 93; U.S. and, 27

Yale Glee Club, 52
Yankee, 25, 34, 106, 110
Young Workers' Liberation League, 244

Zapata, Emiliano, 76, 81
Zedong, Mao, 88, 148
Zulu Force, 150

Critical Human Rights

Court of Remorse: Inside the International Criminal Tribunal for Rwanda
Thierry Cruvellier; translated by Chari Voss

How Difficult It Is to Be God: Shining Path's Politics of War in Peru, 1980–1999
Carlos Iván Degregori; edited and with an introduction by Steve J. Stern

Torture and Impunity: The U.S. Doctrine of Coercive Interrogation
Alfred W. McCoy

Human Rights and Transnational Solidarity in Cold War Latin America
Edited by Jessica Stites Mor

Remaking Rwanda: State Building and Human Rights after Mass Violence
Edited by Scott Straus and Lars Waldorf

Beyond Displacement: Campesinos, Refugees, and Collective Action in the Salvadoran Civil War
Molly Todd

The Politics of Necessity: Community Organizing and Democracy in South Africa
Elke Zuern

About the Cover

Artist: Guillermo Nuñez (Chile, 1930–)

Title: *El pueblo venció en octubre* (1972)

Medium: Serigraph

Photograph by Ignacio Serrano

This work appeared as part of an exhibition at the Museo de la Solidaridad Salvador Allende, a collection that was founded by the University of Chile's Art Faculty, through the Instituto de Arte Latinoamericano (IAL) and the Museum of Contemporary Art, with a mandate to collect pieces of international artistic solidarity with the people of Chile and the Chilean road to socialism. The vice president of the International Association of Art Critics, Mário Pedrosa, known for his militant Trotskyism, was in Chile as a research professor at the IAL, a space that welcomed him in his exile after the João Batista do Figueiredo dictatorship and where he served as the first museum curator. The *Casa de las Américas* played a key role in shipping Latin American art to the Solidarity Collection through the IAL, which was the administrative front of the Solidarity Museum. After the coup d'état of September 11, 1973, the museum's art works shipped during 1972–73 were hidden in the Museum of Contemporary Art at the University of Chile's basement, in a latent juridical secrecy until the return of democracy. Those who participated in the project went into exile and they carried on their backs the project of the museum as the Museum of Resistance. With the return of democracy, and the fall of the Pinochet dictatorship, the museum came back to Chile, joining the solidarity and the new resistance collections, after a long journey. The collections were recently installed in 2006 as a museum space, in a building that formerly belonged to the national intelligence center of the military dictatorship.

Carla Miranda Vasconcello
Translated by Patricia Barriga

Made in the USA
San Bernardino, CA
23 May 2013